Treating survivors of satanist abuse

First and foremost, *Treating Survivors of Satanist Abuse* deals with the experiences that bring children and adults abused in this way to the attention of the mental health services. It records the process of their treatment and the fears and doubts of the therapists as they listen to detailed accounts of perversion and extreme cruelty. Contributors explore the meaning of such experience for the victim, and its impact of terror, alongside the reverberations for professionals who come into contact with such cases. A psychoanalytic critique of these issues is put forward, as well as an analysis of the satanist ritual.

The book also aims to answer other questions. It offers definitions of ritual satanist abuse and analyses some of the reasons for societal disbelief. It considers what changes have to be made in therapeutic technique to deal with patients who are in a trance state. It discusses the ethical and legal issues and initial police response when child or adult patients are reporting crimes in which they have been involved. It makes a thorough appraisal of all the services available in such cases, gives details of organisations with experience of working in the area and a critical bibliography for further reference. Above all, it examines the predicament of survivors who have experienced a major trauma only to face societal disbelief.

Treating Survivors of Satanist Abuse brings together thirty-eight contributors: professionals working in the fields of psychiatry, psychology, psychotherapy, mental health management and the media, victims and carers. It provides essential background information and a wealth of practical advice for others working in the field.

Valerie Sinason is a Consultant Child Psychotherapist working mainly in the field of learning disability and sexual abuse. She practises at the Tavistock Clinic, London, and teaches at St George's Hospital Medical School, London. She is also Honorary Lecturer at the Anna Freud Centre and University College London Psychology Department.

Treating survivors of satanist abuse

Edited by Valerie Sinason

London and New York

First published 1994
by Routledge
11 New Fetter Lane, London EC4P 4EE

Simultaneously published in the USA and Canada
by Routledge
29 West 35th Street, New York, NY 10001

Typeset in Times by LaserScript, Mitcham, Surrey
Printed and bound in Great Britain

British Library Cataloguing in Publication Data
A catalogue record for this book is available from the British Library.

Library of Congress Cataloging in Publication Data
Treating survivors of satanist abuse / edited by Valerie Sinason.
  p. cm.
Includes bibliographical references and index.
1. Ritual abuse victims – Rehabilitation. 2. Ritual abuse victims – Rehabilitation –
Moral and ethical aspects. 3. Ritual abuse victims – Services for. 4. Satanism –
Rituals. I. Sinason, Valerie, 1946–   .
RC569.5.R59T74   1994
616.85′82–dc20   93-41461
                                                                            CIP

ISBN 0–415–10542–0 (hbk)
ISBN 0–415–10543–9 (pbk)

Treating satanist abuse survivors

(1)

In the garden
a green breath rises and rises
I am sitting by the window
On the table your fax
sends murder down the lines

(2)

In the hospital
a woman asks for drugs
A child is dying through her mouth
Neither of them can rest

(3)

In the morgue
the dead child is calling for her mother
As we write
the scars on her head close
like red zips

(4)

In the wood
dead dog hairs grow flesh
Whimper
then howl for a kennel

(5)

We put these things together
Together we find a voice

Valerie Sinason

To my father,
Professor Stanley S. Segal OBE, JP

'And shall not pass them by
Nor throw them crumbs'

(from 'A soldier in Italy', by S.S. Segal, 1943)

Contents

Illustrations

Introduction

Valerie Sinason

> It is so unjust, so unreasonable, that of all people the survivor should have to struggle, all by himself, with some of the greatest psychological difficulties imaginable – with psychological hardships everybody else is spared.
>
> (Bettelheim, 1980)

A 30-year-old woman from a prominent family went to a distinguished medically qualified psychoanalyst for treatment. She had a history of self-mutilation, severe menstrual bleeding and heavy nose bleeds. As a result of both somatic and organic problems he referred her to a close friend, a surgeon, who decided on nasal surgery. Appallingly, an object was left in her nasal cavity during the operation, causing infection, and, when it was removed, a flood of blood. Later medical complications included a severe life-threatening haemorrhage. Two years after the operation there were still medical difficulties.

The psychoanalyst had to deal with his anger towards his medical friend and colleague as well as with his guilt towards his patient. However, after processing more of her history he came to see a link between the repeated haemorrhages and her previous problems with bleeding that existed intra-psychically over and beyond the bungled operation. Indeed, he noted that she 'bled out of longing'.

Once he saw a transferential meaning in her bleeding, the woman was able to tell him some traumatic childhood memories. She said the devil stuck 'needles into her finger and then places a candy on each drop of blood'; a week later she provided a more horrifying memory of genital mutilation with the abuser 'sucking up the blood, after which the child was given a piece of the skin to eat'. She claimed to have eaten an earthworm and had a fear of needles and sharp objects from early childhood.

The psychoanalyst was able and willing to consider such horrifying material both as external reality and internal fantasy. Indeed, his clinical work with the young woman, and other abused patients, impelled him to pursue research into bestiality, what the impact of early anal abuse was (whether by tongue, finger or penis) and the origins of disgust in terms of the eating of faeces. His final stage was to study historical books on witchcraft, and the nature and sequence of his reading and research has been replicated by many contributors to this book.

After noting how such ritualistic aspects of the past live on in the present he came to the conclusion that a secret and perverse primeval devil religion could exist in contemporary reality. However, just a few months later, after a summer holiday, the analyst gave up this line of enquiry and, after looking into his motives as conscientiously as he could, turned creatively to other clinical matters.

That change of approach is not surprising and this book will provide many reasons for it. However, this analyst was at a particular disadvantage. He worked alone a hundred years ago trying to fashion the map whereby we might be able to see how 'unnatural acts do breed unnatural troubles' (*Macbeth* V. V. 73). The psychoanalyst was Freud, the young woman was Emma Eckstein and the surgeon friend was Wilhelm Fliess.

FREUD AND EMMA REVISITED NEARLY A CENTURY LATER

A new motto. 'What have they done to you, poor child?'
(Freud, Letter to Fliess, 14 December 1897)

At the period when Freud was treating Emma Eckstein he had a heavy caseload of sexually abused patients. Outside of specialist forensic psychoanalytic clinics such as the Portman Clinic, London, and the handful of psychoanalysts working in other forensic settings he was probably treating more such patients than his contemporary colleagues. Could it be that a powerful emotional undercurrent coming from Emma at a time when his caseload was particularly trauma-based disconcerted Freud and knocked him from the path he was taking? Almost all contributors talk of the knocks they received when they first spoke about these cases.

Freud understood how Emma as a victim evoked his compassion, whilst Emma as a self-torturer could evoke in him in the transference an understanding of 'the harsh therapy of the witches' judges'. Could it be that the bungled operation by Fliess contained within it not a sadistic recognition of those same wishes and processes but an acting out of them? There are many unanswered questions. Just after Freud considered the idea (Letter to Fliess, 24 January 1897) that perversions contained the 'remnant of a primeval sexual cult' he gave up his line of enquiry and began to change his use of the term 'scene' from meaning a patient's memory to a phantasy.

So how have we fared in the hundred years since Freud first dealt with these abuse cases? In the 1970s in the UK, bruised and battered children were all too often seen as 'clumsy' until the work of Kempe (1962, 1978) in America filtered through. In the 1980s the early pioneers who spoke out about child sexual abuse and sexual abuse and disability were similarly disbelieved. Now, in the 1990s, we face, yet again, ritual satanist abuse. Almost a hundred years after Freud struggled with Emma's material, clinicians now struggle with the same sequence of reading and research.

WHAT IS SATANIST ABUSE?

The split off mind is the devil with which the unsophisticated observation of early superstitious times believed that these patients were possessed. It is true that a spirit alien to the patient's waking consciousness holds sway in him; but the spirit is not in fact an alien one, but a part of his own.

(Freud, Vol. 2, p. 250)

The idea for this book came from the experience of supervising the therapy of a woman with a severe learning disability in Sweden (Sinason and Svensson, Ch. 1). After eight months in which the patient described events that we found unbearable to hear, a picture was painted for us of one aspect of contemporary Satanism. Men and women, dedicated to Aleister Crowley's guiding principle 'Do what thou wilt shall be the whole of the Law', worship Satan as their god in private houses or in churchyards and forests. In so doing they literally turn upside down any moral concept that comes with Christianity. They practise every sexual perversion that exists with animals, children and both sexes. They drink blood and urine and eat faeces and insects. They are involved in pornographic films and drug-dealing as a means of raising money. They are highly organised, successful in their secrecy and have a belief that through this pain and abuse they are getting closer to their god.

It needs to be strongly underlined that the number of children and adults tortured in the name of mainstream religious orthodoxy historically outweighs any onslaught by satanists. There are many satanists who do *not* abuse children just as there are many followers of every mainstream religion who do. However, the cruelty of past and present witch-hunts does not mean that there is no such thing as an evil witch. Arthur Miller's genius in *The Crucible* in linking witch-hunting to fascism has, ironically, blinded us at times to this fact: in contemporary culture a witch-hunt is always seen as cruel and a witch is a biameless victim.

Within this book you will find an exploration of a range of definitions (see Burrell, Ch. 31; Moore, Ch. 28), with Finkelhor's (USA) and Hanks and McFadyen's (UK) being the most commonly used. Some contributors (Goodwin, Ch. 4; Hobbs and Wynne, Ch. 27) consider that creating new terms for an old practice takes this abuse into a supernatural religious area away from its links with torture, physical cruelty and violence. Arnon Bentovim and Marianne Tranter are keen to emphasise the links with other kinds of abuse. Nevertheless, the actual religious element, I feel, does need mentioning as it creates some of the power that ensnares the victims (Bentovim and Tranter, Ch. 11; Pooley and Wood, Ch. 3).

As an atheist with no fears about a real Satan, Freud provided us with a secular understanding of the devil. However, for many abused religious patients (and some practitioners), a hundred years later Satan exists. Worryingly, young delinquents from fundamentalist religious backgrounds are turning to Satanism. They have been told they will go to hell and are turning to Satanism as a way of ensuring they go in style. Where a religious belief is linked to a perversion (Jones, Children of God) there is a far more damaging experience to contend with.

I consider the term 'satanic abuse' unhelpful. It carries with it an assumption of the objective reality of Satan, which is not a shared belief, and I have therefore used the term 'satanist abuse' to highlight the human reality (Goodwin, Ch. 4; Burrell, Ch. 31). Colleagues (Neil Frude, personal communication, 1993) have doubts about the need for a new name. Whilst agreeing that almost all the acts of this kind of Satanism are included in any description of perversion, I think there is a need right now to directly use this term.

PHANTASY OR REALITY

I have almost forgot the taste of fears
I have supped full with horrors.

(Macbeth V. V. 10)

Within psychoanalytic treatment a 'scene' can be internal, external or both. The psychoanalyst Donald Meltzer (1992) brilliantly describes a satanic internal scenario (The Claustrum) in which the individual is at the mercy of a 'malignant object'. Understanding the internal ramifications and structures of perversion sheds crucial light on the way cults operate. However, there is an important differentiation to be made between those who are forced to live in a perverse external world ('Neil Charleson', Ch. 20, and 'Russell Kelsall', Ch. 10) and those at the mercy of their own inner devils.

Bettelheim (1980) was very clear that whilst the psychotic individual could have an internal delusion of a malevolent destroyer, the survivor has faced such a person in their real outside life. It is the final clinical insult to a traumatised human being to deny the authenticity of their literal (as well as their psychic) experience (Hale and Sinason, Ch. 32). However, only seven cases have been successfully prosecuted (Tate, Ch. 23) in this country where ritual abuse was one of the charges. Other cases that are successfully prosecuted (see Bentovim and Tranter, Ch. 11) fail to prove the ritual element. Alternatively, the media (Tate, Ch. 23) change the story. Only occasionally do the media aid the dissemination of truth.

In the *Daily Mirror*, on Friday 13 August 1993, Allan Hall spoke of the abuse of a family by a satanist father who called himself Lucifer. The boys in Rush Springs, Oklahoma, aged 15 and 12, killed him. *The Sunday Times* of 1 August 1993 also devoted many column inches to the case but totally missed out the satanist element. On 5 December 1992 the *Guardian* reported that a couple had been convicted on six joint charges of child cruelty at Guildford crown court. Judge John Bull said only a prison sentence could be justified. However, the jury were unable to reach a verdict on several charges including 'allegations that the couple force fed the two boys with spider sandwiches and made one of them eat his own excreta'.

The issue of belief and disbelief which all clinicians are inevitably faced with is, in the end, 'unhelpful' (Pooley and Wood, Ch. 3). If a child is referred for bedwetting we do not send a forensic expert in to check the sheets. Whilst bearing in mind the possibility of psychosis, fragmented memory and altered states of mind (Conway, Ch. 30; Moore, Ch. 28; Adshead, Ch. 6), clinicians respond to the manifest referring symptom as well as to underlying fears. Pooley and Wood (Ch. 3) comment that as ritual is a part of life and abuse is well documented, the fear of the combined term is rather remarkable.

Where survivors are reporting a clinical trauma that is also a crime in reality, we enter a legal area (Hudson, Ch. 7; Doran, Ch. 26; Adshead, Ch. 6; Police, Ch. 24; Pooley and Wood, Ch. 3) that needs extra attention we can only begin to hint at here. As psychiatrist Adrian Sutton said to me (personal communication, 1993), 'In these cases we have neither the certainty of safety nor the safety of uncertainty.' Where almost every survivor has claimed to witness the murder of babies, there is indeed a complex moral and legal issue. Brett Kahr (Ch. 5) traces for us the historical antecedents of infanticide.

However, as one patient of mine commented, 'I watch the starved or anguished faces of men and women in Somalia and Bosnia and I feel for them. But I also get angry. At least everyone can see what is happening to them. For us, nobody believes where we come from. We are an invisible trauma.'

SURVIVORS AND INVISIBLE TRAUMA

Bettelheim was using the term 'survivor' to describe those who had experienced life in concentration camps, and there is a way that the casual contemporary transfer of such a term to all abusive experiences can devalue the original meaning. However, I consider the clients and patients whose harrowing experiences are described in this book survivors in the true sense of the word.

A woman with marks carved on her body which she could not have caused herself is cowering in the corner of the room. She is terrified that her torturers will find out where she is living. She has moved twice already. A little boy is frightened to have a bath. He is haunted by the memory of his pet budgerigar whose mutilated corpse was placed in the bath with him by his abusing father. A young woman cuts her arms and legs with a knife at night 'just like they did'. A girl with a severe learning disability tells of multiple abuse by men and women. She has vaginal and anal injuries. A small boy knifes his pet dog and drinks the blood.

These individuals share a double trauma. Like many others they have been victims of sexual, emotional and physical abuse. Doctors have confirmed the nature of their injuries (Hobbs and Wynne, Ch. 27) and have differentiated between those wounds which were self-inflicted and those inflicted by others. Psychiatrists and psychotherapists have confirmed the injuries to their minds and their daily functioning.

However, the secondary trauma is often a harder one. With a few notable exceptions, nobody can bear to believe the real nature of what these survivors have experienced (Corbett, Ch. 20; Morris, Ch. 19; Casement, Ch. 2). Our invisible patients have no proper asylum or justice. Only a few reach a proper sanctuary (Bloom, Ch. 33). Whether systemic methods are used (Bentovim and Tranter, Ch. 11; Cooklin and Gorell Barnes, Ch. 13), therapeutic management (Trowell, Ch. 25; Doran, Ch. 26), group work (Pooley and Wood, Ch. 3; Norton, Ch. 12), individual work (Ironside, Ch. 9; O'Driscoll, Ch. 8; Colver, Ch. 14; Corbett, Ch. 20; Morris, Ch. 19; Svensson and Sinason, Ch. 1; Hudson, Ch. 7; Mollon, Ch. 15; Beail, Ch. 18), conjoint work (Hale and Sinason, Ch. 32; Cooklin and Gorell Barnes, Ch. 13) or in-patient work (Bloom, Ch. 33; Norton, Ch. 12), our patients suffer from societal disbelief.

This invisibility and disbelief also creates a major problem for workers. Almost all professionals experience severe stress (Youngson, Ch. 34) or shock, fear, loneliness, treatment, management and ethical dilemmas (Hale and Sinason, Ch. 32; Sinason and Svensson, Ch. 1; Cooklin and Gorell Barnes, Ch. 13). Professionals have to cope with the client's fears and their own, as well as with the disbelief of colleagues and the media (Tate, Ch. 23; Snelling and Scott, Ch. 22), and many have kept these cases secret. Contributors (Trowell, Ch. 25; Doran, Ch. 26; O'Driscoll, Ch. 8; Bloom, Ch. 33; Casement, Ch. 2) point to the need for regular supervision and support and the need for a proper sanctuary (Bloom, Ch. 33). They comment that just to hear about this kind of work is traumatic (Mollon, Ch. 15).

Indeed, on behalf of all the contributors, I need to warn the reader to go through this book at whatever pace is most manageable.

THE AIM OF THIS BOOK

This book, as the first clinical (as opposed to research) book on the subject, aims to facilitate the treatment of satanist abuse survivors whose extreme traumatic experiences pose new technical problems and ethical issues even for professionals who are experienced in abuse work (Bloom, Ch. 33; Hale and Sinason, Ch. 32; Trowell, Ch. 25; Bentovim and Tranter, Ch. 11). It also aims to change the international climate of intellectual opinion by offering a thoughtful reflection on unbearable events. It is hoped that publication of the book will make it tolerable for the intelligent lay person and professional to consider the complexity of these matters.

When I started planning this book as a result of my first supervision experience (Sinason and Svensson, Ch. 1), I found only a handful of brave co-contributors. As the book progressed, the number rose and as we went to press, thirty-five people had wanted to contribute, with many more in the wings (Neil Frude, Norma Howes *et al.*). The knowledge that this book was being planned has already changed the environment (Cooklin and Gorell Barnes, Ch. 13). However, each step forward also brings a backlash with it (Trowell, Ch. 25).

There are colleagues who are scared that knowledge of symptoms of possible satanist abuse will mean we see it where it does not exist. Such fears are not entirely groundless for poorly trained professionals (Bloom, Ch. 33); however, the biggest clinical and social problem is the extent to which we go blind and do not see all the time.

A second major fear is of 'contamination'; that as a result of horror films, conferences and study-days clients and professionals will infect each other with horrific content. It is worth noting that all the clients I have seen or heard of watch horror films *after* they disclose ritual abuse in order to relax and have their internal experience validated. Equally, most workers are trying hard *not* to hear the child!

In America, where abuse issues appeared a decade earlier than the UK, I have seen some transcripts of sessions where untrained fundamentalist 'therapists' have sought for a devil in their clients. However, the greatest difficulty, as I have said, is not seeing rather than seeing what isn't there. As regards 'contamination', no-one suggests that medical students should be restricted in their knowledge of symptoms for fear of a fake epidemic! It is seen as pooling knowledge or intellectual exchange rather than 'contamination' when other professionals compare notes.

There are just a few points I would like to make before the reader stands by the 'fifth window'.

1 *Horror films* Our child and adult patients do not find horror films horrifying. They are a pale shadow of the reality of their experience. Therefore they can be entertaining. They turn to horror films *after* they have disclosed in order to find consolation and recognition. They do not develop ideas or fantasies as a result of watching such films.

2 *Addiction* We are aware of the process of accommodation whereby the abused child becomes addicted to the abuse by way of identification with the aggressor and to avoid the unbearable psychic pain of memory. With satanist ritual abuse our understanding of addiction has to be expanded to include self-mutilation for the purpose of gaining blood and drinking blood, drinking urine and eating faeces.

3 *Power* The addiction is also to power. Having life and death decisions to make over humans and animals as well as a belief of control over after-life is addictive.

4 *Pain/heat/cold* To not feel heat, cold, hunger, thirst and pain similarly means rising above normal human concerns. It is a sign of improvement in therapy when the patient experiences temperature change and pain.

5 *The satanic lie* Those who run away have a great sense of power. They consider that they are indispensable to the group they have left. The circle is not complete without them. The ritual cannot be fulfilled. Such patients have an authority and power (Norton, Ch. 12) and do well creatively (Moore, Ch. 28) and academically.

6 *Nausea, horror and mortality* All belief systems deal with our fear of dying

and death. I consider that some satanists who follow the practices that are most sickening have a particular hatred for the concept of mortality. They are therefore injured by the realisation that parts of the human body come off us and die before the host does. Semen, blood, urine, faeces, hair, fingernails and toenails and skin have a powerful meaning in representing eventual death. A human does not have to do much to overcome his own sense of horror at being mortal. By denying the decay involved in such bodily products and overcoming what is sickening, a perverse sense of power is consolidated.

A CAVEAT

At a Conference on Child Torture at Tromso University in Norway in June 1993, I had the opportunity and pleasure to meet with Sherill Mulhern, an American anthropologist who had researched ritual abuse with the FBI and now lives and works in Paris as Co-Directeur of the Laboratoire des Rumeurs, des Mythes du Futur et des Sectes, in the Anthropology and Science of Religion Department, University of Paris.

She feels strongly that each case of ritual abuse should be properly investigated and that the fact that one case is forensically proved true does not mean that all are or vice versa. She provides some important cautions from her anthropological training that I have found helpful. The fact that different people in different geographical areas report the same events does not automatically mean those events are happening. As an anthropologist she has studied the way similar symbolic, religious or cultural ideas can appear in different parts of the globe without being linked to actual concrete events. She has also watched members of different religious groups become possessed by their gods and enter altered states of consciousness that include somatic change, voice change and an authenticity of emotional affect. She helped to clarify the meaning of trance states and flashbacks. An anthropological input can be extremely helpful in these cases.

CONCLUSION

Psychoanalysis has been increasingly attacked for not taking on board the needs of the abused and the learning disabled. I am proud that this book was conceived as a result of the words and courage of a severely learning-disabled woman (Sinason and Svensson, Ch. 1). I also hope the strong presence of psychoanalytically trained practitioners in this book redresses the historical balance.

I would be failing in my professional duty if I did not again warn the reader that reading a book like this is a disturbing experience. It involves entering a war-time atrocity area in peace-time England. It changes our concept of the contemporary universe we inhabit. However, the price of not understanding or facing truth is even higher.

CONFIDENTIALITY

Finally, names and background details in this book have been carefully changed wherever necessary to protect the identity of individuals and to preserve confidentiality. Any resemblance to real-life family names or circumstances is coincidence.

ACKNOWLEDGEMENTS

In addition to thanking the contributors to this book for their courage and commitment to their patients, I would like to thank particular family, friends and colleagues who have been part of the necessary support network for carrying out this task – my mother, Tamar Segal, Michael Sinason, Marek Sinason, Marsha Sinason, Don and Elizabeth Campbell, Chris Cordess, Estela Welldon, Jenny Sprince, Richard Davies, Wendy Feldman, Neil Frude, Juliet Hopkins, Dorothy and Dennis Judd, Beverley Loughlin and The D16 Child Protection Course, Carol Mallard, Penny Rogers, Bob Parkes and members of the 1993 City Literary Institute Conference on Abuse, Anne Marie Sandler, Tim Scannell, Adrian Sutton, the Portman Clinic, Dr Eileen Vizard, Dr Bob Whyte and members of the 1993 Pitlochry Royal College of Psychiatrists Conference, Peter Wilson, Sheila Bichard and the Tavistock Clinic Mental Handicap Workshop. Particular thanks to Brett Kahr and Marek Sinason for last minute typing and editorial help.

Thanks to Sarah Menguc from Murray Pollinger for believing in this book; to Edwina Welham from Routledge, for her courage and commitment in being willing to take on such a book; and to Liz Allison, Patricia Baker, Fiona Bailey, Bea Devlin, Olivia Eccleshall, Ann Grindrod, Sarah Hill, Simon Josebury, Benedicte Page and Sophie Richmond, for their care and attention to detail. Thanks to all the courageous contributors in this book – the patients, the clinicians, and particularly Anders Svensson, 'Ingrid' and Rob Hale, without whose strength this book would not have been written.

Finally, with particular thanks to Mervin Glasser, who made it possible for me to think and speak about unbearable matters.

REFERENCES

Bettelheim, Bruno (1980) 'Trauma and reintegration', in *Surviving and Other Essays*, USA, Vintage Books.

Freud, Sigmund (1985) *The Complete Letters of Sigmund Freud to Wilhelm Fliess 1887–1904*, ed. J. Masson, Cambridge, MA, and London, Belknap Press/Harvard University Press.

Kempe, C.H. (1978) 'Sexual abuse, another hidden paediatric problem: the 1977 C. Anderson Aldrich Lecture', *Paediatrics* 62: 382–9.

Kempe, C.H., Silverman, F.N., Steele, B.F., Droegemueller, W. and Silver, H.K. (1962) 'The battered child syndrome', *Journal of the American Medical Association* 181: 17–24.

Meltzer, D. (1992) *The Claustrum: An Investigation of Claustrophobic Phenomena*, Perthshire, Clunie Press, The Roland Harris Trust Library.

Part I

Going through the fifth window

Chapter 1

Going through the fifth window
'Other cases rest on Sundays. This one didn't'

Valerie Sinason and Anders Svensson

Valerie Sinason is a Consultant Child Psychotherapist at the Tavistock Clinic, St George's Hospital and the Anna Freud Centre, London. Anders Svensson is a Clinical Psychologist in Sweden.

Names, identities and background details have been changed wherever necessary to protect confidentiality.

> A house has five windows: through four the day is clear and still. The fifth faces a black sky, thunder and storm. I am standing by the fifth window.
>
> (Tranströmer, 1983)

> If you meet a man from Auschwitz you don't ask what he has dreamed – you just listen to what he is telling.
>
> (Anders Svensson, August 1993)

The courage of a severely mentally handicapped woman of 44, who was ritually abused, inspired the idea for this book and is the reason why this chapter was written.

This chapter is the result of a three-year collaboration between the two of us – a child psychotherapist from England and an adult psychologist from Sweden. It was conducted by fax and telephone weekly between Sweden and England and with termly meetings in both countries. We had to stay by the fifth window even when we did not want to.

These events began on an ordinary Monday in 1990 and they were going to influence every day of our week, every month of the year. As Anders wrote in Summer 1993:

> when I was with the family or when I was behind the steering wheel of the car or when I lost my appetite eating lunch, this case and its events filled my thoughts and filled my days. This case was not like any other. Other cases rest on Sundays. This one didn't.

As a psychologist, Anders Svensson was asked to assess a severely handicapped woman of 44 who was suddenly found to be severely bruised, hallucinating and afraid of windows. There was a suspicion of rape. However, as with many rape cases, physical and mental proof of rape do not prove who the rapist was. Ingrid, as we will call her, had lived in a variety of places since she was a child. She was now settled in a group home. She had little social contact outside it as her parents had died nearly a decade ago, two older brothers had married and emigrated and she had only one elderly aunt who kept in contact with her.

When Anders interviewed her for the first time, she was in a state of extreme terror and said she had been raped by a man on Christmas day. At this point the subject of sexual abuse and mental handicap was taboo and there was very little in the academic literature. Anders also had some intangible concern about the date of her rape. So when he found an article about Valerie Sinason and her work with sexually abused handicapped patients in England, he wrote to her asking for her papers.

A month later he disconcerted her by writing to ask if she had written anything dealing with more sadistic abuse as there were some physical signs of sadistic ingredients beyond the cruelty of rape – for example, marks around Ingrid's wrists and ankles. Valerie sent him an unpublished chapter – something she had never done before. Some time later, when she came to give a talk in Stockholm, he sent a friend of his with a note asking for her evening phone number as he did not feel safe calling from his work.

She gave it, as something powerful about secrecy and danger had been communicated, and told her secretary to let her know of any call from Sweden as a matter of emergency. The first telephone call was the starting-point of an unbelievable journey as well as a model of international co-operation. The joint look through the fifth window was beginning.

THE BEGINNING

In our own unpaid time initially, we devised our pattern of communication. After seeing Ingrid each week and recording the session, Anders would type it, translate it into English and fax it to Valerie. Each week for one hour there would be a telephone supervision. Anders saw that time as a lifeline for himself and his team. It mattered that a person far away, not knowing their history, could understand the depth of their worries and difficulties.

We will provide small extracts from sessions to show the way in which Ingrid was capable of communicating her experiences once she knew she was being understood and believed (see Cooklin and Gorell Barnes, Ch. 13). We shall also be showing the way disbelief and shock passed between therapist and supervisor alternately and the way the initial nature of the collaboration changed from being experienced supervisor/inexperienced therapist to an equal journey into territory unknown and unimagined by either. Transference and counter-transference issues were important to understand but perhaps with a case like this the capacity to just be able to be there and stand it was the most crucial.

Session 1

Ingrid showed how the man held her feet and pulled them apart. Then she showed how her hands were tied at the back of her head.

INGRID: Get away! Get away! (She kicks her feet in the air.)
ANDERS: You said you were asleep and the door opened?
INGRID: He locked the door. He hurt me. Mouth. (Puts her thumbs in her mouth to show how it hurt.)

Session 2

INGRID: He held my legs. Out devil. Evil man.
ANDERS: He hurt you?
INGRID: Evil man. Dumb in his head. He made blood come in my mouth. Hurt me. Dirty stuff in my mouth. Spit it out.

Session 3

INGRID: Up up in the night. Wake me up. Look at disgusting film.
ANDERS: You saw a disgusting film?
INGRID: No clothes. Hurt my leg. It is not his leg. It is my legs he pulled.
ANDERS: He hurt your feet?
INGRID: He takes them roughly.
ANDERS: He takes them roughly?
INGRID: With a cord or rope.
ANDERS: With a rope? He tied your legs with a rope?
INGRID: It hurt. Forgot it. Go away. Evil devil. Door. Opened but was locked. Couldn't get away.
ANDERS: You tried to get away?
INGRID: Tied to a chair and he carried me outside.
ANDERS: (incredulously) Outside?
INGRID: I don't know. It is hard.

With Anders just reflecting back her statements Ingrid was able to continue with her narrative in a clear way. She was able to describe being woken up to see a disgusting film, having her legs tied, being naked and not being able to get out of the locked room. The moment Anders found it hard to believe something – that she could be carried outside tied to a chair – she resorted to a handicapped defence of saying she did not know. In the supervision Valerie commented, 'Whenever a handicapped patient says "I don't know!" it means that they do know but don't know if we can bear it.' This was to be her way of showing us right through the therapy when either of us found ourselves shocked by her intelligence, her memory and the harrowing details of her ordeal.

Session 4

Anders entered this session determined to make up for his incredulity when Ingrid spoke of being taken outside tied to the chair.

ANDERS: He carried you outside in a chair.
INGRID: Yes. Cold in the moon. Cold in the outside wood. Can't sunbathe.

When Anders could process his disbelief, Ingrid was able to take her narrative further. She had to deal with her own shock at her experience with limited cognitive ability. To try and make sense of being naked and tied to a chair at night she linked it with the experience of nude sunbathing in sunlight. It was experiences like this that allowed us to travel further. We knew that Ingrid's limited cognitive abilities meant she could not lie or fantasise. She was trying to make sense of something insensible she had actually experienced.

Session 9: through the fifth window

INGRID: He hurt my legs and I said 'Go, go, you devil.'
ANDERS: He hurt you.
INGRID: He is forbidden to do it. Something disgusting in the mouth. Tied me hard. Not sane in his head, not sane.

Later in the session:

INGRID: There were strange colours. It was all white purple up there.
ANDERS: Where?
INGRID: The next floor in the middle of the night. In the other house.
ANDERS: Where did you go?
INGRID: We went down there – to the strange house.

It is hard to convey the shock this session brought to us. Because of the nature of her handicaps Ingrid rarely left her group home and never at night. Now we were beginning to enter material that sounded more like a horror film than therapy sessions with a severely mentally handicapped woman. For Anders, there was an extra blow. Good provision for the mentally handicapped in Sweden is a matter of national pride. 'This cannot happen in Sweden' was to be a regular comment of his. Who would tie up a mentally handicapped woman at night, strip her and hurt her and take her to a different place? Could it be a staff member or a stranger? Either possibility was frightening. After the next session it became worse.

Session 10

INGRID: Fat man took off my clothes and their clothes but the big one kept on his silly long black clothes. Devil women watched films with me. A girl. A girl. Shut up. Sick.
ANDERS: He is sick?

We had moved from considering a rape by one disturbed individual into seeing something organised that involved films and other people. They wore particular clothes when not nude but neither of us could make sense of it at this moment. However, Valerie pointed out that Anders had avoided the first mention of a girl – perhaps because of Ingrid's fear at mentioning her: 'A girl. Shut up. Sick.' In asking if the man was sick Anders was showing how sick he felt at the mention of yet another possible victim and how sick he felt the man must be. Again, the main purpose of supervision in the first year was to help Anders stay with Ingrid's words.

However, when we returned to the next session he stayed with it.

Session 11

ANDERS: There was a girl, you said.
INGRID: Yes. No breasts. Not my fault. I am not her mummy. They hurt her. The girl shouldn't be naked.

This was the worst moment for Anders. Ingrid came from a village where a young child was murdered several years ago. The crime is still unsolved and powerfully affected the whole country. After the murder of the Prime Minister it has had the second biggest impact. The name of the village in Sweden is now synonymous with the event just as Aberfan and Lockerbie carry in their names the memory of events. Therefore any professional in Sweden hearing of any child being hurt cannot help thinking of that murdered child. 'The face and fate of that child impresses itself on us in the same way as the face of Anne Frank', wrote Anders.

Anders also had to consider that a patient of his living in a professionally staffed group home had been taken to a strange house at night with unknown people who made films and hurt their victims. Who were they? Slowly, we were to get more clues about their extensive range of perversions.

Session 19

INGRID: Go away devil dog. They had black dog. Gave us shit to eat. And horrid drink. Yellow and brown. We spit it out.
ANDERS: They gave you horrid food?
INGRID: Don't know.

Anders could not bear the thought of what the ingredients might be and hopefully tried to make her terms symbolic. Immediately, Ingrid was handicapped. As Valerie has regularly written (1992), the moment the therapist cannot bear the historic concrete possibility the therapy is hindered. She said he needed to stay hearing what Ingrid was saying – she was saying it was real shit, not pretend. Again, he had the courage to return and stay with it.

Session 20

ANDERS: They gave you shit to eat?
INGRID: Yes. On a plate. Dogshit too. And red drink. The girl didn't like it and I didn't like it. We were sick and spat it out. Take us in bus to forest and down in the ground.

By bearing what she had said Anders had created an environment in which Ingrid could tell more of her sickening experiences. As more details came of the 'devil black dogs' we began to hear the regular use of the words 'devil' and 'evil' in a different, less symbolic way. For weeks Ingrid had been talking about people in long black silly clothes, who sang disgusting songs, took people to forests at night, anally and vaginally abused children and adults and animals and had underground places, yet only now did the word 'ritual abuse' come to the front of Valerie's mind, together with the fact that Ingrid had been raped on a special Christian day. When she nervously said – after eight months – 'This sounds like ritual abuse', Anders snapped, 'Of course it is.' But after a moment's shock he retracted, 'This does not happen in Sweden. They do not do those kind of things in Sweden.'

It was at this point, even miles away in another country, that Valerie became frightened. In fact, she had never been so frightened before. Richard Davies, Vice Chairman of the Portman Clinic, a psychoanalytic clinic that is part of the Tavistock and devoted to forensic psychotherapy, made an observation. Coming for a weekly meeting with Valerie Sinason he said, 'You look ill. Whenever I see you – you have just had a phone call from Sweden that makes you ill.' Only then did she realise that she – like Ingrid – was keeping a secret. ('Another girl. Shut up.') On telling him about the case, he suggested a presentation at the Portman Clinic. Psychoanalysts Mervin Glasser and Don Campbell then kindly offered an invitation to Anders to come for a consultation and, with the backing of educational funding, Anders visited London.

Informal meetings with Don Campbell, psychoanalyst and Chair of the Portman Clinic, and Eileen Vizard, director of the Tavistock Young Offenders project, proved particularly helpful in understanding the structure of the abuse and its implications. A larger presentation at the Tavistock Clinic Mental Handicap Workshop and the Portman Clinic followed. This mixture of formal and informal presentations helped to differentiate between the dynamics of confidentiality and secrecy. All professionals need to keep confidentiality. However, in this case we had gone beyond keeping confidentiality. We were keeping a secret and being struck dumb with terror – acting out the counter-transference.

For Anders, giving a coherent presentation to the Portman staff group and being listened to sympathetically, was a powerful experience. It made a significant difference to Valerie too – she had been concerned her colleagues would think her mad for supervising and believing such a case. However, people who work in forensic environments, and abuse teams, have got particularly strong digestions. After the meeting at the Portman, Valerie felt enabled to talk about ritual abuse to other colleagues and, on the advice of Eileen Vizard and child psychiatrist Arnon Bentovim, contacted the Scotland Yard Ritual Abuse Research Unit headed by Michael Hames. A visit to the Tavistock by Sgts Keith Driver and Carole Mallard proved extremely helpful in thinking of forensic issues for Anders to take back to the Swedish police, and Carole Mallard's input was essential in understanding the long-term implications for the victim.

On going back to Sweden, Anders was able to go beyond the tiny team of three he had constructed to create a proper support group. The model provided by the Portman had enabled both therapist and supervisor to trust that a group would bear to hear their experience. The formation of such support networks is essential in working with a case of ritual abuse (see Judith Trowell, Ch. 25; Catherine Doran, Ch. 26; Sheila Youngson, Ch. 34). We both found that outside of our small support networks we met with disbelief and, indeed, distancing by otherwise respected colleagues. Anders then gained the economic and emotional support of his line management and was paid for his translation and supervision time. The appointment of a case consultant allowed him to let go of the forensic responsibility as the Portman had suggested, and formal police and case consultant liaison was established.

In beginning to speak more openly, Valerie and Anders both heard of other cases. Forensic psychiatrist Estela Welldon (Portman Clinic) and psychoanalyst Chris Cordess introduced Valerie to other therapists with such cases. At a Conference on Psychosis organised by Free Association Books and Estela Welldon's Forensic Psychotherapy Conference, lunchtime discussions with them and psychotherapists Steve Colver and Liz Campbell provided further understanding. Child psychotherapist Jenny Sprince asked Valerie to write an account of this work in the *Child Psychotherapy Bulletin* – through which she was approached for supervision by child psychotherapists with such cases. Phil Mollon then introduced her to RAINS, the Ritual Abuse Information and Network Support convened by psychiatrist Dr Joan Coleman. When Anders came to England the next time he already had his own English network to regain contact with – including RAINS.

For the next year, Ingrid grew in emotional strength. She began to lose her secondary handicap and her voice became clearer and her sentences longer. She was able to show anger with her abusers and an ability to describe her experiences in a far more coherent way. Something powerfully moral was voiced by Ingrid. 'I am handicapped but I am not mad', she said. 'They are mad. It is my legs, my body.' She felt great concern for the little girl who was to painfully figure further in her account in ways we cannot currently detail and had clearly tried to support her. She carried her on her back when the child was too abused to walk and caressed her when the child could not sleep at night – among other things.

As you will see when you read this book, every chapter discusses the abuse of both children and adults, and the disabled, the mentally ill and the normal; some abducted, some born into the cult and some who just drift in or are brought in on the periphery. It is hard for those who are tortured to have room in their minds for any empathy for others. However, Ingrid's capacity to observe the madness of the non-mentally handicapped and their treatment of children, animals and each other, was inspiring as well as painful. Ingrid is in a place of safety. As with other brave patients mentioned in this book, the police are doing their best to provide security and investigate a crime within a context of international societal disbelief.

We will not provide examples of the harrowing details that were to appear in the next year of therapy. They are congruent with the details provided by patients in the other chapters in this book. Almost all cases include details of murder, cannibalism, drinking blood, urine, semen, eating faeces, bestiality, sadomasochism, etc.

There is another point that needs mentioning. As we passed through that fifth window, the relationship between supervisee and supervisor changed dramatically in the same way that the relationship between patient and therapist changed. For example, Ingrid was able to say to Anders, 'It is not fun. It is not fun for you to have to hear this.' After some particularly harrowing details Ingrid asked 'How are you? Is this too much for you?' Similarly, at times Anders would ask 'Is this a good moment? Are you sure I can discu.s this with you right now?' There were moments last year when Valerie wanted the forensic investigation to go quicker and Anders reassured her 'It cannot go any faster than it is.'

Anders considered that perhaps the most important feature of supervision was having security and not needing to feel defensive.

It was like being a deep-sea diver but feeling secure that the person on the surface boat would stay there supporting me with oxygen. I also knew that the woman in the boat would study with interest anything I brought up from such depths as well as be concerned for my physical and mental well-being.

For Valerie, the supervision experience of this case involved enormous respect for Anders as therapist, having to go so painfully far from normal therapeutic conditions. She likened his job to working with the one surviving victim of the Yorkshire Ripper before he was found. Even in another country she felt frightened and needed her own support system too. At times she was not in the boat but drowning too.

As a result of this journey Valerie now has English ritually abused patients (Hale and Sinason, Ch. 32). Without the collaboration with Anders she would never have recognised it. A visit to Sweden in August 1993 allowed her to meet Ingrid, her aunt, the team and the political chairman, Carl Sonesson of the Malmohus Lans Landsting who has supported the whole structure. All gave their permission for this chapter to be published, even though it is the first such case to be publicly written about by a professional within Sweden.

All of us were and are deeply moved, as workers in the field of mental handicap, that a severely mentally handicapped woman should have such courage and empathy in such extreme circumstances. This book is a testimony to her as a courageous survivor. Since this chapter was read to a conference in Sweden Anders has been approached by other people with such cases from Sweden.

ACKNOWLEDGEMENTS

With thanks to Carl Sonnerson, the Chairman of the County Council, and Karl Eric, Ronneholms Slott. With special thanks also to Maja Makinen Martindale for translating Anders' journal from Swedish to English.

REFERENCES

Sinason, V. (1992) *Mental Handicap and the Human Condition: New Approaches from the Tavistock*, London, Free Association Books.
Tranströmer, Tomas (1983) *Det Vilda Torget*, Sweden, Bonniers.

Chapter 2

The wish not to know

Patrick Casement

Patrick Casement is a Psychoanalyst.

Names, identities and background details have been changed wherever necessary to protect confidentiality.

When confronted by some painful or disorienting truth, one possible defence is that of wishing not to know. As Laub and Auerhahn (1993)[1] have said: 'To protect ourselves from affect, we must, at times, avoid knowledge' (p. 288). Some people, for example, when faced by symptoms that might indicate cancer, choose to increase the risk of death through delaying appropriate investigation rather than possibly have their fears confirmed by proper diagnosis. They prefer to prolong the time of not knowing even though this could be lethal. It is more usually those who can bear to know the truth, whatever that might be, who take the course of insisting upon early investigation. It is this defence of not wanting to know that has also operated, until recently, in relation to the sexual abuse of children.

Society has however come to recognise that *some* children *are* abused, even in their own homes. The former wish of not knowing has therefore shifted, and in some cases it has swung too far the other way into a salacious wish to seek out further abuse even where it may not exist. And that over-zealous interest has rightly created a new caution about such things. But there are yet other children who continue to be abused, some of them in ways so horrifying that most people are unprepared to consider that the emerging accounts could possibly be true. Most often, people who are told of such things have difficulty in believing what they hear, preferring to dismiss it in exchange for some other more comfortable theory.

For some time, evidence has been coming to light that indicates the existence of some adults, and groups of adults, who appear to be addicted to extremes of sexual perversion and corruption that defy imagination. 'These activities include rituals of all sorts, imaginable and unimaginable, which serve a dual purpose: to increase sexual excitement because of the dangers and risk, and to terrify the victims into silence' (Dr Judith Trowell, personal communication). Because these rituals and practices are so evil in their nature they are sometimes described as 'satanic'. For instance, we hear of such outrageous practices as the use of young children in ritual abuse and even the ritual slaughter of babies before the eyes of children, who are forced to witness these acts and to take part in them.

These accounts are so horrifying, it is no wonder that most people wish not to believe them to be true. Therefore, any therapist who begins to hear about such things from a patient is confronted by a very serious dilemma. What if some of these accounts *are* true? Not to believe someone who has actually been a victim of such abuse leaves that person still alone in the torment of their own experiences, and leaves the perpetrators free to continue with these practices undeterred. At the very least, I believe we must keep an open mind when we begin to hear of such things: sometimes we may be hearing the truth – as far as these victims are able to risk telling that truth to anyone.

We should also bear in mind that the telling of these experiences is usually the last thing these victims wish to do. They are always terrified of telling: terrified of the consequences of telling and of not being believed. And these victims often behave as if they have been hypnotically programmed not to remember or, if they do remember, to be either too terrified to tell or unable to tell much that can be verified. For this reason they are most often *not* believed.

I will give just one example from those that have come to my notice. A child, suspected to have been the victim of incest, and then taken into care, told her therapist that she had seen babies murdered and buried. She eventually took the police to where she said they would find the bodies; but no body was found. Had she made all this up? Had she been witness to something else that was to be concealed, but duped into believing that there had been real murders when perhaps there had not been? For sure, if there had been 'satanic' abuse, a false account reported to others would certainly reduce the chances of this patient being believed with regard to anything else that she had witnessed and experienced.

Similarly, might this patient have been hypnotically programmed not to be able to identify where these events had taken place? Or might she have remained unable to risk exposing the perpetrators, amongst whom she claimed had been her own father? (Her mother had already left the home, unable to stay, so this child had no other parent to turn to.) To succeed in bringing her remaining parent to justice would have risked her finally losing the illusion that he could, under some other circumstances, still be a valid parent to her. Or should we put this down to psychosis and/or revenge against the father? I think that an open mind to these different possibilities is essential.

For those who hear such accounts, the wish not to believe them is often very acute. To believe what one is being told by a victim of 'satanic' abuse would mean facing something for which one has no adequate means to deal with or to explain. It means accepting that there could be human beings capable of behaving in ways so evil that we cannot bear to conceive of such a possibility. It means facing an outrage to all that we have come to regard as human. It means facing such degrees of deception and corruption of young children that one would no longer know what to believe. It is much less disorienting to think that these accounts could not be true.

In addition, if these things *are* true, it means facing that we are being told of things that go beyond anything that our familiar theories of personality are able to grasp. No wonder, therefore, that we prefer to keep to the more usual ways of trying to understand such things; in particular, in terms of familiar psychiatric disorders. For it is far less uncomfortable for us to assume that we are merely being lied to, or that the person who dares to tell us such things must be deluded and therefore victim to his or her own psychotic processes, rather than being a victim of something so very much more sinister. We can then dismiss all else that we may hear as phantasy, hallucination or delusion, and we need not have our own sleep too much disturbed by what we have been privy to.

But there is a disturbing degree of consistency in these reports that cannot be so easily explained away. And these accounts are from people who are afraid to tell, and they themselves do not want them to be true. But when memories of 'satanic' abuse are eventually recovered by a patient, in the presence of a therapist able to give sufficient security so that the barriers to remembering can then be lifted, the process of remembering is very similar to that which takes place in the course of any analysis: it has all the signs of being authentic. But the patient is then caught between the terrors of telling (against an inner voice that threatens dreadful consequences against telling) and the fear of not being believed and being treated instead as mad. But the patient desperately needs not to remain so isolated with what cannot be borne alone.

It may be that some accounts which are reputed to be of 'satanic' abuse are delusional, and the narrators may indeed be psychotic in some cases. Then at least our theories, and our more usual views and beliefs, are not necessarily going to be challenged. But we must still face the awful fact that if some of these accounts *are* true, if we do not have the courage to see the truth that may be there (amidst however much confusion that may also be there), we may tacitly be allowing these practices to continue under the cover of secrecy, supported also by the almost universal refusal to believe that they could exist. We may then continue safe in our wish not to know whilst others are still left exposed to those abuses which we, for our own peace of mind, prefer to think could not possibly happen.

When such a patient, claiming to be the victim of 'satanic' abuse, eventually finds the courage to tell someone who is trusted enough to be told, I believe that we owe it to the patient to consider the possibility that there may be truth in the patient's account, even at the risk of this disturbing much of our usual ways of thinking about mental disturbance. The alternative is for us to remain cut off from what could be the kernel of truth that seems repeatedly and uncomfortably to be there, leaving the victim feeling mad because of the isolation from anyone else who will believe what they are trying to tell. Such a person may then have to remain defended by insanity, because it is not possible to maintain the threatened self in an integrated state without the support of another person who is prepared to share the experience of facing what cannot be faced alone.

And when a therapist does have the courage to listen with an open mind, balancing his or her understanding between the more familiar view of this as a patient's phantasy or delusion, and the awful possibility that some truth may actually be contained in these accounts, then clinical experience shows that the victim of 'satanic' abuse can be helped. But the traditional approach, of treating these accounts as psychotic phantasy, is likely to do nothing other than drive that person further into a state of isolation and madness.

In therapy, with a therapist who is prepared to accept that there could be truth in what is being told, a 'satanically' abused patient can gradually recover from the nightmare of those memories from which there had seemed to be no escape except perhaps into insanity. But to enable this kind of patient to recover, the therapist has to take risks with her or her *own* more usual sense of sanity – and often without the security of having colleagues prepared to understand the nature of this work or prepared to support it.

It can be a very lonely business when a therapist is prepared to believe that a patient's account of 'satanic' abuse may actually be true. Colleagues are more likely to criticise the therapist than be willing to believe what they themselves have not yet encountered, or dare to consider with an equally open mind. Professional colleagues will often continue to protect themselves with this wish not to know, leaving the therapist who has been exposed to the trauma of 'knowing' terribly isolated, somewhat as the victim had been isolated from anyone else prepared to know.

It is essential that therapists who encounter 'satanically' abused patients should be able to get support from others who have had similar experience of working with this kind of patient. It is therefore to be hoped that this book will help to facilitate an atmosphere of greater understanding and willingness to offer that support for those who are faced with the terrible responsibilities and impact of this kind of therapeutic work.

NOTE

1 Laub and Auerhahn's paper offers an important discussion of the defence of not knowing.

REFERENCE

Laub, D. and Auerhahn, N.C. (1993) 'Knowing and not knowing massive psychic trauma: forms of traumatic memory', *International Journal of Psycho-Analysis*, 74, 287–302.

Chapter 3

Rituals

The power to damage and the power to heal

Jane Pooley and David Wood

Jane Pooley CQSW is a family therapist and senior clinical social worker at the Hemel Hempstead Child and Family Therapy and Consultation Clinic. David Wood MRCPsych is Consultant Child and Family Psychiatrist at the Hemel Hempstead Child and Family Therapy and Consultation Clinic, and a Member of the Institute of Group Analysis.

Names, identities and background details have been changed wherever necessary to protect confidentiality.

> One Ring to rule them all, One Ring to find them,
> One Ring to bring them all and in the darkness bind them.
>
> (J.R.R. Tolkien, *The Lord of the Rings*)

The use of the word *ritual* in connection with *sexual abuse* seems to provoke a particular reaction, a reaction that often seems to involve a rather horrified question such as 'You don't really believe in that do you?' Given the depth to which human social relationships are pervaded by ritual, and thus its power and significance, this is not surprising. As with anything powerful, its abuse is very frightening. Similarly, the connotation of ritual with religious activity brings in the supernatural dimension and the question of the existence of God and Satan.

However, the question of whether or not one believes in 'it' is usually remarkably unhelpful and serves only to muddy the waters and make thinking more difficult. The existence of *ritual per se* is not in question; nor, these days, is that of the abuse of children for the sexual gratification of adults. Following a brief look at the meaning of ritual in human society, this chapter sets out to examine the way in which ritual activity is used in abuse, the effects it has on those involved and some implications for treatment.

Ritual has been described as a *system of symbolic acts based on arbitrary rules*, and is a feature of all human societies, large and small. Ritual acts are an important part of the way that any social group celebrates, maintains and renews the world in which it lives and the way it deals with dangers that threaten that world.

In *The Ritual Process* Turner (1977) states:

Rituals reveal values at their deepest level . . . men express in rituals what moves them most, and since the form of expression is conventionalised and obligatory, it is the values of the group that are revealed. In the study of rituals is the key to an understanding of the essential constitution of human society.

He describes ritual as 'a periodic restatement of the terms in which people of a particular culture must interact if there is to be any kind of coherent social life'.

Rituals are therefore fundamentally a part of group life. From both psychological and social viewpoints the function of ritual activity may be seen as a way of managing anxiety. Group rituals function as group defences against the anxiety engendered by any threat to group life. It is therefore not surprising that anxiety-provoking events such as social transitions (birth, marriage, death, promotion, retirement, etc.) are deeply suffused with ritual activity.

Similarly, responses to misfortune are also often highly ritualised, the rituals providing both a solution of specific problems and a formal way of re-establishing disturbed relationships. Helman (1990) gives the example of the way medical activity is ritualised, not just in the past but in modern societies. This activity reassures the ill person that they can be cured and, at a primitive level, attempts to restore the cultural sense of being in control of our destiny.

Another form of ritual, the so-called Calendrical rituals, marking various points in time (Christmas, midsummer, etc.), focuses on the relationship between the social and the cosmological, perhaps reducing the anxiety engendered by the realisation of humankind's cosmological insignificance through providing an illusion of control.

Human beings are essentially and profoundly social beings; they do not exist except in relation to groups. Individuals both constitute and emerge from groups in a complex recursive network of continuous interaction and cannot be understood in isolation. The *maintenance of the boundary* of the group both in space and time, *entrances and exits* and *structure within the group*, are all saturated with ritual activity, which serves to reduce the anxiety provoked by the fear of loss of identity within the group, to mark and state roles and relationships for each individual, and to provide a *framework* for group life.

Freud (1921) described one component active in the formation of groups as *the members' idealisation of the leader*. This idealised leader is then introjected and takes the place of the ego ideal. The relationship between members is then seen as 'a number of individuals who have put one and the same object in the place of their ego ideal and have consequently identified themselves with one another in their ego' (p. 147). Groups in which ritual activity is used to coerce and control members into blind obedience are commonly referred to as cults, a word derived from the Latin *cultus* from *colere*, to worship.

When an adult seeks to seduce children into sexual activity a number of problems arise. The child has to be persuaded that there will be a reward sufficient to overcome reluctance and inhibition, and the breaking of taboo. They have to be persuaded to keep silent and maintain secrecy. One method is to use force or the threat of violence. Another is to use more subtle psychological techniques that prey on insecurity and vulnerability. Rituals are a powerful adjunct to this process, especially if used in the context of a group.

Kriegman and Solomon (1985) have usefully applied some ideas from Kohut's self-psychology to the process of idealisation in cult groups. Kohut proposes that certain people who experience early traumatic disappointments in their relationship to one or both parents suffer from 'structural defects in their personalities'. They may attempt to remedy these defects by seeking out new idealised objects with which to merge and complete the self. The leader of a cult group may then seek out this type of person who is particularly vulnerable to recruitment.

Kriegman and Solomon list six 'benefits' that the cult leader offers to potential members:

1 a charismatic leader to merge with and idealise;
2 sibship/peer group support and cohesion;
3 alleviation of all emotional distress, e.g. feelings of anxiety, depression and loneliness;
4 membership of an elite special group;
5 total equality with sib/peers under the loving and idealised leader;
6 a new belief system, set of values and purposes in life, an offer to fill up one's empty life.

Those who are particularly vulnerable to these offers seek:

1 self-support and affirmation through merger with an idealised object;
2 self-support and affirmation by a twinship merger with other members of the group;
3 relief from fluctuations in self-esteem and fragmentation of the sense of self;
4 group support and validation for a grandiose self which masks shame and inferiority;
5 relief from the painful effects of intense envy, jealousy and narcissistic rage;
6 relief from emptiness, valuelessness, loss of goals and anomie.

The authors point out that the cult group employs techniques designed to exploit the formation of an idealised transference in which the convert becomes merged with the 'omnipotent leader'. The leader acts out the role of *saviour and redeemer*. It seems likely that a high degree of ritualisation of the group serves to support and cement this process.

Ulman and Abse (1983) have described the mass suicide in the people's Temple in Jonestown in 1978. Under the leadership of the 'Reverend' Jim Jones, hundreds of people took their own lives. This event followed years of cumulative indoctrination and ritualised acts. Jones formed a group of followers with the promise of power. He instilled fear through degradation by offering an alternative view of the world outside as dangerous and to be guarded against at all costs. The members slowly lost their hold on their own realities and choices, renounced their pride and dignity and submitted to Jones's will.

As these authors point out,

> the psychic stability of both Jones and his followers was founded therefore on a pattern of interaction characterised by his sadistic demand for mirrored grandiosity and their masochistic surrender in the hope of merging with an idealised and omnipotent self object.

Those who have belonged to cults have been members of groups that are characterised by intense collective pathological regression. The regressive identifications with other group members lead to intense ties and attachments to each other and to the group as a whole, ties which are notoriously difficult to undo.

CASE STUDY

A young girl had disclosed sexual abuse by a male paedophile. The subsequent investigation found that, in all, eleven girls had been abused, possibly eighteen, with ages between 6 and 11, and some for as long as six years. The police investigation discovered that the paedophile had a strong interest in the occult. As the story unfolded it became clear that the abuse involved ritual practices and occult beliefs. The girls spoke of magic wands that gave them power, of 'processes' involving increasing degrees of sexual intimacy that promoted them along the path to achieving the status of 'witch', and of prayers to Asmodeus, the Lord of Debauchery.

One of the means of obtaining the girls' loyalty and silence was the use of threats such as 'your mother will die', or 'you will be unable to walk'. These threats held their power through the invocation of magical forces; and indeed, following the discovery of the group, one girl was admitted to hospital suffering from a paralysis.

In this particular group the merger between group member and omnipotent leader was concretised in the act of sexual intercourse. Not only does intercourse enact this process of merger but the 'saviour' leader donated his 'magic' semen which bestowed power upon the recipient. Membership of the group and the rituals involved in entering the group (increasing degrees of sexual intimacy denoting one's place within the group hierarchy) and the ritualised prohibition of leaving the group (provided by threats and magic curses of what would happen should they tell) fostered the sense of belonging to an elite and of sharing something 'special'. The increasing amounts of personal power that were promised to the members, as they completed ever more intimate sexual acts with the leader, offered alleviation of feelings of anxiety, helplessness, depression and loneliness.

The 'power to damage' of the rituals used in this group lay in the way they expressed and confirmed perverse and distorted ways of relating, based on power, coercion, magical thinking, omnipotence and idealisation.

Finkelhor (1986) has defined four principle 'traumagenic dynamics' in sexual abuse that he considers are responsible for the genesis of pathology in victims; *traumatic sexualisation, powerlessness, betrayal* and *stigmatisation.* In this particular group, the experience of powerlessness was heightened by the ritualistic context and the explicit threat of magical powers. Similarly, the experiences of betrayal by one who promised so much, the stigmatisation of having belonged to the group which became notorious in the local community, and the traumatic sexualisation resulting from the ritualised sexual activity, made the trauma suffered by the children particularly intense.

Confronted with having to find ways of helping these children, the clinicians were particularly concerned with the effects the ritualisation of the group had had. It was thought important to treat not only the individuals but also the group as a whole. Unlike the more usually constituted 'stranger' therapy groups, this group already possessed a firm identity which was not easily given up.

Ulman and Abse (1983) remark that 'following the demands and dictates of an authoritarian charismatic leader often generates some secret hostility and rage . . .' and that '[this] destructive hostility [is] displaced onto other groups, or individuals outside the group, or some scapegoats may be found within and sacrificed'. This dynamic almost certainly made some contribution to the high level of hostility that was encountered. The convening of a therapy group for these girls presented them with a situation that directly threatened the enormous power that the abusive group still held over them. The attack on the group leaders, the outsiders, was to be expected.

The vital first step was to provide a sufficiently containing situation in which this hostility and anxiety could be managed. Just as rituals were used to bind this group together in a perverse way, so ritual could be used to free them. It was important to offer exceptionally clear boundaries and structure, and to this end a ritualised way of beginning and ending each session was developed.

At times the hostility and rage erupted into physical attacks upon the therapists, who had to be prepared to hold the girls to prevent them harming themselves and each other. There was a great fear of thinking about their experience, or considering the possibility of a different future, as if life without the group was unthinkable. Any attempt at thinking together was rudely and violently disrupted by flying pencils and glasses, or by overturned chairs and jostling bodies. When two girls were determined to leave the room and rush about the building, one of them forcefully elbowed the female therapist in the breast. The significance of this attack on the 'mother' in the group was confirmed by the later development by the girl of very powerful feelings towards the therapist. Through role play and story telling, she was able to reveal wishes to both fuse with and murder her. In a group story session she turned the therapist into a lesbian lover and then into her mother.

As the group developed, the girls slowly took more responsibility for themselves. In one session, when things were being thrown and obscenities shouted, one girl was heard to say 'Don't swing on that blind, we'll have to pay for it.' It was not broken.

It also became obvious that another source of anxiety was allowing the group to 'choose' in free-floating discussion what was talked about. In order to contain the anxiety, a 'game' was introduced that ritualised the choice of topic. This game became a focal symbol for the group. It involved a large folded paper structure, under the flaps of which were hidden slips of paper on which the therapists had written suggestions for discussion or role play. One member of the group would hold the paper and ask another a question which would then determine the number of moves made by the *operator*. A further question would then be asked and the process would be repeated. Then came the moment to lift up the flap and discover the instruction hidden beneath. The effect of this was dramatic, providing much more containment and making it much easier to think and to talk.

It was both fascinating and surprising that this fragile structure was never damaged even when the group acted out violently with missiles being thrown and people physically provoked. The girls always wanted to play the game and it seemed to offer the opportunity to explore ideas, but not to have to own or take direct responsibility for choosing the topics, as they were selected by 'chance'.

To recall Turner (1977):

> Rituals reveal values at their deepest level . . . men express in rituals what moves them most, and since the form of expression is conventionalised and obligatory, it is the values of the group that are revealed. In the study of rituals is the key to an understanding of the essential constitution of human society.

Thus, in this group, in which rituals had been used in such a destructive and harmful way, defining and supporting a perverse group culture, ritualised actions were found to be a powerful way of redefining the values of the group and helping to create a therapeutic culture. The values implicit in therapy, of safety and containment, of respect and trust, of coherence and identity, were expressed in the rituals that were developed as the therapy group moved towards healing.

The experience of working with this group of children was particularly exhausting and challenging, and required far more than the usual amount of support and discussion from colleagues, friends and family. Out of it have emerged the following principles.

1 When dealing with groups of children sexually abused in a ritualistic way (whatever the underlying belief system), special attention needs to be paid to the existing group culture, otherwise this culture will continue to exert its influence, despite the absence of the original leader(s).
2 Ritualisation of group activity results in the underlying belief systems becoming very firmly held and pervading all aspects of everyday life and relationships. In particular the group becomes very powerfully bound together.
3 Treatment of the group as a whole is important (despite the complications and difficulty) in order to help the group redefine its culture.
4 Treatment of the group needs to be:

(a) firmly structured;
(b) of longer than usual duration;
(c) conducted (or supervised) by experienced therapists.

5 Therapeutic rituals have been found to be a very powerful tool, reducing anxiety and redefining the cultural values of the group, thus allowing new ways of relating and thinking to emerge.

ACKNOWLEDGEMENTS

The authors wish to acknowledge their indebtedness to the children and families with whose experiences they were entrusted, to Peter Taylor who co-conducted the group with J.P., to their clinic colleagues for support and encouragement, and to all the others who lived and worked with them through the experience.

REFERENCES

Finkelhor, D. (1986) *A Sourcebook on Child Sexual Abuse*, Beverley Hills, Sage.
Freud, S. (1921) 'Group psychology and the analysis of the ego', *Standard Edition Vol. XVIII*, London, Hogarth Press.
Helman, C.G. (1990) *Culture Health and Illness*, London, Wright.
Kriegman, D. and Solomon, L. (1985) 'Cult groups and the narcissistic personality: the offer to heal defects in the self', *International Journal of Group Psychotherapy* 35 (2).
Turner, V. (1977) *The Ritual Process: Structure and Anti-Structure*, Ithaca, Cornell University Press.
Ulman, R.B. and Abse, D.W. (1983) 'The group psychology of mass madness: Jonestown', *Political Psychology* 4 (4): 637–60.

Chapter 4

Sadistic abuse
Definition, recognition and treatment

Jean M. Goodwin

Jean Goodwin MD, MPh is Professor of Psychiatry in the Department of Psychiatry and Behavioural Sciences, University of Texas Medical Branch, Galveston, Texas.

Names, identities and background details have been changed wherever necessary to protect confidentiality.

The term 'sadistic abuse' is proposed to designate extreme adverse experiences which include sadistic sexual and physical abuse, acts of torture, overcontrol and terrorisation, induction into violence, ritual involvements and malevolent emotional abuse. Individuals with these extreme childhood histories may present with severe and multiple symptoms and require a prolonged complicated treatment course. Adherence to basic principles of trauma-based treatment is recommended, as is reference to relevant databases, which include not only those concerning severe child abuse and family violence, but also literatures describing torture, the Holocaust, prostitution, pornography and sex rings, cult abuse and sadistic criminals.

SADISTIC ABUSE: DEFINITION, RECOGNITION AND TREATMENT

This review proposes the term 'sadistic abuse' to describe severe abuse, often occurring in childhood, that may include torture, confinement, extreme threat and domination, overlapping physical and sexual abuses, and multiple victim or multiple perpetrator patterns of abuse. The term focuses on the presence of sadistic behaviours, exhaustively catalogued in the works of the Marquis de Sade. Its use does not require a diagnosable sadistic paraphilia in the perpetrator. Krafft-Ebing, who coined the term in the nineteenth century, held that all human beings have potential to engage in sadistic acts. Focus on the presence of extreme abusive behaviours allows systematic data collection about such behaviours without attributing a motivational system as the term 'ritual abuse' tends to do. It facilitates understanding of these cases as part of a spectrum of child abuse accounts that includes mild and moderate cases as well as those more extreme situations. It allows us to test the hypothesis that more severe child abuse will be correlated with more severe sequelae.

THE RELUCTANT DISCOVERY OF SADISTIC ABUSE

The need to name and define this construct has arisen in the last fifteen years as medicine began its reluctant discovery of the sadistic abuse of children in much the same intermittent and ambivalent way that medicine discovered the physical abuse of children in the 1950s and 1960s and the sexual abuse of children in the 1970s (Summit, 1988).

In the 1980s, therapists began to hear accounts from children and adults of extreme sexual and physical abuse. Some children abused in nursery school settings, for example, described scenes in which multiple children were victimised by multiple adults. These adults were described as using elaborate planning to execute multiple perverse acts often including bondage, incarceration, forced eating of non-food, torture of children and animals, sodomy and threatened or actual killings with mutilations (Kelley, 1989; Jonker and Jonker-Bakker, 1991). Some adults with dissociative disorders were recounting similar extreme abuses beginning in childhood often in association with images of altars, ritual orgies, infant sacrifice with cannibalism, and use of candles, circles, chants and other elements or reversals of Judeo-Christian symbolism (Hill and Goodwin, 1989).

Finkelhor and co-workers (1988) estimated that extreme abuse was a factor in about 15 per cent of nursery school sexual abuse cases. Children reporting extreme abuse were more symptomatic, especially around loss of toilet training and presence of sexual and aggressive enactments.

Adults describing extreme abuse in childhood often presented severe and atypical dissociative syndromes with dense amnesia, even for recent violent experiences, and intrusive hypnotic phenomena such as flashbacks seemingly indistinguishable from reality. Some described the deliberate use of hypnotic techniques by perpetrators. Physical and neurological problems complicated the emotional and psychological morbidity (Young *et al.*, 1991).

These apparently new clinical problems tended to split therapists into opposing camps. Some therapists believed that well-organised and powerful groups of perpetrators needed to be detected by law enforcement and deterred by legal or other safety measures from abusing known and future victims. Others believed that therapists were somehow fostering these extreme accounts and that a more sceptical therapeutic stance toward such patients would reveal alternative explanations, both for the patients' accounts and their extreme symptoms (Ganaway, 1989).

Terminology: 'sadistic abuse' versus 'ritual abuse'

'Ritual abuse' was the term first used to describe these new clinical situations. From the beginning there have been problems with the term. It emphasises religious or pseudo-religious practices rather than the extreme violence that lies closer to the centre of the clinical experience. As a new term, 'ritual abuse' implies a new reality rather than a phenomenon indigenous to human history, a phenomenon that can be placed on a continuum of severity of abuse and se-quelae, and connected to bodies of extant knowledge and research about other types of physical and sexual abuse. The term's connotations of the religious and the occult have led to a search for data about 'ritual abuse' in the history of religions rather than in the history of family violence, political torture, crime and sexual perversion. To believe a patient's account of 'ritual abuse' has become subtly connected to a propensity for belief in secret religious conspiracies or in the magical powers of witches or spirits. Questions have arisen about whether clinical work in this area might infringe on basic religious freedoms.

The author (Goodwin, 1993) has proposed substituting the older term 'sadistic abuse' and reserving 'ritual abuse' only for subtypes of sadistic abuse in which pseudo-religious or cult elements predominate. Sadism was defined by Freud's mentor Krafft-Ebing (1894/1965) in the nineteenth century as follows:

> The experience of sexual or pleasurable sensations . . . produced by acts of cruelty, as bodily punishment inflicted on one's own body or witnessed in others, be they animals or human beings. It may also consist of innate desire to humiliate, hurt, wound or even destroy others.

Krafft-Ebing's seven editions of *Psychopathia Sexualis* constitute an encyclo-paedia of clinical accounts of extreme abuse, mostly drawn from perpetrators rather than victims. No element found in contemporary accounts is missing from this nineteenth-century text, published in Latin to deter its use as a handbook for sadistic perpetrators. Death threats, use of religious settings and costumes, bodily mutilations of all sorts, bondage, use of excretions and blood, animal torture and cannibalism, all are well described, not only in Krafft-Ebing but also in the works of the Marquis de Sade who lived a hundred years earlier and whose name Krafft-Ebing gave to these behaviours.

Careful study of de Sade and other sadists can broaden our approach to the study of extreme sexual abuse. The Marquis de Sade (1789/1987) was a famous eighteenth-century libertine, sexual criminal and pornographer. He developed a philosophy largely devoted to rationalising his sadistic deeds by claiming sexu-ality as the fundamental motivation of natural man. He spent most of his adult life imprisoned for sadistic crimes. He poisoned the inhabitants of a brothel with aphrodisiacs, tortured a prostitute in his private chapel, abducted and tortured a beggar, and sexually abducted his wife's younger sister. Even while incarcerated he continued to pay mothers to bring him their daughters as sexual victims; bones were found in his castle garden, probably from sexual victims who died 'accidentally' during sadistic orgies. It was in prison that he began his career as a writer of sadistic pornography. He denied personal sexual interest in homicidal sadism and necrophilia, although he wrote about such practices.

Indeed, when he was recruited as a judge in the aftermath of the French Revolution he refused to execute prisoners on grounds that the guillotine did not excite him sexually.

The case of de Sade as well as other cases collected by Krafft-Ebing would lead us to look for extreme abuse not only in pseudo-philosophic cult contexts, but also in criminal contexts, in the worlds of prostitution and pornography, in extreme family violence and also in settings of political and institutional torture. Use of this broader behavioural category (Durkheim, 1895/1984) facilitates both cross-cultural and historical comparisons.

Terminology: 'terrorisation' versus 'programming'

As we access earlier research about sadism, recent accounts of perpetrators' attempts to gain mind control over their victims come into contextual focus. As Krafft-Ebing noted, emotional terror and successful deception are as important to sadists as the infliction of bodily harm. One study found that the victim's facial expression of pain and terror, achieved by whatever means, provided the sadist's most direct source of satisfaction (Heilbrun and Seif, 1988). As a sadistic serial killer put it: 'The pleasure in the complete domination over another person is the very essence of the sadistic drive' (Dietz et al., 1990). Careful interviewing of sadists and their victims indicates that many methods are used to achieve total domination or 'soul murder' (Shengold, 1989) of the victim. Such methods, used by political torturers as well as by criminal sadists, include: control of basic bodily functions such as eating, sleeping and elimination; physical beatings, physical torture, psychological torture, control of information and misinformation, confinement and sensory deprivation, rape and genital mutilation, witnessed violence and threats, forced labour and poisoning. Galinas (1993) has used the term 'malevolence' to describe the emotional abuse found in these contexts. Induction into violence is an ultimate technique and test of this process in which an initial victim recruits new victims and eventually becomes a co-perpetrator.

This review proposes 'terrorisation' as a descriptor for sadistic efforts to gain absolute levels of control. 'Programming' would be reserved for the subgroup of terrorisation tactics involving combinations of modern hypnotic, behavioural and pyscho-pharmacological techniques. Terrorisation has been described in situations of extreme family violence, in Holocaust and other prison camp settings, and in hostages and other victims of political torture (Goldfield, 1988).

Historical examples of sadistic perpetrators

De Sade is not the only sadist in history whose career combined criminality, family violence, political violence, the creation of a pseudo-religion and involvement in pornography and prostitution. Caligula (Suetonius c. 120/1979) is described as marrying his sister and then killing her after she became pregnant. He is said to have delighted in watching prisoners being tortured. He replaced the heads of the statues of all the gods with his own head and created a brothel for the wives and daughters of his enemies.

Hitler is another historical figure whose sadism emerges not only in the 'final solution' but also in his sexual use of whipping and sadistic pornography, his sexual abuse of a niece who later committed suicide, and his creation of a private pseudo-religion made up of fragments of grail legends and European and Tibetan black magic (Ravenscroft, 1973).

Gilles de Rais (Opie and Opie, 1974), a French noble who fought with Joan of Arc and became the model for 'Bluebeard', and Aleister Crowley (Greaves, 1992), one of the rediscoverers of witchcraft folklore at the turn of the century, are other historical figures for whom the practice of black magic was only one aspect of a sadistic lifestyle that included the perpetration of crimes and family violence and dependence on sadistic sexual practices and pornography.

These historical examples illustrate aspects of sadistic abuse that, while absolutely typical, may strain the credulity of observers unfamiliar with the daily life of a de Sade or a Caligula. Violence is extreme. Victims and perpetrators are multiple. Enormous energy and planning are expended on perpetration. The diagnostic manual (APA, 1987) and recent studies of criminal sadists (Dietz *et al.*, 1990) describe in detail some of these characteristics. We do not yet have adequate data on the psychological characteristics of sadists. Extensive psychological testing on Nazi war criminals showed normal profiles (Harrower, 1976). Milgram's studies (1974) and more recent work (Gibson, 1990) indicate that almost any male can be taught to engage in sadistic behaviour. Females have not yet been studied in detail. Some theorists suggest that the association of pleasure with the process of killing is biological and connected to human evolution as hunters (Nadelson, 1992). Professionals need to acknowledge realistic difficulties in identifying sadistic perpetrators.

RECOGNISING VICTIMS OF SADISTIC ABUSE

In many cases the presence of sadistic elements in the child abuse account is readily available, either in the patient's initial responses to a detailed lifetime violence history or lifetime sexual history. Examples include: (1) patients who describe ritualistic punishments in childhood such as kneeling on chains or being bitten on the nipples (Goodwin, 1989); (2) patients whose sexual abuse led to damage requiring hospitalisation or surgical repair; or (3) patients whose childhood sexual abuse involved bondage, or beatings as a constant precursor of other bizarre elements such as the active pursuit of an incest pregnancy or use of excretions in sexual encounters. Even when such elements are documented, professionals may have difficulty recognising sadistic abuse. For example, the presence of lifetime foster care, of one or more intra-familial murders, of broken bones due to parental abuse, may not be noted in a later psychiatric record or, if noted, may not be connected to symptoms (Goodwin *et al.*, 1990). A child's off-hand mention of being tied up, threatened with a weapon or forced to eat vomitus may not be followed up because the therapist assumes this to be phantasy.

Even when the presence of childhood adversity is known from collateral sources, a lifetime violence history is necessary to understand the childhood environment, to determine whether other types of emotional, physical or sexual abuse or witnessed violence were part of the context, and to understand the patterns developed in childhood for communicating and containing emotions.

In those patients whose accounts of sadistic abuse surface later in treatment, narratives about abusive experiences may be interrupted by dissociative gaps or distortions. In some cases sadistic elements appear only in vivid flashbacks, traumatic nightmares, re-abusive re-enactments or body memories. In others severe post-traumatic, borderline and dissociative symptoms, often in an atypical presentation, coexist initially with a bland childhood history or with a dense childhood amnesia.

The presence of multiple severe symptoms in individuals whose dissociative problems impair both symptom description and the recounting of life history makes it easy for the patient to search for a misdiagnosis. Spirit possession, past life trauma, abduction by space aliens, culture-specific syndromes or schizo-affective schizophrenia become attractive pseudo-explanations when the alternative involves disclosure of severe childhood abuse and neglect.

Even when indicators of severe or sadistic abuse are noted, it is often wiser to pursue the symptoms and childhood memories that are at the surface, postponing use of special memory retrieval techniques until a safe treatment setting has been established. If the patient cannot yet deal with a parent's alcoholism or put into words his responses to it, he will have difficulty metabolising memories of more severe abuse. A prolonged interval of education about normal development and its disruptions and of ego-building to increase skill levels and independence may be necessary before a patient gains enough trust and autonomy to disclose severe levels of abuse.

The most serious risks around recognition and disclosure are conveyed by images of the Jonestown massacre of 1978 (Lasaga, 1980). Here, members of a large pseudo-religious cult committed mass suicide just as airplanes were landing bringing investigators to document the cult's abuses. The psychiatric syndrome that describes such phenomena is 'shared delusional disorder'. In this condition, the partners of a delusional leader come to share the leader's grandiose views about his own powers as well as his persecutory fears of the outside world. Separation is necessary to restore the passive partner's reality testing, but is also a feared catastrophe (Goodwin, 1989). Therapists should refrain from imposing their own beliefs on a victim in a way that substitutes a new set of grandiose delusions and persecutory fears for the old system imposed by the perpetrator.

SPECIALISED TREATMENT TECHNIQUES

Therapists skilled in treating other victims of child abuse should be able to apply similar techniques in approaching patients describing sadistic child abuse. In general, symptoms are more severe in these victims, so more time and more specialised techniques may be required (Chu, 1992). The goals, however, are the same: (1) establishing safety and symptom relief, (2) achieving life history narration without retraumatisation, and (3) defining developmental lacunae and establishing an environment in which behavioural, emotional and cognitive development can resume (Herman, 1992).

For each treatment phase we will describe potential complications and list special techniques which may be useful in that phase. At present we are working from anecdotal evidence. More precise definitions of symptoms, treatment techniques and stages in the natural history of treatment will be necessary as we begin to collect data on larger numbers of patients and design treatment trials.

Safety/symptom control

The autobiographical novel *I Never Promised You a Rose Garden* (Greenberg, 1964/1989) conveys the difficulties that may arise in trying to establish symptom relief and basic safety while treating someone whose abuse and self-defensive self-abuse are longstanding. In the book, as in other complicated treatments, the symptoms become a battleground between patient and therapist with the patient feeling paradoxically that self-mutilation or suicide is the only way to regain a place of safety.

Relevant co-morbid psychiatric syndromes that may be present include borderline personality disorders, compulsions, addictions, eating disorders, paraphilias and masochism. However, the available literature in all these areas tends to underestimate the role of trauma.

Table 4.1 lists technical interventions that may be introduced to achieve symptom control. Severely symptomatic patients with histories of severe abuse by human agency tend to require a great deal of treatment. Symptoms are usually concealed and minimised rather than exaggerated. Requests for increased therapy should be taken seriously, not dismissed as 'borderline manipulation'.

Table 4.1 Safety/symptom control – useful techniques

Treatment plan
Crisis plan
Hospitalisation
Medication
Addictions programming
Medical and nursing care
Hypnosis, imagery
Structured living
Networking

Therapists, however, must refrain from being drawn into over-activity or boundary loss. Over-protective over-activity can lead to self-aggrandising over-activity and even to re-abuse by the therapist. Being listened to remains the patient's most urgent need. Understanding the symptoms is the key to controlling them (Gardner and Goodwin, in press).

When symptoms are uncontrolled, or when the environment is dangerous or unsupportive, serious reconstructive work must be postponed in most cases.

Reconstructing life history

Most psychiatrists are familiar with the Schreber case, a case of florid psychotic symptomatology which developed in a nineteenth-century German judge after several years of psychiatric treatment. Not until a hundred years after his psychosis did it become clear that his symptoms had been re-enactments of his childhood abuse and of his childhood reactions to that abuse (Niederland, 1959). The major risk of reconstructing life history when abuse has been severe is that abreactions will lead to psychotic-level regression and distress which will be so destructive to functioning as to preclude, distort or obliterate the construction which is being attempted.

The techniques listed in Table 4.2 emphasise integrating and pacing insights about life history. Patients often complain they need to know more about gaps in childhood memory when the more urgent problem is grasping the full implications of memories already retrieved. It is important to keep in mind that it is not only childhood abuse that needs to be reconstructed, but also childhood coping strategies, symptoms, rescue and revenge fantasies, and at times in dissociative

Table 4.2 Reconstruction of life history – useful techniques

Physical signs and symptoms
Interviews with collaterals
Narration
Journaling, charting
Group therapy
Sibling group
Natural history of symptoms
Managing anxiety and regression
Hypnosis, imagery
Bibliography, films
Sand-tray therapy
Art therapy
Planning and titrating abreaction
Amytal interviews

disorders, adolescent and adult experiences in these same categories. One of the most frightening aspects of reconstruction is realising how unreliable, fragmented and confabulated the memory system has become.

Abreaction may be accompanied by loss of orientation to time, place and person. Psychotic transferences may emerge when the patient cannot differentiate the therapist from the sadistic abuser. When the victim becomes psychotic it is important to (1) shift the focus to safety and reality issues, (2) screen for non-traumatic causes of the psychosis, such as a coexisting major mood disorder, drug toxicity or physical illness, and (3) identify with precision the post-traumatic issues which led to the break with reality and the roles of anxiety and dissociative processes in mediating the psychotic presentation. Understanding the inter-relationships among triggers, memories, anxiety and dissociative symptoms will help control remaining baseline symptomatology as well as abreactions.

Sand-tray therapy has been an effective modality in allowing continued narration even when regression and anxiety impair verbal capacities.

Even if hypnosis is not used formally, intrusive trance states are likely to appear and the therapist needs to be skilled enough in hypnotic techniques to communicate with the patient in trance and help him gain more control of state changes (Braun, 1986).

Relearning

Once symptom control has been achieved and a working life history has been reconstructed, the victim of severe childhood abuse is ready to embark on treatment as it is more traditionally conceived, with goals of rehabilitation, self-understanding and personal change (see Table 4.3). Here the work of Winnicott, Kohut and related psychoanalytic theorists becomes relevant.

Even at this point the treatment may be complicated by an excessively prolonged course, therapeutic impasses and persistent relational problems due to deficient social skills despite important gains in other areas, such as creativity. Freud's patient 'The Wolf Man' illustrates some of these issues (Gardiner, 1971). He experienced transference psychoses; his need for psychotherapy was lifelong; after he ran out of money he paid for therapy with his paintings and later he paid by being a wonderful teaching case. However, given the multiple and severe abuse in his family and the numerous suicides, his outcome was positive.

Medical economics is at present unfriendly to situations in which long-term out-patient psychotherapy is the treatment of choice. Human as well as economic resources may become depleted. Therapist burn-out can be mitigated through the multi-disciplinary team approach which allows shifts in primary therapists as treatment progresses. For example, a therapist skilled in safety issues might maintain a commitment as a consultant or family therapist even after a more psychodynamically oriented person has assumed responsibility for individual therapy as it becomes more oriented to developmental issues. At this point, managing the treatment plan becomes a therapeutic modality in itself as the

Table 4.3 Relearning – useful techniques

Managing own treatment plan
Formal education
Vocational guidance
Parenting training
Sex and marital therapy
Physical education, body therapies
Dynamic personality
Creative work
Friendships, voluntary families
Wilderness therapy
Volunteer work, political action
Spiritual development

patient learns to distinguish benevolent from malevolent therapeutic environments and learns to create a world not ruled by terrorisation (Turkus, 1991).

Part of the therapist's task is to maintain hopefulness through this prolonged treatment. It is helpful to review in an on-going way the natural history of the victimisation syndrome and the strengths, accomplishments and wellness that have been manifest even during periods of maximal abuse and maximal symptoms.

DISCUSSION

Table 4.4 summarises, in mnemonic form, elements in a patient's account of childhood adversity that may alert the clinician to the possibility of sadistic or severe abuse in the developmental history. Such experiences may remain closely guarded secrets or confused mysteries even in those patients whose abuse was disclosed in childhood. Identification of extreme cases will become a priority as research in this area begins to quantify and differentiate the developmental impacts of different types of childhood adversity.

Use of the term 'sadistic abuse' emphasises the severity of the childhood

Table 4.4 Defining sadistic abuse – a summary mnemonic

Sadistic sexual and physical abuse
Accounts of torture
Despotic overcontrol, intentional terrorisation
Induction into violence
Satanic, cult, and/or ritual involvements
Malevolent emotional abuse and neglect

adversity and the possibility of sadistic or sado-masochistic types of re-enactments and transference. It reminds the clinician to utilise available research data including the child abuse literature and also databases concerning torture and torturers, Holocaust survivors, victims and users of prostitution and pornography, sadistic criminals and their targets, and violence as it occurs in cult and pseudo-religious contexts. Use of the older term, 'ritual abuse', risks distracting the clinician or researcher with arcane details while the extreme violence and destructiveness of the sadistic behaviours may be lost to focused awareness (Eco, 1990).

Treatment of patients who present with histories of sadistic abuse involves trauma-based principles well-described in the treatment of other child abuse survivors. Symptom variety, severity and duration seem to reach higher levels in this group and there are risks of complication and relapse in every phase of treatment.

ACKNOWLEDGEMENT

With thanks to Dr Kluft of the journal *Dissociation*, Vol. 6, Nos 2 & 3, 1993/94, for permission to reprint this chapter.

REFERENCES

American Psychiatric Association (APA) (1987) *Diagnostic and Statistical Manual of Mental Disorders*, 3rd edn, revised, Washington, DC, APA.

Braun, B. (1986) *Treatment of Multiple Personality Disorder*, Washington, DC, American Psychiatric Press.

Chu, J. (1992) 'The therapeutic rollercoaster. dilemmas in the treatment of child abuse survivors', *Journal of Psychotherapy Practice and Research* 1, 351–70.

de Sade, Marquis D.A.T. (1789/1987) *The One Hundred Days of Sodom*, New York, Grove.

Dietz, P., Hazelwood, R. and Warren, J. (1990) 'The sexually sadistic criminal and his offences', *Bulletin of the American Academy of Psychiatry and Law* 18, 163–78.

Durkheim, E. (1895/1984) *The Rules of Sociological Method*, 8th edn, New York, Free Press.

Eco, U. (1990) *Foucault's Pendulum*, New York, Ballantine.

Finkelhor, D., Williams, L. and Burns, N. (1988) *Nursery Crimes: Sexual Abuse in Day Care*, Newbury Park, CA, Sage.

Galinas, D. (1993) 'Relational patterns in incestuous families, malevolent variations and specific interventions with the adult survivors', in P. Paddison (ed.) *Treatment of Adult Survivors of Incest*, Washington, DC, American Psychiatric Press, pp. 1–36.

Ganaway, G. (1989) 'Historical versus narrative truth: clarifying the role of exogenous trauma in the etiology of MPD and its variants', *Dissociation* 2 (4), 205–19.

Gardner, R. and Goodwin, J. (in press) 'Io myth: therapeutic use in sexual abuse survivors', *American Journal of Psychiatry*.

Gardiner, M. (1971) *The Wolf Man by the Wolf Man*, New York, Basic Books.

Gibson, J. (1990) 'Factors contributing to the creation of a torturer', in P. Suedfeld (ed.) *Psychology and Torture*, New York, Hemisphere, pp. 77–88.

Goldfield, A. (1988) 'The physical and psychological sequelae of torture: symptomatology and diagnosis', *Journal of the American Medical Association* 259, 2725–9.

Goodwin, J. (1989) 'Persecution and grandiosity in incest fathers', in J. Goodwin (ed.) *Sexual Abuse*, 2nd edn, Chicago, Mosby Yearbook, pp. 83–94.

Goodwin, J. (1993) *Rediscovering Childhood Trauma. Historical Case Book and Clinical Applications*, Washington, DC, American Psychiatric Press.

Goodwin, J., Cheeves, K. and Connel, V. (1990) 'Borderline and other severe symptoms in adult survivors of incestuous abuse', *Psychiatric Annals* 20, 22–32.

Greaves, G. (1992) 'Alternative hypotheses regarding claims of satanic cult activity: a critical analysis', in D. Sakheim and S. Devine (eds) *Darkness and Light: Satanism and Ritual Abuse Unveiled*, Lexington, MA, Lexington, pp. 45-72.

Greenberg, J. (1964/1989) *I Never Promised You a Rose Garden*, New York, Holt, Rinehart & Winston.

Harrower, M. (1976) 'Rorschach record of the Nazi war criminals: an experimental study after 30 years', *Journal of Personality Assessment* 40, 341–51.

Heilbrun, A. and Seif, D. (1988) 'Erotic value of female distress in sexually explicit photographs', *Journal of Sexual Research* 24, 47–57.

Herman, J. (1992) *Trauma and Recovery*, New York, Basic Books.

Herman, J., Russell, D. and Trocki, K. (1986) 'Longterm effects of incestuous abuse in childhood', *American Journal of Psychiatry* 143, 1293–6.

Hill, S. and Goodwin, J. (1989) 'Satanism: similarities between patient accounts and pre-inquisition historical sources', *Dissociation* 2 (1), 39-44.

Jonker, F. and Jonker-Bakker, P. (1991) 'Experiences with ritualistic child sexual abuse: a case study from the Netherlands', *Child Abuse and Neglect* 15, 191–6.

Kelley, S. (1989) 'Stress responses of children to sexual abuse and ritual abuse in day care centres', *Journal of Interpersonal Violence* 4, 502–13.

Krafft-Ebing, R. von (1894/1965) *Psychopathia Sexualia with Especial Reference to Antipathic Sexual Instinct*, New York, Stein & Day, p. 53.

Lasaga, J. (1980) 'Death in Jonestown: techniques of political control by a paranoid leader', *Suicide and Life Threatening Behaviour* 10, 210–13.

Milgram, S. (1974) *Obedience to Authority*, New York, Harper & Row.

Nadelson, T. (1992) 'Attachment to killing', *Journal of the American Academy of Psychoanalysis* 20, 131–41.

Niederland, W. (1959) 'Schreber, father and son', *Psychoanalytic Quarterly* 28, 151–69.

Opie, I. and Opie, P. (1974) *The Classic Fairy Tales*, New York, Oxford University Press.

Ravenscroft, T. (1973) *The Spear of Destiny*, New York, Putnam.

Shengold, L. (1989) *Soul Murder*, New York, Yale University Press.

Suetonius (*c.* 120/1979) *The Twelve Caesars*, New York, Penguin.

Summit, R. (1988) 'Hidden victims, hidden pain', in G. Wyatt and G. Powell (eds) *Lasting Effects of Child Sexual Abuse*, Beverly Hills, CA, Sage, pp. 39-60.

Turkus, J. (1991) 'Psychotherapy and case management for Multiple Personality Disorder: synthesis for continuity of care', *Psychiatric Clinics of North America* 14, 649–60.

Young, W., Sachs, R., Braun, B. and Watkins, R. (1991) 'Patients reporting ritual abuse in childhood. Report of 37 cases', *Child Abuse and Neglect* 15, 181–9.

Chapter 5

The historical foundations of ritual abuse
An excavation of ancient infanticide

Brett Kahr

Brett Kahr is Lecturer in Psychotherapy, Regent's College, London.

Names, identities and background details have been changed wherever necessary to protect confidentiality.

> Go, go, go, said the bird: human kind
> Cannot bear very much reality.
>
> (T.S. Eliot, *Burnt Norton*, 1935)

In his timeless play, *The Importance of Being Earnest*, Oscar Wilde described that quintessentially gorgonesque character Lady Bracknell as 'a monster, without being a myth'. Audiences often laugh uncomfortably at this description because we know only too well that monsters can exist, and not only in mythology. During the last decade, numerous professionals and members of the public alike have debated the very existence of the monstrous phenomena known as ritual abuse and satanist abuse. Ever since Pamela Sue Hudson (1991), the pioneering social worker from California, began to disseminate her findings concerning the routine torture of extremely young children, the topic has provoked considerable controversy, as well as a flurry of interest in the popular press (e.g. Bennetts, 1993; Rose, 1993), in the reports of investigative journalists (e.g. Boyd, 1991; Tate, 1991), and in professional publications (e.g. Cozolino, 1989; Gould, 1992).

A group of Americans have begun to publish *S.O.A.R.*, a newsletter written by Survivors of Ritual Abuse; and a number of professional organisations have started to study the clinical realities with growing assiduousness. A major panel on ritual abuse will be held in New York in 1994, sponsored by the International Psychohistorical Association; and Dr Jean Goodwin of the University of Texas Medical Branch at Galveston, Texas, has begun preparation for a panel on this subject at a forthcoming meeting of the American Psychiatric Association. In London, the RAINS group for Ritual Abuse Information and Network Support hosts regular meetings for mental health workers, and the Association for Psychoanalytic Psychotherapy in the National Health Service hosted the very first public psychoanalytical conference on this topic in Great Britain, on 4 December 1993, under the title 'Satanist Abuse: Psychodynamic Perspectives', with Dr Robert Hale, Dr Phil Mollon and Ms Valerie Sinason as featured speakers, and Dr Arnon Bentovim and Dr Judith Trowell, two of England's most distinguished child abuse experts, as the chairpersons.

Other contributors to this volume will provide incontrovertible proof regarding the existence of ritual and satanist cults by chronicling work with both child and adult survivors, as well as work with perpetrators, not to mention the discoveries of underground caves and other venues in which the cult tortures would occur. Nevertheless, in spite of the wealth of data, many people have continued to dismiss the work on ritual abuse as a sensationalistic and hysterical outburst from a bevy of overly zealous and paranoid social workers. Others have admitted that though ritual abuse may exist, it occurs quite rarely, in merely one or two isolated cases. Still other people have claimed that cult abuse has only just appeared on our horizons as a new and unusual reflection of our degenerated post-Thatcher and post-Reagan era (cf. Lotto, 1994). In truth, we really do not have any full conception as to the actual incidence or prevalence of ritual abuse or satanist abuse, but we now find ourselves in a much better position to answer this question.

In the pages that follow, I shall review data from ancient history which suggests quite overwhelmingly that the ritualised murder of infants in the context of group meetings and religious ceremonies occurred with unremitting frequency, and that in order to understand contemporary child death and child torture, we must first recognise the insidious practices of our ancestors which have filtered down to the present time. If we can demonstrate that ritual abuse has always been a feature of human life, we may then find ourselves somewhat better equipped to recognise current cases.

In 1974, Lloyd de Mause, an American historian and psychoanalytical scholar, published a pathbreaking essay on 'The Evolution of Childhood', the first serious survey of child care through the ages. Based upon a review of literally thousands of sources, de Mause provided a framework in which we could study the relationships between children and parents. On the basis of his research, de Mause uncovered untold descriptions of abusive practices towards children, ranging from burning, stabbing and flogging, to buggering, drowning and even crushing the genitalia. His work shattered innumerable myths about the idyllic nature of childhood in the past, revealing for the first time that most children born prior to the twentieth century suffered from quite dramatic forms of abuse. De Mause and his co-workers at the Institute for Psychohistory in New York, and other colleagues around the world have subsequently expanded the original research, and now, after twenty years of psychoanalytically informed childhood history, we have a much clearer picture of the brutal realities of our distant ancestors (cf. Taylor, 1985; Schultz, 1986; Rokeah, 1990; Kahr, 1991).

Without doubt, the most disturbing research concerns the history of *infanticide* or *neonaticide*, in other words, the murder of infants and newborns.

Nowadays, we would regard actual, full-fledged infanticide as a rather rare and extreme manifestation of psychiatric disturbance (cf. McGrath, 1992; Morris and Wilczynski, 1993; Wilczynski, 1993); but during ancient times infanticide flourished, so much so that de Mause (1974: 51) described the period of history from Antiquity to the fourth century AD as the *'Infanticidal Mode'*. At first glance, it may sound preposterous to characterise an entire slice of history as infanticidal, but let us begin to sift through the evidence which has survived the decay of the centuries in order to comprehend the broad scope of filicidal behaviours.

At the present time, historians, archaeologists, literary scholars and others have amassed an abundance of strong evidence which suggests that the ancient Greeks, Romans, Egyptians, Gauls, Irish Celts, Scandinavians, Moabites, Ammonites, Etruscans, Taurians, Scythians, Phoenicians, Israelites and many other cultures besides, all killed babies as a routine matter. They did so by resorting to the following treacherous methods whereby children would be stabbed, starved, slashed at the neck, exposed on mountain tops, abandoned in the streets, drowned in rivers, tossed onto dung heaps, flung into deep pits, cooked, burned alive as sacrificial offerings, cannibalised or interred in the foundation stones of bridges and other monuments as good luck charms.

The data can be found in a multitude of sources such as mythology and folklore, drama, historical testimonials, medical writings, demographical records and archaeological remains. This review cannot be comprehensive by any means; instead, I shall mention only the most salient highlights from this body of research. (A more extensive distillation will appear in a special issue of *The Journal of Psychohistory* devoted to ritual abuse, to be published in 1994.) The vast majority of the forthcoming references will be drawn from Greek mythology, as these will be most familiar to an English language readership. Comparable data can readily be found in the source materials of other civilisations (e.g. de Mause, 1987, 1991).

In ancient mythology, references to murderousness of all kinds abound in almost every tale and, sadly, the children do not often escape. In Greek legend alone, we have numerous instances of infanticidal behaviour beginning with the figure of Cronus, who ate five of his children alive, gripped by the fear that his offspring might one day murder him. Zeus, the son of Cronus, did eventually avenge his swallowed siblings by assassinating his father. When Zeus became a parent, he abused his own son Hephaestos by hurling him off of Mount Olympus. Miraculously, Hephaestos survived the murderous, filicidal attack, but he spent a lifetime as a crippled and deformed figure, mocked and humiliated by other deities. Two more children of Zeus almost died, namely Amphion and Zethus, the twin sons from his adulterous union with Antiope, the Queen of Thebes. The boys had been exposed at birth on Mount Cithaeron, but they eventually survived with the succour of some compassionate shepherds.

Other infanticidal figures from the ancient legends include Medea, the protagonist of Euripides's drama, who murders her two children in order to spite her philandering husband Jason; Agamemnon, the warrior who sacrifices his daughter Iphigenia in order to ensure smooth progress from the gods for his campaign; Herakles, the mighty strong-man who killed his children, believing them to be his enemies; and of course, the Minotaur, that tragic underground creature who fed on virginal blood. The Minotaur ate older children, not infants, but as the parents themselves supplied the Minotaur with these youthful trophies, we must acknowledge the filicidal intent. And what about Oedipus? His biological parents, King Laius and Queen Jocasta, exposed him at birth, a fact all too frequently overlooked in much of psychoanalytical theory, which tends to focus only on Oedipus's erotic impulses, to the exclusion of his infanticidal fears. Dr Heisaku Kosawa, the undisputed founder of Japanese psychoanalysis, spoke with Sigmund Freud in 1932 about infanticide, informing Freud of the Japanese equivalent of Oedipus, a figure known as Ajase, the son of the Indian King, Binbashara, nearly murdered by his mother, Queen Idaike (Okonogi, 1989).

In the Old Testament and the New Testament of the Bible, the killing of babies appears as a regular motif. As children, many of us learned about the wisdom of King Solomon in his dealing with the two mothers, both of whom claimed parentage of a certain child. Solomon proposed to cut the child in half so that the two women might share him. One mother disapproved of this solution, but the other woman agreed with Solomon's suggestion. Though the baby did not die in the end, the overt use of neonaticide as a possible juridical solution seems remarkable. But of greater importance still, we must consider the plight of Abraham and Isaac, and that of Jesus. In the tale of Abraham and Isaac, the father prepares to sacrifice his son as proof of his fidelity to God. Abraham refrains from the killing only when an angel intervenes to save Isaac. As a tribute to God, Abraham then circumcises both himself and his son, thus opting for genital mutilation as a *displacement* for infanticide. I would like to suggest that each time a baby undergoes a religious circumcision ceremony, the parents thereby express their unconscious hostility towards the newborn, a form of hostility which related to strong death wishes in our ancestors. In the Christian tradition, the murder of Jesus also epitomises the filicidal tendency. As Lloyd de Mause (1975: 412) has observed, 'Early Christianity, for example, directly acted out the killing of a son under orders of his Father.' Religious practitioners will be rather displeased to realise that the foundational stories of Abraham, the first Jew, and Jesus, the first Christian, revolve around deferred filicide followed by the removal of a body part (the penile foreskin), and around a tale of actual filicide through crucifixion (cf. Bergmann, 1992).

Greek drama also thrives on infanticide as a staple feature. In the story of *Medea*, a brilliant psychological investigation by Euripides, we learn why Medea has murdered her innocent children. Jilted by her husband Jason, who has abandoned her in order to marry Glauce, the daughter of Creon, the King of Corinth, the distraught Medea runs a sword through her offspring as an expression of her bloodthirsty rage. Ancient Greek spectators would have heard the following dialogue (albeit in the original language):

CHORUS:	Do you hear? The children are calling for help. O cursed, miserable woman!
CHILDREN'S VOICES:	Help, help! Mother, let me go! Mother, don't kill us!
CHORUS:	Shall we go in? I am sure we ought to save the children's lives.
CHILDREN'S VOICES:	Help, help, for the gods' sake! She is killing us! We can't escape from her sword!

Clearly, Medea uses her children as receptacles for her own unbearable affects. No doubt they remind her of Jason, the lecherous father, and they also remind her of her own unwantedness which she then kills off. The Chorus chillingly typify Greek attitudes to child murder. They find it troublesome, and yet they do nothing, querying, '*Shall*' we go in, whereas a modern chorus would cry '*Let*' us go in, without delay. The death of children appears in many other works including *Ion*, also by Euripides, a story in which we learn that birds of prey and wild beasts feast on the carcasses of youngsters exposed on the roads. In Act Four of Menander's comedy, *The Girl from Samos*, one of the characters threatens to murder a baby, and the child's grandfather, Demeas, delivers an impassioned speech, expressing fear that he might have to watch his grandson being roasted and killed. In *The Bacchae* by Euripides, a story also told in *The Metamorphoses* by Ovid, a mother called Agave rips off the head of her son Pentheus, one of the most blood-curdling moments in ancient drama, or ancient poetry.

We also have a great deal of data from the ancient Greek and Roman chronicles of the period. Many eye witnesses wrote about the practice of infanticide, including Diodorus, Orosius, Plutarch, Siculus, Tertullian and numerous others. The sacrifices occurred as individual instances, but more often than not in *group* settings of a *religious* nature, similar to the structure of contemporary accounts of ritual abuse. In Sparta, for example, a council of elders would convene to inspect the newborn babies. Those neonates who did not conform to the expectations of the elders would be hurled off the heights of Mount Taggetus into the depths of the Apotheta, the consuming cavern below (Radbill, 1968; cf. Sinason, 1991, 1992).

Medical authorities also endorsed the practice of infanticide. Even the great Roman physician, Soranus, known for his progressive views, included a section on 'How to Recognize the Newborn That is Worth Rearing' in his textbook on *Gynaecology*. Soranus recommended that infants who cried too much or too little, as well as those with physical imperfections, should be slaughtered. The demographers have also provided data about child murder, especially the selective killing of girl babies. In the famous study of 364 families in the *Prosopographica Attica*, only one girl seems to have survived for every five boys, suggesting a strong sex difference in the rates of filicide (cf. Golden, 1981; Harris, 1982; Patterson, 1985).

Perhaps the most compelling data concerning ancient infanticide can be found in the discoveries of the archaeologists. Among the ancient Jews, babies would be sacrificed to Moloch in the Valley of Hinnom, then sent to Gehenna (that is, Hell). The psychoanalytically trained anthropologist, Géza Róheim (1939) reported on the excavation of the ruins of Gezer, nearby, in Palestine. In the rubble, the investigators found a half-skeleton of a girl roughly 14 years of age, and probably of Canaanite extraction. The body had been cut or sawn deliberately at the eighth thoracic vertebra, thus indicating some wilful mutilation. James George Frazer, the noted anthropological researcher, had also discovered skeletons of infants in large jars beneath the floor of the temple in Gezer. The presence of these urns in a house of worship suggests that the infants had been exterminated in the context of a religious ceremony, for sacrificial purposes. Most infants in the last millennium whose parents wished them dead, simply did not merit a burial at all, but ended up instead in a river bed, or on the streets, or in deep ravines. Thus, when parents *did* take the trouble to preserve the bones in specially marked containers, they did so as a religious gift to the upper deities.

Certainly, the best evidence of all for the existence of ancient infanticide came to light during the discovery of the massive Carthaginian burial sanctuary in Tanit, known traditionally by the Hebrew name 'Tophet', a reference to a special cemetery for sacrificed children, near Jerusalem. The burial ground at Tanit had been in use for an extensive period of time, from approximately 750 BC until 146 BC, and it remains the largest burial ground ever uncovered. We can be absolutely certain that the Carthaginians slaughtered their own infants and children in ritualised religious ceremonies, because the burial urns are covered with decorative stone stelae which refer *explicitly* to the sacrifices. More than 7000 stelae from the latter period of the sacrifices have been disinterred during this century alone (Brown, 1991).

Although the tablets of these ancient people had already been discovered in the nineteenth century, the true meaning of the inscriptions did not become evident until the twentieth century, in part because scholars had difficulties undertaking the translations of the stelae. One cannot help but wonder whether anxieties and emotional resistances to this grisly material had interfered with the translation work. Studies of the stelae have nevertheless revealed the routine murder of children from earliest infancy up through the age of 4. We have evidence that the Carthaginians killed boys as well as girls, noble children as well as poor children, and even the highly prized firstborn sons. The veritable breadth of the choice of victims shatters any simplistic notions that only the poor killed their children, to save them from starvation. Lloyd de Mause (1990) has already made this astute observation in his more recent essay on 'The History of Child Assault'. In fact, there may even be evidence to suggest that the wealthy performed infanticide *more* regularly, in order to assuage the envious wrath of their gods.

In his comprehensive and definitive survey of the Carthage sacrifices, Shelby Brown (1991) has summarised the primary *conscious* reasons for which parents killed their offspring. Infanticide seems to have occurred for three main purposes:

1 to please the gods;
2 to appease the gods during periods of war or plague;
3 to obtain personal successes.

As for the *unconscious* factors, we might want to think about the ways in which the paranoid adults of yesteryear, besieged by pestilence and disease, gripped by persecutory imaginal gods, and victimised by horrific forms of intrafamilial child abuse, would use their offspring as receptacles for their own disavowed parts (cf. Winnicott, 1949; Bloch, 1978).

The sacrifices would be executed in the name of the Greek god Cronus, or the Roman god Saturn. Sometimes, parents would kill their young in the name of Herakles, or in the name of other, unspecified figures. Cleitarchus, a writer from the third century BC, provided a description of the death ritual, which Brown (1991: 23) has related to us:

> the child was cremated in the arms of a bronze statue of the deity. The hands of the statue extended over a brazier into which the child fell once the flames had caused its limbs to contract and its mouth to open. The grimace was known as 'sardonic laughter' because the child seemed to die laughing. This text may suggest that the child was alive and conscious when burned, or it may merely describe the initial stages of the child's cremation after it had been sacrificed.

Whether the child died by burning, or whether the adult slit the throat first (as Plutarch has testified), the urns in the Tophet at Tanit contain untold fragments of charred baby bones. Chillingly, investigators found other Tophets at Motya and at Lillibeum in Sicily, at Hadrumetum in Tunisia, at Cirta in Algeria, and at Monte Sirai, Su Cardulinu, Nora, Sulcis and at Tharros, all in Sardinia. One cannot overemphasise the importance of the discovery of the many fragments of baby bone and the inscribed plaques for the study of contemporary ritual and satanist abuse. Many sceptics proclaim that the murder of babies cannot possibly occur, because nobody can find any forensic evidence. But the very existence of the *physical* remnants of infanticide attests to the historical reality of this gruesome form of madness.

Not only did our ancient ancestors practise infanticide, but they often participated in other cult formations, the most notorious of which may be the Roman Bacchanalias which flourished in the second century BC, involving thousands of men and women in sexual perversions and ritual murders, chronicled by the historian Titus Livius. The cult would perform sacrifices to the salacious god Bacchus or to his Greek equivalent Dionysus. According to Arnold J. Toynbee (1965), the cult flourished not only in Rome, but also in Methymna, Pergamum, Erythrae, Rhodes, Cos, Thera, Cnidos, Seleucia-on-Calycadnus, Cyme, Delphi, Corcyra, Sicily, Etruria and elsewhere in Greece and Italy. The initiation rites often included enforced homosexual relations, and those who refused to participate would become sacrificial victims. In addition to the Bacchic cult, the followers of the Hindu god Mithras performed well-known ceremonies in Rome, involving the sacrifice of bulls, followed by ritual baths in the spilled blood.

As the centuries progressed, the prevalence of infanticide does seem to have reduced dramatically, especially once the general quality of child care had begun to improve. However, we still have reports of notable outbursts of neonaticidal and filicidal practices during all epochs of history (cf. Langer, 1974); and scholars have documented particular episodes of widespread infanticide ranging from those in England during the Middle Ages (Kellum, 1974), to the practices in Florence throughout the Renaissance (Trexler, 1973a, 1973b), to the butchery in Slovenia in the nineteenth century (Puhar, 1985), not to mention the all too numerous modern reports which congest the psychiatric and psychological periodicals (e.g. Resnick, 1969; Christoffel and Liu, 1983; Newlands and Emery, 1991). References to baby murder appear so often throughout history that it would require several volumes to document all the eyewitness reports (cf. Tierney, 1989). Often, the killing of children became embroiled with more overtly satanist connections, such as during the Würzburg witch scare of 1629. At least 60 per cent of the accused 'witches' who perished at the stake were young children (Midelfort, 1972).

Sadly, I cannot document the extensive inter-relationships between baby murder and satanism in the context of such a brief report, although other writers have begun to do so in splendid fashion such as Tim Tate (1991) whose work on the history of satanist groups includes detailed surveys of the misdeeds of a panoply of notorious personalities. Tate's book includes studies of: Gilles de Rais, the Breton nobleman and aide to Jeanne d'Arc, who killed more than 800 children in the name of Satan during the fifteenth century; Françoise-Athenais de Mortmart, the Marquise de Montespan, mistress to King Louis XIV of France, who participated in Black Masses, involving the slitting of children's throats, followed by their disembowelling; and Aleister Crowley, the infamous 'Great Beast' of satanism, who claimed to have murdered 150 male children every year between 1912 and 1928. One must also consider Martin H. Katchen's (1992) very worthy essay on the history of satanist religions, as well as the exceptionally revealing work of Dr Jean M. Goodwin (e.g. Goodwin, 1993; Hill and Goodwin, 1993a, 1993b) who has brilliantly linked demonic possession and sadistic acts to profound experiences of child abuse and trauma, thus providing us with important clues for treatment and prevention.

We live in a world dominated by irrationality, obsessed with vampires, occultism, poltergeists, superstitions and devils. Our theatre and ballet depict these themes, as evidenced by the production of the Norwegian musical *Which Witch?* in 1992 at the Piccadilly Theatre in London, and by the launch of *The Witch Boy*, a new piece in the repertoire of the London City Ballet, which also had its debut in 1992. And the archives of modern cinema literally overflow with ghoulish films such as *Rosemary's Baby*, not to mention the fifty-three films listed in the revised eighth edition of *Halliwell's Film Guide* (Halliwell, 1992) whose titles begin with the words 'Devil', 'Devils', or 'Devil's'. In the 1966 film,

The Witches, Joan Fontaine portrays a school teacher who stumbles upon a secret underground coven whose members perform ritual sacrifices. As the motion picture nears it climax, Miss Fontaine enters the chamber just in time to stop the priestess from slaughtering a 14-year-old virgin girl. (As a matter of psychoanalytical interest, Kay Walsh, spouse of the eminent Kleinian analyst Elliott Jaques, played the role of the murderous priestess.) Even seemingly innocent rituals, such as college fraternity initiations, often result in the sacrificial deaths of young students (Bloom, 1991).

Every single contemporary case of ritual or satanist abuse has involved allegations concerning the murder of babies, and to many sceptics in the mental health profession, in the media or in law enforcement, this remains the most difficult aspect of the case to accept (Sinason, 1993). But if one considers the vast history of infanticide, then one begins to realise that baby murder has a long and unrelenting ancestry. In the historical studies of ritual abuse written by Tim Tate (1991) and by Martin H. Katchen (1992), one has the impression that only highly perverse and unusual sadists such as Aleister Crowley engaged in child murder. In fact, the assassination of children has always been a *normative* experience, perpetrated by ostensibly respectable individuals in the course of socially sanctioned ceremonies. As I indicated in an earlier study on the possible relationship between parental death wishes towards infants and clinical schizophrenia in adult life,

> If we can bear to read the writings of the psychohistorians on infanticide, we will understand that the very foundations of humanity have been constructed upon the charred bones of dead infants. Although this murderousness has abated considerably in recent centuries, it has not yet vanished, and I would argue that its modern incarnation can be found in our psychiatric hospitals and on our battlefields.
>
> (Kahr, 1993: 271)

I now wish to suggest that the infanticidal urge of fathers and mothers also seeks expression in ritualistic, satanistic and sadistic forms of child abuse.

Of course, the mere existence of ritual filicide in antiquity does not prove that child deaths occur nowadays in satanist covens. But the historical data confirms that human beings possess the capability of committing such atrocities. As the astute Roman historian Titus Livius, better known as Livy, once observed,

> The study of history is the best medicine for a sick mind; for in history you have a record of the infinite variety of human experience plainly set out for all to see; and in that record you can find for yourself and your country both examples and warnings; fine things to take as models, base things, rotten through and through, to avoid.

We avoid our history at our peril, and at the possible peril of too many vulnerable children.

ACKNOWLEDGEMENTS

I should like to express my very deep gratitude to Ms Valerie Sinason for having encouraged me to write this historical study, and more particularly, I want to thank her for her courageous, pioneering and creative work in the field of ritual abuse studies. I also wish to express my appreciation to Dr Sandra Bloom, Mr Lloyd de Mause, Dr Jean Goodwin, Mr Sonu Shamdasani and Mrs Olave Snelling for their generous contributions to this project, and to Mr John Cooper, Mrs Judy Cooper, Mr Ian Mordant, and Dr Hisako Watanabe for helpful bibliographical suggestions. Finally, I must thank Mr Matthew Lagden, the distinguished classical historian, for his assistance, and for having taught me so much about the ancient world.

The quotation from T.S. Eliot appears by kind permission of Faber & Faber Ltd.

REFERENCES

Bennetts, Leslie (1993) 'Nightmares on Main Street', *Vanity Fair* 56 (6), 22, 24–7, 30–3.

Bergmann, Martin S. (1992) *In the Shadow of Moloch: The Sacrifice of Children and its Impact on Western Religions*, New York, Columbia University Press.

Bloch, Dorothy (1978) *'So the Witch Won't Eat Me': Fantasy and the Child's Fear of Infanticide*, Boston, Houghton Mifflin Company.

Bloom, Sandra L. (1991) 'Everyday sadism: hazing practices and abuse', unpublished typescript.

Boyd, Andrew (1991) *Blasphemous Rumours: Is Satanic Ritual Abuse Fact or Fantasy? An Investigation*, London, Fount Paperbacks.

Brown, Shelby (1991) *Late Carthaginian Child Sacrifice and Sacrificial Monuments in their Mediterranean Context*, Sheffield, JSOT Press and American Schools of Oriental Research.

Christoffel, Katherine K. and Liu, Kiang (1983) 'Homicide death rates in childhood in 23 developed countries: U.S. rates atypically high', *Child Abuse and Neglect* 7, 339–5.

Cozolino, Louis J. (1989) 'The ritual abuse of children: implications for clinical practice and research', *Journal of Sex Research* 26, 131–8.

de Mause, Lloyd (1974) 'The evolution of childhood', in Lloyd de Mause (ed.) *The History of Childhood*, New York, Psychohistory Press, pp. 1–73.

de Mause, Lloyd (1975) 'Psychohistory and psychotherapy', *History of Childhood Quarterly* 2, 408–14.

de Mause, Lloyd (1987) 'The history of childhood in Japan', *Journal of Psychohistory* 15, 147–51.

de Mause, Lloyd (1990) 'The history of child assault', *Journal of Psychohistory* 18, 1–29.

de Mause, Lloyd (1991) 'The universality of incest', *Journal of Psychohistory* 19, 123–64.

Golden, Mark (1981) 'Demography and the exposure of girls at Athens', *Phoenix* 35, 316–31.

Goodwin, Jean M. (1993) 'Human vectors of trauma: illustrations from the Marquis de Sade', in Jean M. Goodwin (ed.) *Rediscovering Childhood Trauma: Historical Casebook and Clinical Applications*, Washington, DC, American Psychiatric Press, pp. 95–111.

Gould, Catherine (1992) 'Diagnosis and treatment of ritually abused children', in David K. Sakheim and Susan E. Devine (eds) *Out of Darkness: Exploring Satanism and Ritual Abuse*, New York, Lexington Books, pp. 207–48.

Halliwell, Leslie (1992) *Halliwell's Film Guide*, 8th edn, revised, John Walker (ed.), London, Grafton.

Harris, William V. (1982) 'The theoretical possibility of extensive infanticide in the Graeco-Roman world', *Classical Quarterly* 32 (new series), 114–16.

Hill, Sally and Goodwin, Jean M. (1993a) 'Freud's notes on a seventeenth-century case of demonic possession: understanding the uses of exorcism', in Jean M. Goodwin (ed.) *Rediscovering Childhood Trauma: Historical Casebook and Clinical Applications*, Washington, DC, American Psychiatric Press, pp. 45–63.

Hill, Sally and Goodwin, Jean M. (1993b) 'Demonic possession as a consequence of childhood trauma', *Journal of Psychohistory* 20, 399–411.

Hudson, Pamela S. (1991) *Ritual Child Abuse: Discovery, Diagnosis and Treatment*, Saratoga, CA, R and E Publishers.

Kahr, Brett (1991) 'The sexual molestation of children: historical perspectives', *Journal of Psychohistory* 19, 191–214.

Kahr, Brett (1993) 'Ancient infanticide and modern schizophrenia: the clinical uses of psychohistorical research', *Journal of Psychohistory* 20, 267–73.

Katchen, Martin H. (1992) 'The history of satanic religions', in David K. Sakheim and Susan E. Devine (eds) *Out of Darkness: Exploring Satanism and Ritual Abuse*, New York, Lexington Books, pp 1–19.

Kellum, Barbara A. (1974) 'Infanticide in England in the later middle ages', *History of Childhood Quarterly* 1, 367–88.

Langer, William L. (1974) 'Infanticide: a historical survey', *History of Childhood Quarterly* 1, 353–65.

Lotto, David (1994) 'On witches and witch hunts: ritual and satanic cult abuse', *Journal of Psychohistory* 21, in press.

McGrath, Patrick (1992) 'Maternal filicide in Broadmoor Hospital 1919-69', *Journal of Forensic Psychiatry* 3, 271–97.

Midelfort, H.C. Erik (1972) *Witch Hunting in Southwestern Germany, 1562-1684: The Social and Intellectual Foundations*, Stanford, CA, Stanford University Press.

Morris, Allison and Wilczynski, Ania (1993) 'Rocking the cradle: mothers who kill their children', in Helen Birch (ed.) *Moving Targets: Women, Murder and Representation*, London, Virago Press, 198–217.

Newlands, Mary and Emery, John S. (1991) 'Child abuse and cot deaths', *Child Abuse and Neglect* 15, 275–8.

Okonogi, Keigo (1989) 'Ajase complex and the mother–child relationship in Japan', unpublished typescript.

Patterson, Cynthia (1985) '"Not worth the rearing": the causes of infant exposure in Ancient Greece', *Transactions of the American Philological Association* 115, 103–23.

Puhar, Alenka (1985) 'Childhood in nineteenth-century Slovenia', *Journal of Psychohistory* 12, 291–312.

Radbill, Samuel X. (1968) 'A history of child abuse and infanticide', in Ray E. Helfer and C. Henry Kempe (eds) *The Battered Child*, Chicago, IL, University of Chicago Press, 3–17.

Resnick, Phillip J. (1969) 'Child murder by parents: a psychiatric review of filicide', *American Journal of Psychiatry* 26, 73–82.

Róheim, Géza (1939) 'The covenant of Abraham', *International Journal of Psycho-Analysis* 20, 452–9.

Rokeah, Zefira Entin (1990) 'Unnatural child death among Christians and Jews in medieval England', *Journal of Psychohistory* 18, 181–226.

Rose, Elizabeth S. (1993) 'Surviving the unbelievable: a first-person account of cult ritual abuse', *Ms.* 3 (4), 40–5.

Schultz, Magdelene (1986) 'The blood libel: a motif in the history of childhood', *Journal of Psychohistory* 14, 1–24.

Sinason, Valerie (1991) 'A brief and selective look at the history of disability', unpublished typescript.

Sinason, Valerie (1992) '"They don't know one hole from another": clinical and historical notes on sexual abuse of children and adults with a mental handicap', Lecture Series on 'Aspects of Child Abuse: Psycho-Analytical and Historical Perspectives', The British Institute for Psychohistory, London, 14 March.

Sinason, Valerie (1993) Personal communication to the author. 3 September.

Tate, Tim (1991) *Children for the Devil: Ritual Abuse and Satanic Crime*, London, Methuen.

Taylor, Karen J. (1985) 'Venereal disease in nineteenth-century children', *Journal of Psychohistory* 12, 431–63.

Tierney, Patrick (1989) *The Highest Altar: The Story of Human Sacrifice*, New York, Viking Penguin.

Toynbee, Arnold J. (1965) *Hannibal's Legacy: The Hannibalic War's Effects on Roman Life. Volume II. Rome and Her Neighbours After Hannibal's Exit*, London, Oxford University Press.

Trexler, Richard C. (1973a) 'Infanticide in Florence: new sources and first results', *History of Childhood Quarterly* 1, 98–116.

Trexler, Richard C. (1973b) 'The foundlings of Florence, 1395–1455', *History of Childhood Quarterly* 1, 259–84.

Wilczynski, Ania (1993) 'Child-killing by parents: social, legal and gender issues', unpublished typescript.

Winnicott, Donald W. (1949) 'Hate in the counter-transference', *International Journal of Psycho-Analysis* 30, 69–74.

Chapter 6

Looking for clues
A review of the literature on false allegations of sexual abuse in childhood

Gwen Adshead

Dr Gwen Adshead is Lecturer in Victimology, Forensic Psychiatry Traumatic Stress Project, Institute of Psychiatry, The Maudsley Hospital.

Names, identities and background details have been changed wherever necessary to protect confidentiality.

LOOKING FOR CLUES: FALSE ALLEGATIONS OF CHILD ABUSE: A REVIEW OF THE LITERATURE

It is clear that sexual and physical child abuse occurs, and occurs frequently within Western society. The theory that most if not all victim accounts are phantasy (Freud, 1924) is no longer tenable given prevalence figures like 10 per cent in the UK (Baker and Duncan, 1985) or up to 62 per cent (females), and 16 per cent (males) in the USA (Finkelhor, 1993; Kendall-Tackett *et al.*, 1993). However, the reality of child abuse is not easily accepted and denial by others is common (Summit, 1988; Bentovim, 1993; Jackson and Nuttall, 1993). The most common form for denial to take is to question the validity of the allegations made by children. Child abuse carries a difficult burden of proof in the criminal courts, especially for sexual abuse. It is possible to read Sir Matthew Hale's seventeenth-century warning about rape (cited in Brownmiller, 1975) – '[It] is an accusation easily to be made and hard to be proved, and harder to be defended by the party accused, tho' never so innocent' – and recognise this sentiment as one commonly expressed about children's allegations of assault, and also the allegations of adults who allege that they were abused as children. It seems plausible to expect that denial will increase in situations where the alleged abuse is horrific in its detail, such as occurs in relation to ritual abuse.

Nearly all the work on false allegations has focused on child sexual abuse (CSA), and this review will therefore have little to say about child physical abuse. The extent to which allegations of CSA are actually false is not well researched. This may be attributed in part to the legal processes which frequently follow such allegations, and which are much less amenable to medical scientific scrutiny, concerned as they are with the collection of evidence, the attribution of guilt and the apportioning of blame. Although it is reasonable to suppose that all false allegations of CSA would be reported (otherwise why make them?), it is well known that many 'true' victims of CSA never tell anyone at all about their experiences, and it is possible for 'true' allegations to be under-reported (Finkelhor, 1986; Kendall-Tackett *et al.*, 1993). It is thus possible that false allegations are likely to be over-represented, because estimates of the total number of allegations that could be made will be inaccurate. To be proved false they have to be investigated, but we know that not all are investigated and many are not even reported.

False allegations made by children

Fifteen years ago, Goodwin (Goodwin *et al.*, 1978) described false accusation prevalence by reviewing eighty-eight papers on incest published between 1972 and 1977. Only one paper documented the frequency of the allegations, and found that 6 per cent were concluded to be false *by emergency room staff* (emphasis added).This emphasis is important in the review of the literature. Very few of the studies available have looked at allegations that were found to be false after a police investigation of the facts or a legal trial of the evidence; rather, social work and health care professionals have made a determination of 'truth'. Whether this determination can have the same factual status as a legal finding is debatable.

The Goodwin 1978 study found the following:

1 that false allegations by children are usually opportunistic, rather than pre-meditated;
2 that such children usually have an adult confederate;
3 that mothers with a psychotic illness are frequently involved in allegations that are later shown to be false;
4 that false retractions are also common.

Goodwin concludes that false allegations are rare. Other workers such as Jones and McGraw (1987) studied incest allegations and found a false allegation prevalence of about 2 per cent. Everson and Boat (1989) studied CSA allegations in child protection offices in the USA and found that the level of false allegations (as determined by social workers) varied with the age of the child. Among pre-school children, the range was 1.7–2.7 per cent, whereas for adolescents the range was 8–12 per cent, with an overall average for all ages of 5–8 per cent. Everson and Boat also noted that some case workers seemed to discover more false allegations than others, and conclude that bias is possible.

Specifically, high rates of false allegations are said to be found in the context of custody disputes (Benedek and Schetky, 1985; Green, 1986, 1991). Mikkelson *et al.* (1992) reviewed twenty-two case reports in detail, and attempted to describe subtypes of false allegation. They conclude that there are four subtypes:

1   allegations in the context of a custody dispute, which were most frequent (approximately thirteen cases out of twenty-two);
2   allegations arising out of psychological disturbance in the accuser (two out of twenty-two; in both cases the allegations were made by the adult caregivers of alleged child victim);
3   conscious manipulation by child or adolescent (two out of twenty-two);
4   iatrogenic cases: where the clinician believes abuse has taken place; particularly associated with somewhat rigidly held beliefs (five out of twenty-two).

The authors point out that these subtypes may coexist. It is noteworthy that conscious manipulation or lying by children appears to be rare and that the majority of false allegations are driven by adults, rather than children themselves (see also Klajner-Diamond *et al.*, 1987; Green, 1991). It is also noteworthy that almost a quarter of the false allegations were driven by the investigating professional.

Other papers have similar findings (Faller, 1984; Green, 1986, 1991). A review of these papers seems to suggest that children very rarely make up malicious false allegations of their own accord: in 98 per cent of allegations, children are *not* deliberately setting out to make trouble for adults. This emphasis is important because there may be a perception by some investigators that children enjoy malicious trouble-making. False allegations appear to be much more likely when adults initiate them (such as in custody disputes), and these appear to be the majority of allegations. Children are vulnerable to pressure, especially from people who they love or fear, or who are in authority over them such as parents and child protection officers. It is plausible to argue that if children can be pressurised into unwanted sexual activity, then they can be pressurised into making and holding false allegations.

False allegations by adults

Adults also make allegations that they were abused in childhood. This may lead to legal action, both civil and criminal, against the alleged offender, with ensuing family disruption. This pattern of false allegations has caused particular concern in relation to both children and adults who disclose that they have been abused in therapy, apparently after pressure from abuse investigators or therapists. This has been described, perhaps somewhat inaccurately, as 'false memory syndrome', and refers to the possible inclusion of false material in retrieved memories (Bartlett, 1957). This issue has generated controversy, and is well discussed by Berliner and Loftus (1992). They point out that little is known about suggestibility within a psychotherapeutic framework, nor is it known whether memories can be 'created' and 'suggested' in the way implied. Such allegations are difficult to prove because it may be many years since the alleged events took place, and because doubt is often thrown upon allegations that are not made at the time of the alleged offence (as is also common for rape victims; see Adler, 1987). It may also be suggested that memories of childhood that are recalled in adulthood are inaccurate.

Remembering childhood: influences on accuracy

One may then ask whether it is true that childhood memories cannot be accurately recalled in adulthood. It may be helpful here to consider some of the evidence about memory retrieval. A detailed review cannot be attempted here (see Baddeley, 1990, for review, cited in Brewin *et al.*, 1993). It is known that the retrieval of memory is subject to a large variety of influences, including the context of retrieval and the nature of the content of the memory. For example, abused children tend to disclose less serious material first, and only disclose details of more serious abuse after several weeks of a therapeutic relationship (Gonzalez *et al.*, 1993). This confirms Finkelhor's view that children who disclose abuse tend to minimise their experience, rather than the reverse (Finkelhor, 1983). This is consistent with the avoidant aspect of post-traumatic reactions, as described by Horowitz (1973), and it may be that there are specific effects of chronic post-traumatic stress on the retrieval of memory. For example, it is known that increased arousal may alter the ability to retrieve memories (Christianson and Loftus, 1987), and increased psycho-physiological arousal is recognised as a feature of post-traumatic stress (Pitman, 1993). Under hypnosis, there is an increase in retrieval of both correct and incorrect memories, and the use in court of material obtained under hypnosis as legal testimony is not recommended (AMA, 1985).

A review of the validity of retrospective reports of early childhood is given in Brewin *et al.* (1993). This paper discusses in detail three objections to the validity of retrospective accounts in childhood: the essentially doubtful nature of auto-biographical memory, the effect of psychopathology on memory and retrieval bias as a result of mood (i.e. depressed patients are more likely to remember bad things than good). The authors conclude that there is little evidence that the recall of adverse events in childhood by psychiatric patients is unreliable.

None of the studies cited by Brewin *et al.* specifically address recall in therapy, nor do the studies appear to address abuse specifically. Herman and Schatzow (1987) found that in a sample of psychotherapy patients who described abuse in childhood, subsequent examination of social services and legal records at the relevant time showed them to be telling the truth. These were patients who had *not* reported their experiences to anyone before, and did not describe any plan to report further. Many of them were unsure of the details of their experiences and were reluctant to accept what they themselves were saying.

More information is required about the effects of traumatic events on the formation and recall of memory in the specific context of abuse. Children under stress may be able to recall accurately until the stress becomes too great (Goodman *et al.*, 1991). After a traumatic event, children may remember things that they wish had occurred (Pynoos and Nader, 1989). In many cases of childhood abuse, the victims may have been drugged at the time of the abuse (Young *et al.*, 1991) or entered a dissociative state as a result of the trauma (Putnam, 1985). It is not known exactly what the effects in childhood of chronic dissociation or drug abuse may be on later recall in adulthood.

This review found no studies which have looked at the frequency of false allegations among those allegations of CSA made by adults. Such a study would be helpful, although very difficult to carry out in practice because of the attendant legal aspects. Psychological disturbance alone could not confirm that abuse took place (cf. rape trauma syndrome, Frazier and Borgida, 1992), even if the patient presents with what are recognised as classic symptoms associated with abuse in childhood (Herman, 1992). Investigating agencies are often unwilling to pursue criminal proceedings, and so legal convictions are rare unless the plaintiff can gain family and social services support and backing (which may not be forthcoming).

It may be safe to conclude only that among those allegations made by adults about abuse in childhood, there will be those that are false. For adults, as for children, it is important to think about the source and motivation of false allegations. It must also be possible that some allegations will be driven by another person who is influential in the life of the alleger, such as a partner or a therapist. This is a particular danger given the current emphasis on retrieval of traumatic memories as treatment for post-traumatic stress, and the use of hypnosis to assist in the retrieval of those memories.

CAN 'TRUTH' BE SCIENTIFIC?

More studies are needed which follow through allegations by children of sexual abuse, from the initial complaint until there is a *legal* finding of guilt or otherwise (including retraction of allegations or the dropping of a case by social services or the police). This is not to say that legal confirmation is the final arbiter of truth since false convictions and acquittals can and do occur.

Three other points are relevant here. The first is that it is well known that denial of offences is particularly strong among those men who commit sexual offences (Segal and Stermac, 1984; Abel *et al.*, 1985; Kennedy and Grubin, 1992). This is true when sex offenders are compared with non-sexual offenders. Many men continue to deny their offences after conviction (Scully, 1990), although they may disclose further undetected offending while serving a sentence (Abel *et al.*, 1988) or while attending treatment groups (Mezey, 1991). Denial is also noted to be increased in those men who batter their wives (Dutton, 1986; Jukes, 1993).

Secondly, if memory biases *are* thought to be operating for adults who allege abuse in childhood, parental reports relating back to a specific time in childhood may not necessarily be free from bias, especially if one parent may be asked to corroborate allegations that will lead to charges against the other (Berliner and Loftus, 1992).

Brewin *et al.* (1993: 92) noted that studies which compare children's recall and parental recall consistently find that parents recall past events more positively than children. Other studies suggest that parents consistently underestimate the seriousness of children's distress compared to children's own accounts (McFarlane *et al.*, 1987; Yule and Williams, 1990).

The third point is that clinician biases are certainly present in the assessment of CSA allegations. Everson and Boat's work (1989) shows that there are factors about children that make some workers more suspicious, and that those workers find more false allegations depending upon their individual view of these factors. There are several studies that suggest that gender and professional group are factors that affect the credulity of those who assess allegations of sexual abuse (Eisenberg *et al.*, 1987; Reidy and Hochstadt, 1993). Jackson and Nuttall (1993) looked at factors affecting whether clinicians believed an allegation or not, and found that age, gender and professional training all affected the likelihood that an allegation would be believed. Older, male physicians were less likely to believe allegations than their younger, female social work colleagues. A professional's own history of abuse also affected the perceived credibility of the allegation, making belief more likely. The emotions of both the discloser and the listener affect what is said and what is heard.

The context of disclosure may be quite different for adults and children. Disclosure may be affected by the questions asked (Berliner and Loftus, 1992) and by the relationship with the questioner. Gonzalez *et al.* (1993) noted that children in therapy took several weeks to disclose their abuse, and months to disclose details of sexual and violent acts.

Adults, however, may be first remembering abuse, or disclosing it, while in therapy which they have initiated for problems unrelated to abuse. It is likely that disclosure and remembering are likely to be a process over time, as for children. It is also well known that those who have been abused are frequently ambivalent about their abusers, and need time to reflect upon their feelings (Jehu, 1988). This point is noteworthy, not least because it challenges the assumption that all those who have been abused are bent on revenge against their abuser, and that this is the basis for their legal action. Many adults who were abused as children are reluctant to disclose this because they are attached to the offender; especially if, during childhood, the offender was the only consistently caring adult (Bowlby, 1953).

In addition, it is important for therapists to bear in mind their professional duties towards the patients. The patient and not the therapist should drive the direction of the therapy (Parry, 1975), while the therapist's job is to help the patient to bear as much as they feel able to (Grant, 1991). Arguably, therapists should not attempt to dig out facts that they think are hidden (Freud, 1910, 1913); not only is this pointless, but it may affect the patients' ability to recall anything (Briere, 1992). Finally it is a point of professional debate about the role of therapists in giving advice (Parry, 1975; Thompson, 1983). It is this author's view that therapists should be *extremely* reluctant to give advice as to whether a patient should pursue legal action against an alleged abuser. This decision should be the patient's, guided perhaps by legal advice obtained elsewhere.

The essential difficulty is that CSA is not simply a behaviour but a crime. Thus the 'truth' about whether the offence took place or not must be determined within a legal framework. It is not possible for health care professionals to determine such a 'truth'. Not only are they not trained to detect crime (cf. police investigators), there is nothing about a health care professional training that enables them to 'know' if someone is telling the truth (Becker and Quinsey, 1993). History-taking and experience of talking to people as patients is not the same as the dialogue of interrogation, which provides the basis for evidence within a legal framework. The role of the investigator is quite different from that of the therapist (cf. Berliner and Loftus, 1992).

If health care professionals do attempt to determine 'legal' truth, they risk subverting the whole legal process which arguably protects us all as citizens. Within the courtroom, and by virtue of the adversarial system, it is possible for biases to be made plain when considering the evidence of witnesses. This may not be so clear within the consulting room, nor will the health care professionals' biases be made known. Rather, the determination of truth will be presented as a clinical phenomenon, and the social function that courts serve – to identify offenders and punish the guilty – will be lost. Clinicians sometimes appear to believe that they are qualified to make such judgements, and thus step outside the limitations of the professional role (Black *et al.*, 1989). Health care professionals need to discuss management of sexual abuse allegations carefully within their professional groups in order to ensure that ethical standards are maintained in this very difficult and sensitive area.

REFERENCES

Abel, G.G., Mittelman, M. and Becker, J. (1985) 'Sexual offenders: results of assessment and recommendations for treatment', in M. Ben Aron, S. Hucher, and C. Webster (eds) *Clinical Criminology: The Assessment and Treatment of Clinical Behaviour*, Toronto, M7M Graphic.

Abel, G.G., Becker, J., Mittelman, M., Cunningham Rathner, J., Rouleau, J. and Murphy, W. (1988) 'Self-reported crimes of non-incarcerated paedophiles', *Journal of Interpersonal Violence*, 2, 3–25.

Adler, Z. (1987) *Rape on Trial*, Routledge & Kegan Paul, London.

American Medical Association (AMA) (1985) 'Scientific status of refreshing recollection by the use of hypnosis', *Journal of the American Medical Association* 253, 1918–23.

Baddeley, A. (1990) *Human Memory: Theory and Practice*, Hove and London, Erlbaum.

Baker, A. and Duncan, S. (1985) 'Child sexual abuse: a study of the prevalence in Great Britain', *Child Abuse and Neglect* 9, 457–67.

Bartlett, T. (1957) *Remembering*, Cambridge, Cambridge University Press.

Becker, J. and Quinsey, V. (1993) 'Assessing suspected child molesters', *Child Abuse and Neglect*, 17, 169–74.

Benedek, E. and Schetky, D. (1985) 'Problems in validating allegations of child sexual abuse. Part 1: Factors affecting perception and recall of events; Part 2: Clinical Evaluation', *Journal of the American Academy of Child and Adolescent Psychiatry* 26, 912–5.

Bentovim, A. (1993) 'Editorial: Why do adults abuse children?' *British Medical Journal* 307, 144–5.

Berliner, L. and Loftus, E. (1992) 'Sexual abuse accusations: desperately seeking reconciliation', *Journal of Interpersonal Violence* 7, 570–8.
Black, D., Harrai Hendricks, J. and Wolkind, S. (1989) *Child Psychiatry and the Law*, London, Gaskell.
Bowlby, J. (1953) *Child Care and the Growth of Love*, Harmondsworth, Penguin.
Brewin, C., Andrews, B. and Gotlib, I. (1993) 'Psychopathology and early experience: a reappraisal of retrospective reports', *Psychological Bulletin* 113, 82–98.
Briere, J. (1992) *Child Abuse Trauma: Assessment and Therapy*, Newbury Park, CA, Sage.
Brownmiller, S. (1975) *Against Our Will*, London, Penguin.
Christianson, S. and Loftus, E. (1987) 'Memory for traumatic events', *Applied Cognitive Psychology* 1, 225–39.
Dutton, D. (1986) 'Wife assaulters' explanations for assault: the neutralisation of self-punishment', *Canadian Journal of Behavioural Sciences* 18: 381–90.
Eisenberg, N., Glynn Owens, R. and Dewey, M. (1987) 'Attitudes of health professionals to child sexual abuse and incest', *Child Abuse and Neglect* 11, 109–16.
Everson, M. and Boat, B. (1989) 'False allegations of sexual abuse by children and adolescents', *Journal of the American Academy of Child Adolescent Psychiatry* 28, 230–5.
Faller, K. (1984) 'Is the child victim of sexual abuse telling the truth?', *Child Abuse and Neglect* 8, 473–81.
Finkelhor, D. (1983) 'Common features of family abuse', in D. Finkelhor, R.J. Gelles, G. Hotaling and M. Straus, (eds) *The Dark Side of Families*, Beverly Hills, CA, Sage.
Finkelhor, D. (ed.) (1986) *A Source Book on Child Sexual Abuse*, Newbury Park, CA, Sage.
Finkelhor, D. (1993) 'Epidemiological factors in the clinical identification of child sexual abuse', *Child Abuse and Neglect* 17, 67–70.
Frazier, P. and Borgida, E. (1992) 'Rape trauma syndrome', *Law and Human Behaviour* 16, 293–311.
Freud, S. (1910) 'The future of psychoanalytic treatment', in *Collected Papers*, 4th edn, 1946, trans. J. Riviere, London, Hogarth Press.
Freud, S. (1913) 'On beginning the treatment', in *Collected Papers*, 4th edn, 1946, trans. J. Riviere, London, Hogarth Press.
Freud, S. (1924) 'The aetiology of hysteria', in *Collected Works*, Vol. 3, edited and translated by J. Strachey, London, Hogarth Press.
Gonzalez, L., Waterman, J., Kelly, R., McCord, J. and Oliveri, M. (1993) 'Children's patterns of disclosure and recantations of sexual and ritualistic abuse allegations in psychotherapy', *Child Abuse and Neglect* 17, 281–9.
Goodman, G., Hirschman, J., Hepps, D. and Rudy, L. (1991) 'Children's memory for stressful events', *Merrill-Palmer Quarterly* 37, 109–58.
Goodwin, J., Shad, D. and Rada, R. (1978) 'Incest hoax: false accusations, false denials', *Bulletin of the American Academy of Psychiatry and Law* 6, 269–76.
Grant, S. (1991) 'Psychotherapy with people who have been sexually abused', in J. Holmes (ed.) *Textbook of Psychotherapy in Psychiatric Practice*, London, Churchill Livingstone.
Green, A. (1986) 'True and false allegations of sexual abuse in child custody disputes', *Journal of the American Academy of Child and Adolescent Psychiatry* 25, 449–56.
Green, A. (1991) 'Factors contributing to false allegations of child sexual abuse in custody disputes', *Child Youth Services* 15, 177–89.
Herman, J. (1992) 'Complex PTSD', *Journal of Traumatic Stress* 5, 377–93.
Herman, J. and Schatzow, E. (1987) 'Recovery and verification of memories of childhood sexual trauma', *Psychoanalytic Psychology* 4, 1–14.
Horowitz, M. (1973) 'Phase-oriented treatment of stress response syndromes', *American Journal of Psychotherapy* 27, 606–15.

Jackson, H. and Nuttall, R. (1993) 'Clinician responses to sexual abuse allegations', *Child Abuse and Neglect* 17, 127–43.

Jehu, D. (1988) *Beyond Sexual Abuse: Therapy with Women Victims*, Chichester, John Wiley.

Jones, D. and McGraw, J. (1987) 'Reliable and fictitious accounts of sexual abuse to children', *Journal of Interpersonal Violence* 2, 27–45.

Jukes, A. (1993) *Why Men Hate Women*, London, Free Association Books.

Kendall-Tackett, K., Meyer Williams, L. and Finkelhor, D. (1993) 'Impact of child sexual abuse: a review', *Psychological Bulletin* 113, 164–80.

Kennedy, H. and Grubin, D. (1992) 'Patterns of denial in sex offenders', *Psychological Medicine* 22, 191–6.

Klajner-Diamond, H., Wehrspann, W. and Steinhauer, P. (1987) 'Assessing the credibility of young children's allegations of sexual abuse', *Canadian Journal of Psychiatry* 32, 610–14.

McFarlane, A., Policansky, S. and Irwin, C. (1987) 'A longitudinal study of the psychological morbidity in children due to a natural disaster', *Psychological Medicine* 17, 727–38.

Mezey, G. (1991) 'Community treatment of paedophiles', *Criminal Behaviour and Mental Health* 1, 169–72.

Mikkelson, E., Gutheil, T. and Emens, M. (1992) 'False sexual abuse allegations by children and adolescents', *American Journal of Psychotherapy* 46, 556–70.

Parry, R. (1975) *Basic Psychotherapy*, Edinburgh, Churchill Livingstone.

Pennebaker, J., Kiecolt-Glaser, J. and Glaser, R. (1988) 'Disclosure of traumas and immune function: health implications for psychotherapy', *Journal of Consulting and Clinical Psychology* 56, 239–45.

Pitman, R. (1993) Biological findings in PTSD', in J. Davidson and E. Foa (eds) *Post-traumatic Stress Disorder: DSM IV and Beyond*, Washington, DC, American Psychiatric Press.

Putnam, F. (1985) 'Dissociation as a response to extreme trauma', in R. Kluff (ed.) *Childhood Antecedents of Multiple Personality Disorder*, Washington, DC, American Psychiatric Press.

Pynoos, R. and Nader, K. (1989) 'Children's memory and proximity to violence', *Journal of the American Academy of Child and Adolecent Psychiatry* 28, 236–41.

Reidy, T. and Hochstadt, N. (1993) 'Attribution of blame in incest cases: a comparison of mental health professionals', *Child Abuse and Neglect* 17, 371–81.

Scully, D. (1990) *Understanding Sexual Violence: A Study of Convicted Rapists*, London, Unwin Hyman.

Segal, Z. and Stermac, L. (1984) 'A measure of rapists attitudes towards women', *International Journal of Law and Psychiatry* 7, 437–40.

Summit, R. (1988) 'Hidden victim, hidden pain: societal avoidance of child sexual abuse', in G. Wyatt and G. Powell (eds) *Lasting Effects of Child Sexual Abuse*, Newbury Park, CA, Sage.

Thompson, A. (1983) *Ethical Concerns in Psychotherapy and Legal Ramifications*, University Press of America, USA.

Young, W., Sachs, R., Braun, B. and Watkins, R. (1991) 'Patients reporting ritual abuse in childhood: a clinical syndrome report of 37 cases', *Child Abuse and Neglect* 15, 181–9.

Yule, W. and Williams, R. (1990) 'Post-traumatic stress reactions in children', *Journal of Traumatic Stress* 3, 279–95.

'You will only hear half of it and you won't believe it'

Clinical accounts

Part II Clinical accounts

Children and families

Chapter 7

The clinician's experience

Pamela S. Hudson

Pamela S. Hudson MSSW is a licensed clinical social worker and child therapist in California.

Names, identities and background details have been changed wherever necessary to protect confidentiality.

As an experienced child and family counselor working in a public out-patient mental health clinic in a rural community on the coast of Northern California, I have successfully treated numerous abused children. Some were as young as 3 years old and afflicted with sexually transmitted diseases but amnesic of any genital contact. Some children were in their teens and suffered from the effects of sexual assault which occurred when they were under 5 years of age. Post-traumatic symptoms of intrusive thoughts or memories, hyper-vigilance and the post-molestation sequelae of anger, shame, guilt and depression (Finkelhor and Browne, 1985) were all familiar territory to me. Furthermore, working with Child Protective Services workers and law enforcement officers had been my on-going practice for the previous seventeen years. You might say I was confident of what to do, what to expect and the possible outcomes in most cases. After twenty-six years of experience in numerous mental health settings such as a large state hospital, a psychiatric/medical/neurological training institute and three out-patient settings, I thought I had seen everything the field has to offer. I was wrong.

It began in 1983 although I did not know it at the time. A 7-year-old child was brought to the clinic presenting symptoms of night terrors, high anxiety and inappropriate sexual activity with a girl of the same age at a day care setting. He and his mother remained in the community only a short while, so he was only seen twice. Months later another mother brought a 7-year-old who claimed that he had observed the two children at the same day care center engaged in some variety of sexual activity. He later admitted that the same girl had initiated sexual activity with him. Referred to Child Protective Services, investigation was hampered by the flight of the first family and resistance on the part of the parent of the second boy. The second boy's mother determined that his sexual behavior was normal explorative behaviour for a child of his age and would not allow him to assist in an investigation. Thus far I had no reason to doubt this mother's conclusion and turned my attention to more pressing cases. But in late 1985 and continuing through 1986, a steady stream of young children were brought to the clinic by their worried parents. What I encountered with these was similar to other sexual assault cases but there were four outstanding differences:

1 phobic behavior,
2 extreme terror,
3 severe secrecy,
4 all attended the same day care center.

Altogether, between 1983 and 1990 I saw twenty-seven children from this day care center and I opened two new cases this year (1993). Nineteen of the twenty-seven had extremely high anxiety levels. Fifteen had temper tantrums and were unable to function in school. Other symptoms included preoccupation with sex, fear of using the bathroom or of entering their own bedrooms. Some were cruel to younger siblings and sadistic towards animals (reportedly acting in a trance-like state). They were often revolted by certain foods and avoided certain colors. Many had severe night terrors. Some exhibited compulsive trance-state behaviors including defecating on the floor in certain patterns and lying spread-eagled on the ground as in crucifixion. As time went on and suspicions rose regarding the 'lack of supervision' at the day care center, parents started removing their children and state-funded referrals ceased.

Removed from the day care setting, the children began to disclose to their families the fact that molestations were perpetrated by the two female day care operators and 'their friends'. Seeing that disclosure did not mean personal annihilation or the loss of their families, as they had feared, the children started making further disclosures which began to sound like those of prisoners released from a concentration camp. Long after hearing about physical/sexual assaults, the families heard of the psychological terrors. Children talked of being placed in a cage or a closed 'box'. One described being in a chest freezer with her feet in ice cubes. Another spoke of being lowered into deep water from the end of a rope. This boy relived the experience (revivification process) upon first entering my office. He dropped to the floor, writhed and screamed, 'Help! Help!'

He was clearly terrified and reliving something but I had no idea what he was re-experiencing. I instinctively extended my hand and cried out, 'Here, grab my hand, I will help you!' I pulled him up off the floor. His older brother, present in the room, simply shook his head saying that the younger brother was 'strange'. Later, the younger boy described in vivid detail banging against bars or a ladder as his body was lowered into the water. The perpetrator was one of the shadowy men associated with the day care center, whom the children called '_____'s friends', or simply, 'the bad guys'. Some of the children had had older siblings in the day care center. These older siblings corroborated the stories of the younger ones. Often, older children tried to protect younger children and when caught feigned innocence yet were punished severely. Older children were encouraged and/or forced to sexually molest the younger ones.

Punishment for not obeying the operators included being hit on the stomach or genitals with a wooden paddle and locked in a closet for the rest of the day. Some children reported being hung 'by the feet' or 'by the hands', being burnt with candles, being anointed with blood, tied to trees, 'poked' with needles (they described being both bled and given injections with syringes). One boy started sticking pins and scissors in the eyes of people in family portraits. The investigative police officer and I listened as this boy both told and demonstrated how the day care operators made him stab 'something', One child spoke of seeing naked people dancing around a fire. A few described the killing of animals and of babies.

It is not surprising that the families became extremely alarmed, each hearing their children's independent, incomprehensible yet persistent disclosures of abuse. Meetings were held between the investigative officials and the parents. Despite everyone's efforts little 'hard evidence' was discovered. However, the day care operators and friends had four months of advance warning of the investigation, giving them ample opportunity to remove anything incriminating and to consolidate their support. The local investigators prepared an exhaustive report but the prosecuting attorney did not file charges, deciding the victims were too young to be credible. Their parents were derisively labeled 'hysterical moms'. The State of California Department of Social Services investigator interviewed seven children and found sufficient evidence of 'child endangerment' to revoke the day care center's license permanently.

Today our county has a Rape Crisis Center which provides examinations of victims of sexual assault but in the 1980s we lacked such a forensic medical evaluation center for children. Those few medical examinations which were performed were done outside of the area and at the parent's expense. Of the children alleging abuse in this particular investigation, all those examined returned results positive for sexual assault.

Meanwhile the reports took on a more occult tone. The children were talking of 'the God below', 'the Devil', participating in a mock marriage ceremony and being 'operated on'. Families reported automobiles following the children home from school and the discovery of human blood on their front porches. Between the disclosures, subsequent events and the children's behaviors, things became a confused tangle. We lacked accurate time references, names and places. I advised that the families log the disclosures and events but try not to interpret the material until we met and together attempted to decipher what was happening and why.

Four families kept in contact with one another during the initial disclosure phase. Advice against speaking together to avoid 'contamination' went unheeded. Supposedly, cross-referencing disclosures contaminates the witness pool for the prosecuting attorney. However, enjoining a family to maintain silence only causes isolation during a crisis and goes against normal human behavior. Common sense suggests that families in crisis should attempt to develop a support system. The parent who believes the child and tries to discover the full truth, even if it means discussing the situation with other parents of other victims, does more for that child's eventual healing than the parent who cannot face the full potential horror and retreats into distance and denial. Threatening an already horrified parent with jail for breaking a court ordered rule of silence duplicates the abuse suffered by the child. If parents were certain that their silence during the investigation would assure their children justice, they would probably make a greater effort to observe the unnatural stricture of silence.

Parents who were not contacting one another were as concerned and as forthcoming in therapy with me as parents who were networking with one another, placing me at the hub of all this activity. Piece by piece, child by child, relative by relative, the picture emerged. According to the children, the day care center operators and friends were engaging the children in sexual activity alone or in groups, systematically torturing children physically and psychologically, and demonstrating to them what horrible things would befall them if they disclosed. The children were made to feel personally responsible for what happened to themselves or to their friends. By reminding them frequently that it was their parents who continued to bring them to day care, the perpetrators alienated the children from their mothers and fathers. Furthermore, the perpetrators called themselves 'the real parents', saying that the ones at home were 'just fakes'. By these means, the perpetrators made the children believe that their only hope of survival was in obeying the day care operators. One boy painted a picture of a tall wooden fence above which floated fluffy white clouds. He said, 'Only the clouds could get away.'

It became apparent that neither I nor the combined experts of several local investigative agencies had previous experience with this particular form of multi-level/multi-perpetrator/multi-victim case. For instance, we understood the *modus operandi* but we did not have the motivation. Sexual perversion – yes. Child pornography – yes. Sadism – yes. But why? Finally, one parent said, 'It sounds like Satanism.' I asked, 'What's that?' When she explained that some people worship Satan, I was skeptical. I clearly knew nothing about cult abuse of any sort, much less satanic ritual abuse.

It is true that isolation fosters independence of thought. No university or religious expert was at hand in our remote community. If anything was going to be done to solve this conundrum, I would have to do it myself. So, since 1986 I have studied in depth the available literature on contemporary occult theory and practice. I have become aware of the destructiveness of certain cults and I have learned something of the techniques of cult-related sadistic abuse. I studied reports of 'shell-shocked' soldiers from the First and Second World Wars, of 'brainwashing' (operant behavior conditioning), dissociative disorders including multiple personality disorders, and hypnosis. Such studies are not offered in institutions which train social workers or law enforcement officers (national and international intelligence organisations are exceptions). Yet lacking an understanding of these subjects will seriously impede the professional clinician trying to help this particular population. Such ignorance may cause misdiagnosis and the prescription of inappropriate therapies. Not only does the patient suffering from ritualistic abuse suffer longer and needlessly when incorrectly treated, but the medical costs are far greater because of persistence of symptoms and the re-emergence of memories (Ross, 1993).

TREATMENT

In *Ritual Child Abuse: Discovery, Diagnosis and Treatment* (Hudson, 1991) I mentioned using play therapy with doll houses, sand tray, puppets, art supplies, board games and numerous toys. I still do. I have used Richard A. Gardner's 'Talking, Feeling and Doing Game' (from Creative Therapeutics, P.O. Box R, Cresskill, N.J. 0726-0317). Now I do not. Children suffering from the effect of ritual abuse are generally talking, feeling and doing too much. I have now shifted from purely non-directive play to a focus on trauma-driven psychopathology as I considered traumatised children need to look at the trauma.

I begin by gaining the child's confidence and instilling hope in the child and family, offering to work towards a reduction in the crippling post-traumatic symptoms. To do this I introduce myself to the child as someone who helps children who have problems. Then I ask whether they have any problems. Their list of problems is carefully noted and I enter into an agreement to help solve those problems. I then explain to them that we are like two explorers discovering things and solving problems together. If the problem is 'bad dreams' or 'nobody likes me' or 'my brother hits me' I start with that.

Even before the traumatic event(s) is explored the healing process has begun because the child is given the respected position of fellow 'mystery solver'. Not only does the child have a sense of accomplishment in the outcome but he helps to guide both the course and pace of treatment. Briere states this relationship best as one of 'Respect, Positive Regard, and the Assumption of Growth' (Briere, 1992: 81). The therapeutic process of exploring potentially distressing material is balanced by support and consolidation (Briere, 1992: 98). A child will tell you when to stop exploring the 'bad stuff'. He will either stop talking or say, 'I don't want to talk about it anymore.'

Whereas I used to think two or three years of therapy would suffice for ritually abused children in most cases, I now believe it might take a lifetime. Doctor Susan J. Kelley, Assistant Professor at Boston College has conducted studies of ritually abused children and their families. Her research covers ritualistic abuse of children, parental stress response to child sexual abuse and ritualistic abuse of children in day care centers, and the stress responses of children who were ritualistically abused in day care centers (Kelley, 1988, 1989, 1990). She recommends that therapists treating this population focus not only on issues related to sexual abuse but also address 'issues related to the wide range of abusive behavior [these] children often experience' (Kelley, 1989: 512). I am presently treating adolescents who were in this particular day care center at age 3 and who have recently been hospitalised for severe obsessive compulsive disorders and suicidal impulses. They are too disturbed to attend school. They were not treated when younger. Of the twenty-four children treated when young, only one is diagnosed with multiple personality disorder and is too disturbed to attend school. That child was removed from therapy prematurely.

Some adolescents with ritual abuse history are being treated in adolescent treatment centers. The 'voices' inside the head of the adolescent who has been ritually abused are not due to a psychotic delusional system but are the various parts of the self or ego states conversing or arguing together. Often, however, some 'voices' or personalities are sociopathic and under their influence the adolescent becomes assaultive or verbally abusive. Then these multiple personality disordered young people are often placed in adolescent treatment centers which prescribe anti-psychotic medication to control the voices and to curb the assaultive behavior. Unfortunately, the underlying trauma is often overlooked by clinicians in these settings because their primary focus is on developing socialisation skills via behavior modification and cognitive therapy. Powerful psychotropic medications have side-effects which become permanent. Physical restraint of an adolescent having a flashback is often necessary but it may increase the youngster's violence as the restraint resembles the start of the abuse itself. I have been interested in the combination of hypnosis and cognitive therapy. Teaching the patient self-help cues to moderate symptoms is also beneficial.

Abused children, described by parents and teachers as 'not really being there', 'possibly drugged' or 'mentally handicapped', may be dissociative. In these cases one needs to bring the mind back into the body via sensory stimulation. After explaining to them that they are *not* stupid, just absent-minded because of their trauma, I recommend that between sessions they take walks, go swimming, jump rope, dance or engage in sports. I may point out interesting things in the environment, a leaf, clouds, music, a golf ball. It is as though one were taking a toddler for the very first walk in a garden. Eventually, with sensitivity, support and encouragement, ritually abused children do 'come back' and take charge of their own happiness.

It is not unusual for small children who have survived ritual abuse in a day care setting to mistrust all teachers and fellow students. School phobia is almost certain to develop and the therapist must prevent this from becoming permanent by a desensitisation process. By gradually introducing the young children to social groups those children will overcome their fears. Add one small, non-threatening child at a time to the young victim's social contacts. These early pre-school relationships will be fraught with acting out, flashbacks and terrors, so close monitoring of the play will be needed. Those older children who cannot function in school should have home study with the parent present during tutorial times. As with young abuse victims, introduce one potential friend at a time to the older child.

Children victimised in a pre-school develop a loathing for school. They enter mistrustful and unhappy. They become easy targets for the aggressive students which only serves to prove that schools *are* terrifying environments. To maximise the chance of success, I spend up to three hours a week conferring with school teachers and administrators on behalf of each of these particular children.

Ritually abused grammar school children with post-traumatic stress disorder are frequently hyper-vigilant and nervous with an inability to concentrate. They are labeled hyperactive with an attention defect disorder and placed on medication which masks symptoms but does not address the precipitating trauma.

THE THERAPIST TREATING RITUALLY ABUSED CHILDREN

Traditionally, mental health clinicians were ever alert to our own counter transference issues. To these we now add the fear of being sued by the client, the client's parents and by the people accused of abusing our client. Also we are subjected to accusations of installing abuse histories. We are discredited because we fail to follow the strictest guidelines in interviewing a possible victim of child abuse. It is prudent to consider every child a possible victim of abuse, but how do we interview effectively yet judiciously? Vocal organisations have emerged which accuse therapists of 'pushing the event' where none exists. How do we prove we did not 'push' an event when these events are difficult to prove in the first place? True, there are some therapists who should not be working in this field. It is also true that some therapy modalities are dubious if not abusive in themselves.

The solution to this dilemma lies in an awareness of the latest research on children's memories and of the nature of leading questioning according to law. What follows is a brief summary of pertinent points.

The experimental psychologist Dr Gail Goodman is an expert on the subject of children's memories (Goodman, 1984a, 1984b, 1993; Goodman *et al.*, 1987, 1990, 1992). Her research has shown that young children have reliable memories for stressful events, especially if personal assault or threatened assault were included. The greater the stress, the more complete the information. Young children are more suggestible than older children but even they have strong resistance to suggestive questioning. In one research project, children were given genital examinations in the course of a medical examination. Most of the children tested following these examinations gave errors of omission rather than commission. They omitted the genital exam or parts of the exam. The children did not deliberately give untruthful answers. Primarily they forgot details surrounding the event. Many errors were due to the children's lack of linguistic skills.

Dr Goodman's research findings showed that free recall responses were fairly accurate but the use of an anatomical doll gave less risk of false reports of genital touching than many might suspect. In most American families genitals are not discussed. Even young and non-abused children absorb the taboo against discussing 'private parts'. This should not be underestimated as a reason for initial non-disclosure of genital examination details. The important finding was that:

Based on the results of our studies it seems unlikely that normal children will easily yield to an interviewer's suggestion that something sexual occurred when in fact it did not, especially if interviewers ask questions that children comprehend. It seems unlikely that normal children will make up details of sexual acts when nothing abusive happened. They are more likely to accept the interviewer's suggestions, these studies suggest, when they are younger, when they are interrogated after a long delay, when they feel intimidated by the interviewer, when the interviewer's suggestions are strongly stated and frequently repeated, and when more than one interviewer makes the same suggestions. Even so, children's reports of specific acts generally remain accurate.

(Goodman and Clarke-Stewart, 1989: 16)

While the use of the free recall question (i.e. 'Tell me what happened') is more acceptable to the court, generally children give only very brief or incomplete descriptions as they have no frame of reference for understanding what kind of information the adult is asking about. Any person who asks a child, 'What did you do in school today?' is familiar with this phenomenon. It is more fruitful to ask, 'Did you pass the spelling test in school today?' if that is what the adult really wants to hear about. Better yet, the knowing adult asks, 'How many spelling words did you spell correctly?'

While the free recall or indirect question is most acceptable, a direct question is generally more effective. Direct questions may be divided into:

1 Misleading, e.g. 'The person who played dolls with you had a white shirt on, didn't she?' when actually she wore a blue shirt.
2 Specific, e.g. 'What color shirt was the lady wearing while she played dolls with you?' (For small children the last six words should be omitted as the sentence is too long.)
3 Coercive but abuse-related, e.g. 'She kissed you, didn't she?' 'He took your clothes off, didn't he?' 'How many times did she hit you with the paddle?' (This last question *could* be asked if the child has already established that 'she' did hit him with a paddle.)

Obviously, coercive questioning is 'leading' as it contains a suggestion of what the answer should be. Leading questions mar an investigation and taint the victim's disclosures. While it is the therapist who is accused, it is most often the defense attorneys who ask the strongly leading and coercive questions. The clinician must never do what the defense attorney is accusing him of doing. The coercive questions that some attorneys can ask are clinically not acceptable.

However, Goodman's research shows that unless you ask an abuse-related question, the child does not understand what you are trying to establish. And even if he or she does, the child is very reluctant to tell you about it. Nevertheless, it is best to start all questioning in a general free recall form and only gradually narrow down to focus on the events under investigation.

My questions start with time, place and person, e.g. 'Last summer you went to summer camp. Did you have a good time? Did you like the other children? Did you like the camp counselor?' If the child shows emotional upset or offers data regarding camp counselor molesting, that is straightforward. If not, proceed very cautiously because from here on the questioning continuum goes down into leading and coercive. If a young child is asked a mildly leading question because circumstances require it, be prepared to argue your decision in court using situational and developmental reasons. Next I might ask, 'What did the camp counselor do when she took the children to the bathroom?' *A rule to remember is that children tell you the least upsetting material first.* The more frightening disclosures come with time and trust. They are not trying to top the last bit told. They are building up strength to face the worst. When abuse is disclosed the best response is an open and neutral one like 'Tell me more about it' or 'Then what happened?'

The other charge leveled at clinicians is that by our kindly support we lead the child to disclose this or that. Dr Goodman's research demonstrates that small children actually give fuller and more accurate accounts of events if questioning is accompanied by some degree of warmth and encouragement. Her examples are videotaped and the results are clear for anyone to see. The warm interviewer obtains more accurate accounts. Children simply want to terminate interviews with aloof interviewers.

The constraints of free recall questioning dictate a client-focused therapy and any disclosure thus obtained will have a better chance of passing legal scrutiny. However, there will be situations in which these constraints might slow the healing process. One teenager said to me that she told her mother of the ritual abuse because 'She made me. You didn't' and the last was an accusation. My commitment to her healing process was viewed as insufficient in light of her distress. All my explanations of respect for her fell on deaf ears. The mother cared enough for her to demand that she talk. I did not demand. Obviously I did not care.

There are no easy answers in working with the young victims of ritual abuse. Must the choice be between healing the child or assisting the prosecution? Children are still not adequately believed. Understandably, parents and clinicians question the value of co-operating. The legal process itself can be abusive.

A case in point concerns a social worker who helped evaluate the children in a day care case on the West Coast. Altogether the social worker spent sixteen weeks on the witness stand. During six of those weeks the attorneys for the defense hammered at her academic training, her professional experience, her method of interviewing the children. The defense attorneys asked about her sex life before she was married, her marital sex life and whether she had been molested as a child. When she refused to answer the last question, she was cited for contempt of court and the defense attorneys demanded that she be jailed. The female judge withdrew, then returned to declare the social worker to be 'molested for the purpose of [that] hearing' and that as such her testimony was presumed to be biased. However, the two other (male) prosecution witnesses, both doctors, were not declared molested. Indeed, they had not even been asked.

Working with children who have been damaged by ritualistic abuse and working against public skepticism, the therapist will feel like a Roman charioteer whose three horses are (1) the child's treatment course, (2) the non-offending parent's reaction to the child's disclosures, and (3) society's systems (schools, police, courts). And like the charioteer's our work is dangerous. We risk secondary trauma from listening to these horrific disclosures, we risk strain helping to heal an entire family, we risk anxiety when cult members attempt to intimidate us by threats to family, person and possessions, and we risk the ridicule of disbelieving media. Each of us will have to weigh risk against reward. I believe that we can provide a real service if we remember that the prize will not be honor and glory but the happy face and peaceful heart of a child.

REFERENCES

Briere, J.N. (1992) *Child Abuse Trauma: Theory and Treatment of the Lasting Effects*, Newbury Park, CA, Sage Publications, Inc.

Finkelhor, D. and Browne, A. (1985) 'The traumatic impact of child sexual abuse: a conceptualization', *American Journal of Orthopsychiatry* 55, 530–41.

Goodman, G.S. (1984a) 'The child witness: an introduction', *Journal of Social Issues* 40 (2), 1–7.

Goodman, G.S. (1984b) 'The child witness: conclusions and future directions for research and legal practice', *Journal of Social Issues* 40 (2), 157–75.

Goodman, G.S. (1993) 'Children's memories: current knowledge, implications for effective intervention, treatment and prosecution of child sexual abuse', presentation given 14 May, San Francisco.

Goodman, G.S. and Clarke-Stewart, A.C. (1989) 'Suggestibility in children's testimony: implications for child sexual abuse investigations', APA Science Directorate Conference on Child Witnesses, Cornell University, manuscript.

Goodman, G.S., Aman, C. and Hirschman, J. (1987) 'Child sexual and physical abuse: children's testimony', in S. Ceci, M. Toglia and D. Ross (eds) *Children's Eyewitness Memory*, New York, Springer-Verlag, pp. 1-23.

Goodman, G.S., Rudy, L. and Bottoms, B.L. (1990) 'Children's concerns and memory: issues of ecological validity in the study of children's eyewitness testimony', in R. Fivush and J. Hudson (eds) *Knowing and Remembering in Young Children*, New York, Cambridge University Press.

Goodman, G.S., Taub, E.P., Jones, D.P.H., England, P., Port, L.K., Rudy, L. and Prado, L. (1992) 'Testifying in Criminal Court: emotional effects on child sexual assault victims', *Monographs of the Society for the Research in Child Development, No. 229*, 57 (5), Chicago, University of Chicago Press.

Hudson, P.S. (1991) *Ritual Child Abuse: Discovery, Diagnosis and Treatment*, Saratoga, CA, R & E.

Kelley, S.J. (1988) 'Ritual abuse of children: dynamics and impact', *Cultic Studies Journal* 5 (2), 299–336.

Kelley, S.J. (1989) 'Stress responses of children to sexual abuse and ritualistic abuse in day care centers', *Journal of Interpersonal Violence* 4 (4), December, 502–13.

Kelley, S.J. (1990) 'Parental stress response to sexual abuse and ritualistic abuse of children in day care centers', *Nursing Research* 39(1).

Ross, C.A. (1993) 'Scientific state of the dissociative disorders field', Paper presented at the Third Annual Spring Conference of the International Society for the Study of Multiple Personality and Dissociation, Dallas, Texas.

Saywitz, K., Goodman, G.S., Nicholas, E. and Moan, S. (1989) 'Children's memories of genital examinations: implications for cases of child sexual assault', Paper presented at the biennial meeting of the Society for Research on Child Development, Kansas City.

Chapter 8

'Daddy eats poo'
Work with a ritually abused boy

Catherine O'Driscoll

Dr Catherine O'Driscoll is a Senior Registrar in Child Psychiatry at the Tavistock Clinic and a Child Guidance Clinic. She was previously Senior Registrar in Psychotherapy at the Cassel Hospital.

Names, identities and background details have been changed wherever necessary to protect confidentiality.

There is currently an explosion of interest in the controversial topic of ritual abuse and an understandable response of professionals is to feel that we should leave it to the 'experts'. However, my experience is of getting involved with these cases before I knew what I was taking on. Such cases take up much more emotional space than work with children who have been abused in other ways. This is an issue that will not go away and all those working with ritually abused children and adults have a responsibility to consider the topic and the counter-transference issues that it engenders. In this chapter I refer to two children I have treated where ritual abuse was not initially mentioned but where I was later forced to consider the possibility. I think one has to be 'forced' to consider the possibility as no-one would willingly think about such material.

I have treated two ritually abused children in therapy in two different work settings. One patient was a boy, David, referred by a foster mother where the father had been imprisoned for sexual abuse, though ritual abuse had not been mentioned in court. The other child, a girl, Angela, was referred by her mother after the mother discovered familial ritual abuse.

For this chapter I propose to concentrate on the boy – although bringing in shared issues. Supervision was hourly once a week; the boy was seen once weekly and the girl was seen intensively. David was 5 when he was referred and Angela was 6. Both were intelligent middle-class children who succeeded in their infant schools despite their occasional moments of dissociation. However, both children had some specific reading problems which had surprised their teachers given their level of intelligence. These difficulties seemed to be emotionally caused. Angela also had a problem with numbers.

One curious feature of both cases on referral to two different settings was that ritual abuse was not mentioned in either file. Indeed, the sexual and physical abuse of Angela was also omitted from the file. It seemed that there was something so disturbing about these cases that the normal practices of *Working Together* (HMSO, 1991) had been disregarded.

With the first case, David, I had no idea that this was anything more than a 'usual' sexual abuse case. As a senior registrar and psychotherapist I was used to working with abused adults and children.

In David's first assessment session he announced out of the blue, while playing with the dolls, 'Daddy eats poo.' When I asked what that meant he replied 'Daddy eats poo – that's what comes out when you go to the toilet – and he drinks wee.' Whilst I struggled to understand what infantile phantasies he might have about his father who had abused him, and wondered internally what rubbish he wished his father would consume himself instead of passing on, he carried on in a matter-of-fact way, 'I do not like that because poo is smelly and nasty and I have never done that. I cannot understand why daddy does.' He was clearly very upset by these thoughts but moved on to talk about his father further. 'Daddy drank beer and had it on his face and a beard on his face.' I wondered about what substances the father had on him but could not take my thinking further.

In the counter-transference I did not think David was trying to tell me of his own infantile wishes or actions to eat faeces. I did not understand what this phantasy could be about, other than thinking it must be a phantasy. I found this first encounter quite disturbing. The pleasant superficial relationship of the rest of the session had a detached quality. I felt I could understand why David's school didn't see him as having a problem as he was easy to engage, but I felt that under the surface he had secret thoughts and phantasies and I was disturbed at what might emerge in therapy.

After twelve weeks of similar experiences in the sessions in which David alternated between pleasant almost-ordinary behaviour and occasionally disconcerting comments or voice-changes I sought supervision. I had become increasingly worried by the kind of matter-of-fact sentences David could utter that had a chilling after-effect. For example, in the midst of an otherwise innocuous session he announced 'Daddy pushed me in front of a car.' Two weeks later he commented 'Daddy put me in a hole.' These comments, like the one in the first session, could have easily been ignored in order to find refuge and flight in the ordinary material. However, there was something so powerful about them that they stayed in my mind.

David had also brought a bear called Bartholomew which he repeatedly mutilated and hacked in a chilling way that was different from his other play behaviour. At times he would make the bear say 'Please don't do it.' Session after session this continued until the bear had little fur, its eyes were cut, scissors had been inserted into various parts of the bear's body and all the clothes, including the trousers and underpants, were cut up too. Many abused or neglected children in therapy cut up and attack their toys as representatives of their own vulnerable experience. However, both David and Angela's treatment of their toys conveyed something even more chilling to me, although I was unsure of its nature. They could both change their voices in a disconcerting way that went beyond ordinary childhood imitation of the adults or television characters to whom they were exposed.

At a point when I was aware of how hard I found it to remember and write up sessions afterwards because of a counter-transference experience of something nauseous, a meeting with David's foster mother provided some external facts. She told me that when David was first fostered with her she was only told he had been physically abused. After strange and disturbing behaviour in her house – including extreme night terrors, fear of certain foods, terror of the bathroom and water, and a fear of magic spells, she asked social services for further clarification of his experience. It was then she learned both of the extreme sexual and physical abuse and a hint of ritual abuse which had been removed from the trial in the same way as it was not present in the file.

After that meeting I did not know whether to believe what I had heard. I did not know much about ritual abuse and did not know if it existed. However, as both David and Angela began to draw strange shapes – pentagrams, hearts – and to speak of blood, doctors that could put pins in babies, poison, fear of death, murder and serious illness, I gave more thought to the possibility. Both had an intense fear of the toilet, yet also a need to go in their therapy time that went beyond normal childhood fears of such bodily processes. Both had a sharp awareness of any slight change in the room, fear of any insect and a painful response to birthdays and major festivals. I began to understand their problems with reading (David and Angela) and numbers (Angela) when she seemed to attribute magical qualities to numbers and both were concerned with the hidden meaning of letters.

When I finally set up a weekly supervision I was increasingly concerned by the material that David, especially, brought to the sessions and by my counter-transference. As a psychiatrist I was also extremely worried about the levels of dissociation in both children.

I began supervision with the following session with David. It is a fairly typical session in which the ordinary feels extraordinary and the extraordinary is said in an ordinary way. It highlights many of the issues faced.

SESSION 32 WITH DAVID, AGED 6

When I went to get David he said he was going to do a drawing. In the room he drew two faces in yellow and said one was a sad face. The second face was a smiling one and he said it was a stupid face. I said it seemed to me as if it were stupid to be happy. He looked earnestly at me but said nothing. Then he continued drawing and said 'nasty things'. I said, 'I think you feel sometimes there are nasty things inside you.' He gravely said 'Yes' and then drew a heart. This was not an ordinary childhood bright red heart. It was disturbingly accurate and had a chilling effect on me. I found myself preoccupied and disturbed but said nothing. David's actions then worried me further. He made a pentagram shape with pencils and brought a grandad doll out. Then he changed it. Again I felt chilled and became preoccupied, but was trying very hard to concentrate. He took a little boy doll out and tied him to a horse with the granny and grandad dolls watching and then the father doll. He viciously sellotaped the little boy onto the horse. 'This boy is being tied up', he said. I said 'You have been tying up that little boy doll nearly every week – have you ever been tied up?' 'Yes', he said, very matter-of-factly, and carried on playing. The little boy doll was then torn off the horse and David said 'No. I haven't been tied up.' He made the little boy lie down and then get up to eat the coloured heart. He then drew small purple circles. After this Bartholomew bear was brought out and he asked me to hold the bear while he cut his fur. I interpreted his anxiety about what I could do and how he wanted to punish the bear at this moment. David said 'I am the nastiest witch in the whole world and I am going to cut up everything including you.' He began cutting pieces of plastic and crayons saying he was making rubbish turn into diamonds. He then started attacking the furniture with the scissors and I stopped this, commenting on his wish to cut me. He then relaxed and took a deep breath and said he was not really magic but was angry with me. I linked this with the forthcoming break.

After hearing me read the session the supervisor said in a shocked voice 'but this is ritual abuse'.

One year later, with both children still in therapy and supervision still on-going, some sessions continued to make me feel too sick to write them up fully. With some sessions that were particularly full of painful actions I felt sick in the session and would try and write them up afterwards but then could not remember anything. This has never happened to me before. I am normally very good at remembering and writing up sessions. However, supervision helped me to process this experience. In these cases the function of supervision was to help me process and hold onto my counter-transference experience, as therapy with these children, unlike with any others, had a particularly chilling and disturbing impact on me. It was a relief to realise my supervisor felt the same way herself both in supervision and with her own cases.

This has meant that it has been a totally different experience being supervised for these cases. I have treated many patients and worked in extremely difficult and dangerous circumstances but nothing has had this impact. It would have been easy to deny the counter-transference and concentrate on the 'normal' material but supervision helped me to keep both in mind. When I felt concerned that my interpretations were avoiding the actual abuse, it became clear from supervision that I was intuitively correct. The importance of an all-purpose interpretation that could sound ordinary and link to the surface normality of what was sometimes said whilst also being appropriate for the secret material was essential.

Unlike work with some children, who needed the actuality spelled out, for these children the actuality was so terrifying that it was easier to address it initially via something ordinary. In other words, far from putting a ritual idea or fact into a child's mind my function as a therapist and with the support of supervision was to stay with the ordinary whilst bearing internally the extra-ordinary.

This is a very different state from that of the therapist who ignores feeling the traumatic level but answers in an ordinary way. Both David and Angela responded to the known affect under my words as well as to my words.

The suggestion that comes up in the discrediting of the possibility of the existence of satanic ritual abuse is that the therapist puts satanist ideas in an innocent child's head. My experience is that the reverse is true. I found myself wanting to run away from the counter-transference induced in me and hoping always for an 'ordinary' session. When David was moved to a boarding school in another part of the country I was quite relieved that his therapy had come to an end and I did not have to participate any longer in the necessary ordeal. Angela is still in intensive therapy and will be so for the foreseeable future.

I realise that I will never finally know what has actually happened to either of these children. This is part of the pain that will be on-going for both the children themselves and all those who come into contact with them. To have the capacity to not know and yet to continue to tolerate the discomfort that is engendered is a very difficult state to maintain. What I do feel strongly is that it is impossible to function therapeutically with such children unless one can at least entertain the possibility that they may have been subjected to ritual experiences that are beyond normal imagination.

REFERENCE

HMSO (1991) *Working Together Under the Children Act 1989. A Guide to Arrangements for Inter-agency Co-operation for the Protection of Children from Abuse*, London, HMSO.

Chapter 9

Psychotherapy with a ritually abused 3-year-old

Deceptive innocence

Leslie Ironside

Leslie Ironside is a Senior Child Psychotherapist in Sussex.

Names, identities and background details have been changed wherever necessary to protect confidentiality.

In this chapter I will focus on work with the first ritually abused child I treated. As a child psychotherapist who has also worked with multiply abused children in contexts without ritual abuse I feel that there are some differential issues that need addressing.

TOM'S REFERRAL, AGED 3

Tom's background was of physical, sexual, emotional and satanist abuse in his family of origin. He and his brother were taken into care when Tom was 3 and then separated when his older brother, who claimed to be possessed by spirits, said he was pushed by these spirits to continue the abuse of Tom. At the point of referral Tom's behaviour caused concern. He fluctuated between withdrawn or violent moods, could go into a trance state and pass out at times of stress. He also exhibited disturbing sexualised behaviour, self-mutilation and sexual and violent attacks on children and pets. Mealtimes were difficult because even the sight of a table knife would seem to 'set him off' onto an aggressive and dangerous path – on one occasion he had stabbed a dog. He was not considered safe with babies or animals as he had been found with his finger in the anus of both a baby and a dog. He used his toys to violate himself.

Actions such as these, especially in a small child, are painful for professionals to hear about let alone to live with and witness regularly. Where foster parents and residential workers with damaged and deprived children can experience 'hypochondriachal concern' (Britton, 1993) it is not surprising that those who care for a satanically abused child have an even stronger response. Tom's behaviour would have been extremely difficult for anyone to bear and the staff at the children's home needed a great deal of extra support.

CREATING A CONTEXT IN WHICH TRUST AND ATTACHMENT MIGHT DEVELOP

In just three years Tom had experienced multiple traumas. My concern was to offer him his own space and time to explore issues and, as he was my first ritually abused patient, I did not know in what ways the process of his therapy would be similar or different.

The initial sessions were dominated by separation anxieties which would, of course, have their natural place in the first stages of working with such a young patient. However, the power of Tom's separation anxieties threatened to attack the important liaison between myself and the caring key worker from the children's home who brought Tom.

It is known that within a professional network working with abuse there can be a desire for action to save the child (Furniss, 1983; Bentovim, 1992). With Tom, the dynamic was even stronger. I found myself struggling with the idea of 'saving' Tom from the influence of the key worker and she too was occupied with getting rid of bad influences.

THEORETICAL CONCEPTS

Freud's (1905: 116) concept of transference describes how a patient can bring to sessions expectations about the worker, the setting and the process of therapy which are not related to the present external setting but more accurately reflect the patient's past relationships and experiences. Arising from this is the concept of the counter-transference. This is the response aroused in the therapist through contact with the patient. It is a useful tool in understanding what the patient is feeling and what is occurring in the session.

The psychoanalyst Melanie Klein (1946) extended the concept of transference to include a whole range of early emotions as well as the projection of infantile feeling states. In describing characteristics of earliest infancy she developed the concept of 'splitting', the occasional division of the meaningful people in an infant's life into ideally good and persecutorily bad. Klein stressed the importance of normal splitting for healthy development but also drew attention to how splitting mechanisms may be used in a more pathological way and as a defence against excessive persecutory anxiety. Drawing on this concept I could make sense of these initial sessions with Tom and the way in which such a splitting mechanism was activated in the counter-transference.

Tom's terror of being on his own with me, whether through fear of what I might do or through fear of abandonment engendered by the escort leaving, had triggered a wish in me to be the 'good object' who understood and protected him. As I interpreted his fears and processed my own responses, after a number of sessions with the worker in the room, Tom was able to manage her leaving.

ALONE WITH TOM

Without the key worker present I found myself wanting her back in the room as I faced on my own the disturbingly fragmented nature of Tom's play. I was extremely aware of the need for two good parents to join together in a non-destructive way. Once I was aware of my need for good liaison with the worker Tom was able to further explore his own need to think in terms of 'goodies' and 'baddies'.

These baddies included a witch that was coming and had to be kept out. Many children, of course, talk in terms of witches, as they are part of common folklore. However, I did find it important to keep in mind that, for this child, the notion of a witch might carry real connotations. Indeed, on a few occasions Tom's worker responded to his panic-stricken state by saying she was a 'better witch' and was more powerful than the 'bad witch'. This was a response that clearly placated the immediate anxiety but, I considered, would have added to the previous intense phantasy.

TOM'S PLAY

Many 3-year-olds find it hard to concentrate on one activity for any length of time, but Tom's play during this early part of therapy was particularly disjointed and fragmented. Certain objects, as had also been noted in the children's home, took on a more significant though complex meaning. For example, amongst his animals, Tom suddenly noticed the toy rabbit and became panicky, petrified and distressed. He moved away from what he facially and bodily made clear was a dangerous and frightening situation. I had to struggle carefully in my mind with the feelings Tom had projected into me in order to try to understand if there was some significance in the particular animal, or if there was some other reason for such a powerful response.

I commented on how terrified he had been at seeing the rabbit under the chair and that this was similar to how terrified he sometimes was at being on his own with me and that perhaps the rabbit also reminded him of something in his past. This brought some relief.

Children in therapy can show many irrational and unconscious fears of different objects in the room. On many occasions the object feared is no longer seen as a symbol. A toy tiger, for instance, is no longer seen as a symbolic representative of a dangerous normal tiger. It can be experienced as if it actually was the real dangerous tiger. The psychoanalyst Hanna Segal (1957) appropriately coined the term 'symbolic equation' to describe this type of behaviour. However, for other children, particularly abused children, the matter is more complex. The toy can represent real terror rather than a primitive phantasy: the scissors can be experienced as the knife that stabbed them.

At a later session with Tom I was forcibly reminded of the importance of keeping his real experience in mind. Tom had taken his shirt and jacket off and had been acting 'the tough man', pretending to shave and go off to work. However, in response to sounds from outside the room he became frightened, spoke of a monster coming to get him and then acted 'fighting and getting the men'. When I queried 'getting the men?' he said 'yes' and turned and lifted his vest to show me some scars on his back which he said were from 'a real mens' (sic). He then became active as a tough karate expert who attacked what he now again referred to as a monster.

I had known that Tom had been scarred through non-accidental injury and we can see here how Tom was linking the present phantasy situation with events in his past and wanting me to know of these events.

SELF-ABUSE

In the second session where I was alone with Tom he arrived with serious and visible marks upon his face where he had been scratching at himself. I struggled with the emotions common to those who work with self-mutilating and suicidal patients – the situation of being faced with treating a person who is both the victim and the perpetrator of the act of violence. These were made even more intense through Tom being so young – only 3.

Though I had been warned in advance by a telephone call, I was shocked at seeing the reality of what he could do to himself. I felt anger with him, guilt as to whether it was connected to therapy as well as a desire to blame the home. Above all of that I felt anger at the thoughts of what I had been told about this child's past experience. I was acutely aware that as well as non-accidental injury he had been subject to the use of an animal claw to scratch at his skin. His brother had spoken of their being threatened with an animal claw and how their mother would 'cut skin off a dog' and catch the blood in a bowl which Tom had been made to drink for being a bad boy.

In response to an earlier occasion where Tom had scratched his face badly, his brother had said their mother had cut off a dog's claw and used it to scratch Tom's face. (I understand a dog was found mutilated and handed in to the police station.) The experience of working with such abused children challenges one's belief in a capacity to help. The impact is so devastating that there is a wish to blame, to minimise the issue or deny its significance.

AFTER SIX MONTHS

In turning to some clinical description six months later I have chosen material that focuses attention on the emotional impact of working with Tom and the internal processing that was necessary to make sense of the material. Prior to the session the worker telephoned in distress to say Tom had been scratching at himself, this time his stomach and groin, breaking the skin and leaving it painfully raw. However, the injury was hidden and so the impact when he arrived did not have the same sense of immediacy as when he arrived with scratches on his face.

At the start of the session Tom rushed in with a teddy bear which he left on the table. He crossed to the sink, turned the tap on and commented on the 'new glass' in the room. He looked worried. I agreed it was a different one and commented on how worrying such a change might be for him. (If the glass could change he might also be worried at what else could.) He took a drink and turned the tap off. 'Where's the tap?' he then asked. I was confused and shocked as he had only just spoken clearly about a tap and had just used it. The question sounds deceptively innocent and it is hard to convey its disturbing affect. Tom was highly intelligent and did not forget the names of ordinary objects. The replacement of the glass had clearly been frightening to him and it had appeared in therapy that in his abuse some objects had been changed or slightly transformed in ways that frightened him. He looked across at the table. I enquired about the tap, trying to get some further idea of what he was referring to and how it related (or not) to the real tap. He began searching the room in panic, 'Where's the tap? Where's the tap?' Suddenly he spotted something on the drainer that brought relief. 'There it is!' He picked up the plug. I simply said 'Oh – you meant the plug.' He replied 'That's right' and filled up the sink as I reflected with him what had happened.

He continued to play with the water, pushing his hands in to the bottom of the sink and out, picking up and putting down the glass and pouring out the water with immense concentration. Hearing some distant voices in the building he looked up, crossed to the door and pushed it and then got his scissors from his box to use as a hand-gun. He went back to the door and pretended to fire. I said hearing the noises made him afraid someone might burst in here and he felt he needed a gun to keep safe.

He then crossed back to the table and began to cut violently at his teddy. It is hard to describe the absolute horror I felt at witnessing this attack. He suddenly seemed quite possessed and the impact of his actions was so powerful that it was as though a real murderous attack were taking place. The combination of both the unbearable nature of what he was doing, the knowledge of his previous attack on his stomach and the difficult technical fact that the teddy was his outside toy led me to ask him to stop doing this. He stopped, but cut some paper and said I was a naughty boy and that it was his teddy – 'not take it'. (My interruption seemed to have been intrusive and to have a stealing quality.) I began to speak of his seeing me as somebody who might now steal his teddy but he then responded in a way that was very confusing. He said it was not his teddy, it was Tom's teddy. He repeated these statements several times – a process of dissociation accompanied by a rapid change in facial expression which happened very fast and with an extraordinary strength and immediacy.

The quality of this material was quite different from the muddle some young children get into linguistically and seemed to indicate a more profound dissociative defence process than is usually seen with abused children.

With Tom in later sessions I would often find myself struggling to deal with what seemed comparatively innocent. I began to realise how difficult I found it to remember what Tom had said or done. Normally I feel quite able to write up sessions with children and consider that my own struggle to recall work with Tom throws light on the 'indigestibility' of the presenting material.

The psychoanalyst Bion (1962) developed an extremely helpful model of an infant's interaction with his/her primary carer. He used the concept of a container and what it contains to describe the process in which a baby projects overwhelming feelings into the mother who receives them, holds them and conveys to the child some sense that anxieties are bearable and meaningful. Very gradually, infants take this experience inside themselves and develop their own capacity to think and metabolise experience. A mother's capacity to contain depends on the external environment, her own state of mind and the strength of the infant's projections. Unfavourable conditions may well interfere with the internalisation process.

Containment is also an important part of therapy and at these points of comparatively innocent material, I found myself having to struggle with and contain an invasive projection that made it difficult to recall what was happening. As Tom had not yet been able to process the experiences he had gone through he had successfully projected into me the struggle to make sense of things.

With the teddy bear material the 'indigestibility' is of a more overt nature and something that I found impossible to adequately address during this particular session. I was left with many questions. Was this something he had witnessed (I thought, for example, of him knifing the dog), or a phantasy or indeed a phantasy about something he had witnessed? Certainly the material was difficult to digest.

The experience of any abuse, but particularly ritual abuse, can make a child feel vulnerable and powerless. The physical, sexual and emotional assaults can be invalidated and denied. This can create a split from perceived reality and lead the victim to begin to disown and dissociate from his/her self. These feelings can be projected into the therapist in turn who struggles to contain and understand intense feelings of vulnerability and powerlessness and the associated defence mechanisms of paralysis, splitting and dissociation.

CONCLUSION

I hope this material illustrates some of the complex issues and difficulties in engaging in individual therapy with a young boy whose life experience included abuse of a satanist nature. The problems illustrated are by no means specific to children who have experienced ritual abuse but may be found in working with such children.

The initial sessions with Tom illustrated the impact upon the network and the importance of close working alliance to support therapy. In working with all abused children the dynamics of the abuse have their impact upon the whole network, but with ritual abuse the ordinary splitting between team members seems even stronger. It is interesting to note how the adult roles seemed to be those of witches or saviours, mirroring, I think, something of the religious overtones of the abuse.

In the treatment of children who have been multiply abused I consider containment to be the key treatment issue. The states of mind are often transitional and the therapist is dealing with different fragments while trying also to keep the other fragments in mind. This fragmentation exists even where the material looks innocent and this is indicative of a dissociation between the activity and the emotional affect that is projected. This aspect of fragmentation is, I feel, further exaggerated when working with a patient as young as Tom. He could not present a consistent narrative as might be expected in an older patient. The tortuous experiences of such a young abused child are extremely fragmented and dissociated, so the therapist only understands in pieces.

The task of the therapist is to try and create a sequence of containing environments whilst paying particular attention to the transition between them. This is a difficult task and is, I think by definition, long-term. However, if left untreated the severe trauma these children have experienced is likely to cause serious emotional problems for them throughout their lives.

REFERENCES

Bentovim, A. (1992) *Trauma-organised Systems: Physical and Sexual Abuse in Families*, London, Karnac Books.
Bion, W.R. (1962) *Learning from Experience*, London, Heinemann.
Britton, R. (1983) 'Breakdown and reconstitution of the family circle', in M. Boston and R. Szur (eds) *Psychotherapy with Severely Deprived Children*, London, Routledge & Kegan Paul.
Freud, S. (1905) 'Fragment of an analysis of a case of hysteria', *Standard Edition Vol. VII*, London, Hogarth Press.
Furniss, T. (1983) 'Mutual influence and inter-locking professional family process in the treatment of child sexual abuse', *Child Abuse and Neglect* 7: 207–23.
Klein, M. (1946) 'Notes on some schizoid mechanisms', in *The Writings of Melanie Klein Vol. III* (1975), London, Hogarth Press.
Segal, H. (1957) 'Notes on symbol formation', *International Journal of Psycho-Analysis* 52: 169–78.

Chapter 10

Fostering a ritually abused child

Mary Kelsall

Mary and her co-foster mother Claire have worked with vulnerable children and adults all their working lives. They have large extended families that include both fostered and adopted children and hold open house in their village home. When 'Russell', a ritually abused 8-year-old came to live with them he joined a family of five – plus pets.

Names, identities and background details have been changed wherever necessary to protect confidentiality.

At the time social services asked us to find a place for 'Russell', aged 8, we considered our family ready and able to make room for a multiply abused young boy. Elizabeth, aged 18, was en route for college, interested in science and athletics. Philip, aged 16, with a learning difficulty, was also about to start local college and was swimming competitively in a team for people with learning difficulties. Martina, who has diabetes, was 14 and, like Philip, keen on music. All of us enjoyed hiking the nearby moorland, riding and swimming.

When social services informed us about Russell we were told he had experienced severe physical abuse. Indeed, his father was imprisoned for a long sentence as a result of it. He had experienced multiple caretakers – over ten by the age of 5 – having been abandoned by his mother at 15 months. We knew he had been moved from his parents to children's homes, to foster homes and to grandparents. However, it was to take him many years before he could say more about the catalogue of horrors he had experienced – much of it beyond the scope of our imagination or experience.

Within 12 months his behaviour had changed our lives completely. We were fighting for his and our sanity. During that one year from the age of 8 until 9 he had stolen hundreds of pounds, and systematically smashed walls, doors and some other furniture into pieces. We lived behind locked doors. Our remaining valuables were secured in a safe. 'Have you got the keys?' became our constant cry. In a sense only Russell became free, his bedroom open. However, the boundaries we had to place around his behaviour needed constant patrolling and took up most of our energy.

He would urinate in any receptacle – waste bins, vases, etc. His excreta was left in piles or smeared on walls. Half-eaten yoghurts, sandwiches and bits of food were hidden in drawers, behind or under furniture. The sight of orange juice disoriented him. He would raid the larder, pick out large cans of fruit and other items and then throw the remainder into the paddock at the side of the house. Mealtimes were always fraught. The sight of cutlery frightened him. He would grab food with his hands and rush away. Seconds were his limit for keeping still.

His disdain for and lack of trust of adults was obvious. Women were cows, bitches and witches. Everyday objects would be sexualised. He described the letter 'M' to his teacher and other pupils as an arse upside down. 'Humping' and who would be having it off with whom was the object of his preoccupation in his conversation. His facility for bringing doom, gloom and embarrassment into social settings was exceptional and soon we became almost isolated.

Nevertheless, we were determined the placement would last. We supported him through his fears – car journeys, night terrors, suicidal bids, headaches and episodes where his mind could not function. Car journeys were always tense and dangerous in spite of numerous invented distractions. In a fraught state he would dangerously fight, kick out and jump around. Sometimes his screaming or frantic searching for a safe place in his bedroom awoke the whole household. I often slept on the floor by his bed holding his hand through the night.

We could only guess at the experiences he had endured that led him to behave in this way. All of us had to deal with the horror of walking into the hall to find him practising hanging himself – swinging down the bannister with a makeshift noose.

Claire was the first to witness the severity of his capacity to dissociate. Three months after he arrived I was going to the cinema with Martina and Philip leaving Russell and Claire at the house. When we drove away he suddenly jumped up and pushed his hand through a glass door panel. Claire rushed across the room to his aid to be greeted by a smiling boy shaking his head in confusion. To Claire's amazement Russell absolutely refused to believe he had smashed the panel. In fact, as we were to learn later, it was not Russell who had smashed the panel. In his dissociated state it was indeed someone else.

Another such incident occurred nearly a year later – also triggered by separation. I had taken Philip to a music lesson and when we returned we found Claire shivering in the kitchen. Russell had been furious that I had left and, despite Claire's attempts to amuse and console him, in the dining room he had exploded. He flung a 17-inch television set at her. In an attempt to get help from neighbours she left, closing the door behind her and hoping he would not injure himself. We all opened the door to find him still rushing around with the room wrecked, two chairs smashed, debris from books, lights, lampshades scattered around. Russell settled himself under the table. Slowly he responded to stroking and cajoling. Again, the boy I carried to bed had no idea he had caused such destruction.

With such an amount of disturbance schooling was not possible. Nor was it easy to find a therapist able to work with this level of disturbance and trauma outside of an institution. Car terrors also meant we needed a psychotherapist who could work with us at home. However, we and social services were determined to gain help so that Russell could stay with us. Eva was a particularly experienced psychotherapist in dealing with children like Russell. However, she lived some distance away. Nevertheless, after a year the funding was found by social services and in spite of the distance, Eva was prepared to come.

With the knowledge that someone was coming, Russell found new ways of expressing his anger. He made an 'anger stick' of rolled-up newspaper and, after drawing pictures of people who had hurt him, would whack them with the stick. When he had finished we would quietly stroke his exhausted body while listening to gentle music. He became accepting of us holding him close as a way of restraining him when he lost control. Slowly some trust built up. Russell knew we would not hurt him and would try hard to prevent him from hurting himself. The marks of non-accidental injury he carried on his body – let alone his mind – made this trust an important step.

When Eva arrived the first time he threw marbles at her across the sitting-room floor with some force. After some time Eva said, 'You seem to have these angries inside you, Russell, and they belong to you. If you want to keep them that is up to you. But I think I know a way of making some of them go away.' Russell was quiet for a moment. She continued, 'If you got rid of the angries, Russell, what would you put in their space?' 'Peace', he replied. 'Right then Russell, let's go start making a space for peace if that's what you want.'

This was to be the start of a life-saving support and treatment. For two years Eva was to visit us monthly, usually staying over with us the night before. Named colleagues of hers would also offer telephone support and their empathy and support are still with us. Sometimes, at peak periods of crisis, Eva was in phone contact with us three times a week.

Because of the distance involved and the enormous trauma Russell had suffered Eva found ways of making her monthly visits even more significant. She suggested that the small playroom used for our meetings should be used for further 'family meetings' in her absence, and that I should record for her a diary of events. The floor of the small room was covered with quilts and pillows and it became the room Russell loved most. It is still his favourite room. It was in this room that Russell was able courageously to tell us of his past and the horrors of his life that we could never have imagined.

Being in this room was a double-edged experience. It offered Russell his first prospect of real peace, but it meant facing frightening memories. We found he needed the physical boundary of being held safely by both of us in order to speak. Indeed, the very first time he came to the room with us without Eva we were confronted by a determined little boy demanding, 'Where's my fucking hold then?'

EXTRACTS FROM MY DIARY/LETTERS TO EVA

DECEMBER: Today, Russell concentrated on telling us the ways in which his body had been tortured and the excited reactions of the adults as they inflicted the pain. Later he drew a picture of his grandparents gloating as they whipped him and burned him with cigarettes. He drew himself crying for help in a pool of tears with grandma saying 'Stop snivelling.' Later he vented anger with his feet and fists on cushions crying out 'So how does this feel, grandad? I was only little, now I am growing, I am stronger, now I can hurt you.'

He spoke about willies wrapped around each other, they were squishy squashy. Later he added, 'Thank goodness my mum was good. You have to have one good one in a family. I know my mum must have been good or I would not be here. Everyone else in my family is bad. They all smile when they hurt you.'

MARCH: Russell visited the neighbours who can keep him safe and they went to the leisure centre. Susan, a student social worker who will be on a residential placement with us, came to babysit. Claire and I went out for a meal. Russell managed our leaving and Susan was calm when we returned. This was the first evening we have managed to go out in eighteen months. We knew he was in safe hands.

APRIL: Russell wants to playfight with me in his room. I am aware I no longer expect this time to become a nightmare of squeezing and near throttling me. Sometimes he regresses into baby ways and he has the trust to know I am a safe mother.

In his Saturday playroom he spoke of the smaller devils who talked him into doing bad things and the bigger devil. He told us he had made a promise to his dad and the devil to be bad about everything; do not love, do not do schoolwork, just be bad, steal and do not tell the truth. 'Well my dad is going to have to forgive me because I am going to break my promise.' Then he added, 'This "bad" – it is right through me. My dad used to say let the bad live and the good die.' He resumed hitting the cushion saying 'Death to hate, pain and evil.'

THURSDAY: Great day celebrating R's second anniversary of coming to live with us. He showed real enthusiasm for his gifts and he managed to sit through the meal. We remembered his first meal, grabbing food with his hands and never sitting at the table for more than a few seconds. With real joy we formed a circle of love singing 'He's a jolly good fellow.'

SATURDAY: He wanted us to create a 'devil land' scenario based on his experience. He told us 'You don't offer sweets to the children to get them in, you drag them in and you put poo and blood and urine in the bottle.' The stark horror he can experience at moments is hard to imagine.

JUNE: Today he kept referring to the 'big people' and alternated saying 'I want to die' and 'I do not want to die.' He was subdued and cold and his teeth were chattering. We wrapped him in a quilt and held him and loved him. Philip was very gentle with R.

DECEMBER: He told us there were twenty Russells. To our surprise he then said 'Here is number six, here is number sixteen and here is twenty', with completely different faces for each.

(We were to obtain extra help from social services and Eva over Russell's multiple personality predicament including a much-needed trip to American experts.)

OCTOBER: This was his anniversary of going into care and he was extremely regressed. He was terrified of a noise in the loft that reminded him of 'devil land' and became terrified of us; we were cows trying to strangle him. Afterwards, as I held and rocked him he relaxed and then with an 'angry stick' he shouted 'You fire master devil I will smash you.' He carried on systematically beating with the stick and saying he was beating the poo master, the fire devil master, the devil poisoners of children and the butcher devil. 'One day I will kill the poo master with a knife. Wham, he is dead. But the fire master devil is forever.' He was exhausted, red and dripping with sweat.

During this week we heard him talk to Martina about the demons. When she expressed interest he explained the hierarchy of devils to her. When she said that she was fascinated as she had never seen one before, Russell quietly said, 'It is awful, Martina. You would not want to know any of this if you did know.' (So much for us protecting our other children.)

NOVEMBER: We are all calm following the anniversary turmoil. Russell played with teddy mobiles and hoped that the Brahms lullaby and the teddies will keep the devils from getting him at night. His hope and belief are stronger. 'You and our family have a love that is stronger than the devil's power.'

By the time you read this we hope that R will have been formally adopted into our family. We had already adopted him forever emotionally but he needs the official piece of paper. Russell has been able to attend school for the past eighteen months with no examination results below 75 per cent. Drawing, painting and creative design are his favourite subjects and he contributes to home furnishings with his wooden handicrafts.

LAST WORD

Russell says,

Mum and Eva have told me some people do not believe that people like me have been abused and that the devil stuff is untrue. Well I say, bollocks. I did live seven years of complete hell, suffering cuts, burnings, stabbings. I was locked in cages and in boots of cars. I was not fed for days. No-one to talk to, no-one to listen, no-one to hear me. But worst of all people always calling me a good little devil. As I grew up, on more than one occasion, I saw myself as the devil in the mirror. I was terrified . . . . Because of all the torture and pain my mind blanked out and caused inside people to come.

(Claire and Mary will hopefully write about the work to integrate these other personalities.)

ACKNOWLEDGEMENTS

With thanks to officers from the Social Services Department, our neighbours, Russell's training club coach, teachers, pony club leaders, friends and relatives. We owe our sanity mainly to Eva and a close friend, Gertrude, who has always been there, a safe haven for Russell and all of us.

Chapter 11

A systemic approach

Arnon Bentovim and Marianne Tranter

Dr Arnon Bentovim, Consultant Child Psychiatrist, Family Therapist and Psychoanalyst, works at the Hospital for Sick Children, Great Ormond Street and the Tavistock Clinic. Ms Marianne Tranter is a Social Worker and Family Therapist in the Great Ormond Street Sexual Abuse Team.

Names, identities and background details have been changed wherever necessary to protect confidentiality.

This chapter is based on our work with three children involved in ritual abuse who were referred to the Sexual Abuse Assessment and Treatment service of the Hospital for Sick Children, Great Ormond Street. The children referred were members of a large family, and there was evidence of widespread physical, sexual, emotional abuse and neglect, affecting all the children in the family. Subsequently the parents and grandparents of these children, together with other adult family members, were prosecuted and found guilty of widespread sexual abuse and sentenced for these crimes. Interestingly, although the defendants were all convicted and received lengthy jail sentences, the allegations in respect of the ritual element were not proven.

SYSTEMIC APPROACH TO UNDERSTANDING ABUSE WITHIN FAMILIES

The systemic approach to understanding the way in which problems can arise and be maintained within family systems originated in the work of Gregory Bateson and his colleagues in the 1950s. They used a cybernetic theory and General Systems theory to understand the communication and relationship processes which led to dysfunction within individuals and families. They were interested in the *pragmatics* of communication, that is the non-verbal, or *analogic* communication which defines the meaning of communication, and defines the nature of relationships (Watzlawick *et al.*, 1967). This is in opposition to the *digital* aspects of communication, the words themselves, which have no meaning unless one understands the context in which they are uttered. Out of these considerations they were interested in the way in which one person could control the other, and they introduced the notion of the *double-bind* which occurs when a particular combination of opposing messages at various levels disqualifies and can paralyse the other's capacity to act. Circular recursive repetitive communication between individuals creates feedback loops which maintain roles, meanings and dysfunctional relationships. Intervening in such dysfunctional patterns led to the development of family therapy as a way of creating change beyond the individual.

Other important aspects of systemic thinking include the notion of *boundaries*. Who controls the boundary is the leader of the system and can define who belongs, who is inside and who remains outside. Belonging can feel life-sustaining and essential, not to belong may feel like a living death. Within the system attachment processes are fundamental to both the creation and the maintenance of such systems.

Social systems are basically constructs based on consensus. Reality is constructed socially by language processes, resulting in a series of beliefs and powerful meaning systems maintained by everyday and ritual action around shared living activities and the larger markers of birth, marriage and death (Anderson *et al.*, 1986). To understand such systems requires a view that the individual, the family and society are dynamically connected (Bentovim and Kinston, 1991).

SYSTEMS AND FAMILIES WHERE ABUSE OCCURS

Research on families where abuse occurs (Bentovim, 1992) shows they commonly have rigid boundaries, are either isolated from community networks or deeply involved with helping agencies, have a powerful inter-generational transmission of abusive patterns (Oliver, 1993), and a set of beliefs, family culture and ways of relating which are in contrast to what are seen as societal norms. Observation of such families shows that they are often on the edge of breakdown patterns (Bentovim and Kinston, 1991).

It is possible to see such families as a trauma-organised system (Bentovim, 1992) because of the way that traumatic events experienced by parents and children can have such long-lasting and organising effects on individuals and families. Re-enactment, flashbacks, triggered memories, avoidance and arousal have a pervasive effect on development, much affected by gender (e.g. identification with the aggressor role in boys, and the victim role in girls). Traumatic experiences also influence subsequent choice of partners, based on parallel experiences and interlocking pathology. Many members of a sibship can be affected and an interlocking extended family system can arise, with multiple forms of abuse, transmitted in a variety of patterns (Oliver, 1993).

Characteristic of such families are the blaming of the victim, the deletion and denial of abusive actions by the perpetrator, and the organisation and undermining of potentially protective individuals both within and external to the family. This is achieved by the creation of a powerful boundary in which absolute loyalty is demanded, and the development of a set of stories, beliefs and meanings which justify abusive action.

SYSTEMS THINKING AND RITUAL ABUSE

McFadyen *et al.* (1993), in their discussion of ritual abuse, define such abuse as *the involvement of children in physical, psychological or sexual abuse associated with repeated activities (ritual) which purport to relate the abuse to contexts of a religious, magical, supernatural kind* (see Jones, 1993). In their discussion of this definition they demonstrate the way in which an extraordinarily powerful self-contained system is created. This is an extremely powerful example of a trauma-organised system. They put forward the view that repetitiveness of ritual action contributes to the trauma of victims, and functions to validate or justify the abuse for the abusers and/or the victims by relating it to some over-arching set of values or metaphysical framework.

The rationale and responsibility for the abuse thus shifts above the heads of individuals involved, and it assumes the character of obligation for abused and abuser alike. Such processes occur in all forms of abuse but are institutionalised in ritual abuse. It achieves the dual effect of indoctrination into a belief system and induction into group practices. Our research (Bentovim, 1992) indicates that involvement of children in sexual activities with others is one of the most powerful factors in inducting them into an abusive role. Thus such rituals confirm identities and loyalty, and as McFadyen *et al.* (1993) indicate, produce a dynamic entrapment and, inevitably, secrecy.

They also induce disbelief, dissuading victims from disclosing abuse, making all aspects of disclosure seem fanciful and fantastic. Thus it increases the authority of the ritual system and constructs a sense of power greater than any other agency, with notions of spiritual connection. Compulsive involvement in bizarre, sadistic, illegal activities, the abuse of others, killing described by survivors, all increase the binding nature of secrecy. Disclosure of such activities would risk prosecution of its instigators, and this is often used as a threat to reinforce the secrecy, and maintain a rigid impermeable boundary to the outside world. These are some of the factors which have a major effect on our therapeutic attempts to process such abusive experience.

REFERRAL: THE 'G' FAMILY

At the time of referral to Great Ormond Street Sexual Abuse Assessment and Treatment Service, the three younger children in the family comprised a girl of 9, Sarah, a boy of 6, David, and a boy of 4, Anthony (not their real names). They were in the care of a local authority and placed with two sets of foster parents.

It was whilst Sarah was going to church with her new foster family that she began to disclose her ritual abuse. She said that her dad had a church, people were wearing black clothes, the witches were making spells about her and they were touching her. They were trying to hurt her with a knife, and they did it to some of her friends. They said that she had to jump off a big wall. She said 'No', but they said they would kill her if she did not do so. Her dad took her to Halloween and they tied her up and touched her, and 'Some of them did it with their willies, and some of them were doing it with their hands.'

There was a man who was taking pictures, some of them were ladies, and the pictures were being put in a book. In the church there were cobwebs on the floor, and there was a star hanging up and it had a devil on it. There was a snake and the star was black and the devil had brown clothes, and it had rude pictures on the walls.

Family background from the social work file

The genogram in Figure 11.1 shows the complexity and size of the family and the extensiveness of sexual abuse and physical violence. We were informed that the family had been known to social services for years and had posed many problems. Social service departments find the management of large families characterised by extreme neglect and abuse difficult because of the ever-growing size of the problem. A sibship of ten presents almost insuperable logistical problems to intervention. It has to be asked whether helping with accommodation, giving support, material provisions, responding to current crises, literally made the Social Service Department take on the role of supportive family members. Thus such actions may maintain problems rather than creating radical change.

Details of neglect and abuse

The details of the case reports indicated that the children had always been subject to poor standards of hygiene and the results of poor financial management. Despite a constant supply of money to improve material standards, the mother could not provide these to an acceptable level and parenting skills did not improve over the years. Clothing was poor and inappropriate to prevailing climatic conditions despite clothing donations. Diet was adequate but of poor quality.

It was extremely difficult for the social worker to describe the chaos within the household. Children as they grew older became more unruly, left to fend for themselves, beyond the mother's control. The mother yelled rather than talked, school attendance became poorer, social isolation became marked and the children had few friends outside their immediate extended families. Appointments for speech therapists, educational psychologists and child guidance clinics were rarely kept and thus the children's needs could not be addressed by professionals. There were gaps in immunisation records and dental and personal hygiene was non-existent.

The children were left unsupervised on the estate and there was regular

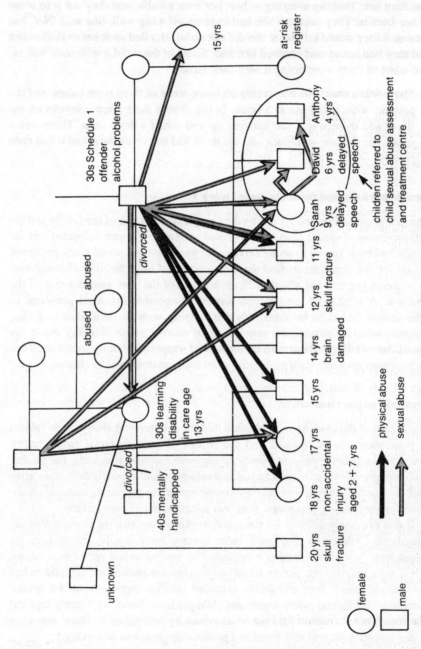

Figure 11.1 Family genogram showing extent of physical and sexual abuse in family at referral

female ○

male □

━━━▶ physical abuse

━━━▷ sexual abuse

at-risk register

15 yrs

30s Schedule 1 offender alcohol problems

divorced

Anthony 4 yrs

David 6 yrs delayed speech

Sarah 9 yrs delayed speech

children referred to child sexual abuse assessment and treatment centre

11 yrs

12 yrs skull fracture

abused

abused

14 yrs brain damaged

15 yrs

30s learning disability in care age 13 yrs

17 yrs

divorced

40s mentally handicapped

18 yrs non-accidental injury aged 2 + 7 yrs

20 yrs skull fracture

unknown

concern and complaints from other families: fears for their safety, climbing on roofs, playing on building sites, eating food from rubbish chutes; acts of vandalism, bullying, stoning elderly people, begging and burglary, although always unproven. There was an appalling history of accidents to various members of the family: falling from the balconies of blocks of flats; one boy hospitalised with a fractured skull; and numerous road accidents.

Allegations of sexual abuse

Many of the children had exhibited behaviour which would be associated with sexual abuse, but there had been little in the way of corroborative evidence to support the allegations made by the children, which were frequently withdrawn. It was the older daughter, and two of the children referred to ourselves who began to allege abuse by the maternal grandparents, leading to action and removal of the children from their parents' care. It should be noted that this action occurred at a time when there was a wave of publicity about sexual abuse, with the establishment of ChildLine and an explosion of referrals to child care agencies. Thus these disclosures occurred at a time when a means existed for children to share what had been a secret and perverse pervasive culture of their family, and professionals were beginning to listen and act. The children began to make widespread allegations about the parents and grandparents which eventually led to their prosecution and conviction.

Background information concerning the family

The mother of all the children had learning difficulties herself, had attended a special school and had been received into care at the age of 13 because of physical and sexual abuse. Her first child was born when she was only 17 years of age, her first husband displaying violence to her and towards the children, particularly after bouts of drinking. Her own sisters had also been extensively abused and there was major concern about their children too. The father of the older children also had a history of learning difficulties and was admitted to a hospital for severe learning difficulties. He met the man who subsequently became the second husband, who had been admitted to the same hospital under a section of the Mental Health Act, as a result of a sexual assault on a girl aged 15. He too had an extensive criminal record and was a heavy drinker. The mother relied heavily on her own parents, could be both hostile and resistant to social work intervention and could not protect the children from known abusers in the social context despite the threat of Care proceedings.

The children's individual histories

The review of information revealed a complex history of special school and boarding school attendances; being subject to threatening and intimidating behaviour;

admissions to hospital due to non-accidental injuries; skull fractures, extensive bruising due to beating, being punched around the ears; serious neglect, being withdrawn, waif-like, frequently craving affection and attention; needing nappies until the third year, having delayed speech development; excessive masturbating and behaving sexually with each other; being involved in violent fights, subject to unlawful sexual intercourse with others, absconding, truanting, alleging rape, self-mutilation; begging, lighting fires, being propositioned by perverted individuals; glue-sniffing, wild behaviour; being used in schools and social contexts as a model for all that was bad and unacceptable. It is also striking to read how surprised workers were at the remarkable improvement in these children's well-being when placed in alternative care, e.g. 'I would never have anticipated the progress that the 15-year-old girl made since she has been in care.' About the 7-year-old, 'Although missing her siblings, she has made great progress since her reception into care, her speech shows significant improvement, she has relinquished the enforced role of little mother.' 'The 4-year-old's clarity of speech is improving, his nightmares have reduced.' It was in the context of living in a different family situation that Sarah was able to begin to reveal the extent and depth of the abusive experiences within her family once released from the bond of secrecy and fear.

Comment on information received from the Social Services Department

This family shows starkly and powerfully characteristics described earlier of the trauma-organised system characteristic of families where the most serious physical abuse, emotional abuse, sexual abuse and neglect occurs. The scene is set for participation in multiple abuse and involvement of the children in ritual abuse.

The parents' limited capacities have been further undermined and maintained both in their family of origin and in the current family by a choice of partners who continue violent and perverse victimising activities. Children are used both as caretakers and the object of anger and sexual response by both parents and grandparents, and are organised in similar patterns between themselves and externally. Although members of the family have provided major concerns for professionals over the years, any intervention had maintained the system and not created any real change.

The culture continued and maintained itself until the change within the social context and the awareness of the deleterious effect of sexual abuse triggered involvement and intervention from the professional network at a different level. Ritual abuse was then being revealed.

THERAPEUTIC WORK

The three children were seen for initial assessment by a child psychiatrist and psychiatric social worker. Sarah was seen first with her foster mother, Mary, and then David and Anthony were seen with their foster mother, Joan. The purpose of the assessment was to offer a second opinion to the local Social Services

Department who had referred them, and in addition to advise about the children's current and future placement needs and the nature of therapeutic help required.

Sarah told us that she had lived with Mary for about sixteen months, and that previously she had lived with her mother. Very quickly and spontaneously she told us that she did not like her father and that he had done something not very nice to her. She told us that she had talked to Mary about this. She also said her grandad had done some very rude things to her that he should not have done and that she felt sad, angry and cross about this. She told us that her mother knew what had happened because she had told her.

Sarah told us that her mother was not very good at cooking meals and that Sarah often had to do this herself; her mother did not wash and iron clothes, they did not always have warm clothes, nor did mother wash or bath the children. When asked how she slept, Sarah told us that she sometimes had nightmares and flashbacks of the rude things that were done to her.

There was some discussion about the fact that Mary and her husband were short-term foster carers and that Sarah knew that later she would go to a 'forever' home. Sarah realised that her own mother could not look after her and she made some comments about the type of home she would like, including the wish that there should be other children there.

After leaving the room, and in fact in the corridor, Sarah told us that she was afraid and at that point she began to sob. She indicated that there were some more things to tell us but which she had not been able to mention. We tried to reassure her that there would be another time when she could talk to us again and a further appointment was made.

On meeting with David and Anthony, our first observation was that both had significantly delayed speech and, although David could express himself and we could understand him, Anthony had great difficulty communicating verbally. Both boys were receiving speech therapy and David was attending infant school whilst Anthony was attending a nursery.

David was able to talk about living with 'aunty and uncle', i.e. his foster parents, and that previously he and his brother and sister had lived with their mum and dad but there was not very much food and that he received more at aunty's. He also told us that he got 'more warmer clothes in aunty's house'. He could remember his father drinking too much and also said 'He sleep with me' but that he had not liked this. He also said father had done rude things, and at this point he said quite clearly 'bum'. Anthony interjected and said 'No', to which David said 'No just me'. He told us it did not hurt but that he did not like it, at which point Anthony said 'I do.'

Joan, the foster mother, gave us a description of David's tremendous progress since being with her in that at first he did not know his colours, his vocabulary was very poor and his speech unintelligible. He could currently make himself understood, could count, knew his colours and could play on his own. She described the boys as rewarding children in that they were very grateful to her and affectionate, both to each other and to other people. However, she mentioned the occasion when Sarah had played with David's genitals during a visit whilst Joan's attention was diverted. Joan said she would be much more worried about possible recurrences of such behaviour if Sarah were living with them.

At first David's speech was not understandable but with help from a special unit and a speech therapist it was currently thought that he would be able to enter mainstream schooling with remedial help. Anthony had no speech at all on arrival at Joan's but this was now developing.

We acknowledged the need for a more permanent placement for the boys and decided to postpone a decision about therapy until this had been achieved. The fact that both boys were developmentally delayed but showing signs of rapid progress also made us think that reassessment of them in six months' time would assist us in our evaluation of their therapeutic needs.

A second meeting was arranged for us to meet with Sarah one week later. We began the meeting acknowledging that she had been very upset at the end of our first meeting, and wondered whether she might be able to help us understand why that was. Sarah started by telling us that when she remembered what had happened to her it made her sad and want to cry. We asked if she was frightened of speaking and she told us that she was worried that someone would get into trouble, and that she had been told by two people to keep what had happened to her a secret.

She started telling us about a scary dream and said it was about her dad doing things to her. She described 'A not very nice building which was very old without any furniture or people living in it. It was cold and had more than one room, although only one floor and there was no-one else there except her and her father.' She told us that the dream was exactly like what used to happen although the place was different. In reality things happened in her bedroom and at times they also happened elsewhere. She then went on to describe what she called the 'church', although it was not an ordinary church, where she was taken both at Halloween and at other times. There were people there, some of whom she knew, both grown-ups and children. She said, 'Some children when I had it had it at the same time', although it was clear that children were also abused at different times. She described adults as wearing long black and brown cloaks with hoods so that they looked like witches. She said she could see people's eyes but did not know what clothes were being worn beneath the cloaks. She told us that spells were made and that things were said in low voices 'different to ordinary talking', in words that she did not understand. She understood some spells were to hurt her and that sometimes the spell was said and then she was actually hurt. She described more than four adults together making a spell in this dark church where the windows were covered so it was dark. She remembered them walking there with her dad and that it was a long way away from where she lived. She estimated that it would be about an hour's walk.

She described drinking what she called 'some funny stuff' whose colour she did not know but which had a sour taste, and when remembering it her face screwed up. She was made to drink it and it made her tummy feel 'yucky' and sometimes gave her a headache. She described men and women in a circle and said that she would be outside the circle. She would be frightened and the people were not kind and she remembered not wanting to be there. She said she was 4 years old when she first went and 6 years old when she went for the last time. David and Anthony did not go, neither did her mother, although she told her mother when she was going and on occasions tried to dissuade her father from taking her.

Sarah said the people did not tell her what they were going to do to her although it was the same sort of thing each time but with differences. She said that she tried not to let them do it to her but that they tied her up by her arms and legs and that she screamed and cried but that no-one attempted to silence her. She described the others being tied up and that she heard screaming and crying. She described a star hanging from the ceiling and drew a brown devil with a snake on the top to illustrate this. She described it as a devil church and said that it was scary. She said that Jesus made her smile and there was no devil in the nice church that she went to with Mary. She said some of the other children in the devil church were her friends whom she knew from home and that their parents were friends of her parents. She said the youngest child there was 2 but there were not any babies, neither were there any animals or birds. She said she saw grown-ups hurting children, doing the same thing as they did to her.

Sarah said she had told some of this to her foster mother but had not told her about the rude things that happened in the devil church. She said similar things happened there as happened at home, although she said 'My dad did not tie me up when he done it in my bedroom.' She said the church was worse because it was more scary. She could recognise her father by his eyes, even with his clothes and hood on, and the adults called each other by unfamiliar names.

Sarah said she had been hurt at her grandad's house whilst she was alone in the room with him and her nanny and aunty were downstairs. She had told her mother about this who had told her grandfather off. He had only hurt her in the home and never went to the church. She added that there were cobwebs on the floor of the devil church and rude pictures on the wall and little spiders on the floor.

Sarah told us that she thought of the church often at bedtime and sometimes dreamt about it but she added, 'It was something that really happened.' She said the grown-ups told her they would kill her if she told anyone what had happened, although she never saw anyone being killed. She told us this was what she was frightened by the previous occasion and that there was nothing else to tell us.

Therapeutic needs

We advised that the children's primary need at the point of assessment was to be placed in permanent substitute families with a view to adoption. They were having infrequent supervised contact with their mother and this would continue providing it was consistent with the overall placement plan. We commented at the time, 'It is of paramount importance that the children's need for a secure attachment to a non-abusing nurturing adult should take precedence over any other consideration.'

Once their placement needs had been met we suggested that Sarah attend a group for sexually abused children at the hospital (Bentovim *et al.*, 1988), and after that she should be assessed for longer-term psychotherapy. In respect of David, we felt his treatment should be delayed for six months, allowing time for a more permanent placement to be made and also, as mentioned previously, for him to reach a developmental level at which he could benefit from group work with other children of a similar age. We thought it rather premature to decide upon Anthony's therapeutic needs other than to comment that he may well benefit from some individual play therapy again once his placement had been secured.

Therapeutic work with Sarah

Sarah attended a ten-session group for sexually abused children run by two female therapists. They noted that she was a bright, talkative member of the group, who was very helpful and able to empathise with other girls' situations very easily. She identified a need to talk in more detail about her experiences in an individual context, and as the local psychotherapists in her area were male, it was thought appropriate that one of her female group therapists at the hospital undertake some individual psychotherapeutic work with her. In general, being able to talk with other girls of a similar age who had had similar experiences was very helpful for Sarah, although it was interesting to note that she did not appear to feel able to share the more bizarre and ritual elements of her abuse.

In individual psychotherapeutic work subsequently she was able to talk in more detail about her overall experiences and to express her feelings of confusion in respect of her mother, to whom she maintained a rather idealised attachment. Because of her father's global abuse of both her and her brothers she seemed to feel less ambivalent about him, and in fact could not recall anything positive about him. The fact that her mother continued to take her to visit her grandfather, even though she knew he was abusing her, seemed to represent an act of considerable betrayal for Sarah, and it seemed that there was nowhere that she felt safe.

Interestingly, in her therapy, she was preoccupied with her concerns for her future placement and this tended to take precedence over her memories of her abuse. It may also have been her way of signalling that she did not feel ready or sufficiently contained to work on the more disturbing aspects of her abuse until she was in a permanent family. The therapist concurred with this view.

Therapeutic work with David

David duly attended a Young Children's Group for children who had been sexually abused and participated well, his expressive language having improved considerably over the months. A psycho-educational approach was used (Vizard, 1986) in which children are helped through story telling, role play and games to be clear about the difference between good and bad touching and the fact that adult perpetrators alone are responsible for abuse. David made quite frequent references to the fact that his father and grandfather had abused him, and seemed to find comfort that such matters could be freely discussed in the group. The group seemed to help David become more self-confident and assertive, and there were no concerns raised during this period of inappropriate sexualised behaviour in the foster home.

Some months after the group ended David was reassessed for individual psychotherapeutic work and began psychotherapy on a weekly basis which is still on-going at the time of writing. His therapist reports as follows. The main themes running through (virtually all) the sessions are his ambivalent feelings towards parental figures and his marked aggression towards extended family, particularly father, mother and maternal grandmother. Quite often members of his extended family were shown jumping to their death or being run over; his grandfather, who also abused him, did not feature in any of his play or stories.

When it was decided he could live with his foster parents on a long-term basis, his play changed dramatically. His parental figures became aunt and uncle (his foster parents). He was ambivalent towards foster father and showed him being kicked out by foster mother. At the beginning of the session David was extremely fearful that his father would take him away, even though he knew that he was in prison. He exhibited no preoccupation with sexual thoughts until the tenth month of individual work when he became sexually excited by the sight of an unclad girl while on holiday at the seaside. The two sessions following this sighting were peppered with talk of girls and mothers 'being rude'. He expressed interest in a 14-year-old girl and seemed to be struggling with reactivation of erotic feelings from his childhood.

It was in the context of discussing these feelings that he revealed, for the first time, that he had been abused as part of a 'dancing ceremony'. He explained that he, his younger brother and his sister had been taken to a forest and tied to trees. Naked men and women danced around them to the sound of music from a cassette radio. Various men had touched their genitalia. He had been threatened with death if he revealed what had happened. This is why he had not disclosed taking part in the ceremony. David found it easier to disclose that his father had abused him, but he was unable to disclose ritual abuse until ten months into therapy. He remained fearful that his disclosure would result in someone 'getting him'. This may be related to the fact that some members of the abuse ring were still at large, or that the fear induced in the settings of a ceremony was strong.

Therapeutic work with Anthony

Great support has been given to Anthony by his foster parents, but apart from the odd one-word reference he has not been able to articulate memories of his abuse and has, therefore, not so far been included in group work. He will be reassessed once he has settled in his permanent substitute family. As has been the case with a number of other children whose abusive experiences occurred before they have acquired language, he may begin to express memories verbally in due course.

COMMENT

A carefully planned multi-disciplinary approach to the management of these children's placement and therapeutic needs has been essential, with close contact being maintained between the Social Services Department, respective foster carers, home-finding team and the therapeutic agency (i.e. the hospital). In addition, some further work was undertaken with Sarah before she had to give evidence in criminal proceedings in respect to her father and grandfather, and one of the members of the therapeutic team had also to give evidence in those proceedings on the children's behalf. Although the defendants were all convicted and received lengthy jail sentences, the allegations in respect of the ritual element were not proven. Once again the difficulty for the police in finding hard evidence to substantiate Sarah's account proved extremely difficult, and thus Sarah's description remained uncorroborated and failed to convince the jury of their veracity 'beyond reasonable doubt'. Finally, we think it important to maintain an open door policy in respect of children who have been so abused as it is vital for them to know that further help is available if and when they should need it.

ACKNOWLEDGEMENTS

We acknowledge the contribution of members of the Sexual Abuse Assessment and Treatment Team to this chapter. They include Dr Clive Britten, Ms Gerrilyn Smith, Dr Tessa Leverton, Dr Theo Mutale and Dr Jill Hodges.

REFERENCES

Anderson, H., Goolishian, H. and Winderman, L. (1986) 'Problem-determined systems towards transformation in family therapy', Journal of Strategic and Systemic Therapies 5, 14–19.
Bentovim, A. (1992) Trauma Organised Systems – Physical and Sexual Abuse in Families, London, Karnac.
Bentovim, A. and Kinston, W. (1991) 'Focal family therapy – joining systems theory with psychodynamic understanding', in A. Gurman and D. Kniskern (eds) Handbook for Family Therapy, Vol. 11, New York, Basic Books.
Bentovim, A., Elton, A., Hildebrand, J., Tranter, M. and Vizard, E. (1988) Child Sexual Abuse Within the Family: Assessment and Treatment, London, John Wright/ Butterworths.
Jones, D.P.M. (1993) 'Child sexual abuse and satanism', Newsletter of the Association of Child Psychology and Psychiatry 15, 207–13.
McFadyen, A., Hanks, H. and James. C. (1993) 'Ritual abuse: a definition', Child Abuse Review 2, 35–41.
Oliver, J.E. (1993) 'Intergenerational transmission of child abuse: rates, research and clinical implications', American Journal of Psychiatry 150(9), 1315–29.
Vizard, E. (1986) Self-esteem and Personal Safety, London, Tavistock/Routledge & Kegan Paul.
Watzlawick, P., Beavan, J.H. and Jackson, D.D. (1967) The Pragmatics of Human Communication, Norton, New York.

Part II Clinical accounts

Adults

Chapter 12

In-patient psychotherapy at the Henderson Hospital

Kingsley Norton

Kingsley Norton is a Consultant Psychiatrist and Medical Director of the Henderson Hospital.

Names, identities and background details have been changed wherever necessary to protect confidentiality.

The Henderson Hospital developed from a treatment initiative founded by Dr Maxwell Jones in 1947 (Jones, 1952). Ex-servicemen who had difficulty settling back into civilian life and others with problems of social functioning (Whiteley, 1980) were treated according to a model which had become known as the 'therapeutic community' (Main, 1946). The hallmarks of this treatment approach were the active participation of patients in their own treatment (and also in the treatment of their fellow patients) and the lessening of the staff–patient hierarchy.

The client group treated, up to twenty-nine in number, are largely selected by the patients themselves and are mainly younger adults in the age range 17–45. Most are single, few having ever married or had sustained relationships with partners. The vast majority (80–90 per cent) have had previous psychiatric treatment, including as in-patients. Over half have been convicted of a variety of crimes and approximately 10 per cent have been imprisoned.

Treatment has been demonstrated to have a marked impact on self-esteem (Norris, 1983); on subsequent use of psychiatric service and on reconviction rate (Whiteley, 1970; Copas *et al.*, 1984). The maximum length of stay is one year, with an average length of stay between six and seven months. Those staying over seven months have a much better long-term progress (at three years' post-treatment) prognosis. Psychological symptomatology has also been shown to improve following treatment at Henderson (at an average follow-up of eight months) and in 50 per cent of all patients, regardless of duration of admission, there is clinically meaningful improvement (Dolan *et al.*, 1992).

Much of the day-to-day running of the community is in the hands of the more senior patients and this includes the chairing of a Monday to Saturday community meeting which is attended by all patients and all staff on duty at the time. Patients are known as 'residents' since this reflects their more active role in their own and others' treatment. Residents have a larger say in who is admitted than do staff. This also applies to discharge, since if this is not at the one-year point, when leaving is compulsory, or through self-discharge (all admissions are voluntary, that is, there are no compulsory admissions, e.g. under the Mental Health Act 1983) it is discharge by the community. Thus were there to be block voting with staff and residents disagreeing it is always the residents' vote which carries the motion. Such voting always involves the whole community, regardless of time of day or night, and is in the context of a large group meeting of all concerned.

The essence of the treatment is working with individuals' strengths and attempting to develop these. Hence, in order to work at the Henderson, staff need to have faith in the therapeutic processes of groups (NB: there is no individual psychotherapy) as a means of allowing individuals to develop a greater sense of responsibility, self-esteem and autonomy through real empowerment.

Mr John Jones was the first resident to openly speak of satanist abuse. His referral was unremarkable in that conventional psychiatric and psychothera-peutic assessments had not revealed any satanic activity. At 30, he had been referred by a Consultant Psychotherapist. The main reason for his referral was his expressed fear of his own violence. This was in the context of marital break-up. The psychotherapist judged that John's potential for violence was too great a risk for out-patient treatment (individual or group).

John stated he grew up in a family where there was a mixture of excessive control and violent discipline. He recalls being beaten repeatedly, particularly by his mother, who would use any blunt instrument which came to hand. On one occasion, she had to be physically dragged from him by his father. Neither parent had a formal psychiatric history or diagnosis.

At the interview for selection to join the community, John did not elaborate many details of his early life. He considered that his teenage years were marked by much bullying and intimidation, especially at school. At this time he saw himself as socially withdrawn, isolated and lacking in self-confidence. Although tall, he felt that he was puny and unable to participate in the sporting ethos of the schools which he attended. By his account, his dealings with other people at this time included an inclination to be arrogant, dismissive and rather distant. This may have been partly brought about by frequent home and school moves caused by his father's occupation.

John did talk about a particular incident during his teens when he had a girlfriend and was challenged in some way by another older and larger rivalrous male. John has little memory of the event save for an awareness that he savagely attacked the man and broke some of his limbs. He was convicted for this offensive behaviour, the nature and intensity of which bore a strong resemblance to the physical abuse John himself had experienced at his mother's hands.

Later John married a partner who had been a victim of sexual abuse within her own family. There were children of the marriage and it was his dealings with the children, considered by the wife to be 'over-rough', which ostensibly led to the marital breakdown. There had also been violence between himself and his wife and there was an injunction against him visiting her.

It was agreed that John had not provided much personal information about himself. However, he had created a vivid impression in the minds of the selection group of the extent to which he had been both abused and neglected and was full of loneliness, anger and despair. There was also concern that he might in fact be somebody who covertly obtained pleasure from sadistic fantasy and/or action.

In the first few weeks following admission, a time when some residents leave prematurely, John settled unusually quickly, forming an idealised and fragile attachment to the community. It was at this point he talked of having been a 'satanist'. Although this talk represented, at least to an extent, an emotional unburdening and self-disclosure, it appeared also to serve the function of keeping others at an emotional distance from him.

John stayed in the community for just over seven months. His sleep pattern was disturbed throughout. He was never in the mainstream of the community and tended to be very much at its margins, although he did find relationships with a small number of residents, both male and female. He talked about having attacked his father and how he 'still liked the feeling of determined revenge'. Following this he appeared to be in touch with genuine sadness and he was on occasion quite tearful. Shortly afterwards he rode his bicycle in front of a car and this was construed by the community as a suicide attempt. The fluctuation between a more caring and upset side to John and his violent phantasies or acts was often abrupt and extreme, and this formed a discernible pattern to his style of relating to the community – care without aggression, aggression without care.

John's wife was due to visit him to discuss their divorce. On the night prior to her visit, John barricaded himself in his room and talked of being 'in touch with a lot of evil forces'. One of the staff members who was on duty that evening described John's terror as being palpable. (It was only later discovered that he had kept a number of weapons, including a large carving knife, which he had taken from the community's kitchen, in his room throughout his stay.)

During the family group (comprising himself, the rest of his small psychotherapy group, together with his wife and her social worker), John's wife indicated that she was still frightened of him. She detailed violent family incidents both towards herself and the baby. John's response to what his wife was reporting tended to be one of disbelief and he was unable to enter into any dialogue with her. His wife also recalled how, when he was an adult, John's mother had comforted him on her lap, in a very infantilising manner, and how she herself had felt totally excluded from this relationship by his mother. As the family group proceeded John became more and more withdrawn, looking upset and eventually becoming tearful. The staff who had been present felt it was as if he were in the presence of a scolding mother.

Following this family group John was more frequently upset and tearful.

During this period he also talked further and in more detail about some of his activities with satanists. For example, he described aspects to do with the ritual slaughter of animals and how he was involved in helping others to cut themselves in a ritualistic way. This included helping certain individuals to commit suicide, although it did not appear that he himself had actually killed another person. In talking of this and other aspects, such as the stench of entrails and faeces, the effect on the group was emotionally stunning. It did not seem possible for either residents or staff to stay emotionally involved with him for long.

Later, when a potential resident who had been a sexual abuser was interviewed for admission at the selection group when John was a member, he was put in touch with huge anger and felt that he wished to destroy the man. This fitted in with his accounts of past vigilante activities. He had described how he would go out in search of 'pimps, drug-pushers and other people'. One victim was a drug-pusher whom John had hit over the back of the neck until he was unconscious before piling his drugs on top of him and then informing the police. Like John's account of his satanic activities, there was something in the way he described the episodes which had an extremely chilling effect on the group members. This was all the more affecting because at times he was able to be a rather engaging personality, in a boyish or childlike way.

John had set an unrealistically early leaving date for himself, but was persuaded by the rest of the community to delay this. However, he eventually left prematurely without saying a proper goodbye or going through the community's usual leaving 'rituals', this aspect perhaps being particularly problematic in view of his experience of satanism. Following his absence, a number of residents and staff were left angry with him, feeling that he had not dealt with all that he might have done in terms of his emotional difficulties, even though he had indicated that he wished to pursue some individual therapy in the future. There was also, however, a sense of relief felt by the community after he had gone.

The staff group considered that by the end of John's stay important aspects of his personality remained seriously split off from one another. He himself had read of a code of chivalry in which, according to him, 'people could be loving and kind as well as strong'. This ideal, representing the functioning of an integrated personality, eluded John. For him, being loving or kind to somebody, usually when he or she was acutely distressed, elicited a compulsive and controlling style which also required some other person to be identified as responsible for the upset. This other person would then become the receptacle of and target for John's split-off aggression and potentially for his violence.

John's divided stance was thought to be inextricably linked to his early, and continuing, powerfully ambivalent relationship with his mother. She had offered either physical abuse or an infantilising and intrusive style of caring which owed more to her own denied and projected infantile needs than to those of her son. Unfortunately, the community also often failed to meet John's more infantile needs, on account of difficulty in finding an empathic response which might have aided him in his attempt to integrate more of his split-off personality fragments.

His needy infantile self thus remained relatively encapsulated and out of touch with a grotesque, grandiose and controlling adult self.

REFERENCES

Copas, J.B., O'Brien, M., Roberts, J. and Whiteley, J.S. (1984) 'Treatment outcome in personality disorder: the effect of social, psychological and behavioural variables', *Personality and Individual Differences* 5 (5), 565–73.

Dolan, B.M., Evans, C.D.H. and Wilson, J. (1992) 'Therapeutic community treatment for personality disordered adults (1) Changes in neurotic symptomatology on follow-up', *International Journal of Social Psychiatry* 38 (4), 243–50.

Jones, Maxwell (1952) *Social Psychiatry: A Study of Therapeutic Communities*, London, Tavistock Publications.

Main, T. (1946) 'The hospital as a therapeutic institution', *Bulletin of the Menninger Clinic* 10, 66–8.

Norris, M. (1983) 'Changes in patients during treatment at the Henderson Hospital therapeutic community during 1977–81', *British Journal of Medical Psychology* 56, 135–43.

Whiteley, J.S. (1970) 'The response of psychopaths to a therapeutic community', *British Journal of Psychiatry* 116, 517–29.

Whiteley, J.S. (1980) 'Henderson Hospital', *International Journal of Therapeutic Communities* 1, 38–58.

Chapter 13

The shattered picture of the family
Encountering new dimensions of human relations, of the family and of therapy

Alan Cooklin and Gill Gorell Barnes

Alan Cooklin is Consultant in Family Psychiatry, Marlborough Family Service, Hon. Senior Lecturer, University College London and Birkbeck College London, Clinical Director, Children and Families Psychotherapy Directorate, past Director and later Chair, Institute of Family Therapy London. He trained as an analyst, group analyst and psychiatrist.

Gill Gorell Barnes is Senior Clinical Lecturer in Social Work, Tavistock Clinic, Hon. Senior Lecturer, Birkbeck College, Consultant for Training Institute of Family Therapy. She worked as a psychiatric social worker and then as a family therapist with Robin Skynner before doing further family therapy training at the Tavistock.

This is a condensed version of our work with this patient which has inevitably had to lose some of its reflective components in order to accommodate to the space available.

Names, identities and background details have been changed wherever necessary to protect confidentiality.

This is the account of one therapist, Alan Cooklin, encountering ritual satanist abuse in a quite unexpected context. As a result of work with a female patient he engaged the help of Gill Gorell Barnes, his partner and colleague. They had worked with child abuse victims and 'adult survivors' of childhood sexual abuse, both separately and together. However, the account told by this woman was different in quality from their former experience. The story challenged their own taboos in relation to former conceptualisations of adult–child as well as family relationships (Cooklin and Gorell Barnes, 1993). It thus constituted a powerful and painful learning for them.

KAREN'S WORK WITH ALAN COOKLIN (1)

I was asked to see a woman of 42, Sheila, who was a futures trader in a finance house. She was the oldest of four sisters. Two of them had emigrated to Canada twenty years ago and were no longer in contact. Karen, her youngest sister (aged

35), an artist and graphic designer, was the only one she kept in touch with. Her parents were lawyers and now in their early 70s.

Sheila was living in New Zealand and had come to England to visit her problematic 18-year-old daughter who studied here. On her second visit she brought her daughter and Karen with her, as Karen was seen as an effective aunt who had been 'into some weird things'. A week after Sheila returned to New Zealand, I received a phonecall from Karen asking if she could be seen in her own right.

She was a tall slim woman with medium length dark hair, quite graceful in her movements, dressed in what seemed fairly expensive clothes and in a fashionable style. She said she was married to a solicitor, Steven, eight years older than herself, and had a lover, Paul, with whom she shared a flat. She divided her time between them and 'other places'. She said she had been previously raped by a 'therapist' who was involved in astrology and that had delayed any search for further treatment.

I arranged to see her for a few sessions and then discuss the possibilities about therapy. On the final assessment session she was in a state of panic. She began to describe in detail both sexual and violent abuse from age 3 at the hands of an uncle that included being locked in a black coal cellar for up to six hours, buggery and torture. I considered she would need to see a woman, but she was adamant that she could not. The possible reasons for this only became clearer as we heard increasingly of her mother's and aunt's participation in the abuse.

She told me of a number of suicide attempts she had made, and it became clear to me that she was now and probably had been for a long time a very serious suicidal threat. I decided to refer her to a general psychiatric colleague to discuss the possibilities of medication and I tentatively agreed to continue seeing her.

A week later she began to describe memories of bestiality. These included being made to behave like a dog with a chain round her neck, tied to the dog and being tied down while the dog entered her. She kept saying in half-breaths 'but then I love animals – they have always seemed so much more human to me than humans'. She also described great violence (as well as need) from Paul, her lover, who on one occasion nearly drowned her in the bath. He would frequently tie her up, rape or bugger her. Neither her husband nor lover offered her any intimacy, safety or a 'way out'.

She agreed to bring Steve, her husband, to the next session. However, he did not come and that precipitated more suicidal threats. A few weeks later, after deciding to leave both men, she made a suicide attempt and I subsequently saw her as an emergency at another institution where I work. She described her mother and her aunt (the mother's sister and wife of the uncle) as all having been somehow involved in 'something' together.

In the next few months she must have made about four suicide attempts of various kinds, and, after much hesitation, she agreed to admission to a clinic. In this clinic she created powerful divisions – some passionately 'for' her, and others 'against' her and believing she was 'breaking up' the clinic. The clinic had an experienced therapist attached to it, who also used hypnotic techniques and Karen had regular sessions with him as well as keeping contact with me. On one of my visits she included her husband, and agreed that GGB (my partner) should also join us as co-therapist.

Steven acknowledged he had been brutal in the past but wanted something different now. He was clearly shocked to learn about Karen's story. He did state he had always seen her mother as a strange, frightening and powerful person. Increasingly he became outraged at the family and, despite Karen's insistence that she would not return to live with him, she began to see him as a real support for the first time. About a month before she left the clinic GGB and I visited the clinic for a staff discussion.

Somehow, dealing with Karen had become a measure for staff competence. A similar process, albeit from a different vantage point was graphically described by Main (1989). Karen also complained that the therapist and other staff were 'too frightened' by the things she was describing. It was agreed with the staff group that she should be protected from both Paul and from her family, unless she explicitly said she wanted to speak to them. However, the resourcefulness with which her mother managed to get peripheral members of staff to put her through to Karen or to deliver postcards was most impressive.

It was clear that these postcards or messages had some very specific meaning for her. A particularly graphic illustration was one which she and the ward staff agreed must represent somebody who could see in the dark. These communications from her family often provoked attacks of intense dissociation with screaming and often some form of self-mutilation.

After another suicide attempt, the clinic consultant decided she could not be contained there anymore. She was transferred to the local psychiatric hospital under compulsory section. After two weeks, however, she was discharged from the local psychiatric hospital. Shortly after, Karen came to see AC and GGB with Steven. She locked herself in the lavatory and then rushed out of the house. In trying to stop her from running into the road Steve's finger was broken. On another occasion she came under the influence of excess medication and GGB and I took her to the local hospital together.

She was very bitter about having been rejected by the clinic, although when she met the consultant, both consultant and therapist from the clinic acknowledged the clinic's inability to contain her, as well as the avoidant reactions of some staff to what she was describing. At this point she decided not to be seen by any of us and I left it open for her to call me.

By this time she had provided increasing evidence that, from at least age 6 and probably age 3, she had been subjected to repeated intercourse, both anal and vaginal, by a large group of people and by animals. It also seemed that she had participated in, and possibly been made to be active in, some ritual mutilations and probably murders of three young children and one young man. She was able to describe with increasing detail where these had happened.

Post-hospital

For ten months since her discharge, I have seen her in a variety of combinations. At Karen's request, GGB and I saw her with Paul and we were surprised at Paul's acknowledgment of the level of violence in their sexual relationship. Although Karen had re-engaged with both Paul and Steven, both relationships seemed to be on a more equal footing. However, at the same time she began to declare intense and passionate love for me.

I have not defined this automatically as 'transference' for the reasons which are spelled out later in this account. My concern was partly the degree of loss of control I had seen in her in other contexts, partly that I would feel responsible for the possibly catastrophic consequences as she gradually faced how 'unrequited' this love would appear to her.

I discussed all of this with her quite openly, and also my own limiting principles in deciding whether I would see her or not: that we should both acknowledge and monitor the possibility of her being harmed by it and that I would stop seeing her if I felt it was harming her. She told me subsequently that this statement had been a relief to her. For a time I saw her together with GGB and a different series of descriptions about herself and her experiences began to emerge. In fact she came to see GGB for three sessions at her own initiative, but soon gave it up, saying she 'couldn't let her get through to me'.

COMMENT BY GILL GORELL BARNES

Over the months Alan had seen Karen, I had formed a distant but concerned relationship with her. On several occasions I had stood outside the lavatory talking to her through the door while she shrieked and retched inside. I would stay until she calmed down and she always took herself back into the consulting room of her own accord. I had also monitored several phonecalls from her when she was in a distressed state, as well as fending off her lover and calming her husband when she was admitted to hospital.

At this same time I had met her once formally to discuss seeing me for some sessions without Alan, but she had rejected this as an idea. I had also visited her in hospital with Alan. On the occasion of her overdosing in the context of therapy, my role seemed to be to 'take charge' of the situation, fetch my car and drive both patient and therapist to the Accident and Emergency Department of the hospital. Karen kept apologising to me for not wanting to live, which I assured her was her business just as it was mine to make sure she was looked after while she was alive.

She seemed to enjoy some humorous womanly chat along these lines and when she stopped to find a lavatory I questioned whether peeing was more important than dying. This and other similar banter led to a shared giggle between us. When she came to see me on her own, therefore, we had some back history. This may have helped her be clearer about why she could not work with me on her own. Apart from the obvious reason, that she was deeply engaged with Alan, which meant that at one level she saw me as a rival, there was an older history; a mother and an aunt who had derided and abused her mind as well as participating in the abuses of her body. At school too she had been constantly chided for her stupidity and her inability to read. (She had a wish *not* to read because of the 'special' books involved in the ritual abuse which she did not wish to understand.)

I think Karen found my belief in her an important alternative image to conjure up in juxtaposition to her own negative image, associated with her recurrent wish to die. She has always made contact to let us know about a suicide attempt, imminent or already undertaken. We would always respond to these messages. Whilst informing therapists of suicide attempts has sometimes been labelled as manipulative, we saw it more in the frame of a need to know whether she had continued meaning in our minds. Often she thanked us afterwards by phone or by letter for 'going on believing in her'. I was helped in my matter-of-fact tone towards these attempts by discussion with friend and colleague Elsa Jones, whose own work with women abused as children (Jones, 1991) has led her to the view that these are memories and experiences that may not be livable with and that the right to kill oneself can be an important path for self-determination (E. Jones, personal communication).

When Alan resumed work with Karen I agreed to consult to the two of them in relation to impasses in the therapy; and we have moved to a more established fluid style of shared work in which I have joined the two of them as consultant, or joined in whenever another family member is present.

KAREN'S WORK WITH ALAN COOKLIN (2)

About six months after Karen was discharged from the clinic she brought her cousin Angela to see GGB and I together. Angela was the only relative she was close to from her father's side of the family, and had nothing to do with the 'group meetings'. Perhaps of most significance, Angela *believed* her. Angela's mother's family had always perceived Karen's mother's family as somehow 'strange and sinister'.

GGB and I remained concerned that Karen might either do something self-destructive to herself in trying to expose the groups, or alternatively might take on more than she could in a crusade to find the proof of what had been done to her and to others. She was talking of going back to Norfolk to the place where she knew the bodies might be buried. At this point we took advice from some colleagues. We were put in touch with a senior police officer who had been researching such groups. He was able to predict many of the situations that arose and eventually met Karen with us.

She was initially frightened by this idea, and thought he might be a part of one of the rings. In the event she was relieved by his matter-of-fact approach and the fact that he positively discouraged her from making a formal statement until she was ready. Our impression was that his down to earth approach, coupled with a considerable sensitivity, played a part in preventing her from trying to prematurely investigate the ring on her own.

COMMENT FROM GILL GORELL BARNES

A particular experience described by Angela conveyed to me something of the fear induced by the group's claim to have 'supernatural' powers. While she was spending time with her boyfriend she reported that Karen's mother had managed to 'break through' her thought processes and set the head of a pig on the shoulders of her lover. She experienced this event as intensely evil. Even though she had no part in the childhood abuse herself, she knew, as did Karen, how to mind-read. What this experience means is open to wide-ranging debate in terms varying from telepathy, projective identification, vivid imagination or hysteria. In our opinion, Angela had in some way been directly influenced by Karen's family, whether this was through the impact of repeated small encounters, or whether through some presumed 'paranormal' experience does not seem to us necessary or possible to clarify.

It is perhaps worth commenting that much of Karen's mental energy had also gone on 'stopping the group getting through'. We found the fact that someone previously – to our knowledge – not involved, could be affected in this way made it additionally pernicious as a phenomenon.

KAREN'S WORK WITH ALAN COOKLIN (3)

From this point on I felt that Karen knew that she knew what she knew. The question of feeling 'mad' and not believed no longer seemed such an issue. However, I am convinced that to be 'believed' is a critical need for anyone who has been through this kind of abuse. Through the discussions with GGB and I together, I also felt she was facing the fact that the love for me, that I had not defined for her in any interpretative way as transference (although she scathingly said that was what I believed), was something she could experience and face not being enacted.

However, I noticed she was wearing increasingly short skirts. Eventually I said to her that although I did not think she wanted to seduce me, I wondered if she didn't want me to see her as a sexual woman in an active way because that was the only way, perhaps, she could perceive a relationship as having any validity. She became enraged and accused me of trying to get rid of her. I responded by suggesting that we make a regular time to meet (which had not always been the case before). In fact I suggested a monthly time to meet and then other sessions as she needed them. She probably correctly interpreted this as a distancing move.

COMMENT FROM GILL GORELL BARNES

Alan consulted me at this point. He was obviously feeling demoralised and trapped by Karen's repeated predictions that she would kill herself, by uncertainty that he would be able to contribute anything that would change her view of herself as evil and worthless, coupled with a sense – which she often reinforced – that he was her only lifeline. He felt caught in a double bind. To continue therapy might be 'worthless' and be experienced as a 'false' relationship. To stop therapy might be experienced as rejection and precipitate suicide and he could see no way to 'leave the field' (Bateson, 1973). He was concerned that her passion for him was as yet related to no adequate therapeutic alliance and he began to see her illusions about him as a potential time-bomb which could provoke further self-destructiveness when challenged.

KAREN'S WORK WITH ALAN COOKLIN (4)

Indeed, a further suicide attempt followed.

After her discharge from the General Hospital I saw her with GGB and Angela. Angela began the meeting angrily. She quoted Karen reporting, 'Dr Cooklin told me that he thought I was trying to sexually attract him and that he was not interested in any way.' I was aware I must neither defend myself nor be tempted to do anything reminiscent of the caricatured professional trick 'I am interested that was how you saw it.' In the event GGB helped me ensure I did neither by consulting to the three of us (Karen, Angela and myself). She said, in front of them, that whilst I might need to remind Karen that her love for me could not be enacted in the way she wanted, it was nevertheless real, not just based on a fantasy, and actually was a potential help and value to Karen.

Both she and Angela agreed that I should see Karen more regularly, and we agreed to convene the foursome from time to time. We also discussed ways in which Karen and Angela could begin to gain support from other members of the family not involved in these groups.

COMMENT FROM ALAN COOKLIN AND GILL GORELL BARNES

Reflecting on this case has raised innumerable questions but has also suggested four useful areas for consideration:

1 the dimensions of family behaviour and how as a therapist one thinks about these (see Table 13.1);
2 trying to find some formulation that would do justice to the way human beings treat each other in situations of ritualistic abuse;
3 considering the impact on the therapist, mistakes that the therapists made and may have learned from;
4 therapy and gender.

Table 13.1 Polarised dimensions of family behaviour

Images of the family (anticipated by the therapist)

Anticipated benign	Pernicious abusive
Connectedness, involvement, benign mutual concern, leading to mutual expectations of loyalty.	Pernicious, malevolent, demands for loyalty to the group based on threats and fear.
NATURE OF ATTACHMENTS	
Mutual attachment with parents attracted to the child's exploratory ways of learning, newness and youth.	Attraction to the child as a source of power and pleasure for the self, and status in relation to the group.
Tenderness and positive identification with the child with concern and love.	Possessiveness of the child as an object of pleasure, exploitation and 'success' in relation to the group's criteria.

Dimensions of family behaviour

How a therapist defines particular families in relation to these dimensions could be useful to him or her in suggesting how children in such families may or may not have been able to process a traumatic event. The question of whether an individual who has experienced such abuse is seen as victim or survivor (Jones, 1991) hinges on what factors allow an individual to learn from, or develop in response to, such experiences in childhood. Some trauma, particularly life-threatening illness *can* become a 'rite of passage' through which a child may increase his/her skill/knowledge (Cooklin, 1993). However, there are many factors which militate against *these* experiences being used positively in later life. These are:

1 The degree of and repetition of the trauma.
2 The fact that it is propagated by those the child believes she/he should trust and on whom she/he is dependent. This also makes it unlikely that the child will find a reliable safe person outside the family who can help him/her.
3 The degree to which the experience is secret and taboo, and therefore, however common, is experienced by each victim as an isolated experience that happened only to him or her (Jones, 1991).

We suggest that until the publication of this book such taboos may well have been inadvertently reinforced by therapists (Cooklin and Gorell Barnes, 1993) because the experiences were not within their expected range of thinking and therefore may not have been picked up when tentatively presented in the course of other clinical work.

Formulations

We have so far found no explanatory formulations of these kinds of unthinkable experiences. There has been little or no guide for the therapist in these situations. A conference convened by the ACPP in which the Nottingham workers spoke was a rare opportunity which allowed shared thinking by clinicians as well as empathy with colleagues who had tried to investigate and prevent re-abuse by such rings (see Chapter 23 by Tim Tate on the Nottingham case).

In our thinking it has not been useful to follow the route sometimes taken in psychoanalytic thinking, whereby meaning may be attributed to specific symbolic representations of relationships via representations of bodily functions, parts or activities. Rather, I would see preoccupations with bodily functions or their parts as a simple and direct manifestation of the experiences of the abuse, in the case of the victims.

Formulation of the abusers

In the case of the perpetrators, a tentative hypothesis might be that in these secret groups are found, not gratification of specific desires or attempts to resolve specific conflicts, but something closer to the goals associated with any closed religious group, viz.:

1 placing life events in a meaningful context;
2 overcoming fear of individual vulnerability;
3 overcoming fear of mortality;
4 avoiding the experience of loneliness/isolation;

However, in the satanist situation it appears that this is not via a moral order but via a search for a 'total freedom'. This 'total freedom' becomes defined as breaking 'taboos' and, as such, defined as giving up all sense of restraint that might be imposed by concern for others. This may require a sense of 'all things are possible'; this may in turn have to relate to a belief that 'anything goes' and ultimately to a belief that, in order for this view to be self-confirmatory that 'everything and anything *must go*'. And all of these beliefs then become placed in the framework of an organised set of rituals.

It seems likely that the process has some similarities to the way atrocities occur in wartime, when people can experience a sense of exhilaration and aggrandisement in the most brutal and unthinkable acts – acts which they could not have imagined they could perpetrate or even think about in their earlier lives. If this hypothesis has validity it raises the interesting question as to whether satanist abuse is less in wartime. (Some elements of this seemed clear in the My Lai trial, probably one of many such events of inhumanity, but one of very few that come to trial.)

Specific therapist mistakes

1 Trying to reinterpret the events in any less unfavourable way than they are described.
2 Becoming too excited or fascinated by finding the 'truth' of what happened. It has of course been a tradition in classical psychoanalytical work for the therapist to concern him/herself with 'inner reality' and therefore feel freed of any requirement to establish the 'truth' of what is being reported. In our work we *are* concerned with the actual past and current realities of the person's experience. However, using a different theoretical framework, based also on constructivist principles (Gergen, 1985) we have realised the importance of seeing the truth as reconstructed description between therapist and client/patient which may change as the perception of self in relation to these events changes.
3 Attempting to be personally unresponsive or distant in one's manner (in a caricature often associated with psychoanalytic therapies). If this happens it will be interpreted as a rejection or abuse by the client as this may replicate to some extent her experience of having 'all the feelings' in herself and being coldly watched by observing adults.
   This point is also aggravated by the fact that many of these children are unable to use symbolic phantasy play as a form of learning. Their phantasies are only associated with either horror or rescue and any symbolic meaning is always dwarfed by the experience. Thus the child is often left with a very concrete or digital (either on or off) kind of thinking, with no interplaying grey areas (Gorell Barnes and Henessy, in press; Cooklin and Gorell Barnes, 1993).
4 Therefore, attempts to interpret symptomatic behaviour, especially if linked to hypothesised destructive wishes, may only undermine the patient's developing integrity.
5 Powerful attachments to the therapist should not automatically be defined as transference.

Therapy and gender

All our assumptions in the past had been that a woman's perverse sexual experiences need to be shared and worked through with a woman rather than a man. Although GGB became highly significant and we suspect a 'safekeeping' presence in Karen's mind, she did not become (to date anyway) a therapist who could be trusted in her own right. This we suspect is in part associated with the degree to which women were the significant active members of the satanist ritual abuse ring, coupled with the fact that Karen maintained in her mind, and probably has not given up, a hope that a man (once her father) would one day show his strength and rescue her.

COMMENT

Many of the views expressed in writing this story have differences both from ideas common to either family therapy or psychodynamic fields. However, it could be suggested that to make this point may in some respects be devaluing the experience of those who have been abused – as though to say 'These poor people can't take the real thing.' An alternative formulation would be to suggest that from people who have been through these horrendous experiences one can learn some things which throw light on how we think about human relations and perhaps how we think about ourselves as therapists.

REFERENCES

Bateson, G. (1973) *Steps to an Ecology of Mind*, New York, Paladin Books.

Cooklin, A.I. (1993) 'Psychological changes in adolescence', in C. Brook (ed.) *The Practice of Medicine in Adolescence*, London, Edward Arnold.

Cooklin, A.I. and Gorell Barnes, G. (1993) 'Taboos and social order: new encounters for family and therapist', in E. Imber-Black (ed.) *Secrets in Families and Family Therapy*, New York, Norton.

Gergen, K. (1985) 'The social constructivist movement in modern psychology', *American Psychology* 40, 286–75.

Gorell Barnes, G. and Henessy, M. (in press) 'Reclaiming a female mind from the experience of child sexual abuse', in C. Burck and B. Speed (eds) *Gender, Power and Relationships, New Developments*, London, Routledge.

Jones, E. (1991) *Working with Adult Survivors of Child Sexual Abuse*, Systemic Thinking and Practice Series (Edited by D. Campbell and R. Draper), London, Karnac.

Main, T. (1989) *The Main Ailment and Other Psychoanalytic Essays*, J. Johns (ed.), London, Free Association Books.

Chapter 14

Cutting the cord
The resolution of a symbiotic relationship and the untwisting of desire

Stephen Colver

Stephen Colver is a member of the Guild of Psychotherapists. He works with adults in individual therapy and is involved in the training of other counsellors and therapists.

Names, identities and background details have been changed wherever necessary to protect confidentiality.

This is an account of therapy with a ritually abused woman several years after she left the cult. It focuses on what Searles (1979: 9) calls 'a symbiotic mode of relatedness', in which a patient is unable to maintain an objective distance between self and others.

At the time of therapy Hannah was 42 and married for the second time to a mature student at a College of Further Education. Her first marriage, according to her, was to a violent man who verbally and physically assaulted her. They had one child who is now an adult. Hannah was adopted at 2 by a couple from a large Welsh town who are now in their 80s. They had one daughter of their own who was two years older than Hannah.

Hannah was seen by me twice-weekly for a year and then intensively for two years. She was referred by Shirley, a staff member of the college where Hannah's husband studied. Shirley told me she had been trying to help a student's wife but felt out of her depth. I suggested Hannah rang me.

When she arrived for her first session I saw a plainly dressed, quietly anxious woman who looked very uncertain. Most of the first session was spent in silence. When she did speak it was in short bursts with much stammering. Her ambivalence was seen in her repeatedly telling me she had not wished to come that day but was glad she was here. After I remarked on this she went on to tell me how Shirley had enabled her to mention things from the past she had never even told her husband. However, Hannah told me nothing of these 'things' other than that Shirley no longer felt able to help her and perhaps I could.

Whilst I noted Hannah's fear and wondered if she might be ashamed to reveal much directly in this first session, I wondered whether I was being teased. I began to feel fairly concerned at what secret things were so difficult to speak about and wondered if Hannah had been sexually abused. In the sessions that followed Hannah began to speak of gross sexual abuse that I found extremely powerful and at times bizarre. The picture Hannah presented me with is as follows.

Although brought up in a rough area of the town, Hannah described her father as a prominent member of the community, having his own business and being at one time a Master of the local lodge. Hannah experienced him as 'above the law' because he had got away with several motoring offences. She also said he 'fixed it' so she did not have to attend school for a period. (Hannah has been semi-literate for most of her life.) Some time after the abuse started she remembers overhearing a conversation between her parents and others in which her father implied that Hannah had been adopted for the purposes of being abused.

> I was on the stairs listening. They were talking about my being adopted and my dad said, 'Well, we had to have a girl didn't we', and everybody laughed.

Hannah went on to painfully describe one of her most powerful memories, which she said had been evoked by seeing a poster with hands on it. The poster had aroused a strong preoccupation with hands and she said,

> I can't remember how old I was. I think about 9. It was sometime after he first started . . . just getting me to touch him . . . . He was on top of me and it hurt . . . there was blood. Then my mother came in – I held out my hand for her to make him stop. I thought she was going to but she just held me down till he'd finished. She just held me down looking at me.

Over time, Hannah presented me with a picture of ritualised and other abuse organised by her father. She once found a book with itemised sums of money and her name in one of the columns. The abuse took place in either a council house or in part of her father's business premises. Hannah remembered a pentagram drawn on the floor, the use of animals, including them being killed over her. She remembered being covered in various unnamed substances and insects which were then crushed on her. Several men had intercourse with Hannah at these sessions and her mother and sister would abuse her too. Moreover, she reported that when adult, a group of these men would enter her house occasionally and rape her there. This latter occurrence continued apparently after her second marriage with her husband knowing nothing about it.

She also spoke of strange smells in the bath, dead infants, a fear, even now, of going to the toilet. Eventually, she was able to tell her husband and he began treatment with a colleague of mine. Although they had been married for twelve years this was the first time she could tell him. Only then could she mention that her father had arranged her first marriage.

I found these accounts extremely disturbing and found myself wondering whether these events had happened historically or in phantasy and hoping they were in phantasy. I recall wondering if they were still happening and if so what should be done about it. It was as if I wished to be the father who upheld the law rather than one who seemed beyond it.

At the same time I was aware of a dynamic in which Hannah told me she was telling 'someone' before me. My feelings about the identity of this 'someone' were confirmed when a frightened Shirley rang me saying Hannah was in a terrible state and had told her a lot more of her occult practices which had continued until recently. It seemed to me important to maintain boundaries so I suggested Hannah should ring.

I was aware of the growth of her curiosity about her natural parents and the way she wished me to experience her relationship with Shirley as teasing and withholding. In time I saw that therapy was the only place where she could explore her feelings and tell her secrets free from the desire of another. In the counter-transference I found this hard as I was aware of my own desire to know, to be effective, to be at the centre. At the same time I was aware of Hannah's fear of the penetrating father who she wished to keep out. Indeed, Hannah's sexual relationship with John in the first year of therapy was minimal and at times in the transference I have been regarded as sexless. Indeed, one curious aspect of the transference was the way that most intensity was between Hannah and Shirley.

Shirley's intervention began when Hannah was having an exploratory gynae-cological operation. She visited often, gave support, time and physical holding. She was the mother who did offer help at the time of sexual intrusion by the doctor/father. Shirley discovered something of Hannah's past, wanted to help and hoped tender loving care would solve the problem. Unfortunately, it brought anguish and bewilderment to both sides although it was perhaps inevitable and unavoidable.

'I feel awful today . . . I suppose I recognise what you have been saying – how much I want Shirley to be my own possession. I don't like to say it but it is true.' She described how physically affectionate Shirley was and how jealous she was of another staff member at the college who, she felt, had a similar relationship with Shirley. Shirley was then experienced as the withholding teasing mother. The following session illustrates this more fully.

HANNAH: I went to college last night and Shirley asked if I would like to come over for a sandwich. We went over and she also invited us for Sunday lunch. So you see I'm getting what I want. What spoilt it though was, as I was waiting for Shirley, the wife of one of the students gave her a big hug, then the husband did and they invited her round for a meal. I thought, 'Why are they doing that?' I couldn't understand it. I thought 'Why does she need them when she's got me?' I felt jealous, I suppose . . . I spent ages thinking about it . . . . Another thing is I feel closer to John at the moment. I don't know why that is. When we got home we virtually went straight to bed. I was tired . . . I just wanted to be held. I can feel close to John when he holds me like he did last night. But . . . I don't like saying this . . . there are times when I'd rather be held by Shirley.

STEPHEN: She doesn't have a penis that intrudes.

HANNAH: Yes! Thank you, you helped me there. The thing is with John –
whenever he holds me I'm always thinking does he want anything
more . . . . With Shirley, it's never there. I know that – and she's had
every opportunity. But she's never done anything but hold me.

As well as seeking the perverse mother at times, one might say Hannah does not
desire the penis because of earlier gross physical intrusion. Whilst this is a factor,
I feel we are dealing with an earlier level of experience. Hannah wants to be
herself the object of Mother's desire. She is to be what Mother lacks and nothing
else must take that place. She identifies with the penis while Shirley is felt to be
the 'lost object that never was' or to provide for 'the lack' (Lacan, 1973).

On this level there can only be a merged relationship with a mother who is
experienced as both bountiful and needing. This means Hannah can have a place
within her and Shirley should never want others. For Hannah, such an ejection
causes pain, loss, rage and a perverse unconscious pleasure. I perceive this to be
a result of the twisting of Hannah's desire for mothering by her adoptive mother.
After a year of therapy, for example, Hannah described this:

They knew I wanted to be held. I don't know how but Mother would respond.
She'd give me signals and I'd go to her . . . I saw her as cuddly. But it always
ended up with them locking me in the cupboard under the stairs or doing
sexual things to me. The only thing I had to hug was my teddy bear and they
did things to that too.

In addition to this twisting of desire I have repeatedly gained the impression from
Hannah that any expression of need and desire on her part was taken and used
against her. To use Hannah's phrase, she 'was punished with it'. This punishment
is expected and unconsciously sought. When Hannah wants Shirley for herself
and feels displaced by another she communicates the affect of her past experience where the parents' natural daughter was always favoured. Something of the
intensity of Hannah's current responses contain an element of retrospective
revenge.

For Hannah, I am to be sexless, without desire and impervious to manipulation
from Shirley or herself. I must not seek to possess her in any way, wish her to be
rid of the past or even desire that she should get better (Bion, 1970). It is
important that she remains at an emotional distance from me. As she herself said
'I can take you to X Street, I can't take Shirley and John. They are too close.'

Some noticeable changes in the transference took place after this. Hannah
began to express more emotion, especially anger, in the sessions. She is on the
verge of expressing anger with me rather than with Shirley, and is becoming
strong enough to loosen the protection she had placed around the therapeutic
relationship. She does not require me to be just a container anymore but feels safe
enough to experience more of what might be termed my potency. Accordingly, I
have found myself making more reality-testing interventions than before. I note

with interest that her sexual relationship with John is now the best it has ever been and this accords with my own perception of her now as a woman.

There have been different crises in the therapy. Faced with the possibility that Shirley might move to another part of the country Hannah became convinced her adoptive mother was living in a church hall nearby and needed her. Hannah was prepared to search this rough area at night by herself to find her, sleeping rough if need be. Her speech became disordered, yet she spoke with conviction about her project. She decided she deserved sexual abuse as a punishment from her mother for past misdemeanours such as washing out the omelette pan with detergent. At that period I needed to see Hannah even more intensively and felt as if I had taken over some ego function for her. I was reminded of Roustang's idea (1982: 141) that the psychotic person uses the therapist as the stage on which to enact their drama. 'The psychotic does not control his thoughts, the other thinks for him; he asks the other to think for him and at every moment becomes his entire fate.' Hannah eventually gave up this delusion and entered a grief process for the mother she never had.

More recently, Hannah is able to differentiate between 'inside' and 'outside' and understand the nature of her relationship with Shirley. She has a greater ability to perceive the language of childhood needs and experiences and the language of ordinary adult relationships. She was able to show she had not understood Shirley's concept of 'friendship' when she saw that as herself being the centre of Shirley's world. She has also struggled with the meaning of the ways people might touch her and what is sexual. This accords with Ferenczi's view that the abuse 'represents a confusion of the languages of tenderness and passion' (Stanton, 1990: 109, 197), the first being pre-oedipal, and that it was the confusion between the two which contributed to the trauma. Hannah is now able to tolerate ambivalence in herself and in Shirley. She can accept that she can love and hate together and this has run parallel with greater self-confidence (Klein, 1952). She is able to desire and plan activities away from Shirley, has become more involved with her husband's work and has started a part-time job.

REFERENCES

Bion, W. (1970) *Attention and Interpretation*, London, Tavistock.

Klein, M. (1952) 'Theoretical conclusions regarding the life of the infant', *Envy and Gratitude*, London, Hogarth.

Lacan, J. (1973) *Four Fundamental Concepts of Psychoanalysis*, Peregrine (1986 edn).

Roustang, F. (1982) *Dire Mastery*, Baltimore, Johns Hopkins.

Searles, H. (1979) *Countertransference and Related Subjects*, New York, International Universities Press.

Stanton, M. (1990) *Sandor Ferenczi – Reconsidering Active Intervention*, London, Free Association Books.

Chapter 15

The impact of evil

Phil Mollon

Dr Phil Mollon is a Consultant Clinical Psychologist and Psychotherapist at the Lister Hospital, Stevenage.

Names, identities and background details have been changed wherever necessary to protect confidentiality.

For many people the existence of intelligent evil is difficult to accept and processes of denial may be extensive. There is widespread reluctance to acknowledge that a person can idealise and become dedicated to evil such as satanist ritual abuse. In the following I describe work with two patients who have been ritually abused. The nature of their anxieties and mental structure is explored. Some of the problems of this work are outlined, including the necessity for the therapist to tolerate feelings of terror and horror, as well as an assault on the sense of reality.

THE TRAUMA OF HEARING OF RITUAL ABUSE

Reactions to earlier clinical presentations have convinced me that hearing of ritual abuse is in itself a significant trauma which evokes emergency defensive measures. These measures consist of vigorous efforts to deny, misperceive or in other ways avoid the impact of the account, e.g. in becoming preoccupied with whether or not what is presented is consistent with established psychoanalytic theory. In verbal presentations people may fall asleep, look ill and appear unable to speak for some time afterwards.

Denial and the difficulties in grasping evil

There is something about the existence of evil that is difficult to grasp and comprehend. It is the idea that someone may be not just a *bit* bad, dishonest or cruel, not just psychopathic, but *dedicated* to being bad. The problem is one of understanding how a personality can become dedicated to destroying trust in goodness and truth in a child, to destroying innocence – and essentially to destroying the mind of the child. Perhaps what contributes to the difficulty is that an evil person may often masquerade as a good person. In this way evil is related to perversion – for as Meltzer (1973) states in his book *Sexual States of Mind*, 'the essence of the perverse impulse is to turn good into bad whilst retaining the appearance of the good'. Is it any surprise then that evil and sexual abuse of children can be closely married?

CLINICAL ILLUSTRATION 1

The following sequence occurred over three consecutive sessions.

Helen is 40 years old – a school teacher; she is in once-weekly psychoanalytic therapy. There had previously emerged extensive material relating to sexual abuse from her father, and in retrospect I can see that there had also been minor hints of satanic elements – e.g. her father' s claim to have paranormal powers and memories of a period in her childhood when disgusting objects, including animal limbs, were put through the letter box. At one session, after about four years of therapy, she reported a rather obscure memory of being in the woods with her mother and father and coming across an animal nailed to a tree; she had recalled her father seeming anxious and saying something like 'They've been here again.' She also recalled that her parents did not seem to like her being a Christian; one day in the same woods whilst walking with her parents they had met a woman whom the parents know; Helen had announced to this woman that when she grew up she was going to be a Christian because she loved Jesus; the woman had been furious with her.

The next session she reported a frightening memory. During the week she had been opening a jar of spaghetti sauce in her kitchen and had accidentally dropped it; some of the sauce had splashed up the walls. On seeing this, Helen had run out of the kitchen in a state of great terror, feeling that it reminded her of something but not knowing what. Subsequently she had recalled a childhood memory of a terrifying scene in the woods. It had been night time and she had been there with her parents and various other people, including children. She recalled there being something said about needing children who were 'pure', and some joke being made to her father alluding to the idea that she was not pure because of his extensive sexual abuse of her. Her brother was led away, this being something to do with his being male. She tried to run away but in her panic found herself running into them again. There was a terrifying figure with a grotesque head, but underneath the costume she noticed grey flannel trousers which persuaded her that the figure was a man dressed up.

I felt that terrifying though this scene sounded, the crucial aspect seemed to be missing. There was nothing in what she described which appeared to relate to the splashes of 'blood'. She then spoke of having felt her parents were trying to steal her soul. She said she felt like screaming, adding that if she did it would be like a scream out of hell. She then recalled that as a child she often used to wake up screaming, as if she were being murdered. I said to her that it certainly sounded as if she felt she was being psychically murdered, and that perhaps she had been in fear of being literally murdered. She looked very shocked and frightened by my remark. She then said that she used to think that she had seen somebody murdered but she had no idea when or how.

She was so frightened and distraught at this point that I let the session run on for a few minutes. What then emerged was how deep and extensive was her anxiety about remembering and telling. She said that she had not been able to remember and to tell me these things because she could not be sure that I was not one of 'them' – anybody could be one of them, a satanist (her father had been in a most respectable position – a 'pillar of society'). I have since realised that ritually abused patients are never sure whom they can trust because they know that satanists often appear eminently respectable in their social roles.

This last session was on a Friday and on Monday morning I received a message to phone her urgently – most unusual since the normal psychoanalytic frame restricts contact to the designated sessions. When I did so, she said she needed to speak to me as soon as possible about what we had discussed. I was able to give her a time later that day and when she arrived she told me that as she had been walking home from her session on Friday she had recalled a shocking scene. She then described this scene in some detail. She was still not sure how old she was – perhaps about 7. It was in some woods. It was night time and it was some special night. Somebody had arrived from a long way away who was called a warlock. A man was brought out from somewhere who looked very ill (unconscious, drugged?). With some large ceremonial knife his throat was cut and Helen heard him making choking noises. Then they seemed to require that his head be held upright and so his hair was somehow attached to a tree. Then a woman knelt down beside him and made another cut in his neck and drained blood into a kind of bowl. Helen thought it was assumed that the man was dead but she noticed that as he lay there he made a gurgling noise. Everyone was sitting round in a circle and a vessel was passed around containing blood. Helen only pretended to drink it, remembering a disgusting warm smell.

She recalled the body being covered in some kind of sheet and peeping underneath at him. She said his expression had been a 'stony grey'. As she was walking away from this scene with her parents, two men passed going the other way back towards the body, one carrying a woodcutter's axe. She heard a loud crack but did not see what happened. She recalled later hearing something on the news about a body being found with its head some distance away. She remembered asking her parents if that had been the man in the woods.

She had been and still was in a state of great shock at the emergence of this memory. She did not know what to do. She had been a witness to a murder and the murderers were still alive and potentially extremely dangerous. She felt in fear for her life. Her fear, which she had often conveyed before, that her parents were powerful people who would somehow get at her if she told about the sexual abuse, had suddenly taken on a new dimension of meaning.

THE DYNAMICS OF HEARING THIS MATERIAL

My own response to the emergence of this and similar material has been a mixture of shock, disbelief, horror, dread and terror – including fear for my own safety. I experience it as an assault on my sense of reality; and I suggest that this is what satanic abuse is – an assault on reality and on the child's sense of reality, an attempt to destroy and possess the child's mind.

A reader who is unfamiliar with such accounts might be left wondering if this apparent memory could be true. To counter such doubts I can say that subsequent communications have provided a full and coherent picture of the ritual context of Helen's abuse.

I am certain that Helen could not have told me about these things until she felt that I could be receptive to them. Moreover, until she told me she could not tell herself. Her perception of the look of horror on my face when she told me of the murder has greatly troubled her. She has felt that she must protect me from further trauma, fearing that I would not tolerate more revelations, whilst at the same time needing to know that I can be emotionally affected by her experiences. It has been important to show her, through interpretation, that I can bear to hear what she needs to tell me and can think about it, and also that I can tolerate knowing that at times she fears that I too might be a satanist; all these aspects of the 'containing' functions are required. Even more difficult for Helen to reveal have been supernatural experiences and powers associated with satanic activities. My clinical experience suggests that this is a common issue in working with satanically abused patients; their fear is that they will be regarded as mad – the dreaded scenario is of finding the courage to tell and then being disbelieved.

THE NATURE OF EVIL: THE SATANIC

There are various psychoanalytic contributions which are relevant to an understanding of evil. First there is Freud's (1920) description of the death instinct, as the constant opponent of life. Then there is Klein's (1957) concept of innate envy, which derives from the death instinct and which aims to destroy what is good, driven by the pain of not possessing the good and desired object (originally the mother's breast). Following in this Kleinian tradition, there are Rosenfeld's (1971) clinical descriptions of destructive narcissism, a manifestation of the death instinct, which organises as a Mafia-like gang around the life-seeking part of the personality and attempts to prevent the patient relating to the therapist; others since have provided similar accounts (see Spillius, 1988). Another work which takes account of evil parts of the mind is Meltzer's study of perversion in *Sexual States of Mind* (1973). Of particular relevance I think is Chasseguet-Smirgel's discussion of perversion in *Creativity and Perversion* (1985). Here she suggests that perversion is actually equivalent to devil worship in that both these attempt to reverse laws, limits and restrictions. She refers to perversion as: 'a universal human temptation going beyond the limits of sexual deviation . . .

the pervert attempts to take the Father/Creator's plan in order to make a new universe from chaos . . . a universe where anything becomes possible' (p.13). I must also mention Erich Fromm (e.g. 1965, 1973) who wrote extensively about human evil and developed the concept of necrophilia, a love of death.

What I find personally most helpful is to have a concept of 'the satanic'. By this I mean an aspect of the psyche – in Jungian terms an archetypal energy – characterised by its extreme destructiveness, an envious hatred of life and love, a gross narcissism that opposes concern for others, a hatred of vulnerability and weakness, extreme pride and arrogance, and above all a *devotion to lies and confusion* as opposed to truth. Satanic literature, such as La Vey's (1969) *Satanic Bible*, expresses a complete reversal of all the normal human values and ideals, and specifically those of Christianity – and thus displays the essence of the satanic as an attack on humanity, as well as upon God.

A Jungian archetype is a complex of attitudes and attributes inherent in the human psyche, that can at times be given power. Those who are identified with the satanic archetype are unlikely ever to seek therapy or analysis, for that would mean acknowledging need and vulnerability, as well as terrible guilt and remorse. A man who claimed to be a reformed satanist did once consult me but, after telling me of a ritual murder of a recalcitrant member of the group, he declined to continue seeing me. On the whole, it is their victims that we see. One consequence of this is that psychoanalysts may not always have adequate concepts for grasping the satanic.

The satanic aim appears to be that of creating an alternative world of permissiveness, power and magic – constructed of lies and asserted as an alternative to the laws of 'God the Father'. Thus, Satanism is concerned with lies and all that is destructive and is closely allied with perversion, especially as described by Chasseguet-Smirgel (1985) and Grunberger (1971) in terms of the wish to avoid the authority of the father. 'Satan' is the 'anti-oedipus', the ultimate narcissist who will never submit to the law, who dwells in Lacan's 'Imagery', the domain of madness and death.

THE IMPACT ON THE CHILD: STATES OF DISSOCIATION

What happens in the mind of the child who undergoes such experiences? My impression is that the grossly perverted and abusive activity in satanic practices is usually so traumatic and confusing that the adult is unable to have conscious memory of it, unless they are still actively involved in the cult. Reports from the USA have associated ritual abuse with multiple personality disorder, which is based upon the defence of dissociation (Kluft, 1985; Braun, 1986; Putnam, 1989; Ross, 1989; Spencer, 1989; Fraser, 1990). The mind splinters in the face of the unbearable. Part of what is unbearable is the recognition that the parent or caretaking adult is indeed dedicated to evil. The memories of satanic abuse do not emerge in clear and coherent form. Rather, the fragmented experiences reappear in the form of scattered clues, bits and pieces of memory that only gradually gather together to form a coherent picture. These psychic fragments reappear against the pressure of enormous resistance and great anxiety, often amounting to terror. They emerge as flashback memories – sudden, vivid and highly disturbing scenes of evil. Neither patient nor therapist want to believe what is being communicated. Both parties have to overcome their inner resistance in order to recover the lost experiences. It cannot be emphasised too strongly that the victim of ritual abuse has been subjected not only to intense and repeated trauma, but also to indoctrination in extensive and elaborate metaphysical beliefs which idealise evil and denigrate truth, trust and love.

Multiple personality disorder must be distinguished from schizophrenia. Indicators of MPD are auditory and/or visual hallucinations, without accompanying thought disorder, substantial amnesia for childhood, as well as more overt signs of personality switching. Often when the more hidden alter personalities are contacted, they will articulate a clear awareness of their function in protecting the host personality from an awareness of trauma. The maintenance of MPD and other dissociative states resulting from ritual abuse is determined by (a) terror associated with horrifying memories; (b) powerful prohibitions against remembering.

SATANIC 'VOICES'

The resistance against remembering is not mere anxiety about reliving a horrifying experience – although it is certainly that. There are powerful prohibitions in the mind of the satanically abused patients I have worked with – prohibitions against remembering and against telling. Very commonly victims of prolonged satanic ritual abuse hear hallucinatory voices which are extremely menacing; often they are described by patients as consisting of 'shadows'. These voices behave like satanic cults. They become enraged and very threatening if they are discovered, for example by a therapist. They threaten death to the one who had disclosed (the patient) and to the one who has been told (the therapist). They claim all manner of destructive occult powers; e.g. they will threaten to 'cause' the therapist to have an accident. They set out to punish the patient for revealing secrets; they will scream and torment the patient relentlessly. They may laugh constantly, taunting and mocking – a cruel mirth that I now think of as 'satanic laughter'. On the other hand they will pretend to be the patient's friends and saviour if he/she does as they instruct – as if they are 'satanic guardian angels'. They present death as a welcoming solution to the torment. Often they will give precise and commanding instructions for suicide. Above all the voices are liars, and it is this that the therapist must expose repeatedly. In short, the 'satanic' voices are characterised by (a) their intense murderous destructiveness, and (b) their lies; this is consistent with biblical descriptions of satan as a *murderer* and as *the father of lies*.

CLINICAL ILLUSTRATION 2: MARY

Mary is a divorced woman in her early 30s from southern Ireland, whom I have been seeing for about five years, much of the time as an in-patient. She was initially described as depressed but had not responded to conventional psychiatric treatments. An alarming feature was her preoccupation not only with killing herself, but also with killing her children, her argument being that this would spare them the suffering of growing up without a mother. Whilst not overtly psychotic and showing no psychotic features on a Rorschach test, she reported loud thoughts urging her to kill herself or damage herself; these were voices which she located in her mind, but experienced as alien to herself. She also complained of 'all the sniggering', a recurrent mocking laughter in her mind. She told me a dream which she felt presaged the onset of her depression some years back. In her dream she has woken up and gone into a room where she sees a woman leaning over a chest; she realises that she has *woken up at the wrong time* and that this other woman did not want to be seen. Later she gave the name 'Hazel' to this inner figure. She identified Hazel with the destructive voices in her mind and came to see that the prime aim of Hazel and her gang was to ensure that she did not remember or reveal secrets of her childhood, representing the chest she was guarding in the dream – the voices would scream and mock her if she attempted to explore any memories. Indeed, for a couple of years of therapy she could remember very little of her childhood – except that she persisted in an idealised view of her parents and could not bear the idea of being critical of them. She and I were aware, however, that there were aspects of her present personality and experience that pointed to sexual abuse; e.g. her feeling that any physical contact with others was disgusting, and that all sexual activity was abuse. She had no relevant memories at this stage.

Much of the early period of therapy focused upon her relationship to the destructive inner voices. Often she appeared to be helplessly in their tyranny. She would be lifeless in the sessions, saying very little but communicating profound despair and an almost total wish to die – like a pure culture of the death instinct, tempered only by guilt about her children. She struck me as like a prisoner kept in a tortured but drugged half-dead state – and she would create a similar feeling in me. Drawing on an analogy she had made with a spectacular SAS rescue of hostages, recently in the news, she commented that the prisoners may not have wanted to be rescued and might indeed have been destroyed in the operation. She repeatedly insisted that she did not want to be 'made better'. The thought of being 'normal' disgusted her, for she felt that this would mean having physically affectionate relationships with others. Even the prospect of being known emotionally in psychotherapy was dreadful for her. She appeared to harbour shame of almost unimaginable intensity; she was in no doubt that to die was preferable to being known. On the other hand she wanted her sessions with me because otherwise she felt so unbearably lonely. She made a number of serious suicide attempts, involving hanging and overdoses.

Looking back through my notes I see that many areas of conventional analytic understanding were covered in this early period – especially processes of false self and the dread of violation, as described by Winnicott (e.g. 1960), and the function of destructive mental organisations, as described by Rosenfeld (1971), Steiner (1987) and other Kleinians (see Spillius, 1988) – but none of this analysis was grounded in an awareness of specific trauma.

Increasingly Mary began to feel that she had experienced some awful episodes of sexual violation early in her life. She felt this because she knew that in her the normal desire for life had been thrown into reverse, such that she experienced a profound disgust with life, and a feeling that to want to live was in itself perverse; any physical contact with others was felt to be obscene. She wished she could remember her childhood, but also dreaded that she might. She felt sure that she must die but wished to know before she did what these experiences had been; she also wanted someone else to know as well why she had to die. In a mood of last resort, as the persisting suicidal despair of this long hospitalised patient continued, it was agreed after much discussion between her, myself and medical staff, that she should have a drug-assisted abreaction in an attempt to recover some of the lost early memories. This was an unusual procedure in the context of psychotherapy, reflecting our hopelessness about the prolonged stalemate in the therapy. Considerable memories of sexual abuse did emerge – yet at the end the sniggering returned, internal voices mocking her, telling her that she would never remember.

Following this she appeared relatively well for some months and left the hospital. Gradually her despair returned, although Hazel no longer seemed such a dominant internal figure. Increasingly, fragments of memory began to emerge and gather in her mind which seemed to relate to ritual abuse. For example, the phrase 'running around like a headless chicken' brought to her mind a memory of a ceremony in which blood from a headless chicken was spilled over a plain white dress she was wearing; she was in a horseshoe of adults dressed in robes. Gradually further elements of the scene were revealed, including the detail that her father, taking on the appearance or costume of Satan, had intercourse with her. Although adopted she came to believe that she was the product of a ritual satanic intercourse between her adoptive father and her biological mother – so that she was identified as the 'devil's daughter'. She recalled that she was made to go to church twice every Sunday, and she now believes that this was done to increase her value as an object of defilement. Many further scenes of horror, macabre, obscene and criminal in the extreme, have since emerged. I will spare the reader many details of these – but consider for example, the image of a baby being fed a bottle of blood. Disclosures of flashback memories have very often been followed by suicidal urges, and I believe this may be typical of ritually abused patients.

Of particular significance in these more recent memories have been her recollections of her father's activity of repeatedly holding her head under the bath water, almost to the point of death, but not allowing her to die as she wished.

This would be accompanied by his threat that he was indeed going to kill her. She would then have to submit to his sexual wishes. She wished desperately that she had been able to die on those occasions. However, her natural biological wish to struggle and survive prevailed; she lived, but lived in order to be abused and defiled. Thus she was left with a sense of her natural wish to live as itself perverse and obscene. Moreover, her father often told her that he loved her and that he did these things because he loved her. She was therefore left with the view that love as well as life is obscene and disgusting. She sees the act of killing herself as the ultimate act of autonomy – being able to do as an adult what she was not allowed to do as a child.

We have spent a great deal of time sorting through some of the tangle of theological and metaphysical beliefs within which she is imprisoned. For example, she has greatly feared her death because she believes that Satan will seize her. She believes the doctrine of her Christian church, that God is infinitely more powerful than Satan, but emotionally she believes that God would not want her and also feels that, in view of her early experiences, Satan must be more powerful than God. As a child she was given the message that she came from Satan and would return to Satan. She believed that if she died without telling the truth of her early experiences, she would be rewarded by Satan and have her spirit used by him for evil purposes. If she died having told the truth, she believes she would be imprisoned and tormented by Satan for all eternity. These have been very real and concrete terrors for her, although for a long time quite unconscious. I am convinced that a therapist working with a ritually abused patient will at some point have to confront the metaphysical belief system, not only of the patient but also of their own; i.e. there will have to be discussion of God, Satan and the supernatural; any glib assumption of the non-existence of these metaphysical realms will be experienced by the patient as an expression of the therapist's naivety and ignorance. Mary has been trapped in her beliefs as firmly as if they had been prison bars. Much of the time she conveys a despair of a depth and intensity that I find almost unbearable to be in touch with.

Mary has also had to face terrible guilt as she recalls participating in ritual abuse of other children, and of recruiting children from play areas for use in rituals. Some of these children were murdered. This guilt is another factor leading her to feel she must take her own life. She had a dream of her hands bleeding – which she understood as expressing her sense of having 'blood on her hands' because of these deaths. A further dream was of cracks appearing in the walls of a house, behind which there were numerous bodies of children. These 'leaks', 'cracks' and 'bleeding' represent, I think, the breaking down of her dissociative defences against her memories.

As she discloses more of her memories, Mary experiences terrors that members of the satanic group will somehow find out and come to silence her. She also fears retaliation of a non-human nature. During one Easter, she awoke and perceived a vision in her room in the early hours of the morning – a woman emanating a strange glow and an eerie sense of peace; she felt in no doubt that this was 'an angel of darkness' attempting to communicate with her and she felt pursued by this figure throughout the weekend, experiencing an urge to kill herself on the satanically significant day of Easter Sunday.

Ritual abuse is associated with multiple personality disorder (e.g. Fraser, 1990). My own view is that there is a spectrum of degrees of multiple personality disorder, ranging from states involving very overt and obvious switches of personality, to more covert forms which become apparent only after considerable psychotherapeutic exploration. Mary does experience herself as a multiplicity of partially dissociated selves, all competing for her voice. We have come to understand that 'Hazel' was originally the main 'protector' personality, whose function was to hide the memories and the child alters; whilst initially appearing very destructive, determined that the secrets should not be revealed, Hazel later became more benign and in potential alliance with the therapist once the memories had begun to emerge. There are adult coping personalities, but also a great many traumatised child personalities. These 'children' are angry with her for not allowing them to die, and thus for prolonging their trauma. Some of the child alters wish to tell me of their experiences and do indeed give detailed descriptions of rituals, whilst others are allied to the satanic and seek to bring about Mary's death in some ritual manner, and also engage in activities such as daubing satanic symbols on her body in blood. There are also parts of her that prohibit communication, that threaten and lie and seek to confuse. Recently she decided she wished to take up Bible study and it became apparent that some of her alter personalities, which she described as 'dark ones' were adamantly opposed to this. All the Bibles in her house disappeared, but she had no conscious recollection of taking them; some days later she found them hidden in an obscure place, burnt and defaced.

I will anticipate here a crucial question. Might not Mary be suffering from a paranoid schizophrenic illness and her apparent memories of bizarre abuse be delusional narratives generated by a schizophrenic process? In answer, I have to say that she does not feel to me to be paranoid. She comes across as a warm and caring person, coherent and rational, aware of how her thoughts might come across to others, and never, to my knowledge displaying any delusional ideas about her *present* reality. She does not hold to reconstructions of her childhood with delusional intensity; rather she would prefer to believe that these things were not true, yet concludes reluctantly that the weight of evidence in her mind points to their truth.

HOW IS ANALYTIC WORK WITH THESE PATIENTS DIFFERENT?

Ritually abused patients have experienced concrete enactments of primitive and very violent scenarios of murder, dismemberment and cannibalism, which for other people are merely phantasies. This leads to a blurring of the distinction between phantasy and reality. For these people, the external world has mirrored extremely primitive levels of the paranoid-schizoid position (Klein, 1946). My experience suggests that, at times, ritually abused patients will perceive the therapist as satanic and as a potential murderer; they will experience terror that they will murder or be murdered by the therapist. This anxiety may at times be extremely concrete.

The therapist's counter-transference will involve a sense of disorientation and loss of bearings – a fear for one's own sanity and grasp of reality. Terror will also at times be a feature. Just as the patient may fear that members of the satanic cult (or angels of Satan) may come to get them as a result of their disclosure, so the therapist may experience similar fears for his/her own safety. Moreover, it is extremely unnerving to encounter murderous parts of the patient which are identified with the satanic, especially if these have been hitherto hidden.

At the heart of the disturbed mind of the ritually abused person are the defences of dissociation, denial and multiplicity. One form that this may take is the building of an extensive false self on the insubstantial sand of denial of trauma. This may account for the years of non-awareness of the ritual abuse – and the ineffectiveness of the therapy which is addressed only to this false self. I suspect that a therapist would have difficulty understanding much of what transpires with these patients without a concept of multiple personality.

Another technical point concerns a reversal of a common analytic principle, especially in Britain, of being suspicious of reconstruction of the past on the grounds that this may involve an unconscious collusion to avoid the more anxiety-laden here-and-now of the transference. In my experience, patients who have been severely traumatised in childhood will be only too happy to have the therapist dwell on the here-and-now – as an escape from the dreaded memories. In these respects, transference can, as Freud's early accounts indicated (Breuer and Freud, 1895), be a resistance to remembering (as well as being in itself a *form* of remembering).

The problem of how best to access dissociated and repressed memories in severely traumatised patients is one which currently exercises me greatly. My impression is that conventional analytic technique alone may often fail to do so. It is indeed noteworthy that after almost one hundred years of dynamic psychotherapy in the Freudian tradition we are still far from anything remotely resembling consensus, either over the role of trauma in development or analytic technique in relation to trauma.

KEEPING AN OPEN MIND

A question I am often asked by colleagues is whether these stories of extraordinary abuse might all be delusion and whether I believe what I am told. In my experience it is usually the patient who wishes not to believe what he/she is communicating. I feel that the psychotherapist has to maintain an open mind about what is real and what is phantasy – holding reconstructive pictures in mind only as tentative hypotheses, ever ready to be revised as further material emerges. In this respect, my attitude to accounts of ritual abuse is no different to that towards any other childhood experience. However, I would rather risk being deluded by my patients – rather risk appearing a fool – than risk abandoning the terrified traumatised child within the patient who is attempting to tell their story.

ACKNOWLEDGEMENT

I am grateful to Mr P. Casement for his crucial support with the almost unbearable clinical work described here, and also to Dr Joan Coleman who was inspired, with others, to set up the Ritual Abuse Information Network.

REFERENCES

Braun, B. (ed.) (1986) *Treatment of Multiple Personality Disorder*, Washington, DC, American Psychiatric Press.
Breuer, J. and Freud, S. (1893–5) *Standard Edition Vol. II*, London, Hogarth Press.
Chasseguet-Smirgel, J. (1985) *Creativity and Perversion*, London, Free Association Books.
Fraser, G. (1990) 'Satanic ritual abuse. A cause of multiple personality disorder', *Journal of Child and Youth Care* Special Issue, pp. 55–66.
Freud, S. (1920) 'Beyond the pleasure principle', *Standard Edition Vol. XVII*, pp. 7–64, London, Hogarth Press.
Fromm, E. (1965) *The Heart of Man. Its Genius for Good and Evil*, London, Routledge & Kegan Paul.
Fromm, E. (1973) *The Anatomy of Human Destructiveness*, Harmondsworth, Penguin.
Gruneberger, B. (1971) *Narcissism*, New York, International Universities Press.
Klein, M. (1957) 'Envy and gratitude', in (1975) *The Writings of Melanie Klein Vol. III*, London, Hogarth Press.
Kluft, R. (ed.) (1985) *Childhood Antecedents of Multiple Personality Disorder*, Washington, DC, American Psychiatric Press.
La Vey, A. (1969) *The Satanic Bible*, New York, Avon.
Meltzer, D. (1973) *Sexual States of Mind*, Perthshire, Clunie Press.
Putnam, F. (1989) *Diagnosis and Treatement of Multiple Personality Disorder*, New York, Guilford.
Rosenfeld, H. (1971) 'A clinical approach to the psychoanalytic theory of the life and death of instincts: an investigation into the aggressive aspects of narcissicm', *International Journal of Pycho-Analysis* 52, 169–78.
Ross, C. (1989) *Multiple Personality Disorder*, New York, Wiley.
Spencer, J. (1989) *Suffer the Child*, New York, Simon & Schuster.
Spillius, E. (ed.) (1988) *Melanie Klein Today Vol. 1* (Part 4, Pathological Organisations), London, Routledge.
Steiner, J. (1987) The interplay between pathological organisations and the paranoid-schizoid and depressive positions', *International Journal of Psycho-Analysis* 67, 69–80.
Winnicott, D. (1960) 'Ego distortion in terms of true and false self', in (1965) *The Maturational Processes and the Facilitating Environment*, London, Hogarth.

Chapter 16

A brief word

Anne McDonald

Dr Anne McDonald is an Acting Clinical Services manager, Consultant Psychiatrist with special responsibility for Forensic Psychiatry, and a Psychoanalytical Psychotherapist in Glasgow.

Names, identities and background details have been changed wherever necessary to protect confidentiality.

I was referred a young woman for help with her uncontrollable bouts of aggression and saw her at the Sexual Assault Clinic because of her history ('she alleges', wrote the general practitioners) of sexual abuse. The referral also stated that she said she was a witch, and I therefore saw her myself, as the team agreed (with some nervous giggling and disbelief) that she might be psychotic.

She was a witch. She was attempting to leave. She had been sexually assaulted, and indeed raped daily by her father; and in the course of being a member of a coven from an early age, had experiences that I would rather not believe possible. She was not psychotic. She was, however, in touch with the psychotic bits of herself in a painful way, and had had first-hand experience of other people's ritualised enactment of their psychotic bits.

She was having uncontrollable and unpredictable bouts of aggression. She was concerned that the coven would pull her back. She sought to convince me of the power she was talking of. I sought to remain analytic.

It is difficult to write about her and do justice to the enormity of the problem. This is not merely a personal problem but a societal one. It is a common analytic problem to cope with depth of feeling and degree of upset in ourselves, our counter-transference, when we work with someone who has been sexually abused. This is more intrusive still, more primitive. It reaches into our own psychotic fears, but we cannot label it as illness and push it away.

In sexual abuse work I insist on the importance of everyone working in a team and having a support system. In this work it is even more imperative. We must be able to listen to our patients, to allow for unpalatable possibilities. Only when we have the support of colleagues can we face those primitive and psychotic fears in ourselves, and we need to do this in order that we may function effectively and be helpful.

Part II Clinical accounts

Learning disability

Chapter 17

Learning disability and ritualistic child abuse

Introductory issues

Joan Bicknell

Professor Joan Bicknell is Professor Emeritus in the Psychiatry of Learning Disability, St George's Hospital Medical School, University of London.

Names, identities and background details have been changed wherever necessary to protect confidentiality.

One major difficulty for those in the medical, legal and social work professions concerned with child abuse is the fantastic and often revolting nature of the accounts of those children who have been abused. Anyone with any sensitivity would prefer to disbelieve them and so guard themselves against the need to diagnose and affirm such abuse. Could this self-protective capacity for denial be even stronger when the child has learning difficulties?

When Jo Ramsden, a young lady with Down's syndrome was first reported to have disappeared and was later found to have been murdered a year ago, local public reaction in Dorset was extreme. There was outrage that her friendliness, naivety and her teenage desire for independence could have been so exploited. The pain of the community from which she was taken turned to disbelief that anyone could have killed her and an accident was thought more likely. Her fragile vulnerability had stimulated in all of us the desire to nurture, blinding us to the motives of those intent on destroying such a human being.

However, in theory, children with learning disabilities are likely to be attractive to those who abuse children in ritualistic settings. Much witchcraft is a celebration of the anti-Christ. Many Christian festivals are celebrated in covens in an inverse way. Evil replaces goodness and imperfection, perfection. Sadistic and selfish impulses take the place of care and concern. Even the crucifix is placed upside down. Could it be in this context that the supposedly imperfect body and mind of the child with learning difficulties is therefore more attractive when evil reigns supreme?

The child with learning difficulties may also be less able to resist abduction and certainly less able to tell of his or her experiences or make the characteristic drawings should the opportunity arise.

Explanations for why a child with learning difficulties misses playgroup or school are also more likely to be accepted without suspicion, knowing the high rate of intercurrent illnesses and hospital attendances for such children.

The picture of the psychological disturbance of the ritually abused child is only now being recognised but it is essentially the picture of the child of normal intelligence whose personality had begun to integrate and who had basic living skills before the abuse occurred. Personality change, psychological disturbance and regression in development are always more difficult to detect when the baseline is not the norm.

Perhaps other characteristic scenarios will emerge. The child with learning difficulties does not often show fears that originate from the vivid imagination of the normal child. Monsters under the bed and fears of the dark are rarely seen in those with significant learning difficulties and perhaps unusual patterns of fear, or even the emergence of fear itself, should put us on our guard.

Children of normal intelligence who may have been ritually abused are often not believed and their accounts considered to be the result of vivid imagination, playground talk, perverse wish fulfilment or a desire for attention. Any evidence from a child with learning difficulties is likely to be dismissed even more rapidly as the capacity for communication and for understanding the concept of truth will be seen as inevitably compromised.

However, abuse may not only be the province of childhood. We know that unemployed, rootless and unsupported girls are particularly likely to be drawn to covens with a promise of food, a roof and companionship. With the sudden acceleration of care in the community but with inadequate provision and a society that remains uncommitted, teenagers with learning difficulties, no longer in the shelter of their own homes or in an institution, may become seduced into believing that witchcraft has much to offer in material things, companionship and a purpose in life, only to find out too late that they cannot escape except by risking capture and death. Once in the coven, they may have pregnancy forced upon them to provide foetuses to further the activities of the coven.

In summary, therefore, both children and young adults with learning difficulties are at risk of ritualistic abuse. Our own sense of revulsion that this could happen may, through the mechanism of denial, leave our clients all the more vulnerable. Atypical symptoms, impoverished communication and a lack of self-advocacy skills may further delay the correct diagnosis and therefore appropriate intervention. So let us all be mindful of the possibility of ritualistic abuse of those least able to defend themselves against both common and uncommon perils of life today.

Chapter 18

'Fire, coffins and skeletons'

Nigel Beail

Dr Nigel Beail is Consultant Clinical Psychologist, Barnsley Community and Priority Services HNHS Trust and Lecturer in Psychology at the University of Sheffield.

Names, identities and background details have been changed wherever necessary to protect confidentiality.

Recent research has demonstrated that the sexual abuse of children and adults who have a mental handicap is a significant and serious problem (Dunne and Power, 1990; Turk and Brown, 1992; Beail and Warden, 1993). However, ten years ago, when a male mentally handicapped patient of mine disclosed sexual abuse to me, I believed this to be rare. At that time, childhood sexual abuse was a controversial issue struggling for acceptance. I was a fairly inexperienced clinical psychologist attempting to provide a psychoanalytic psychotherapy service to mentally handicapped children and adults in Yorkshire. Whilst my work has recently been generously described as 'pioneering' (Sinason, 1992), at the time it felt to be an uphill struggle. In the field of mental handicap, 'clinical psychologist' has meant 'behaviourist' and so I was a bit of an oddity or a novelty. Views like 'such therapy with these people would produce as much a useful result as an engineer using a watchmaker's tools to build a bridge' (Church, 1982) were not uncommon. It therefore did not seem the right time for me to raise what in fact became a controversial issue – 'sexual abuse and mental handicap' – even though I was seeing more and more clients who were disclosing such abuse.

In 1985, in the Yorkshire area, a small group of psychologists who were working psychotherapeutically with mentally handicapped people began to meet regularly to provide peer support and supervision. My experience was soon validated by my colleagues in the group, who were also seeing clients who were disclosing sexual abuse. Then came the publication in 1986 of Valerie Sinason's paper reporting the treatment of a mentally handicapped child who revealed sexual abuse (Sinason, 1986).

RITUALS IN SEXUAL ABUSE

Now the issue of sexual abuse of children and adults with mental handicap is receiving serious consideration. But what about ritual and satanist abuse? Some sexual acts between consenting adults can be heavily scripted or ritualistic and these acts can be perpetrated against children or non-consenting adults and those who are mentally handicapped.

Ian

Ian was a 17-year-old severely mentally handicapped man who was referred to me because he was cross-dressing and being aggressive at home. Both behaviours were deemed totally unacceptable by his parents. Whilst I accepted that Ian's aggression needed to be reduced I felt that his cross-dressing needed to be accepted by his family and managed rather than eliminated.

Ian commenced weekly psychotherapy sessions. During the course of our exploration of his cross-dressing and aggression it emerged that they were linked. After eleven months he began to disclose sexual abuse involving another man who also cross-dressed and forced Ian to cross-dress and take part in some ritualistic phantasy script in the abuser's mind.

Victor

Victor, a severely mentally handicapped man with little speech, was referred because he was being aggressive towards his elderly mother who was finding it difficult to cope with him at home. Concerns were also expressed because Victor was spending time in his bedroom attempting to gag and bind himself. During the course of therapy he disclosed that a gang of men had tied him up and gagged him and anally raped him. Both Ian and Victor were the victims of sexual abuse which was more than contact abuse. They had been subjected to rituals determined by their abusers. For Ian a fetishistic ritual and for Victor a sadomasochistic ritual.

RITUAL SATANIST ABUSE AND MENTAL HANDICAP

At a recent conference on sexual abuse of mentally handicapped people at the Royal Society of Medicine in 1993 I was discussing my work with Valerie Sinason. In the course of our conversation I tentatively mentioned another client of mine who I believed had been the victim of ritual satanist abuse. Valerie then shared with me her own experience of a similar case she was involved with. We both felt great relief in sharing our experiences and when the idea of this book occurred to her she invited me to contribute.

MENTAL HANDICAP AND SATAN

Historically there has been a long association between mental handicap and Satan. These have been reviewed by Ryan in her book *The Politics of Mental Handicap* (1987). In the middle ages and earlier, it was believed that a handicapped child came from the non-human underworld of envious demons, elves and fairies in exchange for a human child. Thus the human child was stolen and replaced with a changeling. Luther believed it was the devil who stole the child and then substituted himself for it. He went so far as to recommend that such children should be killed. Luther also put forward the idea that a handicapped child was a punishment for the sins of parents. A consequence of misdeeds, bad thoughts and sex outside of marriage. Ryan (1987) also states that during the Middle Ages the idea that abnormal children were the result of sexual intercourse between a woman and the devil was common. Also, giving birth to such a child was grounds for branding a woman a witch.

The idea that parents, or the mother in particular, engaged in unnatural practices or indulged in all manner of excesses, recurs in the nineteenth- and early twentieth-century theories of causation as did ideas about possession.

We would expect that such ideas are no longer held. Sadly this is not the case. As Ryan (1987) points out 'that scientific theories rather than religious explanations of mental handicap have come to dominate the field does not therefore mean that other perspectives have disappeared'. Only last year I was involved with a case where the mother of a handicapped child believed that he was possessed by the devil and he was a punishment for her sins. Such myths still consciously or unconsciously prevail, particularly regarding bad sex. Sinason (1992) points out that it is 'not just normal society that contains these fears. It is mentally handicapped people too'.

Ryan (1987) also points out that there has been an association between mental handicap and animality. Such comparisons were made by those nineteenth-century reformers who claimed to be concerned for the welfare of mentally handicapped people. Certainly the conditions in which mentally handicapped people have been forced to live have been appalling. Basically, mentally handicapped people have been and still are treated like animals. In Britain, numerous hospital inquiries in the 1970s have affirmed this and recent exposés in Greece and Eastern Europe have served to shock and appal us.

I would also raise the issue of the continuing use of aversive forms of treatment on mentally handicapped people who have behaviour problems. Methods such as contingent shock, mechanical restraint, Tabasco in the mouth and ammonia held under the nose are wholly unacceptable to the rest of society but continue to be used and debated in the field of mental handicap (Murphy, 1993; Whitaker, 1993). These dehumanising methods are used in the context of 'treatment' but amount to physical abuse.

Associations between mental handicap and the devil and animality would seem to be still around today, and as such render mentally handicapped children and adults vulnerable to physical, sexual and ritual or satanist abuse. Whilst there is now evidence to confirm the existence of physical and sexual abuse of both handicapped and non-handicapped people, ritual or satanist abuse is widely viewed with scepticism.

Many of my clients have disclosed physical and sexual abuse during the course of therapy. Victor and Ian disclosed sexual abuse which also involved a ritualistic element but James's disclosure was of a very different nature.

James

James was referred because he had been engaging in sexually abusive behaviour towards other people at the day centre he attended and in his neighbourhood. His behaviour caused considerable anxiety for his carers and other professionals. I was told at the time James was referred that he had been abducted by a stranger and sexually abused some years ago. James had not received any treatment after the event as none was at that time available. I began to see James for once-weekly psychoanalytic psychotherapy (Beail, 1989).

James is in his 20s and suffers from mental handicap (IQ = 53). His speech is mainly monosyllabic and he has a vocabulary with an age equivalent of 5 years. He had spent most of his early years in and out of institutional care but was eventually placed with a caring family.

Despite James's communication problems I began our sessions by encouraging him to say whatever was in his mind. James needed to be given a lot of encouragement to talk. Eventually he began by telling me he'd been 'naughty' but he blamed other people for this. He also seemed to be saying that he had frightened people and he became very sad at this point. He told me about 'rude thoughts' which got him into trouble and began to cry and mention 'bad dreams'. I encouraged him to tell me about the man who abducted him and the sexual assault which followed. He detailed a horrific sequence of sexually abusive acts that he was subjected to. But every now and again he said either 'fire', 'killing' or 'dying'. I then became aware of the fact that James was in a trance-like state.

In our second session he went into a trance-like state again. He this time said 'shouting and riot, laughing, giddy, swearing and buggering'. Then 'fire, woman, broken ribs, damaged skull, church, graveyard, forest, skeleton, coffins' and 'frightened'.

James's behaviour in these and subsequent sessions was very different to that of other sexually abused mentally handicapped men I had seen for psychotherapy. He always arrived at the session happy and saying he was fine and everything was fine. Then I would ask him to tell me about anything that was in his head. A period of silence then ensued which could last up to 15 or 20 minutes, then he would enter a trance-like state and talk about dreams and nightmares in a state of fear. He frequently said 'fire, coffins and skeletons' and talked about being touched sexually and being raped. 'Shouting and bawling, kill, fire, get raped, get killed, confusing, upset, frightened.' 'I'm hurt, try to hurt me.'

James described needles and pins being stuck into his penis, being anally penetrated and made to eat faeces. He talked about babies being killed. Sometimes he mentioned the other people involved. These included two men whose first names he knew and whose cars he described. He also sometimes said lots of people were present. In the twenty-fourth session he started reciting religious expressions and songs. Then he described his mother taking him to the graveyard and how she laughed as they tried to kill him.

It took a long time to make sense of James's communications. I treated the dreams as dreams and not as a real experience and asked for associations. With some dreams this process would lead to a clear interpretation of the traumatic abduction and assault. On the other hand associations to coffins, fires and so on did not get us very far. Perhaps James was mad – seeing him in a trance and listening to him felt quite mad. But this continued to be repeated over and over again in the sessions. So why was there this compulsion to repeat – what did it all mean? I knew James was trying to master a traumatic experience – he had been abducted and assaulted.

I was aware that since therapy started James had stopped engaging in sexually abusive behaviour towards others but he continued to present as a very disturbed young man. I focused on the traumatic experience I knew he had been through but failed to see that there was more. After sixteen sessions with James I wrote in my notes 'appears to be more like ritual abuse'. But it wasn't until over thirty sessions that I was able to incorporate this idea into my formulation. I began to see that James did feel mad and was confused – probably asking himself, did this really happen and anyway who would believe me? I was unable to think about and accept the real horror of his experience, perhaps for fear of going mad myself and for the fear of not being believed. My acceptance of his experience and my communicating to him that I understood and believed what he was saying brought about major changes in James. The trances stopped as did the bad dreams. He started to come to sessions and tell me about his new enjoyable dreams.

James's level of symptomatology was assessed before therapy started, every eight sessions and after therapy ended, using the *SCL-90 R* (Derogatis, 1983) in a simplified interview format. At intake James's scores were elevated in all symptom areas. Of the 90 symptoms listed, James was being troubled by 70 of them to some degree, especially in the areas of obsessive-compulsive disorder, paranoid ideation and anxiety. After eight sessions there was a small drop in reported symptoms but they then remained at the same level until after the thirty-second session. By the fortieth session the number of reported symptoms dropped to 37 and after forty-eight sessions, when therapy ended he reported only 32.

These assessments were carried out by my research assistant and I was kept blind until therapy ended. The results correlate with the major change which took place in therapy, that is, my understanding and acceptance of his experience, and my communication of this to him. Perhaps it was also important for James to see that I could think about what was in his head and not go mad.

Once I had started to think of the abuse as ritual and satanist I also started thinking about when this had happened. During the course of therapy James gave no indication that abuse was currently occurring. But the way he described the sexual assault at the beginning was as if it had happened only a day or so ago. James had no concept of time and could not give me any clues as to when. However, his description of his family circumstances and the vehicles used suggested that the events took place over ten years ago. This is pure speculation and James is now closely monitored and supervised.

When I spoke about James to my psychotherapist colleagues working with mentally handicapped people in Yorkshire they also had similar cases to report. Having to think the unthinkable (Sinason, 1989) with regard to sexual abuse, we have had to think the even more unthinkable. It is my hope that we will come to accept and deal with this issue a little more quickly than we did with that of sexual abuse.

REFERENCES

Beail, N. (1989) 'Understanding emotions', in D. Brandon (ed.) *Mutual Respect: Therapeutic Approaches to Working with People who have Learning Difficulties*, Surbiton, Good Impressions.

Beail, N. and Warden, S. (1993) 'Sexual abuse of adults who have learning disabilities', unpublished paper, Barnsley Community and Priority Services NHS Trust.

Church, M. (1982) Letter, in *Bulletin of the British Psychological Society* 35, 470.

Derogatis, L.R. (1983) *SCL-90 R Manual II*, Townsend MD, Clinical Psychometric Research.

Dunne, T.P. and Power, A. (1990) 'Sexual abuse and mental handicap: preliminary findings of a community based study', *Mental Handicap Research* 3 (2), 111–25.

Murphy, G. (1993) 'The use of aversive stimuli in treatment: the issue of consent', *Journal of Intellectual Disability Research* 37 (3), 211–19.

Ryan, J. (1987) *The Politics of Mental Handicap*, Revised edition, London, Free Associations.

Sinason, V. (1986) 'Secondary mental handicap and its relationship to trauma', *Psychoanalytic Psychotherapy* 2 (2), 131–54.

Sinason, V. (1989) 'Uncovering and responding to sexual abuse in psychotherapeutic settings', in H. Brown and A. Craft (eds) *Thinking the Unthinkable*, London, FPA.

Sinason, V. (1992) *Mental Handicap and the Human Condition: New Approaches from the Tavistock*, London, Free Associations.

Turk, V. and Brown, H. (1992) 'Sexual abuse and adults with learning disabilities: preliminary communications of survey results', *Mental Handicap* 20 (2), 56–8.

Whitaker, S. (1993) 'The reduction of aggression in people with learning difficulties: a review of psychological methods', *British Journal of Clinical Psychology* 32 (1), 1–37.

Chapter 19

'You will only hear half of it and you won't believe it'

Counselling with a woman with a mild learning disability

Steve Morris

Steve Morris is Director of Respond. Respond is a service for people with learning difficulties who have been sexually abused. It seeks to provide counselling, psychotherapy and survivors' groups. It aims to support and provide a healing experience. It is a community-based service which seeks to be accessible to many people who have found their experiences of other services insensitive. Respond was founded by Steve Morris and Tamsin Cottis as a practical response to the growing number of people with learning difficulties who were disclosing their experiences of abuse and finding no treatment resources. It receives funding from the DOH and the Platinum Trust. Since Respond was established in 1991 it has received over 300 referrals. Respond currently works with twelve individuals a week and provides conferences, consultancy and training to staff throughout the country. Steve Morris is a counsellor, freelance consultant and psychotherapist in training.

Names, identities and background details have been changed wherever necessary to protect confidentiality.

Before becoming Director of Respond I was a senior social worker in various London boroughs and a freelance training consultant on issues of sex education for people with learning disabilities. It was through this work that I first started to receive disclosures of sexual abuse. Sometimes there was clearly documented physical evidence corroborating these accounts of abuse. Indeed, there had been a few successful court cases. More frequently, files produced medical details of sexual abuse that was never taken further. Sometimes this was because of historic disbelief that a person with a learning disability could be abused, sometimes because of the legal problems of people with a severe learning disability. There is also a complex overlap between legal and clinical needs. Some workers could clinically believe a client yet be frightened of the legal consequences. I would frequently hear from young residential workers who heard a disclosure yet were frightened to tell their managers because either they would not be believed themselves or it is not adequately part of the culture to take things on for this population.

In the face of this disbelief many clients have lost hope. With their childhood abuse not believed they go into adulthood with further abuse experiences and do not expect to ever be listened to. As a result of this it is not unusual for clients with a learning difficulty to be referred to me with an apparent absence of feelings. Indeed, many will initially talk to me about the many appalling abuses committed against them without indicating any corresponding feeling or emotion. Their experience of abuse often relates directly to their identity as a person with a disability and it is to anaesthetise this double blow that they lose contact with their feelings.

HELEN

Helen (aged 24, with a mild learning disability) was no exception to this. She was referred as a result of her dangerous self-injuring behaviour. She and her workers had clearly tried a range of other care programmes to see if they would help. However, she remained emotionally incapable of enjoyable leisure or work activities, despite her ability to manage some limited reading and writing.

In our initial meeting Helen spoke of her experience of rape and abuse in the manner of reading a shopping list. However, although her words were out of touch with her feelings, her body provided a different message. For Helen rocked backwards and forwards in her chair looking at the scars that criss-crossed her arms. Her fingers kept picking at the bloodied scabs, causing fresh blood to appear. This evidence of repeated self-injury bore witness to awful trauma.

Helen's painful life experiences were also made apparent by her first hostile yet hopeful statement to me. 'You will only hear half of it; there is another half but they didn't believe it then. They don't believe it now and you won't believe it either, will you?' She was clearly warning me that the featureless shopping list of abuse she had recounted was the easy part and she did not know if the disbelieved half would be able to be spoken about.

Indeed, although she only has a slight speech defect she had succeeded in gaining from the services a very expensive synthesiser and it was clear she did not expect to be heard and listened to with her own voice.

In the first eighteen sessions Helen was to show me the powerful structure of denial and defence she had constructed around herself. Large amounts of alcohol consumed alone in her bedroom or in the local park took away the sharpness of her memories. She told me, 'When I am drunk it is like being in cotton wool . . . taking sleeping tablets lets me lose my memory', and, 'cutting my arm shows them that it's horrible and I'm hurting inside'. As well as a speech synthesiser Helen also chose to wear hearing-aids, even though there was no medical evidence of audio-deficiency. 'These let me hear what I want', she said, 'and then I don't have to listen to what I don't want to hear – look.' She switched them off and completed the remainder of that particular session in silence, not responding to anything I said.

Helen told me (and this was verified by her file) that at the age of 8 she had been sexually abused by an uncle. He had abducted her from her special boarding school by telling the school he was taking her to a family funeral. He had vaginally and anally abused her over a period of days. He was later imprisoned for this. However, she kept making clear that this well-known account was only half the story. Slowly, over a number of weeks, using a series of dreams and a diary, Helen was able to tell me the rest of her account. I was then to understand why no-one could previously bear to believe her.

Unlike many adults with a cognitive deficit, Helen did not spoil the ability she had. Indeed she used this ability to keep a therapy diary. Every week she would push her diary into my hands and deliver the instruction 'You read it to yourself – don't do it out loud. I don't want to hear it.' It was not just me who was scared of what she would say.

In the second session she showed me some drawings. The first was a smiling face. 'Look – this is me when I'm happy.' She pointed to another face with tears coming down its cheeks. 'This is me when I'm sad.' Then, turning over the page, she said, 'This is me when I'm angry.' She pointed to a similar shaped face baring its teeth, adding, 'I've drawn my feelings because I've seen them, and now I want to talk about them.' Her 'shopping list' way of speaking had gone. Now Helen could visually see her feelings because of a dream the previous evening. The process had begun which was eventually to enable her to share the truth.

After showing me the drawings Helen commented 'I do feel happy sometimes and I do feel sad, but I can't feel all of the time because if I did I would die.' Helen was telling me that her experience was so powerful in its awfulness that if she were to allow herself to feel it she worried it could destroy her. Indeed, there had been concerns about her suicidal tendencies as shown by her self-injury. Dreams that Helen had shortly after this, and which she brought to the sessions in the form of drawings, were visual representations of her dying or being near to death.

The next drawing she brought was a round shape with lines dividing it into pieces. 'I dreamed that my brain was going to be cut into little pieces', she told me. Helen was able to relate this unconscious symbol to her conscious struggle with painful memories. 'Sometimes the whole story of everything that happened goes round and round in my head. It hurts my head so much, it's like my brains are being cut.' For the first time Helen was communicating her pain symbolically without resorting to self-injury.

Helen then brought into her therapy a dream which she described as 'the worst dream'. In the dream she was trapped in a fire and died. In her drawing of the dream there was a line of people watching her burn to death in the flames. A similar dream the next week showed a line of people watching her lying in the road after she had been knocked down by a car. Asking Helen what she thought of these people watching while horrible things happened to her, she replied: 'People only see me – they never help me. The men watched me. They watched the bit you don't know. They looked but never helped.'

I knew from counter-transference to the picture that further terrible abuse must have happened as well as from Helen's references to 'the bit you don't know'. It was becoming clear that the legally known account of a sole uncle involved was only a partial one – now she was talking about 'men', not just one man.

The final dream Helen brought to her sessions made it possible for her to tell the 'other half' of her traumatic experience. She used it as a springboard to reveal with chilling clarity what in the early 1970s was completely outside of our thinking and ability to believe. The drawing of this dream showed Helen lying prostrate at the bottom of a steep hill. On the slope of the hill she had drawn four trees, each resembling a penis. 'I've been pushed down the hill. I am dead', she explained.

The dream reminded Helen of being carried down the hill by the uncle who had abducted her. She had told me of how she had been locked and tied to a bed. However, she had never mentioned ritual elements before. Now she completed her account.

As she told it she became pale. Her usual constant movement stopped as her body became rigid. Her facial expressions changed, she looked terrified. I felt terrified. She described how four men had held her by her wrists and ankles while they sang songs. Her uncle, who wore 'long funny clothes', held a chicken over her and strangled it. He then cut the chicken open and collected its blood in a glass. The other men had dipped long sticks into the blood and had used it to draw marks on their faces and bodies. The sticks were then inserted into Helen's vagina. She described how, when she first arrived at the house, she had been given strong drinks that made her feel sleepy. These drinks had been given to her throughout her two days at the house. On the particular evening that she had been taken from the house and carried by her uncle to a churchyard at the bottom of a hill she recalled being almost unconscious. I noticed that now, sitting opposite me, her posture resembled an unconscious figure.

All these years after this terrible event I was able to hear Helen's story. I was able to take on the role of a witness to that half of her experience that could not be believed or heard. The responses of denial in both Helen and those who could not bear her full experience had effectively silenced it. This silence had maintained Helen in a perpetual state of self-injury and self-abuse for nineteen years. Only when someone could witness the truth could Helen bear to share and recognise the extent of her suffering.

Until this point in her therapy Helen had needed to survive an experience that repeatedly brought her close to death. Indeed, whenever she started to remember the experience she became terrified the recollection alone could kill her, in addition to the threats for silence placed on her. Faced with this death-threat whenever the memory surfaced, Helen used denial as a defence against trauma when she could not face the memory of the tortured small child she needed to keep alive.

Hearing such an account is also traumatic. I was aware that the sessions with

Helen took an emotional toll on me. I was silenced and scared. I worried whether I could hold onto these details and where I would be able to take this. I worried whether I would be believed. Would a supervisor be able to support me with such a case if they did not believe it? When I thought about the burden this account proved to be for me I was able to understand more easily why Helen, and many others like her, have not been able to tell their accounts before. Disbelief was not a defence I was able to martial although at times I wished I had.

However, the disbelief from others that Helen had previously experienced had abused her further. It helped to sustain her denial beyond its usefulness, turning it into a destructive compulsion of self-injury. The continued presence of the trauma for nineteen years could only be borne by the infliction of new suffering until therapy began. It was in the context of psychodynamic psychotherapy that Helen allowed herself to face and experience these feelings.

As therapy went on she described further details and further abuse. She was also able to operate at a symbolic level describing her current small bedroom as reminding her of being put in a coffin. She had also begun to watch horror films – something she could not tolerate before. Now she found they offered the solace of a shared experience. Her cutting and other self-injurious patterns have ceased.

Society has only recently begun to acknowledge the reality of child sexual abuse. Abuse of people with learning disabilities has taken longer to acknowledge. If we add to this the currently unrecognised crime of ritual abuse we can see how people like Helen are silenced even more.

Helen's attempts to move the professionals from not knowing to knowing have resulted in a healing which is founded upon shared acknowledgement of inner and outer truth. Denial of ritual abuse and other abuses only maintains people in the long-term effects of those experiences. Recognition of both the nature of abuse and denials is the beginning of an appropriate therapeutic response. I referred earlier to myself as therapist in the role of witness. A witness is able to see, hear and know what others wish to ignore or distort. The legal definition of witness refers to someone who can support an individual's plea of 'not guilty'. The therapist witness can, in this role, assist in securing the freedom of those who have remained trapped in the silencing experience of denial.

It was only in the 1980s that we acknowledged sexual abuse and, after the first cases we treated, we could recognise how our denial had made us blind to previous clients. Since working with Helen I have become aware of painful disclosures by other clients with learning disabilities that never went further because I had no 'hearing aid'. What about 36-year-old John, for example, with Down's syndrome, who told me of masked people who bit his neck and hurt him at night? It was easy to think only of horror films or dreams. But John did not come back for further work.

Chapter 20

A birthday to remember

Neil Charleson and Al Corbett

Neil Charleson was born in Hampshire thirty years ago. He was assessed as having a mild learning disability at 4. He entered the boarding school described here when he was 14. Al Corbett comes from a background in drama, journalism and therapeutic work with people with learning difficulties (disabilities).

Names, identities and background details have been changed wherever necessary to protect confidentiality.

A normal day in the boarding school started with us getting up, washing, stripping our beds. Then we had our breakfast, cleaned up, made the beds, cleaned our teeth, went downstairs, polished our shoes (our indoor shoes, our sandals), then went out to the playground and got the post, went into assembly, went into classes, then there was morning break. Just before morning break we would have our milk. Even after Margaret Thatcher pinched the milk off children we still had milk in boarding school. That was just before morning break. Then we would go to break, come back for more lessons, go to dinner, go to break, then have a quiet reading period when we read proper books.

We were not allowed to read magazines. The most popular book around was *Noddy Goes to Toytown*. What happened was that the rotary club decided to raise money for the senior boys' library, but because they thought we were stupid they started to buy us the complete works of Noddy instead of the dictionary we asked for. So we took them, and the most popular book was *Noddy Goes to Toytown* because it had pictures of Noddy in the nude.

We were happy with the regimentation of the school. We knew what we was going to do, we knew what we was going to eat – that Friday was fish day, that we had chocolate biscuits on Saturday with our milk. We knew what days we was going to watch television and we knew what programmes we was going to watch. It got to the point where you woke up in the morning and thought 'I am going to have an early night tonight. I don't want to watch television tonight.' The only way out of watching television was to go to bed early. There was never a time except when I was asleep that I was on my own. Even then I was in a six-bed dormitory.

I was befriended by an older boy, Steve. At my 14th birthday this friend Steve arranged for me to have a special birthday party. There was someone else at the school who had the same birthday as me. Because I was new at the school, it was all the other lads' friends at the birthday party. The party was held at the school doctor's house nearby. This doctor took us to his house in a Land-Rover which I was really chuffed about. 'I am in a Land-Rover! I am in a Land-Rover! I have never been in a Land-Rover before!' We went to the house and first of all everyone played lots of stupid birthday games. Then the doctor took me to the room where the food was. There were two birthday cakes. Mine had two levels to it. The other cake didn't and I asked why. He said 'Oh you will find out later.'

I was still really excited about everything. I had never been to a doctor's house before and everyone was telling me what an honour it was having a birthday party in such a rich man's house. Then the doctor said, 'I have got one more surprise for you Neil.' I said 'Yes?' He said 'It is in my bedroom. Come upstairs with me.'

I don't know about you, but most people I have spoken to whose parents have a special present for them – it gets kept in the bedroom. So we went upstairs. There was me and four others. There was Steven and the three others around his age. We went upstairs and as we were going up they were singing 'Happy birthday dear Neil – happy birthday to you.'

We got into the bedroom and the doctor pushed me down on the bed, ripped my trousers down and he fucked me. After that the four lads who was with me fucked me one after the other and went downstairs. And left me upstairs. They left me on the floor in a pool of my own blood. The doctor came up with a towel and said, 'Here you are. Clean yourself up and come back downstairs.'

Who do you tell? Who do you go to afterwards when you bleed? Do you go to the doctor? It was then that I stopped believing in life, stopped wanting to feel, stopped wanting to know. The week after that they sent me the little cake on top, the second layer with a knife on top of it. I cut my wrist with the knife. This lad David came in. David, who was later to become my best friend, he came into the common room. I had fainted after cutting my wrists. David came in and fainted on top of me. We were both wearing our Sunday best. A member of staff found us both. She patched me up and I just told her things she wanted to hear, not the truth.

Everything went on. Nothing changed. I wanted to know what I had done, what I had done to deserve what had happened to me and nobody ever answered that, nobody ever tried to answer what I was feeling. It was like a big secret because it seemed to be my fault. I could not tell anybody at that stage because I was so ashamed of it.

The school was a paedophile ring. Four of the school governors was in the ring. The headmaster did not have any knowledge of it, nor the principal. But nearly all the male staff was using the boys. There was a group of freemasons who used to use the boys in ceremonies. They used to worship a boy God and they needed a boy to take on the role of the boy God in the ceremonies. I became the boy God.

One of the lads I started to get on with was diabetic. They told me if I did not do what they wanted me to do his insulin would disappear. There was a case just before of a boy who had refused to do it. He worked as a beater when people went on a shoot for game birds. He beat the ground so the birds would fly into the air and get shot. He 'accidentally' got shot in the arm. They told him if he carried on messing about he would not be so lucky next time – the next time he would not survive.

So I had no-one to tell. the governors had the last word on everything in the school. It was Steven who approached me to take part in the ceremonies. He came up to me and said he was leaving the school and they needed someone to take his place. It was his job to find someone. I ended up participating in the ceremonies for three years. I was only used in the main ceremonies when a new member was coming in. This was at the same time as I was being abused by staff members, sometimes four or five times a day. That was pretty widespread. I was the only person they did it to who had enough speech to tell. It is amazing what people can get away with if they abuse people who can't communicate. When you grow up in special schools you learn that all these able-bodied people do what is best for you, so when it all breaks down it must be your fault.

It goes back to what happened at the birthday party – the guilt I carried. We all know what happens in bedrooms. I was 14 and an adult said, 'Come into the bedroom, I have something for you.' You don't think it is going to end in abuse. It is a birthday party. It is my birthday party. For ages I blamed myself for going upstairs with him. That was my fault. The adult/child relationship is not an equal one. Everything is loaded on the adult side. They have got more experience of life. A child will not survive because he has not yet learned the skills. A sexual relationship between equals – what is based on love – is not wrong and is not abuse. At that time I did not realise the difference and the idea that somebody wanted me for sexual encounter scared me. The idea that a child or young person can be equal with an adult is very false.

I had a relationship with Tim, which had become a sexual one. I was told that if I told anyone about the ceremonies mine and Tim's relationship would be made public. They asked me what I would rather happen, leave school at 16 or be put in care for the rest of my life. Heads I lose, tails I lose. Heads I lose, tails you win.

Everything was my fault. I went into the bedroom. I was gay. What happened to gay lads in school? They got abused. It was all my fault, that was all I knew. My dad had told me that everything that happened around me was my fault, from an early age.

Thinking back to ceremonies, it is very difficult to work out from the start what was real and what was not. Before the ceremony started they would give me high tea with the doctor. He was one of the lodge members and part of the tea consisted of those cakes with sugar rice characters on them. I worked out much later that those sugar rice characters were acid tabs. That makes more sense of the visions I was having. As Head Boy I was given a pendulum, a pendulum of protection. A person was brought into the room topless. The first part of the ceremony was done topless to prove the person was male. I would be wearing a red robe with nothing underneath. There was a big bed in the middle of a circle with a five-forked star. The bed is in the middle. A four-poster bed. On each of the points of the star was a black candle. I was tied to the bed.

The person would come into the room and he would walk around the room anti-clockwise once and then he would untie me. If he did not have a hard-on he would untie me and I would take off my robe. It was my job to give him a hard-on so he could fuck me. He would fuck me then, being watched by all the others. Then he would come over my face. While he was doing that they would take photographs which were kept so he could never break from the lodge. That was also part of my job – to make love to people or get people to make love to me – male staff – so they then could be blackmailed by photographs of us into not telling the police what was going on.

There was one I still feel guilty about – a young man around 18 who was a born again Christian. He found out a bit about the lodge and was going to tell the police. He came to a party put on by a member of the lodge, a governor, and they got him out of his mind on drugs. They took photographs of him giving me a blow job which were delivered to his room the next day.

During the sacrifice they would bring out what they said was a young child's heart and put it in front of me. They said they had sacrificed a child for me so I would be pleased with them. It was difficult to know what was real and what wasn't, especially when the room was going round and you see flashes of light around you and you have just been fucked.

It is funny but in one way it seems like I had all the power. In another way I didn't have any power. The only way I got through it was to think of the whole thing as a horror movie. It was like it was happening to someone else through my body. It was like this horrible nasty person took over my life. It made me very hard in some ways. Recently someone was talking about the horror in Iraq, the children being sacrificed and everything. Everyone was going, 'Oh horror, horror', and I was going, 'It happens in this country. Can we deal with this country?' It was like, 'So what? What is the big deal about that?'

Like anyone who has been abused there are lots of little things I cannot cope with anymore. Many of them seem stupid to people who have not been through this situation themselves – like not being able to be in a room where the song 'Happy birthday' is sung, not being able to cope with anything connected with that. On my last birthday I received one of those cards that, when you open it up, plays a tune 'Happy birthday'. I opened it up and it started to play and I just stood on the opposite side of the room and just stayed there crying. Even the sight of a birthday cake can bring back the thought of the first abuse.

There are other difficult areas, things like being locked in a room, even with people I trust, is very difficult. To have people suddenly grab you from behind if I don't know they are there. I have been known to knee people in the private parts just because they have hugged me from the back without making any sounds. I find it very hard to trust people. Like when I was with my last boyfriend. There was always a question of why he wanted to go out with me. It was beyond belief that he wanted to date me. The unsureness of that area is really awful. The longest relationship I had lasted two and a half months and then it was always me asking him, 'Hey – do you really want to be with me?' which was a big strain on him.

I am also very prone to panic attacks in pubs or if the pub is very crowded I go very much inside myself. Pubs are not my scene anyway. I don't have much of a social life because as soon as someone does get to me emotionally I put up big barriers.

At school, after the abuse, the only contact I wanted with any lad was sexual contact. It was the only way I could show people I cared about them. Later on it became a way of showing people I hated them. For ages, in my later teenage years and early 20s, I had to truly hate a man before I went to bed with him. It became such a close-set idea that sex equalled abuse. The only people I went to bed with were people who I wanted to show how much I hated them.

Outside of the abuse ring in school there was not a lot of sexual contact. There were things like if one of the lads hated to undress in front of everybody he would be stripped every so often, and the usual wrestling matches in dormitories in which pyjamas usually came off. There are lots of regrets, lots of times now when I start getting into ifs and buts. But Sister Patricia, who was Headmistress of my primary school had two sayings:

If Ifs and Buts were pots and pans
there would be no use for tinkers.

and the other one was

If all the land were china
and all the sea were ink
and all the trees were bread and cheese
what would we have to drink?'

I have played the 'if' game but it got me nowhere.

SCRIBE'S NOTE (FROM AL CORBETT)

When in the course of acting as Scribe for the writing of Neil's autobiography we came to this abuse, my initial feelings were revulsion and horror. Disbelief, however, did not enter my mind. This was partly due to my knowledge of Neil as a person for whom telling the truth of his life and getting it heard by a wider public was paramount. My lack of disbelief was also rooted in my on-going work with people with learning disabilities. Time and time again I have heard the most distressing stories of abuse: physical, emotional, sexual, ritual and institu-tionalised, and the roots of all these disclosures seem to come from the person's learning disability, the handicap that prevents them from saying 'no', from speaking up or being believed.

Part III

Outside links
Making the trauma visible

Chapter 21

ChildLine, UK

How children and young people communicate their experiences by telephone

Hereward Harrison

Hereward Harrison is Director of Counselling for ChildLine, UK.

Names, identities and background details have been changed wherever necessary to protect confidentiality.

ChildLine celebrated its seventh birthday in October 1993 and has counselled more than 300,000 children via its confidential, free, national telephone number (0800 1111). Calls cover a huge range of subjects, the most frequent being about physical, sexual and emotional abuse.

ChildLine counsellors have learned much about the way children communicate their worries and experiences. Some of the key learning points have been:

1 Children may phone several times before they have enough courage to speak. This is particularly true of callers with a history of sexual abuse, where children have been 'threatened to silence' and are physically and emotionally traumatised.

2 Children often wish to stay anonymous or give a 'telephone name' to preserve their identity and to try and control overwhelming experiences and emotions.

3 The phone itself affords children the opportunity of testing reactions – 'I know you won't believe me but . . . ', and enables them to make choices in their own time and in their own way. Telephone counselling for children is *not* value free but encourages them to seek safe, realistic solutions, and to avoid further trauma, such as a court appearance, which is often said to be worse than the abuse itself.

4 Children present in a wide variety of ways, some of which appear bizarre, for example, shouting and screaming, talking in groups, sexually explicit language, apparently 'happy' affect while describing horrendous abuse. This does not mean that they have nothing to say, or that they are messing around or are 'hoaxing'.

5 Counsellors have learned that assumptions such as 'This isn't a genuine call', or 'This caller has rung before', are often wrong. 'Second guessing' callers is not only futile but potentially dangerous, as it denies ChildLine's service to children who may be in desperate need, and have no-one they feel they can turn to.

An example of the difficulties involved in hearing and understanding children, from ChildLine's early days, was the assumption that some young males who described sexual intercourse (abuse) with their mothers were inappropriate sex callers. These callers presented in a sexually explicit way, quite different from girls and boys who had been sexually abused by men. It was only after several of these young male callers became very angry with their, mostly female, counsellors that they were accepted as 'genuine'.

6   The whole story often does not emerge until a child has phoned many times. There is, therefore, a danger in categorising a child's problem as the initial problem they ring with. ChildLine's records of calls from children who phone for a period of weeks or months, as in face-to-face psychotherapy or counselling, reveal more of the real nature of the children's experiences and needs.

7   Counsellors, professionals in other agencies and adults generally appear to have a wish, or need, to reconceptualise what children say in adult language. ChildLine has learned to leave the children's words to speak for themselves. We want an accurate account of what is said, not a 'diagnosis.'

We are still learning at ChildLine, and nowhere is this more apparent than in the discussions surrounding 'ritual' and 'satanic' abuse. Children do *not* use the words 'ritual' or 'satanic' (these words are used by some of the small number of adults who phone ChildLine, however). Children do, however, talk about being given 'funny drinks', having to wear 'funny clothes', being taken to 'strange places' and 'having things stuck into me by everyone'. They do talk of 'horrid smells', 'something that's red like blood' and 'cuts on my body'. They talk of assaults on their minds and bodies in a confused, time-jumbled way, and they seem to be living in a recurring nightmare, like hostages or victims of torture who feel they do not belong to the normal world.

Callers to ChildLine who present in this way challenge us to the extreme. The calls are often over a period of weeks or months and may involve more than one counsellor. They frequently involve children who have physical/medical problems, as well as emotional problems. We find ourselves trying to make sense of them in our own terms, as adults, and applying diagnoses, e.g. borderline personality or multiple personality, which may not be appropriate to the children's experience. Giving these callers a label or a psychiatric category has not helped us to understand them or to deal with some of the 'impossible' experiences that we must listen to and tolerate alongside the children.

SUMMARY

ChildLine has a huge sample of telephone calls, more than 300,000, from children and young people. Children remain in control of what they say and what choices they make when they phone ChildLine and, as a result, they have been able to speak to us about their experiences without fear of rejection or unwanted intervention.

The understanding that ChildLine has developed with children can now be placed in a theoretical context, which includes the developmental stages and ages of the children who call and many other influences including gender, culture, intellectual functioning and physical and mental disabilities. Children may give information which cannot be easily understood within this framework and it is here that the limits of our understanding and ability to work with children are most tested.

Children who may be involved in what adults describe as 'ritual' or 'satanic' abuse use ChildLine as one of the few places where what they are saying will be accepted, and where they can remain safe. What they are describing is often beyond our experience and our comprehension. We can, however, apply concepts which have evolved with working, via the telephone, with so many distressed children. The way of working is based on a well-tried psychodynamic model which involves as its prime focus attentive listening, examination of the listener's own reactions and preconceptions and, especially when the work involves counselling children by telephone, the ability to stay with the child, however impossible their story may seem. This response is essential to help the child find a way of dealing with unbearable and often unbelievable experiences, by engaging other adults in hearing and believing their story. Whatever the outcome, the child is in need of sustained help and care.

Chapter 22

Report on the Channel 4 *Dispatches* documentary on Satanic Ritual Abuse, 19 February 1992, and a helpline after the transmission of the programme

Olave Snelling and Sara Scott

Olave Snelling is a TV Producer, and Sara Scott was the Manager of Broadcasting Support Services (Manchester) from 1986 to 1993.

Names, identities and background details have been changed wherever necessary to protect confidentiality.

THE MAKING OF THE PROGRAMME (OLAVE SNELLING)

In the late 1980s and early 1990s there was a noticeable increase in the number of stories carried in the press about alleged satanic ritual abuse. What could be called a mini media explosion took place around child protection cases in Nottingham, Congleton and Rochdale where ritual/satanic abuse was suspected. In the wake of the Cleveland inquiries a few years earlier, allegations of sexual abuse of children were examined. However, when children began to mention ritualistic elements in the abuse, those who believed the children's stories were vilified in the press.

During the late autumn of 1991, Paul Hatcher, a television researcher, brought to my attention the number of newspaper stories dealing with ritual abuse and suggested putting forward a proposal for television. He arranged a meeting with writer Andrew Boyd, who was completing a book on satanic ritual abuse entitled *Blasphemous Rumours* shortly to be published by HarperCollins (1992). Boyd had undertaken careful research for two years in connection with this book. He had decided to begin his research by interviewing doctors, psychologists, psychiatrists and psychotherapists who believed they had come across satanic ritual abuse among their patients. Having established a degree of trust, introductions from one practitioner to another came thick and fast. He initially expected to find only a few individuals who had been involved with the subject, but after six weeks of pursuing contacts he had compiled more than fifty pages of information.

It became apparent that there were a number of medical practitioners who were risking their reputations by publicly admitting they had satanic ritual abuse clients. These represented the tip of a large iceberg. Their conclusions, based on the testimony of their patients, pointed directly to the existence of satanic ritual activity.

I read what I could on the subject of ritual abuse and was appalled at the accounts of satanic abuse in Boyd's book. It included a brief history of satanism, an outline of the beliefs and practices of contemporary Satanism, an overview of self-confessed satanic groups and interviews with a number of ritual abuse survivors and therapists. The accounts from survivors and those who were helping them made it impossible to ignore the allegations. Though it was painful to come to terms with the nature of the abuse which was being described I felt, along with Hatcher and Boyd, that an attempt should be made to bring this issue further into the open.

The programme

To this end a proposal was submitted to the *Dispatches* programme at Channel 4. The channel had previously accepted a programme on the subject of the Nottingham case in which the journalist Bea Campbell had investigated allegations made by children of physical abuse accompanied by what appeared to be satanic ritual. That Channel 4 had been willing to make such a stand was very courageous in the light of considerable press cynicism. Our proposal was accepted and production began in December 1991. Graham Addicott was director. Research material was provided by journalists Eileen Fairweather and Paul Hatcher, in addition to the major source material of Andrew Boyd, who was employed as a consultant and subsequently invited to be the reporter. The programme, entitled 'Beyond Belief', was transmitted on 19 February 1992, coinciding with publication of Boyd's book.

The programme aimed to deal with adult ritual abuse survivors rather than children. (The negative impact of the press vilifying professionals who believed the testimonies of children was acknowledged in the *Report of the Inquiry into the Removal of Children from Orkney in February 1991* (HMSO, 1992)). It featured professionals working with survivors, such as psychiatrist Dr Vic Harris, clinical psychologists Sheila Youngson and Helga Hanks and psychotherapist Vera Diamond. Superintendent Michael Hames of the Obscene Publications Unit, Detective Inspector Kath Adams of West Yorkshire Police and ex-police surgeon Dr Stephen Hempling represented the extent of concern/belief from a law enforcement perspective. Professors Bill Thompson from Reading University and John Newson from Nottingham University expressed their scepticism about claims of satanic/ritual abuse. In particular, Bill Thompson cast doubts on the methods used by social workers to obtain testimony from children about ritual abuse.

The most controversial aspect of the programme was the inclusion of clips from a video made in 1982 and handed to the production team by a professional working with survivors. It was the product of a cult with bases in Brighton and London, which, as a result of our own research and Scotland Yard's, is now the subject of investigation. A report has been submitted to the Crown Prosecution Service by the Obscene Publications Branch for consideration with regard to possible criminal offences committed by members of this cult. One of the survivors interviewed alleged that this portrayed a satanic ritual and part of the programme was devoted to a description of this. However, the programme makers' intention was not to major on the contents of this gruesome compilation video (which was over three hours in duration and which had been handed to the police after production was finished), but to concentrate on the testimony of therapists, survivors and police.

Reaction

Subsequent newspaper reaction to the claims in the publicity (which were stronger than might have been desired) that this video provided new evidence of satanic abuse was swift and strong. It was stated by some newspapers that what had been seen was performance art. In addition, one newspaper attacked the testimony of an interviewed survivor whose memory of satanic ritual abuse was supposed to have been forced to the surface in the course of deliverance ministry by Christians.

The major reaction to the programme, however, was in the form of a helpline. This ensured support to some of the survivors with whose lives it was concerned and an opportunity for viewers who might be affected by satanic ritual abuse to speak to professional helpers.

THE HELPLINE (SARA SCOTT)[1]

Broadcasting Support Services is a charity which operates around fifty media-linked helplines each year. Channel 4 commissioned a helpline to accompany 'Beyond Belief', to open for three hours after transmission and a further four hours the following day. The helpline operated an 0800 number with calls free to the caller.

The number of lines to open was decided upon in the light of previous helplines on sexual abuse that Broadcasting Support Services have managed for Channel 4. The helpline set up following the transmission of a previous *Dispatches* programme, about children and foster parents involved in the Nottingham ritual abuse case, had thirty lines. It was open for five hours and received only 108 calls, a number well below the capacity of the helpline. Unfortunately, the best estimates of likely demand were wrong. Fifteen lines were opened on the night of transmission and five the following day and the helpline dealt with a total of 191 calls. This entailed each counsellor dealing with an average of three calls per hour and several suicidal young women lasted over an hour and a half. Unfortunately it seems that the calls which were answered represented merely the tip of the iceberg in terms of demand. British Telecom recorded 595 attempted calls in the first 5 minutes after the helpline number appeared on screen and 4500 attempted calls in the helpline's first hour of operation. Even if all callers were extremely persistent and tried the number ten times, these figures would still represent 450 callers trying to access the helpline during that hour.

Staff

Counsellors were recruited through RAINS (Ritual Abuse Information Network and Support – see Chapter 29 by Joan Coleman). RAINS was originally set up to provide support to child protection workers involved in the Nottingham and Congleton ritual abuse cases. In order to ensure that calls were dealt with by people with relevant experience, counsellors were asked to travel from various cities. There was considerable anxiety from some members about coping with the helpline or about issues of confidentiality, safety and programme content. None considered themselves 'experts' in the field and feared raising callers' expectations that help was at hand. The staff who worked on the helpline included clinical psychologists, psychiatrists, Rape Crisis counsellors and social workers. All learned from the experience. It provided a valuable, if inevitably limited service to callers and those involved formed an energetic and supportive staff team.

Calls and callers

Almost 50 per cent of calls received by the helpline concerned ritual abuse; 39 per cent of all calls were from current victims or survivors of ritual abuse calling on their own behalf.

Women and men called the helpline in the proportion of 2:1. The same proportion held for current victims and survivors of ritual abuse. This represents a higher proportion of male callers than is generally the case on Broadcasting Support Services helplines dealing with sexual abuse (around 4:1). The two major differences between male and female callers in this category were age (most men were in their 20s or early 30s; women ranged in age from 14 to 60 years) and victim/survivor status (only three of the twenty callers who identified themselves as current victims of ritual abuse were men).

Ritual abuse calls

Approximately half of those calling about ritual abuse on their own behalf had not spoken to anyone before. The level of distress and fear of these callers was very high and is illustrated by the following quotes:

'I'll have to die now. Silence is the first rule and I've broken it.'
'They'll kill me for sure now.'
'I've been out ten years and moved fourteen times.'
'Who are you? Can you trace this call?'

One little girl just cried 'The devil's got me', over and over.

Despite their terror, many callers managed to speak of the things they had seen and done and suffered. Rape, torture, mutilation, sleep deprivation, hypnosis, ritual murder, abortion and cannibalism, all featured in calls. Specific experiences mentioned included:

- being shut in a coffin for three days
- being smeared with blood from a 'sacrificed' child and then being raped
- being tied up and covered with maggots
- having to kill her own kitten when 8 years old
- being prostituted to men outside the 'coven'
- child pornography being made
- death of a sibling from abuse
- extensive use of psychotropic drugs
- having other 'selves' or 'entities' (multiple personality)
- being deprived of food and water for long periods
- being forced to eat faeces and drink urine

Eight callers were currently seeing therapists and two more were receiving support from Christian counsellors. Of these, two had not as yet told their therapists about the ritual abuse – which was on-going. Four had told and not been believed and two more felt concerned that although their therapists were supportive they were not really able to cope.

All bar four of the callers who had suffered ritual abuse had grown up in families they identified as satanists or 'involved in ritual abuse'. Of the four who said they had been recruited as adults (three men, one woman), two mentioned access to their children and blackmail as key issues.

A few callers rang because of concerns about others; spouses, children, grand-children, siblings, who they knew or suspected to be involved in ritual abuse.

Most callers were desperate for belief and for help, but few felt escape was possible except through death. Counsellors were honest about how difficult it can be to find adequate help and how little is available. They talked callers through ways they might put together the sort of support package they needed. They advocated getting a GP referral to a psychologist, finding a safe living situation, seeing a counsellor or psychotherapist and making contact with a local Rape Crisis line. Callers were warned that they might face a long struggle to obtain the help they needed. Some were suspicious of any medical referral as they claimed the groups/'covens' in which they had been abused included GPs, obstetricians and, in one case, a psychiatrist.

The lack of available support was the most distressing feature of the helpline. Everyone working knew the situation and we had used most of the two weeks' preparation time for the helpline contacting organisations and individuals to ask about their capacity/ willingness to undertake the support of people referred by the helpline. *Dispatches'* need to keep information about forthcoming programmes close to their chests until shortly before transmission left little time for this sort of detailed information gathering. Most callers understood only too well the climate of disbelief and misinformation which makes finding support so hard, but their needs were so pressing and the helpline had so little to offer them in concrete terms.

Sexual abuse calls

Thirty-six calls concerned survivors of sexual abuse and four calls were from current victims of sexual abuse.

Many of the callers ringing about 'domestic' sexual abuse had particularly identified with the sadism described in the programme or the issue of multiple abusers. A couple of callers had not been ritually abused, but their abuse had included the production of pornography or they had been abused within a paedophile ring. One teenage boy had been 'recruited' at school and the abuse was on-going.

Professionals

We received half a dozen calls on the helpline from isolated professionals currently concerned about children in their care or supporting adult survivors of ritual abuse. In the week following the helpline a further six such callers were referred to BSS. All were put in touch with others working in the field and were informed of available literature. Some callers believed they had come across evidence of ritual abuse. Two callers rang to defend Satanism. One rang to ask how many people working on the helpline were Christians. (The counsellor in the latter case told the caller that she had no idea about people's private beliefs as they would not be relevant to the helpline.)

Scotland Yard

The Obscene Publications Squad at New Scotland Yard set up a 24-hour hotline to take calls referred on from the helpline. The hotline received about ten calls as a result of such referrals.

CONCLUSIONS

Perhaps the most striking element of this helpline was the similarity of the testimonies of torture and abuse from callers throughout the UK. Counsellors commented on the way in which the programme appeared to have given callers permission to speak of their experiences and their gratitude that someone, some-where, took what they had to say seriously.

The major weaknesses of the helpline were, first, our underestimate of demand and the consequent frustration of many callers who were unable to get through and, second, the lack of suitable sources of support to which referrals could be made. The urgent need for information and training for a wide range of workers and agencies in both the statutory and voluntary sectors was clearly identified.

APPENDIX

Statistical breakdown

Gender of callers:

Female	129	(68%)
Male	62	(32%)
Total calls	191	

Age of callers

Under 16	10
16–30	33
30–60	56
60 +	1

Call concerning current victim (from victim/survivor or concerned other)

Non-ritual sexual abuse	4	(2%)	(some callers were recorded
Ritual abuse	20	(10%)	in both categories)

Call concerning survivor (from victim/survivor or concerned other)

Non-ritual sexual abuse	36	(18%)	(some callers were recorded
Ritual abuse	74	(38%)	in more than one category)
Other abuse	8	(4%)	

Current victims or survivors of ritual abuse calling on own behalf

Female	50	(26%)
Male	25	(13%)

Calls from others (where identified)

Parent	7
Partner	3
Friend	4
Sister	2
Grandma	1
Foster mum	1
Professional	6
Student	2
Member of public	12

Referrals made to:

Scotland Yard Hotline	20	(10%)
Rape Crisis Centres	40	(20%)
SAFE (helpline for Survivors of Ritual Abuse)	9	
RAINS (Ritual Abuse Information Network and Support)	4	
Beacon Foundation	3	
Survivors Helpline (for male survivors)	8	

A number of referrals were also made recommending callers contact Social Services, GPs, psychologists, psychotherapists, etc.

NOTE

1 Sara Scott's contribution to this chapter was first published in the December 1993 issue of *Child Abuse Review*. Reprinted by permission of John Wiley & Sons, Ltd, who retain copyright of this material.

REFERENCES

Boyd, A. (1992) *Blasphemous Rumours*, London, HarperCollins.
HMSO (1992) *Report of the Inquiry into the Removal of Children from Orkney in February 1991*, London, HMSO.
Scott, S. 'Beyond belief: beyond help? Report on a Helpline advertised after the transmission of a Channel 4 film on ritual abuse', *Child Abuse Review* 2 (4).

Chapter 23

Press, politics and paedophilia

A practitioner's guide to the media

Tim Tate

Tim Tate is a writer and television producer.

Names, identities and background details have been changed wherever necessary to protect confidentiality.

> You cannot hope to bribe or twist –
> Thank God! – the British journalist
> But seeing what the man can do
> Unbribed, there's no occasion to.
>
> (Humbert Wolfe, in Punch)

Consider please, the following headline:

141 CHILDREN 'RESCUED FROM ABUSE RING'

How different might the course of the 1987 Cleveland child abuse controversy have been had it started with headlines such as that?

It is a truism to say that we get the press we deserve. It is, none the less, true. And nowhere is the adage better exemplified than in the reporting of child sexual abuse. Whilst individual cases of abuse – whether inter-familial or by so-called 'outsiders' – rarely make headlines, allegations involving multiple victims and/or multiple perpetrators have traditionally proved attractive to both print and broadcast journalists. In the main, however, the reporting of such cases has tended to be of a negative or disbelieving tenor. From Cleveland to Rochdale, Orkney to Nottingham, media coverage of multiple-allegation cases has focused on alleged mistakes by clinicians, social workers or therapists, rather than on the abuse itself.

In 1992 the editor of the *Rochdale Observer*, Steve Hammond, summed up the prevailing press attitude thus:

> To the best of my knowledge newspapers have never got involved in [the] actual child abuse. What newspapers get involved in is the situation that arises afterwards when the parents or guardian believe – rightly or wrongly – that the government agencies are not acting within the law, or they have overstepped the parameters of legal requirements.

The aim of this chapter is to analyse the nature of press coverage in cases of ritual abuse, and to suggest how practitioners can avoid harmful or hostile media reporting by the so-called 'pro-active' approach. This is important as most documented, and certainly all proven, cases of ritual abuse (a list of successfully prosecuted cases of ritual abuse is included in an Appendix at the end of this chapter) involve multiple victims and/or multiple perpetrators: precisely the category which attracts hostile reporting.

All too often, in the face of this prejudice, social services become defensive, terse and unforthcoming and the response of 'No comment' conveniently feeds into an existing perception: namely, that such allegations come from poor handling by social workers rather than the needs and communication of the child. The vast majority of child protection work undertaken by individual departments goes unrecorded and unnoticed and the defensive approach taken by such departments deprives them and journalists of the chance to educate each other.

For a Yorkshire TV *First Tuesday* documentary in March 1992, dedicated to addressing these issues, twenty representatives from the police, social services, parental rights campaigners, children's rights campaigners and the media were invited to role play a common child abuse scenario. They were split into five groups: a joint Police–Social Services enquiry, the Parents, the Caregivers (an aunt and uncle), the Media and the Child. Each group was given the same information. A 6-year-old child was staying with her aunt and uncle and had made an allegation that her father regularly touched her genitals. Each group was asked to decide how it viewed this apparent disclosure and what, if anything, it proposed to do within the next 48 hours. Each group was video-recorded throughout a weekend as it discussed the case. Four journalists were in the media team group but otherwise the groups were slightly mixed with one journalist in the child group.

The most important group for me, the Child group, was made up of two social workers, a children's rights campaigner and a journalist. They were asked to try and feel how the child might have felt throughout the 48 hours and make decisions as to what they might or might not say next.

All participants came in with their own previous experience and made their decisions largely on the basis of that. One disturbing finding was that no-one, until prompted, thought of talking to the child, and the participants in the Child group sat and visibly wilted. The Caregivers group wanted the child taken away on the grounds that the little girl might 'contaminate' their own daughter. Only when the Child group acted strongly, saying no-one had come to talk to them, did the Caregivers group decide to see the child. The Child group then said 'I am the one who caused the problem. I am not saying anything to anybody.'

Some learned from this exercise. The journalist who was placed within the Child group vividly saw how the processes all ignored the child, and was disconcerted by how her own profession would respond to an allegation of child abuse.

The following verbatim exchange between a senior *Mail on Sunday* journalist, Barbara Jones, and John Merry, a freelance rival, exemplifies this attitude:

JONES: What do I find – I mean, I'm saying this quite carefully – I just can't see why anyone would want to work in the field of child sexual abuse . . .

MERRY: Why do you want to work in the field of investigative journalism?

JONES: Oh, that's fine. Because it's varied . . .

MERRY: That's what they would say about child abuse.

JONES: (Forcefully) It's not varied. It's child abuse and it's sexual, and I'm just saying I think there's a lot of iffy people in it.

Later, in the televised hypothetical exercise in which she spoke, Bill Frost, a senior home affairs correspondent for *The Times*, summed up the prevailing journalistic attitude to child sexual abuse allegations:

There is concern fatigue now; the child abuse ritual is perceived to have run its course – I mean as far as good copy [reportage] is concerned. Unless there is some major miscarriage of justice – social services either making a mess of things or over-reacting, then it just doesn't cut the mustard. I mean, if it's true it's commonplace and low-life, and it's impossible to verify anyway.

This, then, is the familiar hidden agenda brought to bear on child abuse stories by many journalists. An inability to stay with the child in such cases is a problem for all professions. Why is the media's response, therefore, so concerning?

The answer is very simple: no social worker, paediatrician or therapist works in a vacuum. Most belong to statutory agencies, or are contracted by such bodies and these agencies are controlled by men and women who sit on social services committees, or police committees whose sources of information are the newspapers and broadcasting channels. Politics is not simply about which party controls the town hall or the House of Commons. Like it or loathe it, child abuse is a political issue. Workers in the field need the support of their managers; managers need the support of their elected members; members need the support of the public to stay elected.

By staying silent, social workers are handing the crucial battle for the hearts and minds of those who employ them to those who would rather they did not intervene in cases of alleged child abuse. The press is a vital conduit – perhaps *the* vital conduit for the creation of a political climate which either enables or obstructs good child protection work.

The process by which the agenda for public debate is set can be depressingly simple. As an example: an aggrieved parent rings their local newspaper to complain that his or her child has been snatched 'in a dawn raid' by social workers and/or police.

A support group of similarly-affected parents claims that their children are being pressured by social workers into making false allegations of sexual abuse. On its own a complaint by one parent is unlikely to yield a response from the media. But when a group of parents makes an approach its complaint is quite likely to be met with some interest: the prevailing view of social workers in child abuse cases is likely to ensure the parents a friendly rather than sceptical reception.

It is in the nature of journalists that they plan the thrust of their story after listening to only one side of an argument – in this case the aggrieved parents. Once assured of the strength of the story they finally approach social services for a comment.

We should note that phrase 'for a comment' because it means exactly what it says. The journalist is looking for a reaction to the story, not information which would enable him or her to ascertain the truth. The best comment of all, from the journalist's point of view, is 'No comment'. Used skilfully towards the end of a story it can seem to imply shiftiness or embarrassed culpability.

Even by the time that phone call is made the agenda is set. Social services are being approached to defend their actions, and by implication there is something unwarranted to defend. At this stage the battle for public opinion is all but lost.

Many of my colleagues might challenge such an apparently simplistic analysis. But consider this exchange from the televised 'hypothetical', involving Barbara Jones from the *Mail on Sunday* and Bill Frost from *The Times*. They had been presented with a scenario involving a single complaining parent, and a reluctant admission by social services that a group of twenty other children at risk had been taken into care in recent weeks. A timely leak suggested that a local professional footballer's child might be one of them. The journalists were working out a strategy for handling the developing story:

JONES: You'd ring up PAIN – Parents Against Injustice – that's one of the first things you'd do. You'd say 'Have these people come to you?' and try and find the support group they'd gone to.

FROST: Yeah, and if we can turn round and get them together with the profes-sional footballer and his wife . . . and, um, turn them into a pressure group – if that's not dictating the course of events too much?

JONES: That's right. Because we've got the experience of it in Cleveland and Rochdale.

The journalists in that exercise were considering a case of 'ordinary' child sexual abuse. Their instinctive reactions were to assume it was a case of false allegations inflated by social workers. They, like most of their readership, viewed the parents as the victims. In a 48-hour period they voiced no thoughts about the children involved.

The journalists were chosen for their previous involvement in covering cases of multiple-allegation sexual abuse. All had some experience of ritual abuse cases. All but one had written hostile articles in which parents were depicted as the victims of over-zealous social workers.

One of their newspapers, the *Mail on Sunday*, had taken a forceful editorial line that ritual abuse did not exist: that it was a 'myth' created by extreme fundamentalist Christians and swallowed gratefully by gullible therapists.

Nor was it alone. The *Independent on Sunday* (12 August 1990) announced:

Over the past two years the British public has been hearing more and more about this apparently new phenomenon, as social workers, psychiatrists, therapists, the NSPCC, voluntary groups and churches all report a growing number of cases of satanic ritual abuse.

But are these satanic abuse survivors' stories fantasy or fact? Are children in Britain being sadistically abused and tortured by witches and satanists in covens?

Are teenage girls being used as 'brood mares', made pregnant and the foetus aborted so that it can be sacrificed and in some cases eaten . . . ?

An investigation by the *Independent on Sunday* has found that nobody has produced evidence to support these claims . . . .

There have been police investigations across the United States, in Canada, the Netherlands and now in Britain. They have produced no evidence.

The apparently well-supported allegations of *Independent on Sunday* writer Rosie Waterhouse failed to recognise that, by 1990, English courts had processed six successful and explicit prosecutions for the sexual, physical and emotional abuse of young children. This information was never publicly volunteered. However, when challenged on this fact, other newspapers and television programmes were unwilling to correct their coverage.

On 7 December 1992 the flagship of BBC television journalism, *Panorama*, broadcast what it described as an investigation into the phenomenon of ritual abuse allegations. The programme alleged that there had never been a proven case of ritual abuse committed by a practising satanist.

In making this allegation, like many newspapers, it clearly overlooked the successful prosecutions (which by then had risen to seven). Its choice of interviewees was also clearly biased. Those shown putting forward the view that ritual abuse was a genuine and observable problem were exclusively from the wilder shores of Christian evangelism; those arguing that the phenomenon existed only in the minds of excitable social workers were seemingly solid sociologists, academics and the police.

Surprisingly for a programme ostensibly dedicated to examining a difficult clinical problem, the programme makers made no contact with the one formal grouping of British professionals dedicated to understanding ritual abuse. RAINS – Ritual Abuse Information Network and Support – had been set up four years earlier. Its membership is almost exclusively made up of social workers, psychiatrists, psychologists and foster parents with direct experience of ritual abuse casework. There are three professional journalists in RAINS. All have extensive experience of ritual abuse cases.

The group was formed in the wake of the backlash against social workers in Nottingham for their part in a long-running case.

NOTTINGHAM

Twenty-three children had been taken into care for abuse at the hands of ten adult family members. Initially seen as a classic example of inter-generational child abuse, the perception changed among social workers when the youngsters began making new disclosures to their foster parents – disclosures which indicated something more than 'ordinary' abuse had taken place.

In 1989 ten adult members of the family were jailed for a combined total of more than 150 years. But the evidence from the children (and corroborated by adult witnesses) of ritual abuse was never put before the court. None the less the ritual nature of the case had been judicially recognised. A year before the criminal prosecution, Team 4 (a handpicked team of therapists from Nottinghamshire's social services department) had taken the case to wardship. In the High Court the judge had stated unequivocally that the children had been the victims of ritual abuse in satanic ceremonies. The decision was subsequently confirmed at appeal.

How then can we understand the press coverage that ensued? Headlines such as 'Satanic Inquisitors from the Town Hall?' and 'Making of a Satanic Myth'?

Led by the *Independent on Sunday*, the media pronounced that whilst the Nottingham children had certainly been abused, the suggestion that there had been a ritual or satanic element to that abuse stemmed directly from social workers. Team 4 was accused of attending seminars on ritual abuse and then conducting 'interrogations' during which the children were asked leading questions. The NSPCC was blamed for introducing witches' costumes and monster toys to play sessions with the victims. And Britain's leading independent specialist on treating sex offenders, Ray Wyre, was alleged to have handed to either foster parents or social workers a list of 'Satanic Indicators' which originated in the United States and which was 'proved' to be the ultimate source of all the ritual abuse stories in Nottingham.

Almost none of these alleged 'facts' are true, and none of the conclusions drawn from them bear even the most minimal investigation.

What follows is a transcript of one of the children's disclosures in which a 3-year-old boy was speaking with his foster mother.

FOSTER MOTHER:	What are you doing, Mark?
MARK:	Witches.
FOSTER MOTHER:	Will you tell me about it?
MARK:	(Mark nodded) You have to get in the middle of a ring and then they laugh at you.
FOSTER MOTHER:	Who laughs at you?
MARK:	Daddy Kieran, Wayne, Michelle, Glenda, Steve, Diana, Grandad; and some others come, more witches. Carla [one of Mark's cousins] have to touch all those willies. Then you get the baby and put it on the floor. They all go 'ha' and put arms up and walk around him.
FOSTER MOTHER:	Is it a baby boy?
MARK:	Yes.
FOSTER MOTHER:	How do you know?

MARK: Him got his clothes off. We see him willy. Daddy Kieran and
                     Wayne jumped on it, like this. [Mark puts his teddy on the
                     floor and jumps on it, shouting 'ha']. Them takes us in the
                     garden and all and whips us, then locks us up in the garage.
FOSTER MOTHER: What happens to the baby they've jumped on?
MARK: They put it in the garages so you can't see it smashed. They
                     paint themselves on the face. They paint them willies.

These words were spoken by a boy just beginning to feel safe after more than three
years of constant mental, physical and sexual abuse. They form a significant part
of his disclosures, recorded on tape by his foster mother for almost two years.

Halfway through those disclosures, unprompted and evidently nervous, Mark
had begun talking about 'witch parties' where several adult men and women
abused him, his brother and their cousins in the course of bizarre rituals. He, of
course, never used the word ritual: indeed, when he had been placed with his
foster parents in December 1986, he had known only a few childish words, most
centred on his genitals or bodily functions.

Mark's younger brother, Dean, also showed signs both of sexual abuse and
severe neglect. By the time he was 18 months old he was eating faeces, even
seeking it out in other children's potties at the playgroup he attended. But
gradually, as Mark and Dean grew more settled at their new home, the nature of
their disclosures changed.

Joan, the foster mother, kept the social workers constantly up to date with the
latest information. In turn Nottingham social services liaised with the local
police, and the first steps in preparing a criminal case against the abusers were
taken. Then, in late winter 1987, Mark dropped his bombshell: he and other
children had been abused at parties – some in other peoples' houses, where adults
dressed up as witches and chanted. It quickly became clear to Joan that this abuse
was different to anything she'd ever come across before.

Although she had never heard of ritual or satanic abuse, she understood that
Mark was trying to tell her about some form of occult ceremonies in which very
young children were sexually abused, tortured and even killed. And even at home
with Joan, Mark didn't feel entirely safe about disclosing what he had experienced.

MARK: Bum bleeds.
FOSTER MOTHER: Whose bum?
MARK: A's, B's and baby C. D has to wipe the blood away with a
                     tissue. We at the monster's house at the party.

Despite her apprehension, Joan managed to avoid prompting Mark with leading
questions or pressing him to disclose against his will. Piece by piece, the details
emerged, starting with a special drink the children had all been given at the
parties and slowly, further details.

MARK: Mum, know them witches? They have sheep.
FOSTER MOTHER: What? Baa baa black sheep, have you any wool sheep?

MARK:	Yes. Them kill them sheep with them fingernails around the neck.
FOSTER MOTHER:	Where does the sheep come from?
MARK:	A witch brings it in a car in a plastic box.
FOSTER MOTHER:	What kind of car?
MARK:	A black one. The sheep bleeds.
FOSTER MOTHER:	Where from?
MARK:	From its bottom and around its neck. [Mark runs his finger round his neck as if he is cutting his throat]
FOSTER MOTHER:	Is it a big sheep or a little one?
MARK:	It's big. Them get spiders and worms in black boxes. We touch them. We eat them. They put worms in our hair.
FOSTER MOTHER:	What do they do that for?
MARK:	Them witches go magic, magic, magic and make you go to sleep. Them witches make D wobble and go to sleep.
FOSTER MOTHER:	Anything else, Mark?
MARK:	No, no, don't want to now.

All the recordings of Mark's disclosures were passed on to Team 4 of Nottinghamshire social services department, a handpicked team of therapists all experienced in child sexual abuse cases. Christine Johnson, the senior worker, saw quickly that the boys' disclosures were pointing at something beyond simple sexual abuse.

As well as all the common behavioural problems you'd expect from a child who'd been sexually abused, he was showing an excessive amount of fear – particularly of toilets, spiders, blood, monsters and what he called witches. I suppose some of these fears aren't unusual to some degree in children of his age. But what we were seeing wasn't a normal degree. This was panic – phobic responses to everyday situations. He was once absolutely terrified when he was given a hot dog to eat. It took a while for us to realise that after what he'd been through he took the words quite literally.

The children were not simply disclosing the details verbally. From their earliest days in care, all the children had been given crayons and paper. Their therapists had encouraged them to draw, knowing that this is one of the most reliable and safe ways for children to reveal what has been done to them. According to Judith Dawson, Nottinghamshire's child abuse consultant, who headed Team 4, this seemingly simple therapy was, in fact, carefully controlled and monitored.

It was a way for these very young children to explain to us what had happened. But we were very careful to prevent them discussing or agreeing the content between themselves. All the groups' children were in separate foster homes and contact was minimal. I was satisfied that the drawings came independently, and as they did, and the mass of drawings grew, each confirmed the other.

Spread out across Nottingham in their foster homes, the children independently built up a convincing picture of a well-organised group of adults repeatedly abusing, and apparently killing, babies and young children during ceremonies.

By the middle of 1989 the Nottingham children had given the most detailed description of ritual abuse ever heard in Britain. In most cases, and with no opportunity for any cross-fertilisation of evidence, these deprived youngsters had independently corroborated each others' stories of ceremonies involving dozens of adults and children.

After some initial reluctance, Team 4 was convinced, and began seeking out guidance on how best to help the children. Judith Dawson saw no alternative.

> We repeatedly looked at the possibility that these children were using some sort of symbolic language to describe what they'd been through. It could have been, for example, that when they talked about snakes these were a symbol for the penises that had really been there. But the children would draw a snake which they said was inserted in their bottom, and they would draw a penis. They knew the difference. It became clear that these kids had been born into a world where good had to be destroyed and innocence perverted. The only explanation for all they told us was satanic ritual abuse .... You tell me – how else can a 4-year-old boy who could barely speak when he came into care, suddenly recite, word perfect, the opening words of an historic satanic chant. In Latin?

While Team 4 was refused permission to speak at, or even attend, professional conferences discussing ritual abuse, officers from Nottinghamshire Constabulary (who refused to accept that ritual abuse had occurred) were permitted to attend meetings and express their views freely. The social workers were not allowed to brief or talk to the press. This made it easier for the papers to scapegoat them. If you do not tell people who are writing what you believe a case to be about they will not know and then they will rely on what they have been told by the people who do not share your point of view.

I was sued for libel over alleged implications in my book on ritual abuse. For the record, both I and my publishers, Methuen, apologised and paid damages to Det. Supt. Peter Coles. We made it clear that we had never intended the detrimental implications found in the text and my book *Children for the Devil: Ritual Abuse and Satanic Crime* was withdrawn.

The ultimate sadness about the Nottingham case, aside from the bestial abuse inflicted on its young victims, is that in the detailed and cautious work carried out by Team 4 lies the best archive of contemporary social work focused on ritual abuse – and it is now locked away for ever.

But there is still a lesson to be drawn from the saga. The media coverage of the case was a disgrace. The lesson is that this was inevitable, given that only one side of a bitter dispute was putting forward its arguments. For Team 4 to have had a fair public hearing, the public needed to hear from Team 4 – and hear first. Perhaps Team 4 could have come to an agreement with the police in formal press conferences at which the difficult conundrum of ritual abuse could have been brought out into the open – and with it the differing views of Nottinghamshire Constabulary.

The timing was difficult. The initial moves to take the twenty-three Nottingham children into care came as the crisis in Cleveland hit its peak. In Nottingham, as in Cleveland, no-one knows how many children were abused and in what context (the *Butler-Sloss Report* made no finding as to the number of Cleveland children who had been abused).

However, had a rational and calculated decision to speak to the press been taken at an early stage in either case, much of the damaging public hostility could have been avoided. The public has a right to criticise those whom it pays to clear up the mess that some men and women create. It feels particularly sensitive over its children, and will want to vent its anger on someone, anyone, when child abuse is mentioned.

For the public to criticise responsibly the public needs information. The only way to give the public that information is via the media. The lesson practitioners must learn is simple. There are certain reporters who will not be educable but in general terms the media is. Journalists want to know the facts. Use the media, before it abuses you.

APPENDIX: RITUAL ABUSE PROSECUTIONS IN BRITAIN

1. Malcolm and Susan Smith/Albert and Carole Hickman, Telford, 9 November 1982.

MS: Three 14-year prison sentences for buggery, wounding and rape of four children (ages 1 year to 15 years); one 8-year and one 5-year sentence for specimen charges of indecent assault; one 2-year sentence for a specimen charge of unlawful sexual intercourse.

SS: One 2-year sentence for aiding and abetting.

AH: One 10-year sentence for specimen charges of buggery and assault.

CH: One 5-year sentence for aiding and abetting rape, buggery and assault.

The evidence presented (and admitted by the defendants) was that a series of sexual and physical assaults had taken place on four children during the course of satanic rituals. The sex frequently occurred on an altar dedicated to the Devil.

Malcolm Smith convinced his child victims that he was 'Lucifer'. Trial judge Mr Justice Drake said the children were 'mesmerised' by Smith's actions and rituals.

Smith carved an inverted (so-called 'satanic') cross on one child's abdomen, inserted lighted altar candles in her anus and vagina and branded her genitals with a red-hot altar knife.

2. Shaun Wilding: sexual abuse of four juvenile boys, Stafford Crown Court, November 1986.

Sentence: 3.5 years in prison.
Prosecuting Counsel, Malcolm Morse, told the Court:

A black magic sort of shrine was constructed. They [the boys] were induced to circle around him while he [Wilding] chanted in a theatrical cape pretending to call up the Devil . . . he gave every appearance, enough to impress the boys, of going into a trance and speaking in strange voices . . . and by pretending to be able to summon up spirits beyond the grave.

All Wilding's victims believed in the rituals and ceremonies. He convinced them his Satanism was genuine. He also sexually abused them.

Wilding pleaded guilty. His defence counsel, Christopher Hotton, challenged only the prosecution's implied suggestion that Wilding had used the Satanism as a trick. Hotton told the judge: 'The defendant has a genuine and longstanding interest in the supernatural and the occult.'

3. Brian Williams: sexual abuse of fifteen juvenile girls/boys, Old Bailey, 23 July 1987.

Sentence: 11 years in prison.

Williams plied his victims with cannabis and vodka before sexually assaulting them on an altar dedicated to Satan. He also forced them to abuse each other.

The rituals were performed with an inverted pentagram drawn on the floor in blood taken from Williams and one of his victims. Each child was 're-christened' with a satanic pseudonym on initiation into the group.

One victim told the Court:

He said he was the Devil in disguise and started out by making us take part in black magic ceremonies. We had to cut ourselves with razors and draw pentagrams with blood on paper. If you cried or refused to go along with what he wanted he would slap you or say he could make one of his disciples kill you.

Sex with the children invariably followed. All the victims believed in the satanic rituals as genuine. One girl was convinced by Williams that she was pregnant and that the child's father was the Devil. All were terrified.

4. Hazel Paul: false imprisonment/grievous bodily harm/assisting sexual abuse of juvenile girl, Old Bailey, 25 July 1988.

Sentence: 5 years in prison.

Paul was convicted of falsely imprisoning a 15-year-old girl and inflicting on her grievous bodily harm during satanic rituals. She also hypnotised the girl and encouraged a male friend to sexually abuse the girl.

The jury heard a 15-year-old boy describe how Paul had ordered him to cut and carve the girl during rituals which also involved placing lighted candles on or around the victim's vagina.

Two other defendants were convicted with Paul of the assaults. The jury heard, and accepted by convicting, the explicit details of Paul's satanic rituals.

5. Peter Mackenzie: sexual abuse of thirteen juvenile girls, St Albans Crown Court, August 1989.

Sentence: 15 years in prison.

MacKenzie was sentenced for four rapes and seventeen other sexual assaults. His victims were as young as 6. An accomplice, John Baxter-Taylor, pleaded guilty to one charge of indecent assault and was sentenced to 15 months.

The Court heard how MacKenzie told his victims he was 'Asmodeus', an historic satanic name principally associated with nineteenth-century French Satanism, and made them recite prayers dedicated to him. He terrified his victims by warning them that unless they took part in the rituals and kept silent about the abuse they would die.

6. Reginald Harris: sexual abuse of two juvenile girls, Worcester Crown Court, 8 August 1990.

Sentence: 2.5 years in prison.

Harris admitted two specimen charges of unlawful sexual intercourse with a 15-year-old girl and her younger sister. The Court heard that he had used satanic rituals to frighten and dominate the children.

Trial Judge Roy Ward said:

You took the trust and affection of these girls to seduce and corrupt them. You aggravated the matter by seeking to obtain dominance of their minds by the pretence of witchcraft or black magic to continue gratifying your desires.

Harris told his victims he was a 'high priest'. The children accepted the rituals as genuine and were successfully terrified by Harris's satanic practice. The Court also heard how he had drawn up a satanic 'coven contract of marriage' to the older girl.

7. A 57-year old satanist (unnamed for legal reasons): rape of 10-year-old girl, Liverpool Crown Court, 3 July 1992.

Sentence: 12 years in prison.

The Court heard how the man had raped his victim (his niece, hence no identification legally possible) two or three times per week between the ages of 10 and 12.

Judge Dennis Clark told the man: 'Your fascination with the occult or devil-worship played a part in impelling you towards this evil behaviour.'

The Court heard details of a 'black magic room' where the abuser kept an altar and ritual equipment. When the child was 12 she became pregnant as a result of the abuse and was required by her uncle to give birth in 'the black magic room'.

The evidence was clearly given that the victim was convinced by and terrified of her uncle's satanic rituals. He threatened to rape her younger sister and kill her pets if she ever spoke of the abuse. On one occasion he snapped the neck of one of her pets in front of her and drowned another.

The Court also heard how, on three occasions before the final interview which led to the man's arrest, social workers had interviewed the girl. She denied any abuse had taken place on each occasion – even though DNA testing subsequently proved it to have taken place.

Chapter 24

Questions survivors and professionals ask the police

Names, identities and background details have been changed wherever necessary to protect confidentiality.

The three main respondents were (1) an Inspector from the north of England, (2) a Sergeant from London (both male) and (3) a woman Police Constable from the Midlands. Sometimes they were speaking on behalf of colleagues with whom they had worked. Where all shared similar views I have grouped their response together (A); individual responses are identified by numbers (1, 2, 3). Unfortunately, they did not feel able to give their names publicly.

Q: What is the task of a police officer on hearing from someone about a crime which involves ritual abuse?

A: You have to listen to any allegations of crime and decide the next stages of the investigation, whether it would be medical investigation, taking a statement, speaking to other witnesses, or speaking to a more senior officer for approval if it involves a murder allegation. You need to establish where it has happened as there are clear police boundaries which are determined by where a crime happens. There are occasions where a judgement is made straight away that the allegation is false or cannot be substantiated.

Q: Are there particular problems with adult victims reporting ritual abuse rather than other abuse?

A: Police officers want a victim who is rational, provides physical and forensic evidence in a fairly short space of time so that the investigation can begin. Ritual victims need much more time, patience and often give disjointed and incorrect information, sometimes deliberately and sometimes unconsciously.

For example, police were in no doubt medically and forensically that one such victim had been tortured, even though they were unsure when she described symbols being daubed on her door and substances being pushed through her letterbox. On setting up a surveillance camera they found the victim daubing her own doors with paint. Nevertheless, they were still prepared to continue an investigation and understand the complexity of contradictory evidence.

Ritual abuse victims may have no clear memory of the abuse, may be or appear to be mentally unstable or be in trance or other dissociated states with the occasional added ingredient of multiple personality.

Q: Is dissociation a general issue regarding rape victims or witnesses to murders?
A: Occasionally rape victims are traumatised to the point of dissociation but it is uncommon. Victims are obviously shocked but it is usually a reaction to a current incident not to something twenty years ago.

Q: How much does the officer's belief in the victim's authenticity play a part in the depth and nature of the investigation?
A: The officer's belief will play a big part in the investigation because if you have any doubts in the beginning the investigation is likely to be superficial. Any line of enquiry that should be followed up will be but the amount of manpower and resources allocated may be limited.

With child, as opposed to adult, abuse, police officers are encouraged to listen carefully to the child and in the main believe the child, and in consequence allegations by children get treated and dealt with very thoroughly.

Q: Does your level in the police hierarchy effect whether your instincts about a case are given support?
1. Even where I have supported junior officers over following up such allegations the amount of manpower needed for proper surveillance might need chief constable backing.
2. Yes. Officers might be given little in the way of support and resources to investigate a ritual case – working a lot of personal overtime to complete the investigation – ending up with additional allegations of crimes being made including murders which they were not allowed to record because senior officers had doubts about the information.
3. Officers have had their belief shaken by lack of support in senior officers. The more distance that supervisor had from the victim the less belief there is.

Q: Have any of the victims you have come across mentioned involvement with the Masons and – if so – do you feel police masonic involvement complicates the issue?
1. This was not anything mentioned by victims I have worked with.
2. Yes. One victim made a statement that we would not get to the bottom of satanist abuse because of the involvement of freemasonry.
3. Yes. One witness I needed to speak to would not speak to a male officer because of her concern that he may be a freemason. Her client had made various comments about mason involvement in satanist abuse.

Q: How can we present cases in a better way in court to be more successful in obtaining a conviction?
1. There is no reason why we should present cases with the victim first. By presenting medical evidence at the beginning – this would immediately allow the

jury to know that something has happened to the victim. We should make greater use of expert witnesses to explain issues like lack of affect in chronic victims – which always has an adverse emotional effect on juries.

2. I think we should make better use of videos for children. Most of the cases have been concerning children rather than adults. There should be more video evidence provided for court and therefore our interview techniques on video must be perfect with absolutely no leading questions so that nothing has to be excluded.

3. Use of the video link – rather than the victim standing in the courtroom. The courtroom itself is a terrifying ordeal. Even behind screens in the court they can still see the jury, the judge and the barristers and literally have to walk through the public area of the courts to get into the witness box.

Q: What do you think of the way some barristers have omitted ritual abuse in order to secure an 'ordinary' abuse conviction out of the fear that the jury would totally disbelieve ritual abuse and thereby disregard anything else the child said?

1. You are trying to achieve a conviction on the evidence you have. There is not an offence for witchcraft or being a witch and if you can present a straightforward case of sexual abuse or serious assault without causing more confusion or disbelief to anybody then it is wise to exclude the bizarre material.

2. Introducing evidence in relation to ritual abuse and bizarre circumstances and obtaining a conviction would surely make it easier on subsequent occasions in court to accept such a subject.

Q: How prepared are police for the emotional impact of hearing about chronic torture and abuse?

1. Not particularly well. There is reliance on the fact that police deal with traumatic incidents on a daily basis and you are expected to deal with that. Perhaps there is more of a support network recently dealing with post-traumatic stress.

2. Officers who deal with child protection work do have multi-agency training. However, overall there is no proper support system working on a daily basis for those dealing with abuse victims.

3. You hear details of abuse of such magnitude and from such an early age and yet – there is always more to come. Some police officers are just not prepared for this.

Q: What was the hardest evidence for you to hear over and above the mental state of the victim?

1. A woman described a ritual from her childhood where an animal was sacrificed. She could hear the cat screaming and was made to drink the blood and also witnessed a baby's head being cut off. Being naive she picked up the head to try and fit it together again and fix it.

2. What did my stomach in was her talking about orgies during a ceremony – animals used for sacrifice and in a sexual way – she was punished for not doing something and made to eat dog excrement mixed with spiders. When she was

sick, as a punishment for being sick she was made to eat more, including the vomit.

3.   I remember a sexual abuse victim who was the scapegoat of the family from her earliest memory. At one point she said she was told she was going to a wonderful party to have a wonderful time only to be the prime victim of abuse in a ceremony. The daily emotional deprivation was enormous – let alone the abuse. She was just so sad.

Q: Why do you think we have so few convictions?

1.   Lack of concrete evidence, both physical and forensic. The victims often speak of videos and photographs being taken – or of being raped – or incidents happening in certain locations and on a number of occasions these facts have never been proven.

2.   Lack of knowledge of what we are dealing with. If you do not understand the methods that have been used on the victims and the reasons why sometimes the victims do not tell the truth then you can be misled to look for evidence and not find it when, with more knowledge, you would have tackled the enquiry from a different perspective. You also have to understand that the adult victim may still be involved in some way and can be passing information back and forth to the group without your knowledge.

3.   Fear at what you are hearing can make you want to actively disbelieve the disclosures which may also mean that you do not carry out a thorough investigation and do not find the evidence. Also the issue of cover-ups or clamping down on cases must be mentioned.

Q: What would make the police task easier in these cases?

1.   A need to have an advice point – a central place where people with experience of these cases can advise other officers and have written material available that would be useful – such as continuing the Scotland Yard Ritual Abuse Research Team.

2.   Additional training – even if it is to do with understanding dissociation and dealing with multiple personality.

3.   A support network for dealing with the distressing material.

Q: What forensic actions or clues would you like police colleagues to take or be on the lookout for?

1.   Children and adults have spoken of being given drugs, and being made to eat or drink alien substances. I think it could be useful in suspected ritual allegations as a matter of course to take a urine or blood sample.

2.   Close-up photographs of wounds or casts of teeth marks of the victim would help to differentiate self-inflicted wounds from externally inflicted ones.

3.   Take note of tattoos, symbols, jewellery items, ritual paraphernalia (ropes, cords, candles, pentagrams, inverted crosses, strange alphabets, chalices, animal parts, effigies). Check the nature of drippings from candles. Make careful notes of all dates of abuse.

Q: What do you think would aid ritual abuse investigations?

1.   The work must be multi-agency, no one agency can deal with it. Not even the police can deal alone, they need the support of others. We need patience, understanding and a greater knowledge of the subject, linked to an intelligence gathering system.

2.   It may be that someone in therapy who is having flashbacks should try and complete as much as possible before reporting to the police.

3.   We need to keep our focus on listening to the child and adult alleged victim rather than critically focusing on how the professionals have handled what they have heard.

Chapter 25

Ritual organised abuse
Management issues

Judith Trowell

Dr Judith Trowell is a Consultant Child Psychiatrist and Psychoanalyst in the Tavistock Clinic. She was the independent expert for the Orkney Inquiry.

Names, identities and background details have been changed wherever necessary to protect confidentiality.

INTRODUCTION

Child sexual abuse has an enormous impact on the children, the families, the alleged abuser and on the community. In addition, the impact on professions is enormous. However senior, however experienced, professionals have to recognise that sexual abuse can enter their minds, their consciousness, their feelings and almost at times their bodies. The impact of ritual organised sexual abuse is much greater than the sum of sexual abuse of a number of children. The terror and the emotional abuse of the children is of a different order and this permeates the families and thence the professionals.

The emotional impact is such that the mind cannot contain it all. This leads to what is known as splitting and projection, or denial or manic flight. Thus the children may become as zombies with most of their humanity, their personality, split off and closed down, or they may deny that anything has happened. But this is at such a price that other aspects of their functioning are distorted or cease. A child may become excited, overactive, rushing about out of control unable to acknowledge anything is wrong (manic flight) or the child may become blaming, attacking, critical of others and feel very threatened, and at times these paranoid projections can become so powerful that the child believes he or she is in mortal danger. At times this may well be a reality. These processes in the children can also, and usually do, involve the families, and then spread into the professional network. Hence the importance of good management.

DEFINITIONS

Management

By 'management' is meant the task of organising and being responsible for the delivery of a service. This requires some knowledge and understanding of the service to be delivered, but above all a capacity to create clear lines of responsibility and accountability and a structure where staff undertaking very difficult and stressful work can be clear about their roles, their tasks, their responsibility. Management also involves staff selection and staff training and development.

The management task is to:

1 appoint competent staff;
2 provide relevant training and in-service development;
3 establish clear lines of responsibility in the hierarchy, from front line workers to middle management to senior management;
4 provide clear routes for decision-making and clarify the place of supervision;
5 provide a flexible structure that can respond to crises and that can recognise overload in an individual staff member or the staff group;
6 provide appropriate leadership and have the capacity to take authority;
7 liaise appropriately with other services.

What is meant by 'ritual abuse'

In the UK the Department of Health have preferred the term 'organised abuse' (HMSO, 1991: 38) and use the definition:

> Organised abuse is a generic term which covers abuse which may involve a number of abusers, a number of abused children and young people and often encompasses different forms of abuse. It involves, to a greater or lesser extent, an element of organisation. A wide range of abusing activity is covered by the term, from small paedophile or pornographic rings, often, but not always, organised for profit, with most participants knowing one another, to large networks of individual groups or families which may be spread more widely and in which not all participants will be known to each other. Some organised groups may use bizarre or ritualised behaviours, sometimes associated with particular 'belief' systems. This can be a powerful mechanism to frighten children into not telling of their experiences.

This wide definition is too loose and fails to address such complex issues as how to deal with children abusing smaller children.

McFadyen et al. (1993) have produced a definition of 'ritual abuse': ritual abuse is the involvement of children in physical, psychological and sexual abuse associated with repeated activities (rituals), which purport to relate the abuse to contexts of a religious, magical or supernatural kind. This is gaining some acceptance as a working definition. Sinason (see the Introduction to this volume) has made a useful distinction in the use of the term 'satanic' and has substituted 'satanist' which avoids the need to make a religious statement about the existence of Satan.

What then are the management issues? As already indicated, the initial problem is to find agreement about what is 'management', what is 'ritual organised (satanist) abuse' and what is 'child sexual abuse'.

Taking the child as the starting-point seems the best way forward, although the most important issue in all instances has been, 'Is it possible to hold the child in mind?' Can the child's best interest come first? A child or some children are thought to have been physically, sexually and psychologically abused, often in a particularly perverted and corrupting way. To investigate this further, a number of agencies all need to be involved. Social services carry the lead role in child protection; they have a statutory role to play. The police have a lead role in stopping crime and protecting the public. Given that sexual abuse is a criminal offence, they must be involved. Health workers need to be involved if the child has been physically or sexually abused. There may be current signs or a significant past history and some family history. Education workers may also have vital information on the child's functioning and a perspective on the family. There may also be involvement with voluntary sector organisations. Hence starting with the child leads immediately to a multi-agency, multi-disciplinary network.

WORKING TOGETHER

In most incidents of organised, ritual (satanist) abuse, there has been a breakdown of inter-agency working. In Cleveland there was a breakdown at middle and senior management level between police, various social services and health workers. This was considered in detail by Butler-Sloss in the *Report of the Inquiry into Child Abuse in Cleveland* (HMSO, 1988). In other cases where there has been a public inquiry inter-agency conflict has been a very significant factor in the handling of the case. In the *Orkney Inquiry* (HMSO, 1992), inter-agency conflict and difficulties played an important role both before and during the exploration of the allegations.

In each geographical area in the UK, there is a body whose task is to develop agreed inter-agency policy and agree procedures on how to handle all forms of child abuse. The Area Child Protection Committee (ACPC) has in England and Wales a role and responsibilities as specified by the Department of Health *Working Together Under the Children Act 1989* (HMSO, 1991). Nevertheless, there have been enormous problems in arriving at agreement on how to handle ritual or organised abuse.

The ACPC is generally composed of:

Social Services Department – purchasers, providers + leisure
Health – FHSA, GPs, etc., hospitals (providers) – management, doctors
Nurses, purchasers, health authorities

Police, probation, voluntary sector
Education – ESW – primary, secondary, tertiary

Why is it taking so long for ACPCs to sort out their response to organised/ritual abuse? The issues seem to be:

1 recognition,
2 training resources for this,
3 massive reorganisation and change in the agencies themselves, particularly Social Services/Health/Education/Police,
4 reluctance to consider it (it wouldn't happen here or does it exist).

Recognition

A consensus seems to be emerging that if ritual abuse does crop up, then it shall be handled as any case of child sexual abuse. Good practice is what is important. This is certainly correct; however, it denies the complexity of organised ritual abuse. It denies the potential awfulness, the impact on the children, families and workers and it denies the difficulties of the all-too-frequent ramifications of the many adults involved – some of the adults may be in the relevant agencies as professionals. We therefore need agreed procedures on how such an eventuality will be handled. There must be an agreed policy.

In the Orkney incident there were enormous problems because professionals did not trust each other. There was suspicion of involvement in the abuse by certain key individuals in the community and there was no policy, no previous planning to help.

Senior management in all the agencies need to ensure there is an agreed view on what is organised/ritual abuse and how it will be handled – when, not if, it arises. This means senior management need to be aware of the possibility and need to think about it. They should either attend ACPC themselves or ensure their representative has sufficient authority to take decisions and agree policy and procedures with colleagues or other agencies. This does not happen often enough.

Training

The training implications follow naturally. In order to handle organised abuse, there needs to be training at all levels in each agency, so that all staff know their agency guidelines and they all have the skills required. There also needs to be inter-agency training involving all levels, but particularly front line workers, specialist interviewers (police and social services) middle and senior managers, training officers and supervisors.

Senior managers need to take the responsibility for ensuring that this is done. The resources have to be found. This includes using skilled trainers and giving staff the time to train. Multi-agency, multi-disciplinary training is vital and essential but it is costly.

Reorganisation and massive change

All the key agencies are undergoing major reorganisation. This is involving the introduction of a whole new way of working: the purchaser/provider division. In each agency, there are now staff who control a budget and with this must pay for other staff to provide the service. There have already been problems with this new system, partly because it is new, but also because the person with the budget, holding the purse strings, may either not know about their responsibilities in the area of child protection or may be in a situation where settling priorities may leave services for children and families competing with other, more pressing needs such as those of the elderly, or community care, or just balancing the books.

In this climate of change and uncertainty it is very difficult for management. Managers are anxious to preserve their jobs, so find it hard to press for resources. There may also be a lack of clarity for them about the exact boundary of their responsibility. In the purchaser/provider split, where does the final responsibility and authority lie? It should be clear, but frequently is not. Is it the purchaser's responsibility to ensure good management in the provider team – good supervision, good training, appointment of competent staff, etc. – or is it the responsibility of the senior person in the provider team? Who finally carries responsibility for an investigation, the purchaser or the provider? This must be made clear at the start, but often isn't.

Does it exist?

The *Cleveland Inquiry Report* (HMSO, 1988) confirmed that child sexual abuse exists. This is therefore a very recent development and it is important to remember that understanding and awareness of the use of children as objects, for sexual gratification of adults, has taken a very long time. Kempe's seminal paper on physical abuse – the battered baby syndrome – was in 1963, and it was almost a quarter of a century later before sexual abuse of children was confirmed by the 'establishment'. The field is growing and developing and those working in this area need to be very careful how awareness is taken forward. Already there is evidence of a backlash, and this should be seen as inevitable and probably appropriate. It is important always to consider the best interests of the child, even if at times this may mean doing nothing about the abuser or taking civil rather than criminal proceedings.

It is not surprising therefore, as the public is getting used to the notion that child sexual abuse really exists, to expect acknowledgement that ritual organised abuse exists and that in some cases this can involve the use of religions, satanic symbols and activity.

In addition to the wish not to know, there is also, sadly, some indication that those involved may be in positions of influence and so may be part of the vociferous clamour that supports the view that it is all in the minds of fanatics.

A more realistic reason not to know, is the resource question. If it does not exist there is no need for policies, procedures, planning, training or, even more worrying, actually recognising that there may be a case in your area of responsibility. Some managers' wish not to know can therefore be understood. Sadly, there is now sufficient evidence to indicate that there are sex rings involving children and adults, some of which involve terror and emotional abuse and the use of rituals and religious activities. It seems unlikely it will disappear. Much more likely is that, as with abuse by women, and adolescent abusers, increased awareness will lead to more recognition that it does indeed exist.

SPECIFIC MANAGEMENT ISSUES

Use of a consultant

When a case of organised ritual abuse is suspected, a number of decisions need to be made. First of these is not to panic, to take time to plan without undue haste but also not to dither and delay too long. If there is not a consultant in the locality senior enough with appropriate experience, it could be helpful to bring in a consultant from outside the area; someone of whatever discipline, who has experience and sufficient respect and authority to influence the decision-making, but who will not take line management responsibility. This person should be able to work at all levels, but must work with senior and middle management to help all involved to think clearly, recognise the emotional impact and, drawing on past experience, offer advice in the planning.

Planning

Careful consideration must be given to the use of planning and strategy meetings, and the use of case conferences. Where there are questions about who needs to know, there needs to be careful discussion and good record-keeping, even if in a separate locked file. The strategy meeting is often the crucial forum for thinking about how to proceed.

The issues to be considered include:

1 Gathering all the relevant information from all the agencies, community groups, etc.
2 If there are to be investigatory interviews, what are the legal steps needed in relation to the children, the alleged abusers?
3 Placement of the children – if removal is decided on, then suitable foster placements must be recruited, or substitute care organised.
4 Physical examination by a competent professional.
5 Interviews of children by a competent social services professional/policeperson team. Consideration needs to be given to the need for a multi-disciplinary input.
6 Work with the parents/carers.

7　Decisions need to be made about who will carry overall responsibility and ensure co-ordination of all involved.

Case managers

In organised ritual abuse, there are usually several children involved. Each child is different and each family is different. It needs to be clarified how this will remain a central focus.

A possible model involves the use of case managers. A case manager may be of any discipline, but needs experience of sufficient respect and authority (see Figure 25.1).

The discipline and agency of the case manager is not of itself vital; what is important is that all the agencies recognise the role. It may be that each family has to have a case manager from police and social services. If this is the case, then these two must work very closely together. If agencies can agree on the case managers, then the way forward is often smoother. The case managers need to meet regularly with the case co-ordinators to ensure the overall handling of the case is correct.

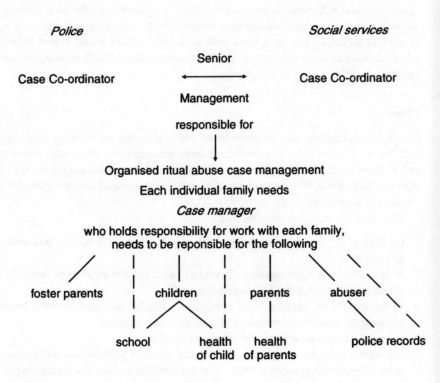

Figure 25.1 Case management model

Supervision

Linked to the appointment of case managers is the need to identify appropriate supervisors. Supervision involves several tasks: managerial supervision, appropriately undertaken by the case manager; case supervision, looking at the content of the work – this is preferably undertaken by an outside supervisor, without line management responsibility in the case. Personal supervision involves considering the impact of the work on the worker. This can be undertaken by the case work supervisor, but back-up facilities for personal consultation or personal therapy may well be needed and should be available without implications for the worker's competence.

Assessment

There are two issues to be considered in relation to assessment. First, staffing; that is, who will do all the work involved. Many areas will not have sufficient skilled professionals, they will need to be found from somewhere. In different areas different arrangements will be made. Skilled workers in adjacent authorities may be released or workers in different areas of the same authorities. But quite often it may be decided to bring in skilled workers. This may be sensible, or it may be a way out in a crisis. What is important is that there is clarity about what is required of these workers, that their skills are confirmed and what the overall management structure will be.

There also needs to be clarification of the assessments required: how these will be carried out, what form of recording will be used, how many interviews are envisaged and who is going to do which piece of the work.

The second area that needs consideration is which aspects of a full assessment are indicated in this case.

The range of tasks include:

Children:	history – physical and educational
Interviews with individual children:	mental state assessment
	developmental assessment
	investigative interviews
	physical examination
	sibling relationships
Parents:	social history
	family interaction
	parental couple assessment
	parent–child assessment
Alleged abuser:	history
	mental state
	interview assessment
	criminal record
	police check

School:	educational functioning of child/children
	peer relationships
	activities
Foster parent:	assessment of child
Substitute carers:	in care

Management need to be involved in the discussion about which aspects of the assessment are needed in this case and how the work will be co-ordinated and supervised.

Equal opportunities

There are many equal opportunity issues that need to be considered. These apply to both staff and children and families. In any form of child sexual abuse there are inevitably conflicts and highly emotionally charged situations. This can be understood as a normal and inevitable sequelae of sexual abuse, which touches very primitive feelings and reactions in the child/children, the family and thence the professionals. Sexual abuse is frequently the abuse of girls by men. This can lead to complex reactions between men and women professionals. Beatrix Campbell has written an eloquent account of the events in Cleveland, highlighting the problems between the police (mainly men) and the Social Services Department (mainly women).

In organised ritual abuse, the issue of gender must be taken seriously in the planning. Constant vigilance is needed to ensure that any emerging problems are recognised and discussed, so that professional conflicts do not reverse the distress and difficulties in decision-making and run the risk of involving the child/children and families.

There are gender issues for the children too. In organised abuse, boys as well as girls may be involved. Where possible, a child's expressed wish to be interviewed by a male or female interviewer/s should not be neglected. In reality, any sufficiently skilled interviewers available will be the gender mix, and only rarely is it that all children can have their choice. This needs to be acknowledged and discussed with them. Gender issues arise in the families depending on the gender of the alleged abuser/s and the impact this has on the child/family members.

Skin colour, race, culture and class are also important issues to consider. All-white interviewers involved with black children and black families can make for a very difficult situation. All too easily, racism and oppressive attitudes and practice can become entangled. Great vigilance is needed to ensure feelings are acknowledged at each stage and practice monitored to ensure good practice and decision-making. Culture and class are more subtle dimensions but there are still prejudices, and judgements are often made on the basis of these rather than objective data.

Disability needs special consideration; where a child has a physical disability, he or she can be particularly vulnerable to exploitation.

Deaf children or children with a speech disability are often targeted. Where a child or a family member has a physical disability, it is very important that the professionals consider the implications for the child and themselves. Where a child has a learning disability, particular management issues arise which require specific decision-making in planning the interviews and, of course, a specialist interviewer.

CONCLUSIONS

Management in organised ritual abuse is a challenge, but there is sufficient knowledge now to enable managers to draw on the experience of others. In summary, management needs to ensure good practice, as rational and objective decision-making as possible and minimal further trauma to the children. Working together with other agencies is essential. No one agency has all the skills or all the knowledge. It is a sign of strength not weakness to use a consultant, for staff to have personal consultation or therapy. This work is very stressful and staff and middle managers need this to be recognised. Their work load may appear reduced during such a case. Above all, management should think beyond assessment, investigation and any court work. Post-protection work will be needed for the children, families and substitute care. Staff and their managers will also need time to recover.

REFERENCES

HMSO (1988) *Report of the Inquiry into Child Abuse in Cleveland 1987*, Lord Justice Butler-Sloss DBE, London, HMSO.

HMSO (1991) *Working Together Under the Children Act 1989. A Guide to Arrangements for Inter-agency Co-operation for the Protection of Children from Abuse*, London, HMSO.

HMSO (1992) *Report of the Inquiry into the Removal of Children from Orkney in February 1991*, Lord Clyde, Edinburgh, HMSO.

McFadyen, A., Hanks, H. and James, C. (1993) 'Ritual abuse: a definition', *Child Abuse Review* 2, 35–41.

Chapter 26

A Service Manager's perspective

Catherine Doran

Ms Catherine Doran, Service Manager of Child Protection in the London Borough of Haringey, is currently seconded as a Child Protection Consultant to the London Region of the Social Services Inspectorate. She has been a specialist in the field of child protection for the last ten years after secondment on a Department of Health training course on Child Sexual Abuse at the Tavistock Clinic. Her background is as a social worker. She is still a practitioner in this field but her main focus of work is around policy, training and the management of Child Protection Services.

Names, identities and background details have been changed wherever necessary to protect confidentiality.

Local authorities face major dilemmas in how to effectively protect children who are being victimised by adults in an organised and ritualistic way. The organisational and ritualistic elements of sexual, emotional and physical abuse make planning, investigation, gathering evidence and protecting children much more complex. What we know about ritualistic abuse is that it includes all the known components of abuse but the systems of silencing are more powerful throughout the network and more difficult to get to grips with.

It is only within the last five years that professionals have been able to intervene effectively in individual family systems in detecting, investigating and protecting children from further abuse. It was only in 1991 with *Working Together* (HMSO, 1991) that there was government help in assisting this process. The *Memorandum of Good Practice* (HMSO, 1992) also acknowledges that we are at a starting-point in effective multi-disciplinary management and practice.

With organised sexual abuse rings we are only beginning to build up the expertise to successfully investigate, as only a relatively small number of workers have been involved in such cases. However, it is not just an issue of experience that makes these cases difficult. Many social services departments and local police child protection teams are aware of possible networks of abuse operating in their areas but are frequently 'stymied' evidentially, emotionally and practically.

Timing is a crucial issue. There is not only the clinical timing of how to support and protect a child from further victimisation, or the emotional impact of a dropped lost case, but also the right timing evidentially. Managers and workers have to balance forensic and clinical needs and there is a painful tension between the two. Rings of any kind evoke more fear in the professional system. There are often two polarised responses to this. There can be a strong impulse to give up or a rush to save the child or children precipitously. These dynamics are reflected in all areas of child abuse but the nature of an organised ring accentuates them.

While these areas of work – organised abuse and satanic ritualised abuse – are still relatively unresearched, managers of child protection services have to accept that they need to work alongside specialist clinicians.

If I suspected in my own authority an organised ring which had possible satanic ritual elements to it I would ensure that, prior to even beginning to plan any intervention, I had the guaranteed involvement of specialist clinicians – people who have the experience of working with such victims and survivors. This is because the real knowledge of the experience can only come from the victim and work with the victim and not from a secondary level.

Many authorities are currently developing their guidelines around organised and ritual abuse. When interventions of this nature are being considered we know that it is imperative that senior management at all levels, i.e. Director of Social Services, Senior Health Managers and Chief Superintendents, are involved in acknowledging and sanctioning the planned processes of investigation. It is my belief that it is imperative, even at this early stage, that we call upon experienced professionals in this area of work. Many professionals who are skilled in other areas of abuse – like Child Protection Co-Ordinators – can be inexperienced in these areas and yet be pressurised to be seen as a specialist in this task.

My reason for arguing the case for specialist clinicians is that I believe that we have to have an understanding of the organisational and belief systems that these children are living in, and also the layers of silence, fear, denial and disbelief.

To even begin to plan forensic interviews with satanically abused children we have to accept that the skills needed to structure and sift through bizarre and shocking material are enormous.

Workers need to know the time, place and details of what has happened to understand the child's experience. They have to understand the children's point of view of the context of where the sexual and physical abuse takes place. But the core of what they need to find out in the interview is not about the rituals but about the abusive experience. Nevertheless, the rituals will actually be the layers that will stop them getting to the abusive experience, i.e. the evidence. They will also impede all the other professionals in the network without prior experience or training. This is not the same with individual family systems. Those professionals who have greater experience of sexual abuse and understanding of the continuum of awfulness can often facilitate those children into providing greater detail.

Without knowing the details of what happens in organised and satanic abuse workers will be overwhelmed and partially immobilised by what they are hearing.

This makes individuals unable to sift through what they are hearing in a balanced, forensically acceptable way.

It is important to point out that professionals accept that the guidance in the *Memorandum* (HMSO, 1992) provides a very good foundation and structure. However, it is important that professionals, in their planning for interventions and interviews, are clear that the protection of children and the evidence needed for that purpose should over-ride the need for forensically acceptable evidence. As Ray Bull commented (ACPP Study Day on the *Memorandum of Good Practice*), it is important that although professionals try to achieve a minimum shared structure, there needs to be flexibility to ensure the child's best clinical/ protection needs.

I do not believe that workers have to go into an interview room with a child and believe that child was satanically sexually abused. The three things workers should hold onto in that room are (1) they are in that room because there is a high index of suspicion that something has happened to that child which is causing distress to the child and professional concern, (2) they are holding the fact that satanic abuse does exist and can happen, but (3) they are also holding the possibility that it might or might not have happened to this child.

My limited contact with cases of ritualistic sexual abuse has always produced fear, anxiety and disbelief in both myself and the professional system. The fear and feelings of being overwhelmed and disorganised, however, must not over- take or cloud the task.

In all the cases I have been involved in, there seems to be a pattern in the way children's and adults' accounts are told. The ritualistic and sexual abuse are so intertwined that, to the outsider, it becomes difficult to separate the two and often, evidentially, one cancels out the other. The rituals are often so bizarre and unreal that they have the effect of invalidating the testimony of the child and adult. Interviewers can become paralysed or allow the rituals to overtake the interview.

Careful planning of forensic interviews in these cases of suspected ritualistic/ organised abuse is imperative. Interviewers have to devise techniques not only to break through the silencing factors, but also to help the child focus on the evidence. Bizarre rituals (which are also part of the abuse) 'mask' and negate the sexually and physically abusive acts.

I once interviewed an 8-year-old girl who was recounting her grandfather raping her. She also talked about witches, masks, eating spiders and drinking urine. Keeping the child on track was difficult. The fine balance between hearing and acknowledging her abusive rituals and focusing her on the *crime* was my clinical objective. The layers and layers of ritualistic abuse would have to be dealt with in therapeutic sessions.

One key factor in interviewing these children is to create a sense of strength, knowingness and calm. The 8-year-old girl asked me, 'Do you know about witches and spiders?' I said 'I do. But I will need your help to understand it better. But first, I want you to tell me all about your grandfather and you.' We would return to the witches and spiders later. My main focus in a forensic interview was to separate the sexual abuse from the abusive rituals. This, I feel, is a daunting task for both the interviewer and the child.

REFERENCES

HMSO (1991) *Working Together Under the Children Act 1989. A Guide to Arrangements for Inter-agency Co-operation for the Protection of Children from Abuse*, London, HMSO.

HMSO (1992) *Memorandum of Good Practice on Video Recorded Interviews with Child Witnesses for Criminal Proceedings, London, HMSO.*

Chapter 27

Treating satanist abuse survivors
The Leeds experience

Chris Hobbs and Jane Wynne

Dr Chris Hobbs and Dr Jane Wynne are Consultant Community Paediatricians in the Departments of Community Paediatrics and Child Health, St James University Hospital and Clarendon Wing, Leeds General Infirmary, Leeds.

Names, identities and background details have been changed wherever necessary to protect confidentiality.

Work in child abuse in Leeds started in the late 1960s when a paediatrician and social worker began to recognise physical abuse and neglect. In the early 1980s a wider group of professionals turned their attention to sexual abuse and by 1985 the number of children referred to paediatricians had increased rapidly to about one hundred in that year. From the beginning there was an appreciation of the need for multi-disciplinary work in child abuse and for links between investigative and treatment programmes.

Attention was drawn to the importance of the paediatric contribution. Buggery, for example, is a common although previously unrecognised form of abuse and was associated with a pattern of clinical signs, symptoms and descriptions by the child (Hobbs and Wynne, 1986). One interesting observation was that clinicians traditionally had never looked at the child's anus or the prepubertal female genitalia.

The finding that buggery was a common form of abuse led to considerable disbelief. There was extensive correspondence in the medical journals and, at the time of the 'Cleveland Crisis', front page publicity and criticism over methods of diagnosing sexual abuse and more specifically anal abuse. The influential *Cleveland Inquiry Report* (HMSO, 1988) confirmed the reality of child sexual abuse and there is now much more information and agreement about the signs and symptoms of sexual abuse than five years ago (Royal College of Physicians, 1991).

In 1990 we examined 130 children who were both sexually abused and battered (Hobbs and Wynne, 1990). Over a four-year period there were seventy-seven girls and fifty-three boys of all ages with a peak age between 2 and 7 years. The series included four children who were killed, six with fractures and twenty-two with burns or scalds, including children with scars from earlier inadequately explained burns. Most of the children had abnormal anal and/or genital findings.

This group is important as it has helped us recognise the violent and sadistic nature of many cases of sexual abuse. It has moved thinking away from the 'loving gone wrong' notion of sexual abuse and highlighted the important link between violent sexual abuse and fatal child abuse (Hobbs and Wynne, 1993).

The link between sexual abuse and burns continues to be found in work in Leeds. The premeditated and sometimes repetitive way that adults may deliberately burn children made us consider torture as the only accurate description. However, several medical colleagues were unwilling to entertain this possibility and diagnosed unlikely or exotic diseases. Only when the children were protected did the marks stop appearing.

Other cases where unusual or bizarre findings have been noted relate to the specific findings from anal or genital abuse. With the experience of the past few years and the arrival of information from North America on ritual abuse, another piece of the jigsaw began to slot into place. Some of the more bizarre findings from the examinations began to make sense.

LEEDS RITUALISTIC STUDY GROUP

Ritualistic abuse of children is a particularly disturbing form of child maltreatment that has recently come to the attention of health care professionals, mental health professionals and law enforcement officials.

(Kelley, 1993)

In 1991 a group of professionals who had experienced cases of child abuse that included ritualistic elements, started to meet. The group was multi-disciplinary and provided an opportunity for discussion. What was clear from the outset was that these professionals had heard experiences described by children which were bizarre and incompletely understood. In some cases, observations made about children in foster care or in residential homes provided more information. The group invited an academic theologian who had no experience of working clinically with children. He was able to freely question clinical information and professional experience.

In addition to the background of work on child abuse in general, other work in Leeds on child sex rings (Wild and Wynne, 1986) provided an understanding of complex social organisation in child abuse. In these rings there was no recognition of satanic or ritualistic abuse. However, the powerful forces which bound the children together in secrecy were understood as well as the way the children themselves could appreciate and use power. One important lesson learned from this earlier experience was just how effectively the secrets were kept. These extensive rings involving hundreds of children had been identified mainly in a single area in the south of the city. In other similar socioeconomic districts in the city nothing had been discovered.

The important factor appeared to be the presence of interested and aware professionals (in this case police officers working with social workers) with adequate time, enthusiasm and energy who were able to conduct the investigation and secure numerous successful prosecutions. It was hypothesised that other rings must exist elsewhere, both in other parts of Leeds as well as other cities, but were unrecognised.

The principal task which the study group set itself was to arrive at a definition of ritualistic abuse and this was achieved (McFadyen *et al.*, 1993). The definition which was agreed was:

> Ritual abuse is the involvement of children in physical or sexual abuse associated with repeated activities ('ritual')which purport to relate the abuse to contexts of a religious, magical or supernatural kind.

This definition emphasises the group's primary concern for the abused child. Two important points were the repeated nature of the abuse and the religious function. The definition, however, removed any assumptions about the perpetrator's intentions and did not exclude abuse taking place in non-group contexts. As the approach was primarily from a psychological perspective, the term 'ritualistic' was preferred to 'satanic' or 'occult'. Several members said they could think of cases of ritualistic abuse that were not linked to occult practices. However, it was acknowledged that religion usually had important social contexts and that the existence of 'satanic groups' seemed logical even though experience of the group was limited. The group is linked to the Area Child Protection Committee which produces guidelines for the investigation of organised and ritual abuse.

From a paediatric point of view, ritual abuse appears to be associated with serious long-term consequences for the child. Interestingly, some of the children who have caused the greatest concerns have revealed the most worrying information only after they have been taken into protective care and then often well down the road of protection, support and therapeutic help.

By providing an opportunity to share disturbing and at times frightening information, the group has enabled a clearer understanding to emerge. The work feels very much like a starting-point in an extremely complex area where most professionals tread with cautious reluctance. However, the children's accounts encourage us to continue.

REFERENCES

Hobbs, C.J. and Wynne, J.M. (1986) 'Buggery in childhood – a common syndrome of child abuse', *Lancet* ii, 792–6.

Hobbs, C.J. and Wynne, J.M. (1989) 'Sexual abuse of English boys and girls: the importance of anal examination', *Child Abuse and Neglect* 13, 195–210.

Hobbs, C.J. and Wynne, J.M. (1990) 'The sexually abused battered child', *Archives of Disease in Childhood* 65, 423–7.

Hobbs, C.J. and Wynne, J.M. (1993) 'Fatal child abuse', Chapter 18 in *Child Abuse and Neglect, A Clinician's Handbook*, ed. C.J. Hobbs and J.M. Wynne, Churchill Livingstone, Edinburgh and London.

HMSO (1988) *Report of the Inquiry into Child Abuse in Cleveland, 1987*, Lord Justice Butler-Sloss, London, HMSO.

Kelley, S.J. (1993) 'Ritualistic abuse of children', in *Baillière's Clinical Paediatrics, International Practice and Research. Child Abuse*, ed. C.J. Hobbs and J.M. Wynne, London, Baillière Tindall 1 (1), 31–46.

McFadyen, A., Hanks, H. and James, C. (1993) 'Ritual abuse: a definition', *Child Abuse Review* 2, 35–41.

Royal College of Physicians (1991) *Physical Signs of Sexual Abuse in Children*. A Report of the Royal College of Physicians, London.

Wild, N.J. and Wynne J.M. (1986) 'Child sex rings', *British Medical Journal* 293, 183–5.

Part IV

Common elements and issues in satanist abuse

Chapter 28

Common characteristics in the drawings of ritually abused children and adults

Mary Sue Moore

Dr Mary Sue Moore is a clinical psychologist and psychotherapist. She is a Consultant Psychologist at the Boulder Mental Health Center in Boulder, Colorado, and the Psychology Department of the University of the Colorado in Boulder. Her main research has been on symbolic process in children's drawings, attachment and psychotherapy and psychosomatic processes. She lectures in Europe and Australia.

Names, identities and background details have been changed wherever necessary to protect confidentiality.

INTRODUCTION

This chapter addresses, in a preliminary way, the use of drawings in evaluating and treating individuals who have a history of physical or sexual abuse. In particular, characteristics of the drawings of ritually abused children and adults will be described and compared to the drawings of individuals abused in non-ritualised ways. One danger in writing a brief overview such as this, is that the details of fundamental concepts must be drastically curtailed. These concepts provide the theoretical framework for the use of drawings in clinical settings, and are crucial to understanding why some interpretations of drawings can be considered valid and reliable, and others are simply the observer's opinion. Specific drawing characteristics associated with a history of abuse can be considered valid 'indicators' only when correlated with other independent sources of information in a multi-dimensional assessment of a child. Because of the subjective nature of the projective and interpretive processes, it is never appropriate to base an allegation of abuse or assign a diagnostic label to an individual simply using a drawing. Given these limitations – one specific to this context, one fundamental to the study of drawings – this chapter will focus on the valuable and relevant reflections of abuse experience that drawings can provide.

The human figure drawings of sexually, physically or ritually abused individuals will be given special attention, partly because they offer a valid and reliable measure of self-expression. These drawings are elicited according to standard procedures and can be scored according to standardized scales (Harris, 1963; Koppitz, 1968). Examples of physically or sexually abused children's human figure drawings will be compared to those of children with ritual abuse history, with an analysis of what appear to be significant similarities and dis-similarities (Moore, in preparation). The dynamics of self-experience and the projective aspects of drawings are equally valid in the drawings of adults and children, and both will be considered here. In the case of a ritual abuse history, the adults' and children's drawings show striking similarities, reflecting not only the highly organised rituals, but the severity of the abuse, and the defenses it triggers.

THE EXPERIENCE OF RITUAL ABUSE AND DRAWINGS

As discussed elsewhere in this book, news events in recent years, and reports from law and health authorities in both the US and UK have led to the realisation that cult-related ritual abuse of children is a more than infrequent reality (Kelley, 1988; Cozolino, 1989; Hudson, 1991). The perpetrators of ritual abuse have integrated practices which terrorise their victims, threatening them or their family members with death or dismemberment if they tell anyone about their experience (Kelley, 1989, 1990; Hudson, 1991). This tactic, a regular part of the ritual abuse pattern, is designed to ensure the continued existence and practise of religious rites in the group. In some cases it so traumatises the victims that they totally dissociate the memories of the abuse. In others, the threats and physical abuse accompanying them result in conscious denial in an effort to avoid the feared repercussions of telling anyone outside the group about the experiences.

Children who have been forced to participate in cult religious rituals very rarely come forward initially. It is usually another person – child or adult – who names them as a victim (Kagy, 1986; Snow and Sorensen, 1990). This differs from the behaviour of children abused in other ways, where the victim or survivor seeks someone to help with feelings or physical distress associated with nightmares or memories. Even in the presence of physical evidence of their abuse, ritually abused children will often deny knowledge of anything related. Often they have been told that devices which will detect any attempt to tell someone about their experience have been surgically inserted into their brains or bodies (Kaye and Klein, 1988). These children have developed dissociative defenses to defend against internal or external pressure to talk about the abuse, believing their families' lives and their own depend on their 'not knowing' (Bowlby, 1979; Sinason, 1986). Only when the cult practices are completely exposed, the information made public and perpetrators have been apprehended – and/or when the children have received psychotherapeutic treatment for some time and begin to believe they and their families can be protected from the threatened retribution – may the victims gain access to some memories of the abuse and begin to draw or discuss the events (Gould, 1987; Kelley, 1988).

This process of uncovering dissociated knowledge, and expressing it in graphic verbal detail is paralleled in the drawings of children who have been ritually abused. Below, I will describe the ways in which the drawings of ritual abuse victims vary – from each other and from the drawings of children with a history of physical abuse or incest. A clear pattern is seen in cult abuse victims' drawings: during the period when the knowledge is dissociated – both children's and adults' drawings appear to look 'unremarkable': outlines of 'hollow' bodies are drawn, human figures lack individuality or vitality – until the point in time at which they begin to remember and tell others about their abuse experiences – and their drawings shift dramatically, suddenly revealing the horrific memories in graphic – often bizarre – detail (Kelley, 1988; Speltz, 1990; Burgess and Hartman, 1993; Young, 1993).

BENEFITS AND LIMITATIONS OF DRAWINGS

Given the fact that the projective process makes all drawings a communication of the self-experience of the artist, and the subjective process makes all viewers of drawings an active participant in the interpretation of drawings, how can children's drawings be useful in evaluation and treatment? How can we use them reliably? Drawings are very evocative, and as a result are used in many clinical settings. Despite the necessarily subjective nature of our understanding of drawings, there is a communicative quality to such productions which is universally understood. Albee and Hamlin (1950) showed that persons asked to judge the relative degree of emotional adjustment of clinic patients, by placing their human figure drawings in sequence from 'worst' to 'best' adjusted, achieved high degrees of reliability and a high correlation to the patients' levels of adjustment as recorded in their clinic files. Training in the use of drawings did not improve the judgments or reliability ratings of judges (Moore, 1981). Our aim is to determine how to utilise this universal communicative aspect in drawings – especially human figure drawings – in a valid and reliable manner, without distorting or denying the message in the drawing.

We have a general sense of what is disturbing in a drawing that is highly consensual. However, drawings by traumatised children and adults are particularly likely to evoke a strong counter-transference response from a viewer. The responses can take many forms, but two that are common are (1) to be unconsciously distressed by the images there, and to immediately defend against that unpleasant response by denying or 'not seeing' what is there, or (2) to have the drawing elicit sudden feelings or memories from our own past which start to flood us, and cause us to be engulfed in our own projections, not those of the drawing. In either case, by over-identifying or denying the validity of expression, we are shutting down our receptive capacity, and the patient's expression goes unexamined, unheard.

A way of limiting subjective distortion in response to a drawing – to allow the use and not misuse of one's unconscious response to a drawing – is to evaluate all drawings using a standardised measure, such as the Goodenough-Harris developmental scales (Harris, 1963) or the Koppitz Emotional Indicators Scale (Koppitz, 1968), as the initial step in the evaluation process. The scale scores indicate deviations from the norm; they are not measures of pathology.

Once these standard measures have been used, the drawing can be studied in a completely different manner, utilising clinical skill and considering unconscious communication in projective material. At this point it is useful to consider what is most striking about the drawing, how the process of its creation was unusual or what the intensity of impact is on the observer. Similarities to other clinical drawings can be noted at that point, allowing hypotheses to be generated regarding the meaning of the drawing to the individual, much in the way dream material is used with adults, and play sequences are used with children in psychotherapy. This analysis of the drawing does not concern empirical comparison to other drawings, it is a reflection of what this particular drawing, from this patient, communicates to us, and evokes in us. Here, our subjectivity is not a liability, it is a benefit – a necessary part of our receptive role with the patient. I have discussed this procedure in detail elsewhere (Moore, 1990).

We run the greatest risk when we inadvertently confuse these two uses of a drawing. When we are moved by a drawing, and want to 'know' what the meaning is, we may be tempted to be more absolute in our interpretation or statements about the drawing than is warranted. It is important to be aware that the drawings of traumatised individuals will be most likely to elicit this extreme response from us, and we will be tempted to make stronger statements than we normally might. This powerful impact is a tremendously important part of the communication of the drawing, but it must be used clinically, not as evidence on which to base an allegation or diagnosis.

It is extremely important to remember that observers of a drawing have no special access to the levels of representation in a drawing, and that some 're-presentations' in a drawing will be non-symbolic in nature – accurately reflecting a body experience that is held in a kind of 'experiential' memory. These graphic features of a drawing, along with symbolic representations, will enable us to understand more fully the drawings of abused or traumatised children (Moore, 1990; 1993). Recognising that some features are non-symbolic, we can hypothesise about the child's experience, and can do further non-intrusive investigations along the lines of our hypotheses.

MULTIPLE MEMORY SYSTEMS AND SELF-EXPERIENCE

Grigsby et al. (1991) and others have articulated the idea that we hold knowedge in a multi-modular memory system – comprised of separate memory systems, some of which are non-verbal (Cohen and Squire, 1980). In a modular memory system certain aspects of experience are recorded in interactive patterns as 'procedural' knowledge or memory. 'Procedural' memory is one type of non-declarative memory, which records habit-forming and skill-learning experiences, but is generally not accessible to verbal recall. By contrast, declarative memory or knowledge can be verbalised. In some instances, procedural and declarative memory are linked (Nadel, 1992); however, experiencing traumatic affect during an event can result in a complete dissociation of the declarative from the non-declarative procedural knowledge. This theory of multiple memory systems provides a relevant framework within which to consider multiple levels of self-expression in projective communication – in this instance, drawings – more fully.

Recent studies have shown that procedural memory is fully functional even in early infancy. A tendency to enact (Terr, 1990) or portray in drawings (Burgess and Hartman, 1993) 'unremembered' as well as remembered early traumatic experiences is documented in research studying the behaviour and physiological sequelae of traumatised children (Eth and Pynoos, 1985; Udwin, 1993 review of literature).

These findings have obvious relevance for human personality organisation, and for the levels of self-knowledge projectively reflected in drawings. Any experience perceived as life-threatening is permanently registered in our non-declarative memory – irrespective of whether the experience is accessible to declarative memory. Non-declarative, procedural memories cannot be articulated verbally but will influence behaviour in specific ways, such as in habit formation (Herman, 1992). Traumatic experiences held in either declarative or non-declarative memory can be represented in a drawing (Kelley, 1988).

In the drawing of a human figure, the process of projection allows for many levels of self-experience to be accessed and depicted simultaneously. Given the multiple levels of expression in a drawing, it is very important to remember that procedural knowledge may not be symbolic in nature. Non-declarative memories may be depicted graphically – with an accurate reproduction of the object or parts of the body involved – and placed physically on the body where the physical experience was experienced 'procedurally'. Declarative memories will be symbolically represented: reflecting the complex self, in forms which contain the meaning given to 'simple self' and body experiences (Bollas, 1992). Thus, a rich tapestry of self-experience is interwoven in the final product, however sketchily it may be manifested (Moore, 1990, 1993).

DEVELOPMENTAL BASIS FOR ANALYSIS OF DRAWINGS

Once children have the hand–eye co-ordination and fine motor control needed to draw, they progress through an ordered sequence of developmental stages in drawing (Koppitz, 1968; Kellogg, 1969). These universal, identifiable developmental stages provide a basis for the use of drawings in cross-cultural studies which seek to understand children's development. The universality in stages of drawing capacity directly reflects human brain development, with cognitive capacity, experience of affect and motor control mediating the resulting production on paper (Hammer, 1980). Initially used as a measure of intellectual and cognitive capacity (Harris, 1963), it has long been apparent to clinicians that the projective drawing task also elicits personality factors (Hammer, 1980). What has been experienced – consciously or unconsciously – is projected onto the drawn human figure, house or tree (Klepsch and Logie, 1982).

RE-PRESENTATIONS OF TRAUMA, PHYSICAL AND SEXUAL ABUSE IN DRAWINGS

The impact of trauma on children has been documented widely (Finkelhor *et al.*, 1988; Terr, 1990; Drell *et al.*, 1993), and traumatic experiences of many types will be reflected in children's drawings (Burgess and Hartman, 1993). There are characteristic features and deviations from the norm in drawings of children who have had a history of physical or sexual abuse (Goodwin, 1982; Wohl and Kaufman, 1985). It is important to note that while we see identifiable evidence of traumatisation in drawings, we cannot determine from a drawing alone what the trauma was. Simply recognising that the child has been traumatised will be of help in treatment planning, while we obtain more information regarding the exact details of the child's experience(s).

A common characteristic in drawings of abused children – equally valid for any child or adult drawing – is the representation of anxiety through intensity of line pressure and excessive shading. Chronic heightened anxiety is common in children and adults with traumatic histories (Eth and Pynoos, 1985; Udwin, 1993). Anxiety is reflected by one or more of the following features in drawings: excessive shading, small figures, rigidity in the drawing process, over-worked or heavily drawn lines (Hammer, 1980; Burgess and Hartman, 1993). As anxiety is reduced, the process of drawing becomes more spontaneous, and excess shading or over-working of lines decreases.

Ten-year-old Martha's drawing (Figure 28.1) is almost obliterated with anxious shading. Her history includes severe physical and sexual abuse from infancy, as well as being witness to chronic domestic violence which resulted in physical injury of both parents.

Figure 28.1 additionally illustrates the way in which the process a child goes through in creating a drawing can reflect traumatic procedural memories. Martha drew her human figure with care; however, when adding facial details she reversed the drawing process involved in placing eyelashes on the eyes. Normally, children and adults draw lashes away from the eye, placing the pencil at the edge of the drawn eye, moving away from the eye in the drawing process – the way the lashes grow. However, children from abusive homes who have been frequent witnesses to violence – either between parents or against themselves – more often draw the lashes as Martha did, placing the pencil above or below the drawn eye, and making a line which crosses the boundary into the eye. Procedurally, this re-enacts the painful experience of violent images entering the child's eyes as they witness or are the victims of physical abuse (Moore, in preparation).

Drawings by abused children indicate the levels at which certain information

Figure 28.1   Martha, 10 years 10 months. History of severe physical and sexual abuse since infancy

is held in memory, and thus provide important guidelines regarding work with the child in psychotherapy or other treatment. Where experience is depicted graphically, verbal memories may not be available, and questioning or probing about traumatic experiences may be experienced by the child as intrusive and anxiety-provoking, if not retraumatising.

Martha's drawing (Figure 28.1) provides us with an example of graphic 're-presentation' (graphic depiction of body parts traumatically injured, or depiction of traumatic events themselves) as contrasted with symbolic representation of the same material (see Figure 28.2). She has drawn a body with pencil scratches covering the torso, especially in the genital area, where she has drawn a 'vagina'. This heavily shaded 'person' reveals Martha's intense anxiety about herself and her body. The dark 'hole' drawn (and scratched over) in the genital area 're-presents' one area of traumatic impact in a graphic, non-symbolic manner. She has drawn the body part, not a symbol for it. The drawing of a penis on the body of a male figure would be an equivalent non-symbolic depiction.

Graphic, rather than age-appropriate, symbolic features indicate that primary memories of abuse experiences are held in non-declarative memory, and are not necessarily accessible to declarative, verbal memory. Making interpretations about that part of the drawing or memories of abuse would very likely be experienced by Martha as frightening, intrusive and retraumatising, because she may not have access to words or symbols to represent her memories of those events in her history. In cases such as Martha's, where graphic representation may reflect a body or procedural memory which is totally inaccessible verbally – held only in non-symbolic form – interpretations addressing the intense anxiety and fear reflected in the drawing, which would 'give her the words' to articulate the affect, would be most appropriate initially (Lanyado, 1985; James, 1989).

By contrast, Elizabeth's drawing reflects the symbolic quality of memory she holds about her history of sexual abuse.

Eight-year-old Elizabeth's human figure shows a 'lady' with a very large decorative flower placed strategically on the body – where her genitals would be. Elizabeth's history includes a documented incestuous relationship with her father, who fondled and had intercourse with her from the time she was 6 years old. She also witnessed his sexual abuse of her older sister. Elizabeth's drawings indicate that memories of her abuse are held in reflective memory, possibly repressed and not available to immediate recall, but none the less held in symbolic form. Here, traditional, metaphoric interpretations of her experience could be therapeutic, helping Elizabeth to tolerate the painful memories and affects.

The symbolic representation in Elizabeth's case allows us to hypothesise that she has developed psychological defenses to deal with the experience of incest. Memories are not necessarily dissociated in such a case, as they most likely would be if a 'vagina' were drawn rather than a 'flower'. We do not know whether memories are verbally accessible or repressed in a case of symbolic depiction, but traditional psychoanalytic interpretations can be made without risking a retraumatisation of the child by triggering memories which are not psychologically defended against and contained in some way. In my experience, traditional metaphoric interpretation is appropriate when the child's drawings and play in psychotherapy shift from a predominantly graphic mode to a symbolic one.

'DEVELOPMENTAL AGE' OF DRAWING AS 'TRAUMA INDICATOR'

The developmental age of a drawing – when it is a year or more below a child's current age – may indicate a period in the child's life when traumatic stress disrupted normal development in some way (Moore, 1990, 1993). Thus, in some cases, a 'delayed developmental age' in a human figure may serve as a 'trauma indicator', in much the same way that Koppitz's emotional indicators reflect emotional distress in the child (Moore, 1990). Figure 28.3 illustrates the way in which a drawing's developmental age can bring to light unresolved traumatic abuse experiences.

Figure 28.2 Author's rendition of drawing by Elizabeth, 8 years. Incest relationship with father from 6 years; witnessed sister's sexual abuse

Five-year-old Mark drew this 'person' (overleaf) during a psychological evaluation resulting from aggressive behaviour at school. The developmental age score for Mark's human figure is 2½ years. Due to the discrepancy between Mark's chronological age and the developmental age of his drawing, his parents were asked whether they recalled anything happening when Mark was '2 or 3' that might have been traumatic for him or the family. Mark's mother then recounted his experience of being taken to a day care center at age 2, where he had been slapped, gagged and shut in a closet as a punishment for screaming.

Mark's drawing simultaneously expresses – graphically and symbolically – multiple levels of self-experience and self-knowledge (Moore, 1993). His actual physical experiences of abuse are communicated in specific features of the drawing (distorted 'mouth', multiple lines in mouth) and the time of the trauma is reflected exactly in the developmental age of the drawing. Additionally, tradi-

Figure 28.3 Mark, 5 years 6 months. Physically abused, gagged and shut in closet in day care setting at age 2 years 6 months

tional interpretation of projective drawings (Hammer, 1980) would suggest that the figure's 'oversized mouth' is a symbolic representation of Mark's unconscious anxiety about his oral aggressive impulses. Both actual abuse experience and constructed meaning (including defenses and coping strategies) can be expressed in a single feature of a drawing. It is important to remain open to multiple levels of communication in what might seem to be an 'obviously symbolic' drawing.

SPECIFIC SEXUAL ABUSE INDICTORS

Koppitz's Emotional Indicators appear frequently in the drawings of sexually abused women and children, and do not appear in statistically significant numbers in the drawings of those without an abuse history. This is equally true for victims of incest and ritual abuse (Young, 1993). The drawings of those who endure the most severe trauma, or who experience it over the longest period of time, show the greatest number of emotional indicators (Hibbard and Hartman, 1990).

There are also specific features which are often present in the drawings of sexually abused children. Graphic re-presentation of genitals on a figure is associated with a history of sexual abuse (Hibbard and Hartman, 1990)). Another re-presentational, non-symbolic indicator is the depiction of two people – where a penis from one penetrates the body of the other.

Mortensen (1991) found that children in Scandinavia who have had more culturally accepted exposure to nudity in family activities show the same frequency (less than 10 per cent) of the drawing of genitals as is seen in the US (Koppitz, 1968). Accentuated or bizarre drawings of genitals are associated across cultures with severe psychological disturbance in the child. Heightened anxiety related to procedural memories of severe abuse may be indicated in heavy shading, scratching out, darkening or obliterating drawings of breasts or genitals. In addition, heavily scratched areas and repeated, overworked lines drawn across the body may be reflective of procedural memories of physical pain and damage to the body in children who have a history of physical abuse (Moore, 1993).

Drawing a person with at least one hand where a finger or the thumb is greatly out of proportion – sticking straight up or out to the side – is common in older sexually abused children. This may or may not be a symbolic expression of sexual preoccupation: traditionally, children who emphasise the fingers on hands were thought to be indicating anxiety about masturbatory activities. It may equally well be a graphic portrayal of the 'object' involved in forced finger penetration by an abuser, or symbolic representation of a penis. Such a feature can also represent anxiety-provoking memories of being forced to use the hands in some way – to masturbate an abuser's genitals, for example. Our understanding of these features must always allow for multiple determination of their source and meaning to the individual child.

CHARACTERISTICS OF RITUAL ABUSE EXPERIENCE

To understand the possible meanings in the drawings of ritually abused children and adults, we must remember what documented accounts of ritual abuse experiences have emphasised in terms of the psychological and physical torture victims endure (Wheeler et al., 1988). Many of these experiences are graphically and procedurally reproduced in drawings. Typically, children have hands and feet tied, may be gagged, are forced to watch dismemberment and beheadings of live animals, forced to eat or drink faeces or urine, have their heads held under water or pushed into a toilet, are beaten, sexually assaulted, often drugged and told they have had instruments 'inserted into their body' by surgery while drugged, are forced to watch or take part in the sexual and physical abuse of other children; often they are told by the robed or costumed adult perpetrators that they can be heard and observed by 'Satan' or the perpetrators anytime, anywhere, and that any attempt to tell outsiders will result in the torture and death of family members or themselves (Gould, 1987; Hudson, 1991). These experiences constitute torture at the most extreme level, and have the effect of dehumanising the child, who is treated as an object without emotions or physical needs, creating a physiological and psychological state of terror in the child. Primitive survival defenses are triggered in the child, invariably including dissociation as a major defense (McElroy, 1992). This is not abuse as an aspect of a relationship, this is chronic 'abuse by terrorists'.

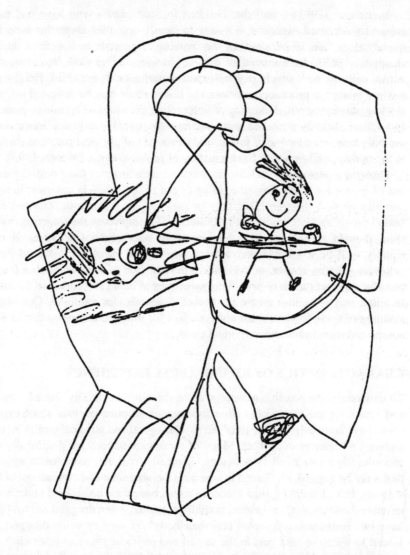

Figure 28.4 Girl, 4 years. Ritually abused, tied to tree observing another child being sexually abused

Source: Hudson, 1991

EXAMPLES OF RITUAL ABUSE DRAWINGS

The drawings of ritual abuse victims depict all of the experiences described in the literature on this type of abuse. Importantly, a single victim may draw very different drawings over time in treatment, even after disclosure of involvement in ritual abuse practices. This process exactly parallels the psychological change in the individual as chronic dissociative states are gradually replaced by other mental states, and memories become verbally or visually accessible. Overt somatic and psychological symptoms generally increase dramatically during this period, and victims' drawings reflect the horrendous events and treament they received at the hands of perpetrators.

Examples below illustrate specific characteristics common to ritually abused adults' and children's drawings. Use of the original drawing was not always possible; however, sketches made by the author of specific parts of the drawings are included, and are labeled as such. The complete, original drawings will be published at a later date.

INDICATORS OF DEHUMANISING TREATMENT

The experience of being tied to a tree and watching another child being raped is depicted in Figure 28.4 (Hudson, 1991).

Striking evidence of the experience of having hands and feet bound or tied is found in many of the drawings of children and adults alike. Bizarre or 'torn off' depictions at the ends of the arms are very common in these drawings, and are unusual in drawings by incested and non-abused individuals. Figures 28.5 a, b, c are the author's renditions of the torsos from three ritually abused adults' drawings; the complete figure (d) was drawn by a 4½-year-old child.

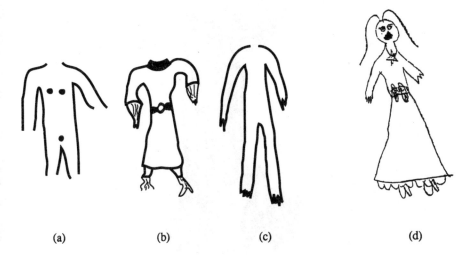

(a)   (b)   (c)   (d)

Figure 28.5 (a, b, c) The author's renditions of three ritually abused adults' drawings; *(d)* drawing by 4½-year-old ritual abuse victim; pentagram at neck, jagged ends on arms, distorted eyes

Source: Hudson, 1991

Figure 28.6 Drawn by a 9-year-old victim of ritual abuse

Source: Hudson, 1991

Figure 28.7 Drawing of perpetrator by 4-year-old ritual abuse victim

Source: Hudson, 1991

Figure 28.8 Horned, costumed figure drawn by 4-year-old victim of ritual abuse
Source: Hudson, 1991

Frightening witch and devil costumes are depicted in both adults' and children's drawings. As in Figure 28.5, these figures show jagged endings to the arms, or claw-like hands. One lacks arms altogether. All have damaged mouths, possibly reflecting the experience of being forced to eat or drink blood, faeces or urine.

Children are often drugged and told they will be cut open, and objects – such as transistors – put inside. They are tied down on tables and cut or sexually abused in this position while others watch. Two adult drawings from separate countries graphically depict the experience of being flattened on a table, tied down. One patient describes 'being in hospital where lots of people watch the operation'. She also says her 'brain is being cut into pieces'. The second woman's drawing shows 'wires attached to the brain', eyes covered, body flat on a table.

Objects used in ritual abuse practices are often depicted in drawings: blood may be shown dripping, from hands, from objects or, symbolically, from a blackened sun.

Candles are frequently used in ceremonies and may be added to a drawing, or become the central focus of a drawing. Other objects or figures that appear frequently are the numbers '666' and rows or clusters of multiple, large, dark, phallic shapes. Pentagrams and crosses used in most cult ceremonies are often depicted. Crosses are drawn upside down. Figure 28.5 d has a pentagram at the neck; the copy in Figure 28.10 was in the corner of an adult victim's drawing.

REFLECTIONS OF PHYSICAL, SEXUAL OR RITUAL ABUSE IN CHILDREN'S DRAWINGS: DIFFERENCES

Displacement of genitals to the face is common in cases of incest, as opposed to cases of ritual abuse or sexual abuse by someone who has no relationship with the child (Moore, in preparation). Depiction of the human figure will necessarily involve projection of self-experience, an important aspect of which will be the identification with the other. The face on the human figure is most closely linked to the concept of self. Thus the sexual abuse experiences with a parent, whether 'known' consciously or unconsciously (Bowlby, 1979), will be indicated as one aspect of self–other experience. This understanding of genitals displaced to the face is supported by both attachment theory and object relations theory which propose that the child creates an understanding of him or herself in relation to 'the other', usually a parent.

An additional difference between some children's experience of sexual abuse and the experience of ritual abuse is that some incestuous relationships involve seduction of the child by a parent who describes the behaviours as 'loving' and tries to gradually arouse the child without causing physical pain, or using force in the abuse. This reduces the child's perception of physical, life-threatening danger, and generally reduces traumatic impact related to extreme pain.

SIMILARITIES IN EXPERIENCES AND DRAWINGS OF ALL ABUSED CHILDREN

Some aspects of abuse experience are common in all settings: primitive survival defenses are triggered if the child believes his or her life is endangered during the experience. Also, dissociative defenses which are a natural part of any child's coping mechanisms to deal with trauma are used instinctively, and later the child may learn to trigger this defense consciously when faced with repeated abuse experiences (McElroy, 1992; Putnam, 1993). At times, an incestuous relationship with a parent leads to ritual abuse experiences, when the adult introduces the child to the cult setting. The traumatisation of the child is intensified in such cases, when the parent initiates practices within the relationship that are later carried out brutally by strangers, while the parent watches (Janoff-Bulman, 1985).

Figure 28.9 Author's renditions of two adult ritual abuse victims' depictions of blood dripping in human figure drawings

Figure 28.10 Author's rendition of adult ritual abuse victim's drawing of pentagram; reproduction of pentagram from Figure 28.5(d)

Source: Hudson, 1991 (Figure 28.5 (d))

INDICATORS OF DISSOCIATIVE PROCESSES IN DRAWINGS

One physical mannerism that often indicates the triggering of a dissociative state is the eyes rolling upward (Perry, 1993). In a graphic re-presentation of this process, some adult and child ritual abuse victims draw the eyes as though rolled back into the head. Additionally, drugged states or terror are often depicted dramatically in the eyes of human figures. I believe these are not reflections of a dissociative state, but graphic re-presentations of the eyes of others as seen by the children during abuse. Some examples are shown in Figure 28.11. The eyes clustered at the left of the page (Figure 28.11 a, b, c) are copied from three ritually abused adults' drawings. The eyes to the right (Figure 28.11 d), are traced from Martha's drawing (Figure 28.1), for comparison. Martha's experience of chronic, sadistic physical and sexual abuse was probably similar to the experience of many ritual abuse victims. Eyelashes drawn into the eye are present in both samples.

Other features in the drawings of abused children and adults seem to reflect the experience of dissociation (Putnam, 1993). Examples include bodies drawn with parts left off, limbs drawn as one-dimensional 'sticks' (see Martha's drawing, Figure 28.1), figures drawn close to the edge of the paper so body parts seem to be 'cut off' by the edge of the page, and the 'hollow' undifferentiated, undetailed, 'unsexed' figure mentioned earlier. Figures 28.5 a and 28.5 c illustrate a type of 'hollow figure' drawn in dissociative states.

SUMMARY

The differences in abuse experiences of children in incestuous or physically abusing families, and those who have been victims of cult abuse practices are directly reflected in their drawings, at the graphic, re-presentational and symbolic levels. Similarities in the experience are likewise reflected in drawings across populations and cultures. Thus drawings can be used as effective means of communication of a child's mental state, quality and accessiblity of memories, and likely degree of traumatisation in the past.

The wish to know the 'Truth' about a drawing – to understand its many meanings completely, to be able to decipher its intentional and unintentional reflections of self – is natural. Unfortunately it cannot be realised. We can become more knowledgeable about similarities in drawings from individuals with similar life experiences, and can generate hypotheses about an individual's

(a)   (b)   (c)   (d)

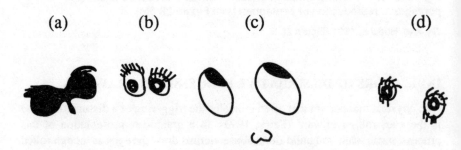

Figure 28.11 (a, b, c) Author's rendition of adult ritual abuse victims' drawings of eyes on human figure; *(d)* reproduction of eyes from Figure 28.1, chronically abused girl of 10 years

Source: Hudson, 1991

'possible' earlier experience and the meaning contained in a drawing, by comparing the characteristics of a single drawing to the 'common characteristics' in drawings by others whose history has been documented. But we must always remember that specific drawing characteristics associated with a history of abuse can only be considered valid 'indicators' when correlated with other independent sources of information in a multi-dimensional assessment of a child. However broad our knowledge base, however skilled we are in understanding and interpreting our clients' communications, we – as observers – can never understand a drawing in an absolute, objective sense. Precisely because of the subjective nature of the projective and interpretive processes, it is never appropriate – or ethical professionally – to make an allegation of an abuse history, or assign a diagnostic label to an individual – based simply on a drawing.

REFERENCES

Albee, G. and Hamlin, R. (1950) 'Judgement of adjustment from drawings: the applicability of rating scale methods', *Journal of Clinical Psychology* 6, 363–5.

Bollas, C. (1993) *Being a Character: Psychoanalysis and Self Experience*, London, Routledge.

Bowlby, J. (1979) 'On knowing what you are not supposed to know and feeling what you are not supposed to feel', in *A Secure Base: Clinical Applications of Attachment Theory*, London, Routledge.

Burgess, A. and Hartman, C. (1993) 'Children's drawings', *Child Abuse and Neglect* 17, 161–8.

Cohen, N.J. and Squire, L. (1980) 'Preserved learning and retention of pattern-analyzing skill in amnesia: dissociation of knowing how and knowing that', *Science* 210, 207–9.

Cozolino, L. (1989) 'The ritual abuse of children: implications for clinical practice and research', *Journal of Sex Research* 26 (1), 131–8.

Drell, M., Siegel, C. and Gaensbauer, T. (1993) 'Disorders of infancy: post-traumatic stress disorder', in C. Zeanah (ed.) *Handbook of Infant Mental Health*, New York, Guilford Press.

Eth, S. and Pynoos, R. (eds) (1985) *Post-Traumatic Stress Disorder in Children*, Washington, DC, American Psychiatric Press.

Finkelhor, D., Williams, L. and Burns, N. (1988) *Nursery Crimes: Sexual Abuse in Day Care*, Newbury Park, CA, Sage Publications.

Goodwin, J. (1982) 'Use of drawings in evaluating children who may be incest victims', *Children and Youth Review* 4, 269–78.

Gould, C. (1987) 'Satanic ritual abuse: child victims, adult survivors, system response', *California Psychologist* 22 (3), 1.

Grigsby, J., Schneiders, J. and Kaye, K. (1991) 'Reality-testing, the self and the brain as modular distributed systems', *Psychiatry* 54, 39–54.

Hammer, E. (1980) *The Clinical Application of Projective Drawings*, Springfield, IL, C.C. Thomas.

Harris, D.B. (1963) *Children's Drawings as Measures of Intellectual Maturity*, New York, Harcourt, Brace & World.

Herman, J. (1992) *Trauma and Recovery*, New York, Basic Books.

Hibbard, R.A. and Hartman, G. (1990) 'Emotional indicators in human figure drawings of sexually victimized and nonabused children', *Journal of Clinical Psychology* 46 (2).

Hudson, P. (1991) *Ritual Child Abuse: Discovery, Diagnosis and Treatment*, Saratoga, CA, R&E Publishers.

James, B. (1989) *Treating Traumatized Children: New Insights and Creative Interventions*, Lexington, MA, Lexington Books.

Janoff-Bulman, R. (1985) 'The aftermath of victimization: rebuilding shattered assumptions', in C.R. Figley (ed.) *Trauma and its Wake*, New York, Brunner/Mazel.

Kagy, L. (1986) Ritualized abuse of children. RECAP: Newsletter of the National Child Assault Prevention Project. Winter Issue, 1-2.

Kaye, M. and Klein, L.R. (1988) 'Clinical indicators of Satanic cult victimization', in B.G. Braun (ed.) *Dissociative Disorders: 1987 – The Proceedings of the Fifth International Conference on Multiple Personality/Dissociative States*, Chicago, IL: Rush University.

Kelley, S. (1988) 'Ritualistic abuse of children: dynamics and impact', *Cultic Studies Journal* 5 (2), 228–36.

Kelley, S.J. (1989) 'Stress responses of children to sexual abuse and ritualistic abuse in day care centers', *Journal of Interpersonal Violence* 4 (4), 502–13.

Kelley, S.J. (1990) 'Parental stress response to sexual abuse and ritualistic abuse of children in day care centers', *Nursing Research* 39 (1), 25–9.

Kellogg, R. (1969) *Analyzing Children's Art*, Palo Alto, CA, Mayfield.

Klepsch, M. and Logie, L. (1982) *Children Draw and Tell: An Introduction to the Projective Uses of Children's Human Figure Drawings*, New York, Brunner/Mazel.

Koppitz, E.M. (1968) *Psychological Evaluation of Children's Human Figure Drawings (Ages 5–12)*, Florida, Academic Press.

Lanyado, M. (1985) 'Surviving trauma – dilemmas in the psychotherapy of traumatised children', *British Journal of Psychotherapy* 2 (1), 50–62.

McElroy, L. (1992) 'Early indicators of pathological dissociation in sexually abused children', *Child Abuse and Neglect* 16 (6), 833–46.

Moore, M.S. (1981) 'Diagnostic implications in the human figure drawings of learning disabled children, aged 6–12', US, Dissertation Abstracts International.

Moore, M.S. (1990) 'Understanding children's drawings: developmental and emotional indicators in children's human figure drawings', *Journal of Educational Therapy* 3 (2), 35–47.

Moore, M.S. (1994) 'Reflections of self: the use of drawings in the evaluation and treatment of children with physical illness', in D. Judd and A. Erskine (eds) *The Imaginative Body*, London, Whurr Publications.

Moore, M.S. (in preparation) 'Symbolization and re-presentation in children's drawings: the impact of trauma.'

Mortensen, K. V. (1991) *Form and Content in Children's Human Figure Drawings: Development, Sex Differences, and Body Experience*, New York, New York University Press.

Nadel, L. (1992) 'Multiple memory systems: what and why', *Journal of Cognitive Neuroscience* 4 (3), 179–88.

Perry, B. (1993) *Neuro-development and the Neurophysiology of Trauma (I and II): The Alarm-Fear-Terror Continuum*. The Advisor, 6 (1&2), Chicago, IL, American Professional Society on the Abuse of Children.

Putnam, F. (1993) 'Dissociative disorders in children: behavioral profiles and problems', *Child Abuse and Neglect* 17, 39–45.

Sinason, V. (1986) 'Secondary mental handicap and its relationship to trauma', *Psychoanalytic Psychotherapy* 2(2), 131–54.

Snow, B. and Sorensen, T. (1990) 'Ritualistic child abuse in a neighborhood setting', *Journal of Interpersonal Violence* 5(4), 474–87.

Speltz, A.M. (1990) 'Treating adolescent satanism in art therapy', *The Arts in Psychotherapy* 17, 147–55.

Terr, L. (1990) *Too Scared to Cry: Psychic Trauma in Childhood*, New York, Harper & Row.

Udwin, O. (1993) 'Annotation: children's reactions to traumatic events', *Journal of Child*

Psychology and Psychiatry and Allied Disciplines 34(2), 115–27.

Wheeler, B., Wood, S. and Hatch, R.J. (1988) 'Assessment and intervention with adolescents involved in Satanism', *Social Work* 3, 547–50.

Wohl, A. and Kaufman, B. (1985) *Silent Screams and Hidden Cries: An Interpretation of Artwork by Children from Violent Homes*, New York, Brunner/Mazel.

Young, M. (1993) 'Empirical Evaluation of Creativity', unpublished thesis, School of Professional Psychology, DU, Denver, Colorado.

Chapter 29

Satanic cult practices

Joan Coleman

Dr Joan Coleman is an Associate Specialist in Psychiatry at Heathlands Mental
Health Services, Surrey.

*Names, identities and background details have been changed wherever necessary
to protect confidentiality.*

My introduction to satanist ritual abuse (SRA) began without my awareness in
1982 when I treated a woman with a history of recurrent self-injury. In November
1986, she began talking about child abuse and pornography involving what
appeared to be a well-organised paedophile ring. A nurse colleague, Eileen
Reeves, established some rapport with her and from that time onwards we
worked together. During the next year she described an increasingly horrifying
catalogue of events, which included abduction of runaway boys who were then
used by the group for sex, pornography and homosexual prostitution; she claimed
to have seen some of these boys being tortured and finally murdered and she went
on to describe the disposal of their bodies.

Some years later, we were to read very similar accounts in the press, concerning the deaths of Jason Swift, Barry Lewis and Mark Tildesley; accounts
which would seem unbelievable without the police evidence, but we were struck
by the resemblance. The patient eventually described how she had witnessed, in
about 1976, the ritual sexual abuse and murder of three tiny Vietnamese children
who had been brought to Southampton from the USA amongst the first contin-
gents of 'boat people'. The abuse involved candles, inverted crosses, participants
who were either naked or wore robes and masks, blood collected into a chalice
and drunk. She gave us a little time to absorb all this before adding that much of
the children's flesh was eaten prior to the remains being burnt.

We have since heard similar accounts many times and as a friend once warned
me, 'You can get used to anything.' But we shall never forget the horror, fear and
isolation of that winter.

My second cult victim, a young teenage girl, referred to me in 1989 by Diane
Core, founder of Childwatch, brought in a new and disturbing feature – the

description of young children, born into the cult, who were unable to walk or talk, having been kept from babyhood in hanging cages, within the basement of a large house. She described them as dirty, naked and unkempt, with matted hair and expressionless faces. They did not cry or scream, she said, but whimpered occasionally; usually they played with their fingers or the bars of the cage. They were brought out only for abuse or experimental operations performed by the cult leader, who, she thought, was a doctor. Some of them were sacrificed.

Other cases have followed. All were involved as children and some have multiple personality disorder (MPD).

Ritual Abuse Information Network and Support (RAINS)

As a result of these cases, we began to contact other professionals in this field. There had already been considerable publicity regarding the case in Nottingham when we met Christine Johnston and Judith Dawson. In September 1989, shortly after the Reading conference, 'Not One More Child', convened by Norma Howes, the four of us, together with Jeff Hopkins, who lectures to social workers at Keele University, met in Manchester. This was the first meeting of RAINS. There were then five members. The membership increased rapidly, without any publicity, and by July 1993 numbered 150, all professionals working with ritual abuse victims.

DISCLOSURE MATERIAL

The following information applies to the activities of transgenerational satanic cults. These are not all proven facts but are a composite of descriptions provided by a number of survivors, mainly my own patients. One point especially requires emphasis: that SRA is not confined to ceremonies but is a way of life. Most of the procedure regarding indoctrination of children is carried out at home, much of it by their mothers.

Structure of cults

The structure is hierarchical, usually with anonymity at the top. Frequently, those high in authority are prominent also in their ordinary lives and include doctors, lawyers, teachers, clergy, police, politicians, ambassadors and aristocrats. Almost every occupation is represented. Members are of both sexes and many are involved from the cradle to the grave. Those not born into Satanism are recruited in, usually as children or adolescents, rarely after young adulthood.

Some cults are divided up into groups of seventy or eighty adults which may be known as *Circles* or *Lodges*. These are subdivided into *Covens* of thirteen. Each circle has a *High Priest* and *High Priestess* who exercise authority over the members most of whom may be known as *Disciples*. Some survivors talk of other officials such as the *Scribe*, who keeps a written record, the *Thane*, who organises equipment and procedure at ceremonies, and the *Head Disciple*, who oversees training of children; also the *Witch*, who is venerated for her wisdom and knowledge of cult history. They speak, too, of *Commanders*, the policy makers, who hold high authority. These meet regularly with other officials, at hotels or conference centres.

All members are given, at some stage, commissions to perform for the cult. These may involve acting as couriers, desecrating graves, attending outings, securing certain objects used in ceremonies and so on. A major commission, especially for teenage girls, is recruiting.

MOTIVATION AND PRACTICES

According to survivors, the religious aspect seems to be supremely important for some members; for others, the quest for power, sexual gratification or financial profit may dominate. All these can overlap, but control over the members is essential if perpetuation of the cult is to be achieved and secrecy maintained.

Religion: worship of Satan

Satanic worship is manifested by the holding of ceremonies, the denigration of Christianity and the instruction of children. Satanic ceremonies, *Sabbats*, occur usually in the middle of the night and take place in barns, churches, churchyards, crypts, cemeteries, tunnels, caves, cellars, ruined abbeys, castles or derelict houses (Kaye and Klein, 1986); also in heath or woodland, on beaches, or in so-called *Satanic Temples*, which are usually no more than a room in a private house, warehouse or shed designated for this purpose. The number of participants varies; small weekly ceremonies may be attended just by the coven of thirteen, but the large ceremonies associated with satanic festivals involve many more members. (For dates of Satanic festivals, see Appendix.)

Accounts are consistent regarding robes with hoods or masks being worn for parts of each ceremony (Hudson, 1991); at other times the participants are naked. The colours of the robes, walls, curtains or covers are usually black, red or purple (Kaye and Klein, 1986), but for some special ceremonies important members wear gold, silver or other colours. Satanic symbols or cult emblems are seen on robes, walls or covers. There is almost invariably a circle which may be drawn or marked on the ground or made with string or twine. Often there is a floor covering of polythene, or sometimes a tarpaulin.

Descriptions of the equipment used are also very consistent. The most essential object seems to be an altar, which may be just a table, or possibly a tomb, rock or tree stump if out of doors. This is covered with a cloth, often displaying a cult emblem. Usually, there is an inverted cross. On the altar are candles, bowls, chalices, a dagger or knife and often a sword. There may also be a horn or bell, to mark the beginning or end of the ceremony. There are several large books and sometimes a human skull or a goat's head, which may be stuffed, or from a newly killed animal. Several survivors have spoken of small apothecary's scales being used in the ceremony. Also playing a part are drugs, alcohol, body paint, live insects, spiders, frogs and snakes. Some have mentioned demons or sometimes Satan himself appearing at ceremonies and most eventually come to believe that these are cult members in costume. Some of the demon masks are grotesque and very terrifying (Kaye and Klein, 1986).

Other patients have spoken of certain objects, such as a wheel, cords and natural twine called *woodvine*, animal costumes, flame torches, caskets for body parts and *poppets* or *curse dolls* which are all used in certain ceremonies (Tate, 1991). All have mentioned the use of live animals for sex as well as for sacrifice; also body substances such as blood, urine, faeces and semen. Additional equipment used for disposal of remains will be described later.

The procedure of ceremonies appears to take the same basic form in most groups with variations during special ceremonies. Some groups are more orthodox than others. Frequently a fire is lit. Readings from the books, chants and prayers to Satan are standard components; also child sexual and physical abuse, smearing and consumption of body substances and sexual orgies. There is usually some type of blood sacrifice to Satan, often a cockerel or small animal, less frequently a large animal or a human being.

The paraphernalia used in ceremonies is placed in the charge of different cult members who are each responsible for cleaning and safeguarding that piece of equipment. Those articles which are too large to conceal easily may be hidden in lock-up garages. Some, such as stuffed goats' heads, swords and daggers, may simply be placed where they will not be noticed, for example, in shops selling military memorabilia or antiques. The books are kept in a safe. Any equipment in members' houses will rapidly be removed at the first whisper of any police or social work interest in their children.

Prior to a ceremony, the ground is prepared with a tarpaulin or a large sheet of polythene, in order that no traces of blood or other body substances will be left. We have heard too, of devices for rapid concealment of incriminating material in the event of interruption. It is, after all, legal to hold witchcraft and even satanic ceremonies. It is only for the accompanying crimes that satanists can be convicted.

Survivors state that victims of human sacrifice may be:

1 *Foetuses* – usually resulting from criminal abortion of female cult members; occasionally obtained from private abortion clinics by doctors, nurses or technicians within the cult.
2 *Babies and young children* – these are unregistered children of cult members; if sacrificed at birth, parents simply announce that the baby was stillborn. If an older child, it might be combined with the parents moving house or separating.
3 *Runaway children* – many are not reported missing (Randall, 1988). They

may be from deprived families and will perhaps have run away previously. There will be little expectation of them returning.

4 *Adults* – Sometimes vagrants and others of no fixed abode are used. Also occasionally, adult members who have stepped badly out of line and are considered a security risk. Other cult members may see this as an example and would be afraid to report it.

Survivors claim that the bodies of sacrificed victims are usually destroyed completely or are buried. In the case of foetuses most of the flesh is eaten (Hudson, 1988, 1991). Regarding older victims, survivors have described a range of disposal means: large bonfires in isolated areas, furnaces in basements or factories, straw burning stoves on farms and even, in some cases, crematoria. Several have mentioned tubs or baths of acid, others have described the use of industrial mincers and the subsequent product being fed to dogs and pigs. Burial grounds within large country estates are quite frequently mentioned, as well as the use of newly dug graves in cemeteries. We have heard of bodies being weighted and placed in river beds. Some of these methods seem incredible until one remembers the wide variety of occupations of cult members.

Satanists believe that the power of the cult is enhanced by killing and ingesting what was, shortly before, living flesh and blood. The younger and more innocent the victim, the greater the transference of power (Crowley, 1926). At the same time it is an offering to Satan. In orthodox cults it seems that the sacrifice is performed by the High Priest, the victim being stabbed in the heart; this is followed by cutting of the throat and draining of the blood. In these groups, the number of participants is greatly reduced at this stage. In less conformist groups we have heard of death by many different methods and participants. Some have described multiple sacrifices in ceremonies lasting several days.

We have heard how young children are trained with dolls so that the techniques of sacrifice and dismemberment become increasingly familiar. Another step in their training is to have to kill and burn their own pets. When participating in ritual sacrifice, initially, their small hands are held round the dagger.

Many other specific ceremonies have been described; those most often mentioned are initiation, marriage (Hudson, 1991; Gould, 1992) and punishment ceremonies. Others have included abortion or induction with full-term delivery in some female cult members, followed by sacrifice of the foetus or baby (Hudson, 1991).

Destruction and desecration of Christian symbols are an integral part of Satanism and Christian morality is scorned and deliberately flouted. An example of this is the *Black Mass*, which patients describe as taking place in a Christian church using a parody of Catholic Mass, but with Satan substituted for God and prayers accordingly altered or recited backwards (Melech, 1986). There is sacrilegious use of the altar, church candles, crucifix, font, etc., as well as the Host. Crucifixes or candles may be used for sexual penetration of women or children (Terry, 1987; Snowden, 1988). In addition, anti-Christ symbols such as crossed fish and inverted crucifixes (Kaye and Klein, 1986), are used in ordinary ceremonies which often start with special dances and prayers to Satan to 'cleanse' the area of Christ's presence. Desecration of graves is also a denigration of Christianity.

Cult children are instructed and trained in ceremonial procedures, prayers, chants and the interpretation of the readings, some of which are in a foreign language (Kaye and Klein, 1986). They are also taught about the philosophy of Satanism and the reversal of good and evil; they are told that Satan is more powerful than God and will ultimately triumph and rule this world and the next (Snowden, 1988; Harper, 1990); that Christ is Satan's enemy and must be spurned. Christian churches can be entered only for purposes of mockery or desecration.

Power: indoctrination and its reinforcement

The level of mind control over children is one of the major aspects of satanist abuse and one which distinguishes it in nature and degree even from other types of ritual abuse. One patient who was subsequently in the cult formerly called 'The Children of God', renamed 'The Family of Love' (Ritchie, 1991), is adamant that the satanist abuse was infinitely worse. It is extremely systematic and employs many brainwashing techniques such as the use of drugs and hypnosis, psychological confusion, sexual abuse, pain, torture, disorientation and near-death experiences.

Psychological abuse and mind control

Most children born into cults to which both parents are committed, receive little if any love and affection; sometimes, however, one parent deliberately shows warmth to the child, gaining its trust by saving it from abuse by the other parent. This process is repeated over some time, then suddenly the 'loving' parent becomes rejecting and hostile, subjecting the child to even greater abuse, resulting in emotional pain and confusion.

This pattern of breaking trust and causing bewilderment is repeated continually. Children are told they are 'special' because they are in the cult; they must not touch or associate with those 'the other side of the wall'; at the same time they are reminded that they are evil and must be punished. They are often threatened with exclusion. Anything that the child begins to enjoy, or become attached to, is either contaminated, or snatched away and replaced by something obnoxious; one patient described being given, for her fifth birthday, a pyjama case with a teddy bear on the front; inside, she found the rotting flesh of a dead animal. Children may be given pets such as puppies, only to be forced, when devoted to them, to watch or participate in their sadistic destruction (Hudson, 1991).

Many survivors can remember, when little, being taken to parties at which there were clowns or conjurors and a mouth-watering banquet of food. The children watched the adults eating, while they themselves were forced to eat rotting meat or excrement; later they were abused by the clowns and conjurors. Others recall being abused by Santa Claus. Similarly, adult members abuse cult children while posing as teachers, doctors, nurses, social workers, clergy, police and so on; thus ensuring continuing distrust of carers and figures of authority.

The use of drugs and hypnosis adds to the children's confusion (Snowden, 1988; Gould, 1992). Many adult survivors speak of 'orange drinks', tablets, or sometimes an injection being administered prior to a journey or a ceremony. Consequently, memories of the more traumatic experiences are sometimes hazy or distorted.

Indoctrination is aided by deception regarding the so-called magical power of Satan, which is a special form of psychological abuse. If children can be convinced that Satan is both omnipotent and omniscient, the power over them is vast. Threats are common and are usually linked to reminders of Satan's magical ability to know when members are talking. Victims are warned that betrayal will result in the death of a family member, their confidante or themselves (Hudson, 1991). They may be forced to attend special ceremonies in which 'demons' are summoned and they are told to hold the 'poppet' or curse doll; they may then be told that 'death by fire' or some other disaster will ensue on a certain date, if they fail to conform. Most take these curses very seriously. Sometimes macabre objects are used as threats – lumps of raw meat on the doorstep, blood on the front door and chickens' claws or animals' eyeballs in the bed, have all been described.

Children are taught that certain colours, especially the combination of red and black, have magical significance (Gould, 1992); numbers, too, play a prominent part. The figures 3, 6, 9 and 13 are all important and 666 was Aleister Crowley's 'Sign of the Great Beast' (Russell, 1980; Parker, 1993). This symbol is said to be tattooed on the scalps of some members; I have seen it on an adult's buttock, done in infancy. Satanic cult children are given 'magical numbers' and 'magical names'. Some are told that certain years as well as dates of satanic festivals are especially powerful.

The child's own birthday is very significant and when certain ages are reached there may be further initiation ceremonies. Most cult children grow up dreading their birthdays, which are always associated with especially traumatic ceremonies centred around the child. The abuse is greatly magnified at this time and the 'birthday presents' (see Charleson and Corbett, Chapter 20) usually evoke terror.

All satanic symbols are said to have magical properties, including the circle which surrounds the site of the ceremony. Children are told that they are safe within the circle, but outside it they are unprotected. Some adults still insist that no human being or animal can cross the magic circle once a ceremony is in progress.

Often children are given apparently insignificant objects to keep, which they believe hold a magical, protective power. Should they lose or part with these they will be vulnerable and subject to punishment. They also act as reminders not to talk about the cult. In addition, children are told that these can harm outsiders, so it is not easy for therapists to acquire them. Objects range from soft toys and small model frogs, snakes or spiders, to ordinary looking photographs, rings, stones or perhaps a piece of cord or rope.

Survivors tell how, as children, they were taught that spiders and insects were Satan's agents, who were watching them and reporting back to him. Some say they were forced to swallow eyeballs 'so they could be watched from inside'; others speak of early operations undergone, during which, they were told, something was implanted in them which would, by Satan's magic, result in terrifying consequences should they talk (Snowden, 1988; Hudson, 1991; Gould, 1992). One of my patients regressed and relived the experience of having a small 'bomb' implanted in her abdomen. For years, she lived in fear of this exploding. A visible abdominal scar was consistent with her account.

Much of the procedure of the actual ceremonies is designed to introduce a strong element of magic and mysticism; the darkness, lit only by sombre coloured candles with aromatic fumes containing drugs which alter perception (Harper, 1990); the chanting and whispering of prayers in strange languages (Kaye and Klein, 1986); the dark robes, drapery and frightening masks, and the inclusion of men dressed as demons or even as Satan.

Sexual abuse, degradation, pain and torture

In many cases this abuse starts in infancy and continues indefinitely. As stated earlier, it is relentless and occurs both within and outside ceremonies (Snowden, 1988; Hudson, 1991; Gould, 1992). It is correctly assumed by the cult that any disclosures from very young children will be confused and inconsistent; they will therefore be attributed to nightmares, fantasies and storybooks or, more recently, as in Rochdale in 1990, watching horror videos. After a few years the children are usually too frightened to talk at all, unless they have been completely separated from all cult members. Even then, objects, toys, letters or cards can still act as warnings to silence them. Hence the insistence of social workers, for which they have been so frequently criticised (see the Orkney Report, HMSO, 1992), that where there is any suspicion of ritual abuse, children should receive no messages or presents from their families. As a rule, it takes several months of separation before children feel safe enough to start disclosing.

They are abused by parents and other cult members, especially the High Priest and Priestess. The sexual abuse usually involves oral and anal before vaginal penetration in very young children, and soon it includes penetration with objects and administration of electric currents, which cause extreme pain. Often, as stated, Christian symbols are incorporated in the abuse.

Part of the training of most cult children involves their use as child prostitutes for paedophiles not necessarily belonging to the cult. This usually takes place in their own homes and is organised by their parents who are paid for their services

(Stratford, 1988). The perpetrators pay more for photographs or films of these sessions. The purpose appears to be not solely commercial, but partly to degrade the child, who can later be blackmailed to conform (Hudson, 1991).

Often the children are left, apparently abandoned, in a variety of places. Eventually they are 'rescued' and told that Satan has saved them from death. One survivor described being left alone, naked and cold, at the age of 4, for three weeks in an underground room, while her mother went abroad. Her only company was the corpse of a woman she had seen being killed. She was given water, but no food; she was told that if she was hungry enough she would eat the rotting flesh of the woman. She was finally taken out by her father, who then sodomised her.

All my patients have admitted that they were forced from a young age to be perpetrators. They have described how as 4-year-olds, they were made to poke objects into the orifices of younger children and to assist in torture. Initially, they may be very reluctant, but some of either sex, as they grow older, seem to find it increasingly easy to sexually abuse and inflict pain on the younger children. Some girls grow up more afraid of their elder brothers than they are of their parents.

Both children and adults are given tasks to perform, and failure to complete them results in punishment. This may be fairly mild, but the punishments for suspected treachery include being gang raped; immersed to near drowning in baths; suspended, manacled, from a bridge or boat; given electric shocks; tied to the wheel and lashed; being subjected to a mock trial in a foreign country; worst of all, being forced to watch or assist in the killing and mutilation of other adults who have betrayed the cult.

Misuse of dissociation

As a result of such trauma, most cult children learn to dissociate at a very young age. It is the only way they can survive. They teach themselves to become detached from the pain and abuse and later describe how they were able to look down on the scene as if it were happening to another child (Putnam, 1989).

The adult cult members are well aware of this ability – no doubt they used it themselves, as children – and sometimes they deliberately inflict pain severe enough to break through the dissociation. Trances can be used by the perpetrators who, through hypnosis, can programme children to enter them when faced with difficult questions, thus avoiding answering. Satanists are also well acquainted with the mechanism of multiple personality and abuse it to their own advantage. By subjecting very young children to a prolonged, unbroken series of intensely traumatic experiences, they can induce into them personalities of their own design, which they can summon when required and which are trained to bear allegiance to the cult; these can be programmed, probably by post-hypnotic suggestion, to perform acts which might be alien to the true intentions of that person but which may nevertheless protect them from further punishment and torture by the cult (Snowden, 1988; Young, 1992).

There are various methods of summoning the cult-induced personalities. Sometimes the name of that personality or another word will be the cue. Cues are induced deliberately and the victim is programmed to respond in a certain way (Young, 1992); triggers are more haphazard and produce a variety of responses including dissociation, phobic anxiety or a sense of guilt and treachery. They need not necessarily be spoken words, but can be objects, symbols, written messages, certain music, a voice on the telephone, a place name on a signpost and countless other stimuli. Triggers do not act solely upon victims with multiple personalities; nearly all cult victims respond to them in one of the above ways. This may result in retractions, or in determined efforts to attend cult ceremonies or in self-injury as a means of avoiding them.

Sexual gratification and licence

The sexual activities apparently include almost any type of practice with anyone, irrespective of age or gender. There are no restrictions upon anything that is desired, including sado-masochism, bestiality (Snowden, 1988) or necrophilia.

Financial profit

Satanic cults cannot rely entirely for their financial resources upon members' donations and extortion, although both of these do apparently play a part. It is doubtful whether most ordinary cult members gain financially; in fact, they are more likely to be the victims of extortion. However, some members high in the hierarchy do, we are told, acquire vast wealth. The bulk of this is obtained from trading in drugs, pornography and snuff videos. Individual members, as indicated, may gain from using children for prostitution. Some survivors have also spoken of arms dealing but this would seem to be less common.

Cult members are apparently bribed and rewarded for conforming behaviour and for informing on members who are 'stepping out of line'. Rewards can be financial (help with holidays, mortgages, new cars, etc.), or string-pulling to further their careers, sometimes with the aid of Masonic connections. They may also be rewarded with high office within the cult.

CONCLUSION

These descriptions are all taken from accounts by British SRA survivors and they correspond closely with those in the international literature.

There was incredulity regarding the Holocaust, until irrefutable evidence was presented. Twenty years ago we were struggling to accept the reality of non-accidental injury to children and, more recently, child sexual abuse – and many still do not acknowledge that this occurs, not rarely, as we once thought, but with remarkable frequency (Search, 1988; La Fontaine, 1990: Ch. 2).

Credibility and scepticism regarding SRA were convincingly discussed in the

New Law Journal (Rolph, 1990). Burke's famous phrase with which Mr Rolph completed his article is as apt as ever:

All that is necessary for the triumph of evil is that good men do nothing.

(Burke, 1790)

APPENDIX

The following are the dates which most survivors claim consistently to be those of main satanic festivals. There may be variation within a few days in individual groups and some groups have their own special dates. (Some, observed less commonly, will be placed in brackets.) Some of these dates are also Christian festivals. As most ceremonies start just before midnight and end in the early hours of the next day, two consecutive dates will be given.

31 December–1 January	New Year
1 February–2 February	Candlemas
2 February–3 February	Calling the Devil
20 March–21 March	Equinox, Heralding of Spring
Maundy Thursday–Good Friday ⎫	
Good Friday–Holy Saturday ⎬	Easter Festival
Holy Saturday–Easter Sunday ⎭	
30 April–1 May	Walpurgis Night
1 May–2 May	Beltane
20 May–21 May	Coming of Summer
20 June–21 June ⎫	
21 June–22 June ⎬	Summer Solstice, Midsummer
31 July–1 August	Lammas
25 August–26 August	Lammas, in some groups
20 September–21 September	Equinox, Autumn
29 October–30 October ⎫	
30 October–31 October ⎬	Samhain, Halloween, November Eve
31 October–1 November ⎭	
20 December–21 December	Winter Solstice
21 December–22 December ⎫	
22 December–23 December ⎬	Christmas Festival
23 December–24 December ⎭	

Birthdays and cult marriage anniversaries of important members are celebrated throughout the group. Members' own birthdays are also celebrated.

This list of festival dates, compiled from British survivors' accounts, compares closely with the American list (Katchen and Sakheim, 1992).

REFERENCES

Burke, Edmund (1790) *Reflections on the Revolution in France.*

Crowley, Aleister (1926) 'Of the bloody sacrifice', Ch. 12, in *Magick in Theory and Practice*, New York, Castle.

Gould, Catherine (1992) 'Diagnosis and treatment of ritually abused children', in *Out of Darkness* by D.K. Sakheim and S.E. Devine, New York, Lexington.

Harper, A. (1990) *Dance with the Devil*, Eastbourne, Kingsway Publications Ltd.

HMSO (1992) *The Report of the Inquiry into the Removal of Children from Orkney in February 1991*, Lord Clyde, Edinburgh, HMSO.

Hudson, Pamela (1988) *Ritual Child Abuse, A Survey of Symptoms and Allegations*, USA, Privately published.

Hudson, Pamela (1991) *Ritual Child Abuse, Discovery Diagnosis and Treatment*, Saratoga, CA, R & E Publishers.

Katchen, M. and Sakheim, D. (1992) 'Satanic beliefs and practices', in D.K. Sakheim and S.E. Devine (eds) *Out of Darkness*, Lexington, MA, Lexington Books.

Kaye, Maribeth and Klein, Lawrence (1986) *Clinical Indicators of Satanic Cult Victimization.*

La Fontaine, Jean (1990) *Child Sexual Abuse*, Cambridge, Polity.

Melech, Aubrey (1986) *Missa Niger: La Messe Noire*, Northampton, Sat Anubis.

Parker, J. (1993) Ch 9, *At the Heart of Darkness. Witchcraft, Black Magic and Satanism Today*, London, Pan Macmillan.

Putnam, Frank W. (1989) *Diagnosis and Treatment of Multiple Personality Disorder*, New York, Guilford Press.

Randall, G. (1988) *No Way Home. A Survey of Homeless Children*, London, Centrepoint.

Ritchie, Jean (1991) Ch. 2, in *The Secret World of Cults*, London, Angus & Robertson.

Rolph, C.H. (1990) 'Credibility', *New Law Journal*, 6 April, 498.

Russell, J. (1980) *A History of Witchcraft*, London, Thames & Hudson.

Search, Gay (1988) *The Last Taboo*, Harmondsworth, Penguin.

Snowden, Kathy K. (1988) *Satanic Cult Ritual Abuse*, Richmond, VA, Richmond Psychotherapy Associates.

Stratford, Lauren (1988) *Satan's Underground*, Eugene Oregon, Harvest House.

Tate, Tim (1991) *Children for the Devil, Ritual Abuse and Satanic Crime*, London, Methuen.

Terry, Maury (1987) *The Ultimate Evil*, London, Grafton.

Young, W. (1992) 'Recognition and treatment of survivors reporting ritual abuse', in D.K. Sakheim and S.E. Devine (eds) *Out of Darkness*, Lexington, MA, Lexington Books.

Chapter 30

Trance-formations of abuse

Ashley Conway

Dr Ashley Conway is an Honorary Psychologist at Charing Cross Hospital and is in private practice.

Names, identities and background details have been changed wherever necessary to protect confidentiality.

The proposal of this chapter is that during episodes of physical or sexual abuse the victim's normal cognitive functioning is impaired as a result of dissociation, and information may be processed in a different way to that of normal consciousness. The consequences of this effect will be observable in cognition, affect and physiology. Phenomena observed during formal hypnotic inductions may provide a good model for understanding this process, and a framework for therapeutic strategies.

DSM-III-R (APA, 1987: 269) describes the essential feature of dissociative disorders as a 'disturbance or alteration in the normally integrative functions of identity, memory and consciousness', and says that the disturbance or alteration may be sudden or gradual, and transient or chronic. It also states that a common predisposing factor is sexual abuse or another form of severe emotional abuse in childhood, and that dissociative states may occur in people who have been subjected to periods of prolonged and intense coercive persuasion, including brainwashing and indoctrination by cultists. Spiegel (1988) reports that there is increasing evidence linking the experience of trauma and dissociation, citing a number of studies reporting a prevalence of severe physical trauma among patients with multiple personality disorder, and says that these patients report slipping into a dissociative state during periods of abuse, at first spontaneously and then deliberately. Dissociation may be an immediate defence, protecting the individual from the overwhelming pain and fear accompanying the trauma. Thus dissociation may be viewed as an adaptive response, where repression leading to amnesia is conceived of as a mechanism for protecting the individual from the emotional pain that has arisen from the disturbing events (Nemiah, 1985). However, as Spiegel points out, this adaptation has its price – while dissociation may help the individual to defend against the experience of physical helplessness, it does so at the risk of eventual psychological helplessness, of being taken over by spontaneous episodes of reliving the event, or by dissociated personalities and, in the extreme case, of multiple personality disorder.

There is a close connection between dissociation and hypnosis. Modern definitions of hypnosis suggest that the state is not one that is uniquely brought about by induction of one person by another using a formal process in a controlled way, but that hypnosis represents a phenomenon that is naturally occurring, and is part of a normal continuum of consciousness (see for example Wickramasekera, 1988; Booth, 1990). Nemiah (1985) has stated that hypnotic phenomena are merely dissociative phenomena elicited by the hypnotist, and that hypnosis may reproduce all of the symptoms of dissociative states (such as amnesias, somnambulistic states, localised paralyses, anaesthesias and hallucinations). Dissociated patients tend to be unusually highly hypnotisable, and there are reports (see for example Horevitz, 1986) that there is a high incidence of severe punishment or abuse in the childhood of highly hypnotisable subjects, such observations suggesting a common aetiological process. Spiegel and Spiegel (1985) report that hypnotic phenomena occur naturally, with or without formal induction, and that certain individuals under stress may shift into spontaneous trance states, that may in extreme cases take the form of dissociative symptoms. Spiegel (1988) suggests that traumatic experience early in life impels certain individuals to maintain high hypnotisability through developmental periods when they would ordinarily begin to lose this extreme capacity. Hilgard's (1977) neo-dissociation theory of hypnosis is one of the most influential theories in hypnosis. This holds that the unity of consciousness is illusory, and a central regulatory mechanism is postulated, that facilitates or inhibits the selective activation of multiple subsystems (such as attitudes, habits, cognitive or affective style) which make up the total personality. When activated, any subsystem continues with a measure of autonomy, and behaviour associated with the activated subsystem may be carried out with little or no awareness. Conway and Clarkson (1987) define hypnosis broadly as 'an altered state of consciousness consisting of the temporary or intermittent loss of contact with the current consensually defined reality'. They suggest that hypnotic inductions occur naturally, and that taught techniques of 'how to hypnotise' are subconsciously derived from these naturally occurring hypnotic inductions. They propose that information received during a naturally occurring trance state will not be processed normally, and may have the power of a hypnotic command. The conditions under which Conway and Clarkson (1987) suggest such a process is most likely to occur include: shock, pain, physical contact, double binds, over- and under-stimulation, extreme confusion, discounting of independence and the potency of the message giver. Any combination of these factors can be present in situations of abuse. Discussing spontaneous trance states, Rossi and Cheek (1988: 137) report 'It is not dangerous for a human being to enter hypnosis spontaneously during a time of stress, *provided that there is freedom from frightening suggestions during the time that he is in hypnosis*' (my emphasis). In abusive situations it is very unlikely that this condition will be satisfied, and very likely that there will be frightening suggestions made. Victims are likely to experience an invasion of the psyche as well as the soma.

Rossi (Rossi, 1986; Rossi and Cheek, 1988) has formulated an explanatory psychophysiological model of spontaneous changes in state, incorporating recent research on neurotransmitters and 'information substances', and the older literature on state-dependent learning. During shock and stress it is postulated that a special complex of information substances are suddenly released by the limbic-hypothalamic-pituitary-adrenal system, which encode all the external and internal sensory impressions of the situation in a special state of consciousness. These memories may then become dissociated from normal states of consciousness. Different combinations of neurotransmitters and information substances will produce different states in the organism; learning, memory and behaviour will all be dependent on that state. Memory and learning may become apparently dissociated or lost when the neurophysiological state is different, and be re-experienced when it is returned. Information is encoded at deep psychobiological levels, and such information may become state-dependent to a specific psychophysiological state of stress. Conway (1993a) additionally emphasises the inclusion of hyperventilation as a factor significantly affecting state. Physiologically, hyperventilation has effects of interfering with normal neuronal function, reducing cortical blood flow, reducing oxygen availability (the Bohr effect), destabilising pre-existing lateralisation of cortical activity, and influencing the EEG in general (Engel et al., 1947; Brashear, 1983; Lum, 1983; Conway, 1993a). Psychologically, hyperventilation can cause feelings of unreality, impaired intellectual performance and concentration, flight of ideas, loss of inhibition, confusion, dissociated states and memory impairment (see for example Allen and Agus, 1968).[1] Hyperventilation may be triggered by fear and pain. Nemiah (1985) reports that the dissociation experience of depersonalisation is sometimes brought on by acute anxiety accompanied by hyperventilation and, under conditions of extreme stress, the avoidance of normal contact with reality produced by hyperventilation may in some ways be adaptive. Turner and Gorst-Unsworth (1990) suggest that torture victims may learn to hyperventilate to dissociate from the impact of the violence. Lum (1981) has stated that during ritual mutilation ceremonies, of tribal initiation or voodoo, hyperventilation enables initiates to stoically endure otherwise extremely painful procedures. He also points out that hyperventilation powerfully aids the induction of hypnosis, with a number of standard procedures for hypnotic induction employing deliberately induced hyperventilation. Lum (1984) additionally states that the hypocarbia resulting from hyperventilation provides a sound physiological basis for many of the clinical manifestations of hypnosis. The same is likely to be true for dissociative states in general. Conway (1993a) proposes that both psychological stress and hyperventilation independently affect cortical laterality, and that the production of specific states may be dependent on both specific ventilation and hemisphericity.

The significance of these observations here is that at the time of the trauma a victim may go into a trance state. In most traumatic situations this phenomenon may occur spontaneously. In situations of ritual abuse it is possible that it may also be deliberately induced by another person (see Coleman, Ch. 29 this volume). Under these circumstances, messages received by the victim may have the power of hypnotic commands and include post-hypnotic suggestions to be carried out at a later time. Under hypnosis subjects may be given a command to be carried out at some future time, without remembering that they have been so instructed. Nemiah (1985) suggests that this may provide a model for some of the phenomena of dissociation. Mathews and McLeod (1986) have demonstrated experimentally that triggers to psychophysiological change can be responded to outside of conscious awareness. Conway *et al.* (1988) have demonstrated that cues to trigger apparently spontaneous episodes of hyperventilation may occur outside of conscious awareness, and that, therapeutically, hypnosis may be used to uncover such triggers. This non-conscious cuing could well account for apparent 'spontaneous' episodes of altered states, and it is of course quite possible that a cue to go into a different state could be deliberately implanted.

As noted above, the dissociation, which may be adaptive at the time of trauma, has its price, and may become the problem itself. The cost to the victim is of psychological helplessness, being taken over by apparently spontaneous episodes of altered states, during which cognition, physiology and affect may all be adversely affected; all systems can become state-dependent in their function. The client may have some sense of where this is coming from (for example, in the form of flashbacks), or the dissociation may be maintained from ordinary consciousness, inhibiting insight and, in extreme cases, may present in the form of multiple personality disorder. Statements made during an abusive episode, while the victim is in an altered state, will be enhanced in their power by not having the assessment of intact consciousness. Thus 'This is happening to you because you are bad / want it to / because you like it / deserve it / you are making it happen', etc. will have particularly powerful and destructive effects. The altered state may be cued by almost any stimulus, a word or phrase, tone of voice, a sight, sound, smell, feeling, taste or sensation which may have become classically conditioned to that state. Wide eyes may act as reminders of the frenzied eyes of an abuser, a specific pain may trigger a state, or breathlessness may cue a state reminiscent of asphyxiation during abuse. If the abuser is psychologically sophisticated, this effect might be exploited deliberately, by providing cues to the required altered state which may be frequently experienced in daily life. Compared to many other examples of extreme trauma, in situations of abuse, there will almost always be an additional complicating factor – some kind of threat not to tell. If the victim is told that if they tell they will be killed, disbelieved, hated, tortured, go mad, die, etc. the injunction against speaking, and usually even remembering, is so strong that overcoming it becomes one of the greatest barriers to change. The threat cues the altered state, so that the thought of telling, or perhaps even remembering, can trigger the state, which is most likely to be the physiological and psychological experience of extreme fear. Evidence for the presence of dissociative states may be observed in phenomena such as flashbacks and spontaneous age regression, and it is of course quite possible that what is recalled is only the tip of the iceberg. There are two very important implications of a state-dependent model: (i) the memory of the traumatic event will not be readily available in 'normal' consciousness, creating major difficulties for therapy; and (ii) when the psychophysiological state is re-accessed, recall of the trauma will be facilitated, but it is also very likely that the original traumatic emotion, cognitions and physiology will also be re-accessed. This means that, even in a therapeutic context, gaining access to the state is likely to be retraumatising.

The goal of the therapy in the long term is most likely to be to facilitate reintegration – to enable the state-bound commands, beliefs and physiological and affective reactions to be accessed and integrated, to be unlearned. Initially, therapeutic strategy may involve the first aid of helping the client to more effectively exclude the state, and subsequently, as more control is gained, to work within the state to dehypnotise the client and encourage integration of the various parts. Medication may help to exclude the troublesome state, and it is interesting to note that both beta-blockers and benzodiazepines used in anxiety management both have the effect of suppressing ventilation and causing a rise in arterial carbon dioxide (Joorabchi, 1977; Folgering and Cox, 1981; Gorman et al., 1985), helping to avoid hyperventilation. Learning breathing control will help to exclude episodes of uncontrollable hyperventilation triggering an altered state, and there is considerable evidence that such strategies are successful in the treatment of anxiety and panic. Cognitive strategies to reinterpret bodily sensations in non-catastrophic ways have also been shown to have beneficial effects in reducing panic. For therapy within the state, Nemiah (1985) suggests administration of Pentothal as one option, but in seriously abused clients offering some control may be preferable. Voluntary hyperventilation (see for example Nixon and Freeman, 1988) may serve to help re-access the physiology, affect and thoughts of the traumatised state, and at least offers clients some control (slowing breathing) if they begin to feel very distressed. Behavioural techniques, such as exposure to feared stimuli, or systematic desensitisation, whether in reality or in imagination, may help to access the state and extinguish conditioned responses. Emotion gives the state its energy, and when emotion is suppressed hyperventilation frequently results (Conway, 1991, 1993b). Psychodynamic therapy involving catharsis will help to release the energy of the state, and expressing the emotion brings about a beneficial change in ventilation (Conway, 1990). In discussing dissociative amnesia, Nemiah (1985) recommends restoring lost memories to consciousness as soon as possible. He suggests using free association to fragments of memories, and also the possibility of using Pentothal or hypnosis. He goes on to state that once the memories are obtained the suggestion must be made to patients that they will retain them in consciousness after waking. I believe that in situations where there has been the possibility of extreme abuse, it is very important to offer the client the option of retaining the amnesia. Nemiah does caution that when the amnesia is very firmly fixed, one must consider the possibility that it is protecting the patient from a 'continuing difficult situation'. The idea of using hypnosis in therapy is logical because, as discussed above, patients who have dissociative problems are likely to be highly hypnotisable. The idea of using hypnosis to reintegrate dissociated parts is not a new one; it was described by Morton Prince at the turn of the century. Hypnosis facilitates access to, and control over dissociated states (Spiegel, 1988). It may seem paradoxical that hypnosis, which may in some ways be associated with losing autonomy, can actually help enhance control. Clients can be given control in terms of planning, goal-setting, strategies, targets for therapy, interpretation and so on, just as in forms of therapy not employing formal hypnosis. The use of *self*-hypnosis can be emphasised, and clients can be encouraged to fluctuate in and out of the altered state as they feel appropriate, thus increasing their sense of control. Horevitz (1986) has suggested that in deeply traumatised individuals, hypnosis might first be used as a tool for relaxation, ego-enhancement and ideal-self techniques, to build the inner resources to cope with the material itself, which can be dealt with subsequently.

In the treatment of abuse victims therapists are very likely to be dealing with altered states of consciousness, irrespective of their therapeutic model or their conscious awareness that this is what they are doing. A radical argument might then be that in fact a lot of psychotherapy in general is about the process of dehypnotising clients. I believe that this is particularly true for individuals subjected to serious abuse. An insight into the process of formal and informal hypnotic techniques is therefore valuable. There is a popular belief that hypnosis enhances recall of memory. There are certainly reports of remarkable benefits occurring to patients whose amnesia has been lifted during a hypnotic intervention (see e.g. Nemiah, 1985). From his remarkable reports of evoking recollection by directly electrically stimulating specific areas of the cortex, Penfield (1952) concludes that a memory record continues intact, even after the subject's ability to recall it disappears. Stimulation of a particular site will cause the subject to feel again the emotion which the situation originally produced, with the same inter-pretations which were made in the first place. Thus, he says 'evoked recollection is not the exact photographic or phonographic reproduction of past scenes and events. It is reproduction of what the patient saw and heard and felt and under-stood.' Spiegel (1988), interpreting hypnosis as a structured and controlled form of dissociation, states that it makes sense that therapy employing hypnosis can be particularly useful in helping trauma victims mobilise and re-experience images associated with the trauma. At the same time hypnosis can provide control, by enabling the client to retrieve material in manageable pieces. It can also help the client to manage the affective response to the memories, and memories can be restructured in a way that allows their incorporation into consciousness.

However, using hypnosis to aid recall is not without difficulties in itself. Hypnosis increases the productivity of recall, but also increases the likelihood of confabulation. Additionally, it is likely to produce greater confidence that material recalled is accurate (Perry, 1992). Hypnosis can be deliberately used to create pseudomemories, for therapeutic purposes, and it has also been demonstrated that the hypnotist can deliberately or unwittingly provoke pseudomemories by asking leading questions under hypnosis (Perry *et al.*, 1988). Inaccurate memories in hypnosis can be confident ones, and highly hypnotisable subjects are more prone to confuse real and imagined memories than are less hypnotisable subjects (Sheehan, 1988) and Lynn *et al.* (1991) report that when target events of pseudomemory suggestions are not publicly verifiable, the pseudomemory rate is invariably higher. Orne (1986) states that, typically, memories from different periods in the patient's life are combined, that phantasies, beliefs and fears may be mixed with actual recollections and that, although some 'memories' may represent a psychologically meaningful truth, they cannot be assumed to be historically accurate fact, even though patients may show a therapeutic improvement from working through such memories. For these reasons, he points out, the American Medical Association has indicated that previously hypnotised witnesses should not give testimony in court concerning the matters about which they have been hypnotised. In an experimental situation Barnier and McConkey (1992) found that hypnotisability rather than hypnosis itself was associated with false memory reports, and as it has been observed that there is a relationship between dissociation and hypnosis, these cautions are likely to apply generally to the clients here, whether or not hypnosis is formally induced. Additionally, Watkins and Watkins (1992) draw attention to the danger that simulations of multiple personalities can be artificially created by hypnotherapists who wish to exercise their suggestive hypnotic leverage, and emphasise the importance of open suggestions, so as to avoid such contaminating leading suggestions.

There are other cautions to be applied in using hypnosis – secondary or multiple personalities may emerge at this time (Nemiah, 1985). Accessing a state/memory associated with a trauma in itself will to some degree reinflict some trauma on the client, and uncovering traumatic content too early may be overwhelming to the client, and threaten the therapeutic relationship. Spiegel (1988) points out that the enhanced receptivity of clients in hypnosis constitutes a potential vulnerability, and that transference problems, as well as fear of being overwhelmed by the dysphoric affect, may be intensified by hypnosis.

Notwithstanding these reservations, the use of hypnosis can be therapeutically very powerful for abuse victims, both in terms of techniques of formal hypnotic work, and in terms of hypnotic processes in general. Spiegel (1988) suggests that the hypnosis is structured as an exercise to be started and concluded by the client. The therapist should be sensitive to when the client has had enough, and he recommends that the client should 'feel comfortable remembering consciously as much but no more than they care to'. This process can enable clients to face the helplessness of the original situation, without reinflicting helplessness upon them. Clients can be given the option of slowing or terminating the hypnosis at any time, and be given strategies for rapidly returning to a psychologically safe place. Spiegel and Spiegel (1985) describe a technique of using a screen, or number of screens to picture scenes, or different aspects of events, while maintaining a physical sense of relaxation, actively using a process of dissociation – to separate psychological from somatic distress. Smith and Titus (1992) describe a technique of symbolic confrontation with a perpetrator, to help discharge emotion, and report that patients can benefit from this process without actually involving the other party.

Ideomotor signalling (see for example Rossi and Cheek, 1988), which involves subjects in hypnosis subconsciously giving non-verbal signals in reply to the therapist's questions, can be very valuable in these situations. Questions asked could include for example: 'Would it be OK for you to know about the cause of your problem? Was there a particular incident that occurred that is still affecting you now? Is there a lot of feeling attached to this event? Would it be OK for you to remember/tell me about it?' and perhaps 'Do you need to understand what happened to be able to achieve your goals?' Automatic writing may be used in the same kind of way.

To maintain the client's sense of control I use a technique of hypnotically induced dreaming. Having first checked out with the client via ideomotor signalling that it is acceptable, two lines of approach may be used: (i) suggest that the client has a dream which provides some useful information about what took place and (ii) suggest that the dream be used to express and release a manageable piece of feeling. Clients can be given the suggestion that they will remember what is useful for them to remember at this time. Rossi and Cheek (1988) suggest a hypnotic technique of asking for an unconscious review, so that therapeutic benefit may accrue in some situations without the client's conscious awareness of what happened. This review may be followed by a review open to consciousness.

Because of the association between hypnosis and dissociative states, hypnotic techniques can be utilised despite the fact that no formal hypnotic induction procedure has been undertaken. This can be particularly valuable where the client associates the idea of hypnosis with a repetition of experiences of loss of control. Indirect approaches may be more appropriate for these clients, where the high suggestibility of the clients can then be utilised as a therapeutic ally. Kluft (1992) has reported that when nursing staff were taught to constructively use the inherent trance-proneness of dissociative disorder patients, significant benefit was achieved for all concerned. Gruenewald (1984) reports a client who frequently went into dissociative episodes during the therapeutic session, and was requested to 'return' as soon as feasible. Then material that had emerged during the dissociation was used for further therapeutic work. Simply asking the client to focus attention on a particular body sensation, and wait for an association to come to mind, can access an important state, and its associated affect and memory. Other techniques, constructively using dissociation phenomena to help in the process of reintegration, might include asking the client to imagine themselves as they are now, going back in time to the traumatised child: 'What would you like to say to the child? . . . What can the child appropriately learn from this experience? . . . Who does it tell us about? . . . Who caused it to happen? . . . For whose benefit? . . . Who was in control of the situation? . . . Did you survive? . . . 'etc. This kind of strategy is likely to encourage a dissociated state, but keeps in touch with the present. New messages can be given to the child, and old beliefs re-examined. Where there is not full recall of events, general messages can be given about things that may have been said in the past, which need not go on having an effect in the present and future. Clients can be given cues or anchors to safe feelings, thoughts and relationships, to help them stay in touch with current reality. Using spontaneous altered states, threats can be re-examined and harmful post-hypnotic suggestions, for example to hurt themselves rather than tell, can be examined and assessed. All of this will have much greater impact if it is done in contact with the disordered/distressed state. If there is no contact with the state, then the therapeutic message is less likely to have a positive effect. The therapist therefore needs to be finely tuned to detect the presence of the altered state. Sometimes it will be very obvious, with a dramatic affective reaction, at other times it may be much more subtle, when cues such as changes in breathing, skin tone, sweating, eye focus or gaze, voice tone, etc. may need to be closely observed. Likewise, an awareness of trance phenomena can be helpful in 'bringing a client back' from spontaneous trance; using a matter-of-fact tone of voice, or requesting simple factual information will help.

Dissociation may in some ways protect the trauma victim from the pain and distress of the past, but it may also make it difficult for the client to be fully present in the therapeutic situation, and dissociation may occur in the face of the challenge of therapy. Rossi and Cheek (1988: 137) propose that it is 'reasonable to assume that such spontaneous hypnosis, unrecognised and ignored by those properly responsible, could become a source of danger not in itself, but as a result of professional unawareness of significant changes in the patient.' Understanding the phenomena of hypnosis may help us to become more effective in our therapeutic work of de-hypnotising our clients.

NOTE

1 Hyperventilation occurring to the experience as a consequence of fear, pain or as a learned dissociation technique, and hypoventilation brought about by being choked or suffocated may, paradoxically, have similar effects, of inducing cerebral hypoxia and a physiologically altered state.

REFERENCES

APA (1987) *Diagnostic and Statistical Manual of Mental Disorders (Third Edition – Revised)*, Washington, American Psychiatric Association.
Allen, T.E. and Agus, B. (1968) 'Hyperventilation leading to hallucinations', *American Journal of Psychiatry* 125, 632–7.
Barnier, A.J. and McConkey, K.M. (1992) 'Reports of real and false memories: the relevance of hypnosis, hypnotizability, and the context of memory test', *Journal of Abnormal Psychology* 101, 521–7.
Booth, P. (1990) 'La situation de l'hypnose en Angleterre', Paper presented at 'The International Congress: 'L'Hypnose 101 ans apres', Paris, 28–30 September.

Brashear, R.E. (1983) 'Hyperventilation syndrome', *Lung* 161, 257–73.

Conway, A.V. (1990) 'Blood, breath and tears: a psychodynamic model for therapy of hyperventilation associated panic attacks', *Biological Psychology* 30, 297.

Conway, A.V. (1991) 'Grieving and breathing', *Bereavement Care* 10, 2–3.

Conway, A.V. (1993a) 'The influence of psychological factors and hyperventilation on lateralisation of electrodermal activity in cardiac and normal subjects', unpublished PhD thesis, University of London.

Conway, A.V. (1993b) 'Breathing and feeling', in B. Timmons and R. Ley (eds) *Behavioural and Psychological Approaches to Breathing Disorders*, New York, Plenum.

Conway, A.V. and Clarkson, P. (1987) 'Everyday hypnotic inductions', *Transactional Analysis Journal* 17, 17–23.

Conway, A.V., Freeman, L.J. and Nixon, P.G. (1988) 'Hypnotic examination of trigger factors in the hyperventilation syndrome', *American Journal of Clinical Hypnosis* 30, 296–304.

Engel, G.L., Ferris, E.B. and Logan, M. (1947) 'Hyperventilation: analysis of clinical symptomatology', *Annals of Internal Medicine* 27, 683–704.

Folgering, H. and Cox, A. (1981) 'Beta-blocker therapy with Metoprolol in the hyperventilation syndrome', *Respiration* 41, 33–8.

Gorman, J., Fyer, A., Ross, D. *et al.* (1985) 'Normalization of venous pH, pCO_2, and bicarbonate levels after blockade of panic attacks', *Psychiatry Research* 14, 57–65.

Gruenewald, D. (1984) 'On the nature of multiple personality: comparisons with hypnosis', *The International Journal of Clinical and Experimental Hypnosis* 32, 170–90.

Hilgard, E.R. (1977) *Divided Consciousness: Multiple Controls in Human Thought and Action*, New York, Wiley.

Horevitz, R. (1986) 'Terrifying imagery in hypnosis', in B. Zilbergeld, M.G. Edelstein and D.L. Araoz (eds) *Hypnosis Questions and Answers*, New York, Norton.

Joorabchi, B. (1977) 'Expressions of the hyperventilation syndrome in childhood', *Clinical Pediatrics* 16, 1110–15.

Kluft, R.P. (1992) 'Enhancing the hospital treatment of dissociative disorder patients by developing nursing expertise in the application of hypnotic techniques without formal trance induction', *American Journal of Clinical Hypnosis* 34, 158–67.

Lum, L.C. (1981) 'Hyperventilation and anxiety state', *Journal of the Royal Society of Medicine*, 74, 1–4.

Lum, L.C. (1983) 'Psychogenic breathlessness and hyperventilation', *Update*, 913–23.

Lum, L.C. (1984) 'Physiological changes during hypnosis', in D. Waxman (ed.) *Psychological Influences and Illness – Hypnosis and Medicine*, London, Royal Society of Medicine and Macmillan.

Lynn, S.J., Milano, M. and Weekes, J.R. (1991) 'Hypnosis and pseudomemories: the effects of prehypnotic expectancies', *Journal of Personality and Social Psychology* 60, 318–26.

Mathews, A. and McLeod, C. (1986) 'Discrimination of threat cues without awareness in anxiety states', *Journal of Abnormal Psychology* 95, 131–8.

Nemiah, J.C. (1985) 'Dissociative disorders (hysterical neurosis, dissociative type)', in H.I. Kaplan and B.J. Sadock (eds) *Comprehensive Textbook of Psychiatry*, 4th edn, Baltimore: Williams & Wilkins.

Nixon, P.G.F. and Freeman, L.J. (1988) 'The "think test": a further technique to elicit hyperventilation', *Journal of the Royal Society of Medicine* 81, 277–9.

Orne, M. (1986) 'The validity of memories retrieved in hypnosis', in B. Zilbergeld, M.G. Edelstein and D.L. Araoz (eds) *Hypnosis Questions and Answers*, New York, Norton.

Penfield, W. (1952) 'Memory mechanisms', *Archives of Neurology and Psychiatry* 67, 178–98.

Perry, C. (1992) 'What is hypnosis?', *Hypnos* 19, 169–79.

Perry, C.W., Laurence, J., D'Eon, J. and Tallant, B. (1988) 'Hypnotic age regression techniques in the elicitation of memories: applied uses and abuses', in H.M. Pettinati (ed.) *Hypnosis and Memory*, New York, Guilford Press.

Rossi, E.L. (1986) *The Psychobiology of Mind–Body Healing: New Concepts in Therapeutic Hypnosis*, New York, Norton.

Rossi, E.L. and Cheek, D.B. (1988) *Mind–Body Therapy*, New York, Norton.

Sheehan, P.W. (1988) 'Confidence, memory and hypnosis', in H.M. Pettinati (ed.) *Hypnosis and Memory*, New York, Guilford Press.

Smith, R.D. and Titus, E. (1992) 'Hypnotic personalization/confrontation: a controlled abreaction technique for multiple personality disorder', *Treating Abuse Today* 2, 6–10.

Spiegel, D. (1988) 'Dissociation and hypnosis in post-traumatic stress disorders', *Journal of Traumatic Stress* 1, 17–33.

Spiegel, D. and Spiegel, H. (1985) 'Hypnosis' in H.I. Kaplan and B.J. Sadock (eds) *Comprehensive Textbook of Psychiatry*, 4th edn, Baltimore: Williams & Wilkins.

Turner, S. and Gorst-Unsworth, C. (1990) 'Psychological sequelae of torture', *British Journal of Psychiatry* 157, 475–80.

Watkins, J.G. and Watkins, H.W. (1992) 'A comparison of "hidden observers", ego states and multiple personalities', *Hypnos* 19, 215–21.

Wickramasekera, I.E. (1988) *Clinical Behavioural Medicine*, New York, Plenum.

Chapter 31

A personal review of the literature

Su Burrell

Su Burrell is a Specialist Clinical Lecturer in Social Work/Child Protection in the Children and Families Department of the Tavistock Clinic. Her background is in Forensic Child Psychiatry and Child Protection. She is a founder member of the Standing Committee on Sexually Abused Children (SCOSAC) which is a network and consultation resource for professionals working with sexually abused children. Su is an established child protection trainer.

Names, identities and background details have been changed wherever necessary to protect confidentiality.

INTRODUCTION

This review of the literature on the 'satanic' and 'ritualised' abuse of children is subject to a number of restrictions including space and, on occasion, the strength of the author's stomach. The emotional content of the debate surrounding the existence, or otherwise, of 'satanic' and 'ritualistic' abuse has led me to include a short statement regarding my own beliefs and, as a consequence, types of literature which I do not feel qualified to review. The aim of this chapter is to provide a brief review of the literature which promotes good professional interventions with children, families and the professional network, with particular focus on the child. For the sake of comprehension, literature relating to the historical background of Satanism, overview texts and definitions will also be included.

Recently, a young relative described to me how a school friend had visited Winnie the Pooh's tree in London whilst on a visit. Inadvertently, I must have conveyed a glimmer of disbelief, for I was immediately confronted by 'You're just stupid! It is true, she left a jar of honey and it was gone the next day. So there!' I am of course well aware that Winnie the Pooh, Paddington Bear and Father Christmas, etc. do not exist in the flesh, and that therefore my young relative's account was not truth. Was it a lie? I include this episode to illustrate that the beliefs of children, fuelled by their own imaginations but initiated and sustained by adults, and by the media, are not always truth. The belief described here appears relatively benign, but this is not necessarily true in relation to all beliefs that children hold. Father Christmas, for example, has a major religious component, but is presented to children in different countries, with similar religious beliefs, in ways that range from the most benign figure to an extremely cruel and punitive 'bogey man'. This is an enormous topic, and beyond the scope of this chapter, but serves to illustrate that there are beliefs held by children, of which adults generally do not disabuse children.

Given the controversy surrounding the subject of 'satanic' and 'ritualistic' abuse, I believe it would be useful to briefly set out my own beliefs. My religious background is Church of England and Quaker, and I attended a church school. I studied theology as an academic subject up to the age of 18 in order to clarify confusions about beliefs. For the last three of my school years I was described as an existentialist and seen as a non-Christian. I place no religion or creed in any hierarchical ordering, but do believe that we are all capable of 'good' and 'bad' and, with some provisos, believe all adults to be responsible for their own actions. I am wary of any belief held in an extreme way, or to the exclusion of all others, although I respect the beliefs of others and their right to these beliefs. I do not believe that anybody has the right to necessarily act on their beliefs if their beliefs impinge in any harmful, negative or judgemental way on others. My professional background is in Forensic Child Psychiatry and Child Protection, and the above remarks are made within the framework of Law.

A significant amount of recent literature on the subject of 'satanic' and 'ritualistic' abuse is written from a base of strong religious belief or 'anti-religious' belief. I do not feel qualified to review this literature and readers wishing to study the debate in greater depth, or who themselves hold strong beliefs, should approach the relevant churches, groups and agencies for advice on relevant reading.

DEFINITIONS AND TERMINOLOGY

That all forms of child abuse may contain elements and components that are ritualised is well accepted in the field of child protection (for example, Pithers 1990; Wood, 1990). In a very helpful article David Jones (1991) argues that the creation of separate labels such as 'satanic' and 'ritualistic' abuse convey little benefit for clinicians and, further, that practitioner objectivity could be jeopardised by their use. He suggests that it is more helpful to consider the extent to which psychological or physical abuse coexist with sexual abuse in any individual case, and that the scope of the abuse alleged can then be described without invoking a new term.

The most helpful definitions of 'ritualistic' abuse appear to be those based on the typology of ritual abuse set out by Finkelhor and his colleagues in *Nursery Crimes* (Finkelhor *et al.*, 1988). Briefly, the authors define three types of ritual abuse: cult-based ritualistic abuse; pseudo-ritualistic abuse and psychopathological ritualism. Later authors have expanded on this or focused on particular aspects, such as an emphasis on the children abused (McFadyen *et al.*, 1993) or to point out the difficulties of distinguishing the motivations of perpetrators in 'cult-based ritualistic abuse' and 'pseudo-ritualistic abuse' (Kelley, 1988, 1993). The definitions of Finkelhor *et al.* (1988) attempt to avoid suggesting that all rituals in child abuse are 'satanic'.

In *Working Together Under the Children Act* (HMSO, 1991) the use of 'bizarre or ritualised behaviour' sometimes associated with particular 'belief systems' is included under the term 'organised abuse'. This is described as a generic term covering abuse which may involve a number of abusers, a number of abused children, different forms of abuse and some degree of organisation. It has been argued (Jones, 1991) that multiple victims may exist without any religious or indeed satanic component, for example child sex abuse rings.

Clearly the definitions of 'satanic' and 'ritualistic' abuse have a major impact on diagnosis. Lack of space precludes listing symptoms that are seen by writers in the field to be diagnostic. There are several lists of symptoms and symptom clusters in the literature including Finkelhor *et al.* (1988), Gould (1987), Hudson (1991), Kelley (1989, 1993), Snow and Sorenson (1990), Waterman *et al.* (1990) and Young *et al.* (1991).

BACKGROUND

In *Satanism and Occult Related Violence. What You Should Know* (Langone and Blood, 1990), the authors describe those activities covered by the modern use of the term 'Satanism'. They divide practitioners of Satanism into four categories: dabblers; self-styled or psychopathic satanists; religious satanists; and satanic cults. The authors clearly state that most satanic practitioners do not abuse children, and of those that do the majority are known to belong to the self-styled or psychopathic and satanic cult categories. These categories would fit with Finkelhor's first two types (Finkelhor *et al.*, 1988). They also clearly state that child abuse perpetrators using satanic practices may not be satanists.

Lloyd (1991) outlines the controversies in the subject of the ritual abuse of children, and argues that the continued lack of consensus regarding terminology and criteria is likely to ensure that the controversies continue.

Hill and Goodwin (1989) use descriptions of satanic rituals given by historians using pre-Inquisition primary sources, and compare these to modern patient accounts. In an extremely useful and succinct article, Kelley (1993) lists the research on ritualistic abuse of children reported in the literature in relation to the characteristics outlined by Hill and Goodwin (1989).

The history of Satanism, satanic religions and satanic beliefs and practices, is described by Katchen (1992) and by Katchen and Sakheim (1992). Both the broad-based British journalistic texts (Boyd, 1991; Tate, 1991) include well-referenced chapters on the background to Satanism and modern day satanic rituals. *At the Heart of Darkness* (Parker, 1993) and *Ecstasies* (Ginzberg, 1989) were helpful background texts. I was unable to read *The Satanic Bible* (La Vey, 1969) which he describes as satanic thought from a satanic point of view, but some readers may wish to and it is still available.

Multiple personality disorder (MPD) and the false memory syndrome

A significant amount of recent literature, particularly that which pertains to adult survivors of 'ritualistic' and 'satanic' abuse, had focused on MPD; this diagnosis is very uncommon in Britain but in recent years has been increasingly used in the United States of America. Practitioners in Britain working with abused children and adult survivors of abuse do, however, frequently encounter dissociative states. Whilst these subjects are not directly within the scope of this review readers are referred to Dr Sandra Bloom's chapter in this volume (Ch. 33). Briere (1988), Van-Benschoten (1990) and Young *et al.* (1991) I found helpful, as also Ganaway (1990), Greaves (1992) and Putnam (1993). Richard Ofshe (1992) is perhaps the best-known exponent of the false memory syndrome.

JOURNALISTIC OVERVIEW TEXTS

There is of course a multiplicity of newspaper articles, of which some are more useful than others, but none cover the subject in anything like the detail of the two British texts, both of which are recommended. *Blasphemous Rumours* (Boyd, 1991) and *Children for the Devil* (Tate, 1991) are both well researched, relatively easy to read and provide a comprehensive overview of the background, current problems debate and difficulties. The former is currently out of print, although available in British libraries.

SINGLE CASE DESCRIPTIONS

Perhaps the best-known single case description recounted by an adult is *Michelle Remembers* (Smith and Pazder, 1980). This is enormously credited by a number of writers as the first published account of satanic ritualistic abuse, and viewed by some as causal to all the cases that have since come to light. Although Freud (1897) later changed his view, his account of his work with Emma E. is perhaps one of the earliest published accounts. (See Introduction.) However, neither of these texts is a particularly easy read for students of this field and they are not recommended as initial reading. *Ghost-Girl* (Hayden, 1991) is the account by an educational psychologist of her work with a pupil in a small special needs class, who has a diagnosis of elective mutism. Torey Hayden recounts, using the child's words and descriptions of behaviour, her growing realisation that the 'ghost girl' has been subjected to abuse. It is a warts and all account and is highly recommended, particularly to students and trainees.

MULTIPLE CASE DESCRIPTIONS: ASSESSMENT AND TREATMENT

The majority of texts describing 'satanic' and 'ritualistic' abuse of more than one victim are helpful in both positive and negative ways in terms of assessment protocols. A smaller number are excellent in terms of treatment approaches.

RE: INTERVIEWING AND ADVOCACY

In the *Memorandum of Good Practice on Video Recorded Interviews with Child Witnesses for Criminal Proceedings* (HMSO, 1992a) the British government lays out guidelines for interviewing children who are the victims of, or witnesses to, violent or sexual offence. Both the *Cleveland Inquiry Report* (HMSO, 1988) and the *Orkney Inquiry Report* (HMSO, 1992b) are more helpfully read in their entirety. Practitioners who are required to act as advocates for children who have made allegations of sexual abuse, particularly if it includes a satanic or ritualistic component, must be familiar with the above documents. Practitioners have found themselves open to accusations of bias if their reading on the subject of 'satanic' and 'ritualistic' abuse can be seen to lack balance. Practitioners who have attended conferences on this subject, however excellent the speakers, are open to accusations of brainwashing (Summit, 1991; MacFarlane, 1992). Both *Community Care* (Anon., 1989; Cervi, 1990; Ivory, 1990; Sone, 1990) and the now amalgamated *Social Work Today* (Wood, 1990; Eaton *et al.*, 1991; Hopkins, 1991) have produced helpful articles in relation to 'satanic' and 'ritualistic' child abuse investigations in Britain, particularly in relation to the impact on practitioners. It is important to balance such reading with, for example, articles by Kenneth Lanning, the designated FBI investigator for 'satanic' or 'ritualistic' abuse (Lanning, 1992a), and articles by Sherrill Mulhern (1990), an anthropologist who has worked with Kenneth Lanning. Both these writers have a genuine concern regarding the professional and lay response to allegations of 'satanic' and 'ritualistic' abuse. *In Pursuit of Satan* (Hicks, 1991) is more emotive but still helpful.

The number of research based textbooks on the subject are increasing and the following are all recommended. *Nursery Crimes* (Finkelhor *et al.*, 1988) is an American national study of sexual abuse in day care and pre-school facilities: 13 per cent of reported cases had elements of 'satanic' or 'ritualistic' abuse. In *Behind the Playground Walls* (Waterman *et al.*, 1993), which had its origins in a study funded by the National Centre on Child Abuse and Neglect in the USA, the authors' primary aim was to document the particular problems of children who have made allegations, and on treatment approaches. Gontalez *et al.* (1993) look at the patterns of disclosure and retraction in psychotherapy. *Out of Darkness* (Sakheim and Devine, 1992) is a collection which endeavours to offer a variety of perspectives on the subject of ritual abuse, and to encourage critical evaluation. They believe that the more practitioners and clinicians understand about the history, beliefs and practices of satanic religion, about those who present as survivors and about treatment approaches, the better their practice will be.

There are a number of journal articles and papers which generally focus on one multiple case description. I found the following available and interesting: Bottoms *et al.* (1991); Kelley (1989); Snow and Sorenson (1990); Hudson (1991). As previously stated, the reader is advised to exercise caution where authors are writing from the point of view of professionals involved in the case, because of allegations of bias. Jonker and Jonker-Bakker (1991), writing about the Oude Pekela case in the Netherlands, have been particularly criticised. However, it is not always possible to find articles of equal scholarly merit to those mentioned above, which are written from a different perspective.

The majority of newspaper reporting of cases involving a component of 'ritualistic' abuse cannot be described as balanced, nor are they written to increase the understanding of practitioners. Caution is advised with articles by the Reachout Trust (Davies) and to a lesser extent by Childwatch (Core, 1991), as both agencies appear to present somewhat extreme views and, whilst the articles are written with the best intentions, they are not good starter texts.

It is clearly useful for practitioners working with children who give accounts of abuse that have a bizarre or ritualistic component, to study accounts of work with children described by other practitioners. This is particularly true in terms of the process of 'disclosing' and of helpful and unhelpful treatment interventions. The current climate and good practice dictate that we are vigilant about keeping a balance in terms of material. For this reason, caution is also advised when using the practitioner manual type of text to inform work with children (Ryder, 1992).

SUMMARY: RECOMMENDED READING

The majority of literature on 'satanic' and 'ritualistic' abuse cannot be described as 'easy' or 'light' reading. I undertook the task of this review a year ago, and some texts took many months to read. Added to this are the problems engendered for practitioners by the controversy around the subject; particularly front line workers who may be required to interview, assess, act as advocates for and draw up treatment plans for children who make allegations. Therefore, for readability and balance the following texts are highly recommended: *Ghost-Girl* (Hayden, 1991); 'Ritualism and child sexual abuse' (Jones, 1991); 'Ritualistic abuse of children' (Kelley, 1993) and *Behind the Playground Walls* (Waterman *et al.*, 1993). To this list I would also add the *Cleveland Report* (HMSO, 1988), the *Orkney Inquiry* (HMSO, 1992b) and the *Memorandum of Good Practice* (HMSO, 1992a), *Working Together Under the Children Act 1989* (HMSO, 1991) and *Out of Darkness* (Sakheim and Devine, 1992).

ACKNOWLEDGEMENTS

With grateful appreciation to Ms M. Walker, the Tavistock Library, SCOSAC's database, and to those colleagues who loaned texts.

REFERENCES

Anon. (1989) 'Facing the unbelievable', *Community Care* 14 Dec, 14–16.
Bottoms, B.L., Shaver, P. and Goodman, G.S. (1991) 'Profile of ritualistic and religion-related abuse allegations reported to clinical psychologists in the United States', Paper presented at the Ninety-Ninth Annual Convention of the American Psychological Association, San Francisco.
Boyd, A. (1991) *Blasphemous Rumours: Is Satanic Ritual Abuse Fact or Fantasy? An Investigation*, London, Fount.
Briere, J. (1988) 'The long-term clinical correlates of childhood sexual victimization', *Annals of the New York Academy of Sciences* 528, 327–34.
Bringewatt, M.J. (1991) 'The Minnesota Family Sexual Abuse Project', in M.Q. Patton (ed.) *Family Sexual Abuse: Frontline Research and Evaluation*, London, Sage.
Cervi, R. (1990) 'Rochdale is on the rack: ritual abuse in Rochdale', *Community Care* 20 September, 2.
Core, D. with Fred Harrison (1991) *'Chasing Satan': An Investigation into Satanic Crimes Against Children*, London, Gunter Books.
Davies, M. (n.d.) Reachout Trust, unpublished paper.
Eaton, L., Cohen, P., Downey, R., Lunn, T. and Wilson, M. (1991) 'Ritual abuse: fantasy or reality', *Social Work Today* 23(5), 8–12.
Finkelhor, D., Williams, L. and Burns, N. (1988) *Nursery Crimes: Sexual Abuse in Day Care*, Newbury Park, CA, Sage.
Freud, S. (1897) 'Emma Eckstein', *Standard Edition Vol. 1*, 242–3, London, Hogarth (1971).
Freud, S. (1897) in J.M. Masson *The Assault on Truth: Freud's Suppression of the Seduction Theory*, London, Penguin (1985), pp. 100–6.
Ganaway, G. (1990) 'A psychodynamic look at alternative explanations for satanic ritual abuse in MPD patients', Paper delivered at the Seventh International Conference on Multiple Personality/Dissociative States, Chicago, November.
Ginzburg, C. (1989) *Ecstasies: Deciphering the Witches' Sabbath*, London: Penguin 1992.
Gonzalez, L.S., Waterman, J., Kelly, R.J., McCord, J. and Oliveri, M.K. (1993) 'Children's patterns of disclosures and recantations of sexual and ritualistic abuse allegations in psychotherapy', *Child Abuse and Neglect* 17(2), 281–91.
Gould, C. (1987) 'Satanic ritual abuse: child victims, adult survivors, system response', *California Psychologist* 22(3), 1.
Greaves, G.B. (1992) 'Alternative hypotheses regarding claims of satanic cult activity: a critical analysis', in D.K. Sakheim and S.E. Devine (eds) *Out of Darkness: Exploring Satanism and Ritual Abuse*, New York, Lexington.
Hayden, T. (1991) *Ghost-Girl: A True Story*, London, Macmillan.
Hicks, R.D. (1991) *In Pursuit of Satan: The Police and the Occult*, New York, Prometheus Books.
Hill, S. and Goodwin, J. (1989) 'Satanism: similarities between patient accounts and pre-Inquisition historical sources', *Dissociation* 2(2), 39–43.
HMSO (1988) *The Report of the Inquiry into Child Abuse in Cleveland 1987*, Lord Justice Butler-Sloss DBE, London, HMSO.
HMSO (1991) *Working Together Under the Children Act 1989. A Guide to Arrangements for Inter-Agency Co-operation for the Protection of Children from Abuse*, London, HMSO.
HMSO (1992a) *Memorandum of Good Practice on Video Recorded Interviews with Child Witnesses for Criminal Proceedings*, London, HMSO.
HMSO (1992b) *The Report of the Inquiry into the Removal of Children from Orkney in February 1991*, Lord Clyde, Edinburgh: HMSO.

272   Common elements and issues in satanist abuse

Hopkins, J. (1991) 'Trial and error', *Social Work Today* 23(8), 21.
Hudson, P.S. (1991) *Ritual Child Abuse: Discovery, Diagnosis and Treatment*, Saratoga, CA, R & E Publishers.
Ivory, M. (1990) 'Ritual abuse – the blight on the path to partnership', *Community Care* 27, 7.
Jones, D.P.H. (1991) 'Commentary: ritualism and child sexual abuse', *Child Abuse and Neglect* 15(3), 163–70.
Jonker, F. and Jonker-Bakker, P. (1991) 'Experiences with ritualistic child sexual abuse: a case study from the Netherlands', *Child Abuse and Neglect* 15(3), 191–6.
Katchen, M.H. (1992) 'The history of satanic religions', D.K. Sakheim and S.E. Devine (eds) *Out of Darkness: Exploring Satanism and Ritual Abuse*, New York, Lexington.
Katchen, M.H. and Sakheim, D.K. (1992) 'Satanic beliefs and practices', in D.K. Sakheim and S.E. Devine (eds) *Out of Darkness: Exploring Satanism and Ritual Abuse*, New York, Lexington.
Kelley, S.J. (1988) 'Ritualistic abuse of children: dynamics and impact', *Cultic Studies Journal* 5(2), 199–236.
Kelley, S.J. (1989) 'Stress responses of children to sexual abuse and ritualistic abuse in day care centres', *Journal of Interpersonal Violence* 4(4), 502–13,
Kelley, S.J. (1993) 'Ritualistic abuse of children', *Ballière's Clinical Paediatrics* 1(1), 31–46.
Langone, M.D. and Blood, L.O. (1990) *Satanism and Occult Related Violence. What You Should Know*, Weston, MA, American Family Foundation.
Lanning, K.V. (1992a) 'Commentary: ritual abuse: a law enforcement view or perspective', *Child Abuse and Neglect* 15(3), 171–4.
Lanning, K.V. (1992b) 'A law enforcement perspective on allegations of ritual abuse', in D.K. Sakheim and S.E. Devine (eds) *Out of Darkness: Exploring Satanism and Ritual Abuse*, New York, Lexington.
La Vey, A.S. (1969) *The Satanic Bible*, New York, Avon.
Lloyd, D.W. (1991) 'Ritual child abuse: understanding the controversies', *Cultic Studies Journal* 8(2), 122–33.
Lunn, T. (1991) 'Confronting disbelief', *Social Work Today* 22 (May), 18–19.
McFadyen, A., Hanks, H. and James, C. (1993) 'Ritual abuse: a definition', *Child Abuse Review* 2, 35–41.
MacFarlane, K. (1992) 'Scapegoating professionals: what does it mean for the field?', Paper presented at the Ninth International Congress of the International Society for the Prevention of Child Abuse and Neglect, Chicago, September.
Mulhern, S. (1990) 'Ritual abuse: defining a syndrome vs. defining a belief', Paper presented at the Eighth International Congress of the International Society for the Prevention of Child Abuse and Neglect, Hamburg, September.
Ofshe, R.J. (1992) 'Inadvertent hypnosis during interrogation: false confession due to dissociative state; mis-identified multiple personality and the satanic cult hypothesis', *International Journal of Clinical Experiential Hypnosis* 40(3), 125–56.
Parker, J. (1993) *At the Heart of Darkness. Witchcraft, Black Magic and Satanism Today*, London, Pan Macmillan.
Pithers, D. (1990) 'Stranger than fiction', *Social Work Today* 22(6), 20–1.
Putnam, F.W. (1991) 'Commentary: the satanic ritual abuse controversy', *Child Abuse and Neglect* 15(3), 175–80.
Putman, F.W. (1993) 'Dissociative disorders in children: behavioral profiles and problems', *Child Abuse and Neglect* 17: 39–45.
Ryder, D. (1992) *Breaking the Circle of Satanic Ritual Abuse: Recognising and Recovering from the Hidden Trauma*, Minneapolis, CompCare Publishers.
Sakheim, D.K. and Devine S.E. (1992) *Out of Darkness: Exploring Satanism and Ritual Abuse*, New York, Lexington.

Smith, M. and Pazder, L. (1980) *Michelle Remembers*, New York, Longdon & Lattes.

Snow, B. and Sorenson, T. (1990) 'Ritualistic child abuse in a neighbourhood setting', *Journal of Interpersonal Violence* 5(4), 474–87.

Sone, K. (1990) 'Ritual abuse: fact or fiction', *Community Care* 12 July, 30–2.

Summit, R. (1991) 'Sexual abuse: what can we teach, what must we learn', Paper presented at the First National Congress on the Prevention of Child Abuse and Neglect, Leicester, September.

Tate, T. (1991) *Children for the Devil: Ritual Abuse and Satanic Crime*, London, Methuen.

Van-Benschoten, S.C. (1990) 'Multiple Personality Disorder and satanic ritual abuse: the issue of credibility', *Dissociation* 111(1).

Waterman, J., Kelly, R.J., Oliveri, M.K. and McCord, J. (1993) *Behind the Playground Walls. Sexual Abuse in Preschools*, New York, Guilford Press.

Wood, H. (1990) 'Exposing the secret', *Social Work Today* 22(12), 18–19.

Young, W.C., Sachs, R.G., Brown, B.G. and Walkins, R.T. (1991) 'Patients reporting ritual abuse in childhood: a clinical syndrome. Report of 37 cases', *Child Abuse and Neglect* 15(3), 181–9.

Chapter 32

Internal and external reality
Establishing parameters

Rob Hale and Valerie Sinason

Rob Hale is a Consultant Psychotherapist, Psychiatrist and Adult Psychoanalyst at the Tavistock Clinic. Valerie Sinason is a Consultant Child Psychotherapist.

Names, identities and background details have been changed wherever necessary to protect confidentiality.

Since 1991, we have collaborated on four pieces of clinical work involving ritually abused patients. In devising a suitable way of working with children and adults who had gone through such extreme experiences we found our technique, theory and practice challenged repeatedly and, in some significant ways, in need of change. However, these processes have allowed us time to reconsider the central tenets of our practice and we will raise the issues that we have found to be most central.

We have the permission of our patients to illustrate our points with clinical descriptions.

THE HISTORICAL TRUTH AND CONFIRMATION

We have found that with these patients in particular, as well as with other abused patients, it is crucial to discover as near to the historic truth as possible and have it confirmed. Where possible the real event needs to be objectively validated by someone who is not involved in the therapeutic relationship and whose task is to do precisely that – i.e. a police officer. However, in the current social climate the forensic investigation can be as hindered by disbelief as the therapy and the medical treatment. Whilst psychotherapists are usually primarily concerned with the patient's emotional truth (Langone and Blood, 1990) regardless of whether it is corroborated by external reality, for ritual abuse survivors this is not adequate. We see the survivor's need to establish what happened with us as a way of making such experiences thinkable.

Survivors all too often find their experiences disconfirmed by all the professionals they meet – therapists, psychiatrists, police, teachers, friends, doctors, priests – as well as by their abusers. 'Mummy asked me if I had a good sleep when she had been helping them hurt me in the night', said 10-year-old Jane, who had cerebral palsy and a mild learning disability. Her father had been imprisoned for sexually and physically abusing her but she had been referred by her foster mother after describing ritual abuse at the hands of both parents and others.

Perhaps even more painfully, survivors can find their sense of the facts questioned by their own actual experiences. For example, Rita, aged 24, a postgraduate student from the southwest of England, puzzled over how, as a child, she went to bed bloody and smeared yet woke up clean in a clean room. As with Jane, every morning was a disconfirmation of her night-time experience. Only her internal injuries remained as proof of what had happened at night. In other words, there is a real objective event that needs to be validated. Unfortunately, for this kind of abuse the current onus is on the victim to prove the fact. Such victims are guilty until proved innocent.

James, a young man with cerebral palsy who was abused by his family and others, said:

> I was put in a cage with a lion roaring. I know it was only a little cage and lions don't fit in little cages. They live in zoos. But I heard it and saw it. I told my mum and she laughed at me and she was there so I didn't tell the policeman in case he said I was stupid too. But there was a lion.

Once James realised we would not laugh at him or call him stupid he could describe being given 'a smartie that made me feel funny' and the issue of drugs could be discussed and how that might have affected his observations. 'I don't like my mum's cat. It hisses at me and scratches me' was his next comment. Taking a deep breath he was then able to consider how the drug might have made him experience the cat as a lion – especially as his mother told him it was. For James, it was important to help him differentiate reality from a deliberately planted false memory that exploited his disability. For Malcolm it was not always possible to differentiate at times between a drug-induced false memory or a defensively elaborated phantasy. Malcolm, aged 27, a lawyer, could clearly describe the expensive furnishings in the place where he was ritually abused. However, whilst in a trance state he spoke of being in a huge palace where everyone, including some famous people, could fly. Faced with such ranges of information the therapists must maintain the position of not knowing what is fiction or faction at the same time as accepting the basic fact of abuse.

Where patients correctly experience another's response as irrational disbelief they can then unconsciously fabricate to a point where everything will be rationally disbelieved; this makes them angrily in control of a further rejection. By the same economic action they have also protected their allegiance to the cult. They are literally serving two masters. The problem then becomes that at times some patients do not know what is fact and what is faction – their own faction.

WORKING TOGETHER

Whilst *Working Together* (HMSO, 1991) represents an optimum multi-disciplinary code for professionals working with abused children, a child or adult in individual as opposed to family, marital or group psychoanalytic psychotherapy would normally expect to see a single therapist.

Although our work as co-therapists began almost by accident, we now find it a useful model that we have chosen to apply to other ritual abuse cases. Working together allows us to share the horrifying nature of the accounts we hear, share the counter-transference and offer legal back-up for each other in the event of formal proceedings.

It also provides the possibility of a division of labour with one person taking on the main burden of the external liaison and management role and one taking the main emotional weight of the experiences. These cases cross so many legal, ethical and technical boundaries that it is essential to have one allocated person carrying the management issues as a priority task.

With two therapists who are not the same sex there is also the chance of dealing with important gender issues. There are some memories that Rita is not able to recount with a man present and at such times Valerie sees her alone with Rob coming in later. Similarly, Malcolm did not want Valerie present when he discussed some aspects of same-sex abuse. Where there are new physical injuries Rob's medical knowledge has proved crucial.

Whoever has been closest to the details of torture feels the most physically contaminated whilst the other is allowed initially to feel clean. These experiences are so powerful it is essential to work with someone you trust.

EXTERNAL LIAISON

Adult and child patients who are revealing criminal acts (murder, cannibalism, bestiality, pornography, drug rings, snuff movies, assaults against children, adults, animals) need to know that the therapist represents the best aspects of justice and will liaise with the outside world where necessary. Whilst child psychotherapists are used to such liaison over abused children, it is not so usual a task for adult-trained psychoanalytic psychotherapists. Whilst adult psychiatry and social services perform such functions, psychoanalysis and psychoanalytic psychotherapy are used to working in the inner world alone, except within psychiatric hospitals or forensic units.

When Rita, Jane, James and Malcolm revealed gross abuse by their families and others, as well as gross abuse that they had been forced to commit on others, we were aware that therapy was no substitute for justice. RH made links with the police concerning the status of the criminal cases. He also made links with hospitals and medical consultants over the injuries our patients had suffered. At crucial points we made such links together. One of the most uncomfortable aspects of this task was the way we as professionals were denigrated and disbelieved – a shadow of what our patients had experienced. In discussing with social services and medical services the abuse Jane had experienced we were denigrated for 'listening to that disturbed woman' – her courageous foster mother. In taking Rita to hospital for a medical examination after anal and vaginal injury following a ritual assault, the aggression towards her and us was palpable. As all our patients, in identifying with their aggressors, had carried out on their own bodies a further attack, self-mutilation needed to be differentiated from external attack. Very few agencies were prepared to bear that double issue. The self-mutilator is hated in the same way as a suicidal patient.

SELF-MUTILATION

Marks on the body of victims do not always aid the 'body' of evidence. There can be the same difficulties differentiating between fact and fiction with physical signs as exist verbally. There are the injuries which are externally given and those which are self-inflicted. Skilled forensic medical work is needed to differentiate. This is still in its early stages. As Hobbs (1993: 6) points out we are still at a stage 'when even major questions such as what is the normal size of the hymenal opening have not been fully addressed'.

Both Jane and Malcolm had marks on their backs that could not have been self-inflicted, as well as cuts they had inflicted on themselves with scissors and breadknife respectively. However, there were often injuries they were unsure about.

We see this physical acting out 'as a substitute for remembering a traumatic childhood experience' which 'unconsciously aims to reverse that early trauma. The patient is spared the painful memory of the trauma, and via his action masters in the present the early experience he originally suffered passively' (Campbell and Hale, 1993: 289). It therefore represents a form of body memory (Vizard, 1989). This memory can contain the elements of destructiveness, eroticism, disgust and excitement. As well as mastering trauma and memory the other primary purpose is the torture and survival of the object. In 1917 Freud ('Mourning and melancholia') showed how in the suicidal patient the ego could kill itself by directing against it 'the hostility which relates to an object . . . in the external world'. We are seeing one self of the patient, in identification with its abusers, perpetuate the attack on the shared body.

With some patients with a severe learning disability, whose capacity for symbolic functioning is further damaged, self-mutilation can be the sole way of communicating what has happened (Sinason, 1988, 1990, 1992). Referrals of sexually abused adults with a learning disability to Valerie Sinason at the Tavistock Clinic revealed self-injury to be the commonest referral problem. Only when the externally inflicted abuse was tackled could the patients deal with their own copycat identification.

THE 50-MINUTE HOUR

It became immediately clear with our first shared clinical work that 50 minutes was not an adequate time for adolescent or adult patients in a trance state. Such states require 1 hour 30 minutes to 2 hours, as a time in which a flashback can be experienced and described. Standard session time is only possible for those whose dissociation or denial make a coherent narrative impossible, or who come for therapy long after the abuse has happened and need and want to forget it. Standard time is also appropriate for child patients whose external experiences have not been adequately acknowledged by legal agencies and who are not in a context where they can explore their experiences safely.

Rita, our first shared patient, was in a trance state during her second session. She was staring at the wall with a look of abject terror on her face. One hand was rubbing her face violently, the other was tearing at a crucifix round her neck; 50 minutes had gone – the time offered – and the two of us had clinical appointments to go to that could not be changed.

Rita was describing or rather re-enacting a terrible birthday scene from her childhood. We were uncomfortably aware of the time and yet she showed no signs of being even remotely finished. Rather clumsily VS asked when that 'birthday' was. 'What does that matter?' snapped Rita angrily – torn out of her re-enactment.

She then asked vulnerably 'Do you believe me?' – seeing the intervention as a sign of disbelief and dislike. VS apologised for asking a clumsy question about the date at that moment, but said it was not to do with belief or disbelief and clarified that she and Rob had arranged for 50 minutes and could not extend that time today, although it was clearly not the right time for Rita to leave. She added that Rita could stay in the waiting room downstairs until she was ready to leave. Rita kept her face turned away. 'You don't believe me', she whispered. RH said she was really angry with us about the time and interruption and it was easier to think we did not believe her. After that session we allocated 2-hour slots.

At one point, at a particularly difficult time of the year because of the satanist calendar, Malcolm missed several sessions as he was in need of hospitalisation. He made clear he needed two long intensive days to process his memories. We had found that until a memory was shared, painful though it was for a patient to go through it, no relief was possible. Rita also had a backlog of such memories and we trusted her own sense of what she needed. Like Malcolm, she made good use of the time offered. Two 6-hour sessions with 10-minute breaks was a very major difference in the time usually allocated to patients.

THE CHAIR OR THE COUCH

Patients who had experienced torture from an early age could not be expected to lie down and trust the therapist's behaviour. Eye-to-eye contact was the safest option although still frightening.

Working in VS's room in the Child and Family Department, with its toys and dolls, was frightening to several ritually abused patients. James, a young man with Down's syndrome, who had seen fetish dolls cut and pierced prior to the same actions being applied to adults, covered his eyes. Rita found the sound of children shouting distressing and worried what was happening to them. Malcolm found particular colours triggered hypnotic states and the toy animals upset all of them.

When we worked in RH's room in the adult department the view of the tree through the window triggered trance states in patients who had been abused in forests.

TOUCH

Within psychoanalytic psychotherapy there is minimum physical contact. This is not just to protect patient and therapist from potentially abusive experiences. Words are the currency for treatment and are symbolic. Whilst child patients need contact at times it is extremely rare with adolescents and almost non-existent with adults.

We found that at times touch was essential with ritually abused patients for two purposes. The first was for protection of the patient physically and the second was for mental containment. When Rita spoke of any cult event one finger immediately moved to poke her eye. We found that if VS held her hand it limited her self-injury. Once Rita was speaking freely her hand could be released again.

When Jane experienced a flashback of her abuse she was in such a primitive state of terror she needed to be held. At times both James and Malcolm needed a hand held to stop them scratching themselves. The hand represented a parent who did not aid and abet abuse but tried to prevent it.

Where Jane and Rita described the most disgusting physical experiences they had been involved in – licking anuses and penises, eating faeces, being smeared with faeces, blood and semen, sucking and eating dismembered penises of animals, having spiders in their ears and mouths, snakes in their vaginas – physical contact assured them that they were still human and capable of human contact; they were not in fact lumps of shit. Jane felt monstrous as a result of a noticeable handicap to begin with and what she had gone through made her feel even more disgusting. The experience of these survivors was akin to concentration camp survivors at liberation.

SECURITY OF THE THERAPISTS

Ritually abused patients need to know that their therapists are well-supported, and that if anything untoward should happen they would have a colleague who would have access to the relevant details.

Jane was terrified that we would die because she had told us the nature of the abuse she experienced. 'They said there is a bomb inside me and if I tell you what happened it will go off and kill you and me.' Rita kept back the names of some of her abusers for fear we would be in danger for possessing that kind of information. Malcolm said everybody he had told about his abuse had been burgled.

It was both a counter-transference issue and a reality issue for us to take our security most seriously. All clinical files are kept in safe places at our Clinic. However, the files for these patients went through a double security procedure.

RH had worked at the Portman Clinic and had spent many years in forensic work. VS had worked with violent adolescents. However, both were aware at times of feeling physically frightened at being caught in the reality of these cases. RH commented that when involved with criminals or murderers he could leave them at work and not fear they would come round and invade his home life. However, these cases went home with him.

One fear was the possibility of the perversion of the judicial system as an inherent part of satanic organisation in two of our cases. The law must be honourable and reflect an innate sense of justice. Where patients had clearly not received just treatment from the law we had cause for concern.

COUNTER-TRANSFERENCE AND GENDER

The counter-transference experience with ritually abused patients is unlike anything either of us had ever experienced before. Taking in the reality of another's real-life hellish experience, in addition to the phantasies and feelings about it, is very different from work with those with an unimpinged-on inner life. We had to deal with feelings of terror, shock, fear, excitement, confusion, disgust, nausea, physical contamination and a deep challenge to our view of the world in peacetime.

There was a slight gender difference in responses. Sometimes with female patients VS would be on her own with them for an agreed amount of time if there were accounts they felt unable to tell initially to a man and RH would join later. VS would feel smelly, disgusting, evil and contaminated and experience RH as clean, pure and coming from a different world. She could feel angry he had been spared some of this. On entering the room feeling clean RH could experience VS as dirty and contaminated and feel angry that he would soon be dirtied as well. At times VS felt like a bad witch and was experienced so by RH. At times RH would be experienced as a saviour.

After such sessions VS and RH spent 30 minutes processing the experience and RH would provide refreshments and take a nurturing role. The situation was reversed when external liaison was involved and VS felt protective of RH who was demonised as the medical consultant who 'believed' his patients.

RH and VS became very interested in the role of nausea and disgust as the strongest counter-transference issues. Meta to the painful aspects of counter-transference was a strong sense of moral duty that such cases should not and could not be palmed off and ignored.

DISGUST AND NAUSEA

In working with abused children VS had noted (Sinason, 1988) that nausea was a common counter-transference feeling she experienced. She linked this to the infantile experience of having an orifice intruded on by unwanted milk-intake (whether from breast or bottle) where being sick was the only means of coping. RH had been taking this further on a biological level. He noted that Johnson-Laird and Oatley (1989) – two psychologists – had shown that disgust was one of the five basic irreducible emotions. Disgust serves a purpose of eliminating that which is noxious. It is normally felt when something is taken in by the mouth but the same emotional state is produced when something is pushed into another orifice contrary to the biological function.

For perversion to occur there has to be a crossing of the body boundary. The abused child has to accommodate the breaking down of the disgust function. Children are normally extremely sensitive to smell and as they grow up become increasingly insensitive. However, ritually abused children are made to become immune to disgust at an early age. All our patients had to eat faeces, drink urine, blood, semen. The established perverted adult has learned to love this affect in order to survive. Adult perversion can only transgress or cross the body boundary if the adult has been the passive victim of infantile transgression.

CORRUPTED ATTACHMENT AND THE BREAKDOWN OF JUSTICE

Corruption involves turning something on its head and making the opposite be the truth and that applies particularly to a moral value system. Patients ritually abused by family members or trusted neighbours and professionals face developing a lethally morally corrupted attachment. Whilst normal religious belief and family life involves upholding the good, abusers with satanist belief (or other religious beliefs that allow child abuse to occur) glorify the corrupt and bring up the child in a religiously sanctioned polymorphous perverse world.

Although a child born into such a cult family is born into a corrupt system the child has an innate sense of justice and of what is healthy and what is disgusting. What then gets corrupted is both the natural sense of justice and the biological protective function of nausea. The creative life force has been transformed into a destructive force and what keeps the person alive is destruction – instead of milk you have blood and shit. Stoller (1975) powerfully describes such perversion as an erotic form of hatred.

When Jane was given a budgerigar and grew attached to it she was forced to kill it and eat it. Rita found her slaughtered pet dog in her bed. James was sexually abused by his mother with his father standing by laughing before being made to abuse his baby brother. Malcolm was made to lie on a female corpse. How do humans have the resilience to survive this upbringing with some kind of moral code still in place? Our adult patients used a wry humour to show both the terrible extent of their experiences and the existence of a moral code. 'I read a book about a serial killer – it was a real easy read compared to what I have been through', said Rita. 'I was involved with a case involving snuff movies and had to watch them', said Malcolm. 'It was quite relaxing.' Despite their nightmarish experiences, their innate moral sense came through in that such statements conveyed both a painful truth and an exaggeration of normal values for the purpose of underlining them. Winnicott (1964: 96) had a strong conviction about 'innate tendencies to morality' which is not societally generated although it can be influenced by society.

COINCIDENCES

The loss of a belief in coincidences is a surprising side-effect of ritual abuse with serious consequences.

When a child shouts angrily to a parent 'I wish you were dead!' he is not able to see it as a coincidence if, unluckily, a parent did then die. The childhood magical belief in causality would then become dangerously crystallised without help.

For most Western children life does not throw up too many such unfortunate timings. Indeed, one of the tasks of parenting is to try and protect a child from as many such situations as possible. As Winnicott (1964) comments 'a mother . . . takes the trouble to avoid coincidences. Coincidences lead to muddle. Examples would be handing a baby over to someone else's care at the same time as weaning.' Avoiding loaded coincidences in early childhood protects a child from using omnipotent defences. Like the mouse on the elephant's back in Aesop's fables that proudly boasts 'Didn't we shake that bridge!' the little child defends against smallness and physical powerlessness by the defence of denial.

These magical defences – if they persist too long – can destroy the beginnings of play and symbolic understanding. If the parent, as well as the child, shares this difficulty there is a double handicap. Winnicott describes a boy waking up at night and calling his mother a witch. As she was quite clear that she was not a witch, when he asked if witches existed she could calmly reply. When 4-year-old Tania woke up having a nightmare and screamed when she saw her mother 'Get out monster – I want my real mummy', her mother felt both devastated and monstrous. She could not contain her child's fears and angrily retaliated – making Tania's fear of monsters and bad mothers worse.

With ritual abuse there is a very different process. We have found that abusers have deliberately destroyed a belief in innocent coincidences in order to foster magical thinking in the child. They have blurred the line between phantasy and reality. The ritually abused child and adult then regards coincidence as causality, which increases omnipotent magical thinking and an inability to differentiate fact from fiction.

For example, imagine Winnicott's child waking up at night terrified of witches to see his mother, in ceremonial attire, laugh mockingly at his question, abuse him and then make no mention of what had happened next morning – all the ceremonial regalia being stowed away. Jane was told that every time she saw a spider it meant Satan was watching her because she was not good enough. There were always spiders in her house. When she found a spider in her classroom she was in extreme terror. A spider would never be an ordinary spider. Malcolm was told by his satanist abusers that his parents were not his real parents – Lucifer was his real father. When as a child he woke up with a nightmare and screamed 'You are not my real daddy' – his father mistook this for the ordinary way a child waking from a nightmare cannot differentiate between the nightmare world and reality for a while. When Rita received telephone calls in the early hours she could not trust it was a wrong number. It was mainly experienced as a message from the cult. When James saw the toy dolls in Valerie Sinason's room he was terrified of dying because the sight of a doll for him meant a curse that would happen.

CONCLUSION

These cases have taken an enormous amount of time both within the clinical sessions and in outside liaison and thinking time. They have challenged our theories and taxed to the extreme our affective response to the patients' material. Like our colleagues in this book we are on a learning curve. We are very aware of how much we need to learn in order to develop our services and contain and help our patients more effectively. In learning from our patients we have to allow them to tell us how to treat them. Rita told us 'The Tavistock is not the right place but it is the best of what is available. What I really need is a 24-hour sanctuary that is neither a psychiatric hospital nor a convent with therapy as an integral part.'

REFERENCES

Campbell, D. and Hale, R. (1993) 'Suicidal acts', Chapter 12 in J. Holmes (ed.) *Textbook of Psychotherapy in Psychiatric Practice*, Edinburgh, Churchill Livingstone.
Freud, S. (1917) 'Mourning and melancholia', *Standard Edition Vol. XIV*, London, Hogarth Press.
HMSO (1991) *Working Together Under the Children Act 1989. A Guide to Arrangements for Inter-agency Co-operation for the Protection of Children from Abuse*, London, HMSO.
Hobbs, C. (1993) 'The evaluation of child sexual abuse', Chapter 1 in C.J. Hobbs and J.H. Wynne (eds) *Baillière's Clinical Paediatrics: International Practice and Research, Child Abuse*, London, J.M. Baillière Tyndall.
Johnson-Laird, P.N. and Oatley, K. (1989) 'The language of emotions: an analysis of a semantic field', *Cognition and Emotion* 2, 81–123.
Langone. M.D. and Blood, L.O. (1990) *Satanism and Occult Related Violence: What You Should Know*, Weston, MA, American Family Foundation.
Sinason, V. (1988) 'Smiling, swallowing, sickening and stupefying. The effect of abuse on the child', *Psychoanalytic Psychotherapy* 3(2), 97–111.
Sinason, V. (1990) 'Individual psychoanalytic psychotherapy with severely and profoundly mentally handicapped patients', Section 1, 71–81 in A. Dosen, A. Van Gennep and G.J.

Zwanniken (eds) *Treatment of Mental Illness and Behavioural Disorders in the Mentally Retarded*, Proceedings of the International Congress, 3–4 May 1990, Amsterdam, Logon Publications.

Sinason, V. (1992) *Mental Handicap and the Human Condition: New Approaches from the Tavistock*, London, Free Association Books.

Stoller, R.J. (1975) *Perversion: The Erotic Form of Hatred*, USA, Pantheon.

Vizard, E. (1989) 'Consequences of child sexual abuse: incidence and prevalence', in *The Consequences of CSA*, ACPP Occasional Paper No. 3, 10–20.

Winnicott, D.W. (1964) *The Child, the Family and the Outside World*, Harmondsworth, Penguin.

Chapter 33

Creating sanctuary
Ritual abuse and complex post-traumatic stress disorder

Sandra L. Bloom

Dr Sandra L. Bloom is Medical Director, The Sanctuary at the Northwestern Institute of Psychiatry, Fort Washington, Pennsylvania, USA, and President, The Alliance for Creative Development.

Names, identities and background details have been changed wherever necessary to protect confidentiality.

FROM PERSONAL EXPERIENCE

In 1980, two years after completing my psychiatric training, I was asked to see a young university student who had accused a man of raping her. The police had investigated the case, discovered that her accusations were false, and she was then referred for psychiatric treatment when she became anxious, depressed and suicidal, having recognised that her experience of reality was distorted. When I began treating her, I understood that she was suffering from a dissociative disorder, but I cannot say that I really knew what a dissociative disorder actually was, other than a weird constellation of neurotic symptoms, presumably expressing some covert sexual or aggressive conflict. I began seeing her in weekly psychodynamically-oriented psychotherapy, and I developed a strong therapeutic alliance with her. Gradually, she improved, and she appeared to develop insight into her behaviour, and then her functioning improved. Eventually, she successfully completed college and postgraduate studies.

By 1985, I had been running an in-patient unit in the general hospital of a middle-class, semi-rural community in America for five years. In this capacity, I had already been personally involved in hundreds of cases of the most severe variety. I received an emergency call from this same young woman in 1985 from another state to which she had moved. She requested in-patient hospitalisation after she once again became seriously depressed and suicidal. In no way was I prepared for the situation that greeted me when I entered her hospital room that day to perform the admission evaluation. There before me sat this woman that I thought I knew so well. And yet, it was not precisely her. Instead, this person had the mannerisms, the gestures, and the speech of a 5-year-old child. She gave her phone number and address appropriate to that age, where she had lived eighteen years previously; and her mother confirmed the veracity of these domestic details.

I immediately grasped that I was in the presence of another 'personality', but I was profoundly shocked. I had trained at a time when multiple personality disorder was, at best, a rare and highly exotic phenomenon that I would never expect to see and, at worst, a figment of the imagination of some eccentric therapists. At the time, Dr Richard Kluft was on the faculty of my psychiatric training institution, but his work, although considered interesting, was also regarded with much suspicion, since he had begun to claim that the syndrome of multiple personality disorder was anything but rare.

I found myself totally unprepared with a plan as to how to address this clinical situation. Fortunately for both me and for my patient, her trust in me was well-established, and the child alter quickly revealed the history of paternal incest and sadism, a history later corroborated by other family members, information that had lain hidden for so long. I realised that I had in fact communicated many times before with this alter, usually over the telephone, blithely unaware that I was conferring with anyone other than my patient in a seemingly 'regressed' state. I had never discovered, because I had never *asked*, that there was an absence of continuity of memory between the adult self and the alter personality, and that, in fact, my adult patient had little or no recall of our previous telephone contacts. When I finally grasped the situation, many hitherto confusing aspects of this case became clear for both the patient and for myself. Using traditional and non-traditional forms of intervention, including videotaping the child alter for the adult self to 'meet', the two selves became integrated and they have remained so ever since.

Certainly, I was pleased with the outcome of this case, but like so many of my colleagues with similar experiences, I was devastated by the apparent huge gap in my body of knowledge, and by the emotional demands placed upon me to grasp the reality of horrendous childhood maltreatment. The gap became an increasingly huge one as I began asking more pointed questions, and began receiving confirmatory responses about the abusive childhood experiences of other patients, many of whom I or members of my treatment team knew well, and who confirmed with great relief that they had been hoping someone would ask them for a long time. More startling and unexpected was the often rapid and dramatic improvement that these patients made once their horrific experiences had been validated and understood.

The pain I finally allowed myself to see in the lives of my patients made it morally necessary that I ask myself several discomfiting questions. How could my psychiatric knowledge be so woefully lacking that I could have missed understanding dissociation and its origins in traumatic experience for so long? How could I have had so little knowledge about the real events of childhood? And even when I knew about the realities of childhood, why had this information played so small a role in treatment formulation? How could it be that, within apparently respectable, financially secure and loving homes, so many children could be undergoing such experiences of torture, torment and neglect? How was I to cope with the overwhelming demands made upon my empathic capacities, in order to provide the necessary empathy so that *validation* and not *denial* could be my therapeutic stance? And most importantly, perhaps, what kind of world do we really live in when the *modus operandi* of the death camps and totalitarian regimes applies equally well to the well-heeled, Western, nuclear family? What is wrong with *us*?

Thankfully, at about this time, researchers and clinicians from around the world were beginning to share information gained from various traumatised groups about the biopsychosocial and moral implications of trauma. It became clear that there is a universal human response to trauma regardless of the particular traumatic experience, a response that has become known as post-traumatic stress disorder (PTSD). As data on PTSD has continued to accumulate, a new and meaningful cognitive framework has evolved and coalesced, with major implications for theoretical formulation, diagnosis and treatment, as well as forming the basis for major social policy change (Herman, 1981, 1992; Figley, 1985, 1986; Van der Kolk, 1987; Courtois, 1988).

It is within this context of experience that my comments on ritual abuse survivors must be understood. Ten years ago, if a patient had come to me and told me that he or she had been sexually and physically abused in a satanic cult, and that this person had been forced to engage in the most degrading of acts, participating in the sacrifice and cannibalism of infants and adults, I would probably have diagnosed such a patient as suffering from some form of paranoid disorder, and I would have tried anti-psychotic medications in order to treat the delusions. I would have labelled such dissociative experiences as psychotic. I would have found any excuse to get such patients out of my practice and out of my life. I could not bear to believe that such things could be possible. But now I recognise that there is a very long continuum of human pain and human possibility.

We now specialise in the treatment of adults who have been abused as children. Our treatment context is a 22-bed in-patient unit called 'The Sanctuary', located in a private psychiatric hospital in suburban Philadelphia. The name derives from a reference made in one of the early books on trauma by the psychologist Steven Silver referring to 'sanctuary trauma', that experience which Vietnam veterans suffered when they returned from the war and sought refuge within Veterans Administration institutions, only to find these institutions to be further traumatising (Figley, 1986). Struck by the concept, we began reflecting on how many psychiatric patients have been retraumatised within psychiatric institutions themselves, and we began to have a dialogue about the necessary components of a system that would not create that kind of traumatic experience, but rather one which would instead provide an environment within which true healing could be promoted. The result is the 'Sanctuary Model' of in-patient treatment (cf. Bloom, in press a, b).

We treat patients who present with many different psychiatric syndromes, including multiple personality disorder (MPD). Patients suffering from MPD comprise about 20–25 per cent of our in-patient population, and about one-quarter of those claim to have been ritually abused. Although the ritually abused patients have certain distinguishing characteristics in their presentation, which will be discussed later, in the main, they differ little from other patients who suffer from severe and complex post-traumatic syndromes.

ASPECTS OF TREATMENT

One of the difficulties in treatment concerns the dangers when these patients seek help from poorly trained therapists. Adults who have been abused as children often present with a complex array of symptoms that have been unresponsive to other interventions. One beginner therapist error would be an adherence to the naive belief that abreaction alone will cure the person. Abreaction can be effective for a single traumatic event in adulthood; however, people abused in childhood suffer not only from PTSD, but also from severe developmental problems as a result of the abuse and the chronic PTSD symptoms. Abreaction is only a relatively minor part of the recovery process.

Another beginner error is the use of splitting, believing that the patient is unequivocally good, and that the parents or perpetrators are unequivocally bad, and that the solution to the patient's problem is simply a *parentectomy*. People who have been abused as children have had a serious insult to their attachment systems, and it is possible to do even further damage by creating yet another bind for the patient over divided loyalties. Because of traumatic re-enactment, the patient will often unconsciously set up therapists to do exactly that, so that they do not have to work through or contain their own ambiguity or ambivalence about their families of origin. Trauma leads to increased, not decreased, attachment difficulties; and separation under these circumstances is an enormous undertaking, certainly not a 'simple solution'. The decision about how to interact with the perpetrator must reside with the patient, not with the therapist, and this may be a process which takes many years to negotiate successfully, and to resolve.

Another typical novice error would be to become an unwitting part of the patient's re-enactment of trauma, and to believe that it is possible to re-parent the patient and hence undo the damage of the abuse. Recovery can only work if the survivors can learn to re-parent themselves. Premature confrontation can do more harm than good, as Christine Courtois (1988) has cogently pointed out in her excellent book on the healing of the incest wound.

In treating suspected survivors of ritual and satanist abuse, as well as survivors of complex post-traumatic stress disorders, the most important starting-point is the provision of a safe environment. We agree with Dr Judith Lewis Herman (1992) that the establishment of safety is the first stage in all the treatment regimens. This includes biological safety, psychological safety, social safety and moral safety. Safety is a particularly difficult issue for the ritual abuse survivor who has often had few real experiences with safety outside of the confines of the decidedly unsafe cult system. Firm treatment contracts must be agreed upon that limit the self-damage of the patient, so that the therapist too can feel safe with the patient. An unwillingness to engage in such a contract bodes ill for the success of the treatment. Clinicians are advised to evaluate their treatment plan with great care, and to obtain close supervision.

In our work at The Sanctuary, we have been struck by the way in which even seemingly trivial details can make patients feel extremely unsafe and terrified. For example, most therapeutic groups occur with patients sitting in a circular arrangement of chairs. This has been the established model of group treatment for nearly one whole century. But unlike other patients, the cult survivors cannot tolerate being in a circle, a situation which almost immediately triggers dissociation, since many of them had undergone experiences of profound abuse in a circular cult gathering. This is particularly the case when music groups occur on the ward, which can sometimes trigger memories of ritual chanting in the satanist cults. The patients do not become exhibitionistic within the group setting; instead they find it intolerable and they make efforts to withdraw and isolate.

In the general milieu, there are also characteristic forms of re-enactment behaviour that occur. Our staff team has also noticed the profound tendency for cult abusers to band together rapidly in order to form a mini-cult which then isolates this subgroup from the general community and excludes others. These patients will often articulate the thought that no-one else can understand them, developing a certain kind of elite atmosphere that forces a split in the community, and then sets these patients up for experiences of rejection.

Also noticeable is the preoccupation with 'triggers', once the cult abuse has been admitted. Virtually anything can serve as a trigger for flashbacks, including certain articles of jewellery, paintings on the wall, holiday decorations; in fact, almost anything that contains a highly charged symbol. This is particularly problematical since many of the triggering symbols are inherent in every single cultural context, such as triangles, circles, stars, moons, etc. Triggers for dissociation that are apparent in everyday surroundings are quite typical for all forms of childhood abuse victims. What distinguishes the ritual abuse survivor from the others is this patient's insistence that the environment remove the triggers rather than recognise that they need to become desensitised to the triggers. This angry insistence, when it occurs, can be seen as a re-enacting tendency on the part of the survivor to exert power and control over the environment, reminiscent of the way power and control was exerted over them. The treatment team needs to be sensitive to the patient's need to alter and master the vicissitudes of the treatment environment, without succumbing to the temptation of being controlled by the patient, thus unwittingly playing a role in a re-enactment.

Once one has provided the right sanctuary environment for patients, then one can progress to the next two stages outlined in Herman's (1992) very clear and carefully considered model. The next stages in the process are remembering and grieving, and then establishing a reconnection with ordinary life. The stage of 'rememberance and grieving' focuses on the reconstruction of memory and the metabolism of the attendant affect. The purpose of this stage is to tell the story, to transform the horrific imagery and repetitive re-experiencing of the trauma into a cohesive narrative, attached to previously dissociated affect, that can then become a part of a true memory rather than a living reality. This is an extremely difficult stage for the ritual abuse survivor to negotiate. It requires the establishment of a safe attachment to other people when attachments within their experience have been consistently traumatising and dangerous. Within the context of such a relationship, the patient must learn 'affective re-education', meaning that the severe deficits in affect management must be corrected.

In the final stage of reconnecting with ordinary life, this is often rather difficult for survivors who have never had anything which approximates an ordinary life in the first place. These patients have never experienced a sense of ease with other human beings, and they have little if any sense of humour. Their thinking is often magical and concrete, particularly in the early stages of recovery, and they lack the capacity for self-soothing in other than the most primitive and often destructive of ways. But with carefully considered and monitored in-patient containment, it is possible to plant the seeds of an alternative way of living and being, one which patients can gradually begin to internalise.

Although there are specific techniques and skills that are being developed to deal with the population of abuse victims, more important than any particular technique is the understanding of how to establish a *context*, a sanctuary, in which new therapeutic options and skills can be developed.

It has become increasingly clear that we have reached the limits of usefulness of the individual model of treatment. This is not a realisation unique to the mental health field. The limits of our current models of thinking about clinical problems and about world problems become increasingly obvious when faced with the extreme traumatic degradation of global, economic, ecological and social systems. We need a new paradigm within which we can develop innovative methodologies that enable us to address critical problems that affect both individuals and groups. The concepts of treatment that are evolving within 'The Sanctuary' are rudimentary steps towards the development of the orchestra as a whole. The instruments can be damaged and in need of repair, or perhaps they can be just simply out of tune. The musicians, as well as the conductor, can be ill, out of sorts, unpractised or inadequately trained. Even if the instruments, the musicians and the conductor are all functioning properly, the orchestra requires the musical direction of the composer, a proper acoustical setting and a culture within which the making of music is appreciated and welcomed. Harmony is only achieved when all of the components successfully interact with and play off of each other.

It is vitally important that the world of psychiatric knowledge be reconnected to and utilised by the world in general. Our work with victims of the most extreme forms of trauma serves as a social laboratory for necessary social change, as well as serving as a reminder of the need for improvements in our clinical repertoire, particularly in view of the fact that the mental health profession has failed these patients for years, through our ignorance and blindness. But the pain that our patients have suffered as children and as adults is not in vain if from their pain, and from their attempts at self-healing, we can learn some vital lessons about healing the world within which we all live.

> Rejected by mankind, the condemned do not go
> so far as to reject it in turn. Their faith
> in history remains unshaken, and one may well
> wonder why. They do not despair. The proof:
> they persist in surviving – not only to survive,
> but to testify.

> The victims elect to become witnesses.

> (Elie Wiesel)

ACKNOWLEDGEMENTS

The author would like to thank J. Foderaro, R. Ryan, J. Vogel, M. De Arment and E. Mayro for their assistance in the preparation of this chapter.

REFERENCES

Bloom, S.L. (in press a) 'The Sanctuary Model: developing generic inpatient programs for the treatment of psychological trauma', in M.B. Williams and J.F. Sommer Jr. (eds) *Handbook of Post-Traumatic Therapy: A Practical Guide to Intervention, Treatment, and Research*, New York, Greenwood Publishing.
Bloom, S.L. (in press b) 'The Sanctuary Model: a short-term hospital approach to the treatment of chronic PTSD', in R. Kleber and C. Figley (eds) *Beyond Trauma*.
Courtois, C. (1988) *Healing the Incest Wound: Adult Survivors in Therapy*, New York, W.W. Norton and Company.
Figley, C.R. (1985) *Trauma and Its Wake. Volume I*, New York, Brunner/Mazel.
Figley, C.R. (1986) *Trauma and Its Wake. Volume II*, New York, Brunner/Mazel.
Herman, J.L. (1981) *Father–Daughter Incest*, Cambridge, MA, Harvard University Press.
Herman, J.L. (1992) *Trauma and Recovery*, New York, Basic Books.
Van der Kolk, B.A. (1987) *Psychological Trauma*, Washington, DC, American Psychiatric Press.

Chapter 34

Ritual abuse

The personal and professional cost for workers

Sheila C. Youngson

Sheila C. Youngson is Consultant Clinical Psychologist, Counselling and Therapy Service (Children and Adolescents), Wakefield and Pontefract Community Health NHS Trust.

Names, identities and background details have been changed wherever necessary to protect confidentiality.

It is in the nature of human beings to resist bad news. We have only to reflect on our own experience of losses we have suffered to perceive the stages that need to be gone through before unwanted and unsolicited news is accepted as reality, and belief in fact established. It is a process that takes time, and a process that proceeds from denial through gradual and growing acceptance to belief, with many stages, stops, starts and stumblings on the way.

Knowledge of ritual abuse *is* 'bad news', and the effects on professional workers are profound. I have been working in the field of ritual abuse for four years, both as a child therapist and as a supporter and supervisor of other therapists. This personal and professional experience has resulted in much new learning; and I have reached the understanding that ritual abuse is certainly quantitatively different to other child abuses, and in some aspects is also qualitatively different. Experienced and 'seasoned' workers, some of whom have been working in child protection agencies for many years, have said that, prior to working with ritually abused clients, they had been certain that they would not be surprised or shocked by any new account of abuse. However, they found themselves deeply affected by ritual abuse: challenged, confronted, overwhelmed, sometimes to the extent of being unable to maintain personal and professional roles and boundaries.

At least two inter-related factors seem to be at work in producing this situation. First, workers have to listen to extreme accounts of gross abuse and assault: sexual, physical, emotional, psychological, involving many children and adults. Second, these accounts are so extreme, in terms of both the quantity and detail of sexual and physical and psychological torture and trauma, and in the recognition of the structure and organisation and systems supporting such acts, that workers cannot always or often accommodate the information into their established views, concepts and constructs regarding fundamental issues, such as how human beings relate to each other. For example, and here the aim is to inform and illustrate, and not to shock or sensationalise, workers have to hear and respond to: accounts of multiple sexual abuse; penetration with sticks, animals; eating faeces, decayed foodstuffs, worms, mice; near suffocation and drowning, to the point of loss of consciousness; people being tied up, suspended by ropes, cut, given electric shocks; people deprived of sleep, buried alive in coffins, small children left in total darkness for hours; pretend operations that convince children that a live animal has been placed inside them that will start to eat them if they talk about their experiences; accounts of murder, dismemberment, and eating body parts, and drinking blood. Further, workers have to hear and respond, professionally and therapeutically, to their clients, as and when these clients recall and relive their experiences. They have to cope with their clients' defensive systems which may have resulted in varying degrees and forms of dissociation, so that accounts can be delivered without appropriate (to us) emotion. They may have to recognise that some clients have been involved in 'true cult-based ritualistic abuse' (Finkelhor et al., 1988), that has instructed and promoted a belief system that justifies such abuses and assaults. This can even render clients vulnerable to remaining in contact with, or returning to, such groups, and they may on occasion miss and yearn for the physiological and psychological states and arousal that such groups and systems and activities produce.

It is in circumstances like these that workers are asked to continue to act and react professionally, and with professionalism, at and during the time that their personal responses to the material they are encountering threaten to overwhelm their every sense (the quantitative difference); and through time they come to realise that such information cannot be subsumed into readily available and understood categories of human behaviour (the qualitative difference).

It may be that this first factor, where personal reactions and understanding, and acceptance, lag far behind the immediate need to respond professionally, is not new, and could be very familiar to those professionals who were working in the field of child sexual abuse in the 1980s. It seems, however, that in the field of ritual abuse in the early 1990s, it is the addition of the related second factor, which necessitates a re-evaluation of fundamental beliefs and principles, that causes workers the greatest stress, and leads to the by now familiar and often ultimately realistic statement: 'My life will never be the same again.'

The personal and professional emotional cost to the worker is immense.

AN ATTEMPT TO EVALUATE AND DESCRIBE THE NATURE OF THIS COST

I have been a member of a national support group for workers in the field of ritual abuse for over three years. The aims of this group, called RAINS (Ritual Abuse – Information Network and Support), are (a) to build up a body of knowledge about ritual abuse, the psychological consequences for victims, and the most appropriate and efficacious therapeutic interventions; and (b) to provide a place and space for professionals to share and discuss their personal reactions to this work, as well as the professional problems and difficulties that result, and to receive informal support, understanding, supervision and encouragement from those similarly involved and affected.

Members of RAINS believe that they are working, directly or indirectly, with children and/or adults who are, or have been involved in ritual abuse, as defined by Finkelhor *et al.* (1988): 'abuse that occurs in a context linked to some symbols or group activity that have a religious, magical, or supernatural connotation, and where the invocation of these symbols or activities, repeated over time, is used to frighten and intimidate the children'.

The membership of RAINS, in July 1993, stood at over 140 professionals, including psychiatrists, paediatricians, general practitioners, nurses, clinical psychologists, social workers, foster carers, probation officers, independent counsellors and therapists, police officers, solicitors and clergy.

In 1992, having reflected on my own personal and professional experience, and having heard many other professionals talk of their stress and distress following work in this field, I decided to investigate the nature of this stress and the possible precipitating factors, in the hope that ways of helping, assisting and advising workers would be indicated, as well as providing information and impetus for managers and supervisors who needed to know how workers were affected, and how they could be supported and supervised most effectively.

Subsequently, I decided to conduct a detailed, heuristic survey, by means of a questionnaire sent to the then 120 members of RAINS.

THE SURVEY RESULTS[1]

Personal and professional details

Seventy-one questionnaires were returned, fifty-six from women and fifteen from men. The majority of respondents (94 per cent) were aged between 30 and 60 years of age. All professional groups were represented in the returns, and 72 per cent had been involved in work in the field of ritual abuse for between one and four years.

Changes in behaviour and in emotional and physical health

The questionnaire considered changes in behaviour, and in emotional and physical health, that had occurred since the respondents began work in this field. The results showed that 97 per cent of respondents had experienced some or major negative changes, in varying numbers of areas. Commonly expressed difficulties were: disturbed sleep and nightmares; loss of appetite and resulting weight loss;

psychosomatic symptoms such as headaches, indigestion and nausea, leading to an increased sickness record; and changes in affect such as increased anxiety, fear, distrust of others, anger and hostility, depression and sadness. Any expressed positive changes were minimal or unlikely.

Changes in social life and relationships

Respondents were also asked about any changes in inter-personal life and relationships: 54 per cent spent less time in social activities; and of those in a partnership, 50 per cent had experienced some or serious difficulties in the relationship since beginning work in the field of ritual abuse and 38 per cent had experienced some sexual difficulties.

Support and supervision

Seventy respondents felt that there was a need for additional support and supervision because of the nature of this work. Some agencies recognised this need before or after being asked, but 41 per cent of respondents recorded that they still did not have the quality or quantity of personal and professional help that they required.

Safety and intimidation

Eighty-six per cent of respondents said that they worried more about their own safety or that of their partners/families/friends because of their work in ritual abuse, and 66 per cent had taken some extra safety/security measures. Five respondents recorded that they had received threats and intimidation in connection with both previous work and current work in the ritual abuse field, and twenty-one respondents believed that they had received intimidation and threats only since beginning this work. The most common form was either silent phone calls (nineteen respondents) or threatening/warning/abusive phone calls (thirteen respondents, ten of whom had ex-directory telephone numbers). It was noted that whilst some intimidation or threat was not open to question (i.e. calls that named the worker and client), others were open to interpretation, which had a differing emotional cost.

The discussion following these survey results in my previously published paper (Youngson, 1993) considered three hypotheses which, it was suggested, future research could usefully test. These were that: workers in the field of ritual abuse are currently professionally isolated; ritual abuse work is qualitatively different from other work; and ritual abuse work may involve threat and intimidation. The following is the 1993 discussion on the first two hypotheses, which further highlights the professional and personal difficulties inherent in this work.

RITUAL ABUSE WORK IS PROFESSIONALLY ISOLATING

This hypothesis proposes that professional isolation results from at least five sources. First, the need for additional confidentiality in such cases, especially when court cases are pending, can deprive workers of their usual routes to peer group support and supervision. Second, there is a lack at present of expert advice and supervision, as many current front line workers will know more about ritual abuse than do their line managers and supervisors. Third, and associated, the lack of much published research and knowledge about this form of abuse, its characteristics and efficacious treatment approaches, leaves workers feeling deskilled, inadequate and helpless. Fourth, a frequent unwillingness amongst non-involved peers and managers at all levels to become involved in such a contentious and potentially professionally and organisationally threatening area results in workers feeling undermined, unsupported and ostracised. This unwillingness, and sometimes disbelief in the existence of ritual abuse, can grow into hostility towards workers, and can lead to professional marginalisation, involving ridicule, scapegoating and, occasionally, transfer to other parts of a service. Fifth, the sometime therapeutic requirements of this client group challenge the usually ascribed professional boundaries, and therapists can find that they need to be more active and directly responsive than they are with other clients. This, in turn, is often unacceptable to, and criticised by peer groups. This situation and the issues involved are well described by Sakheim and Devine (1992).

RITUAL ABUSE WORK IS QUALITATIVELY DIFFERENT

This hypothesis proposes that direct work with children and adults who have been involved in ritual abuse is experienced as significantly more complex, more difficult, more challenging and more professionally 'draining' than clinical work with other client groups. It is suggested that this results from at least four sources. First, that the prolonged, often lifelong, systematic, repetitive and extreme physical, sexual and emotional trauma that ritually abused clients suffer, results in frequently extreme psychological and psychiatric disturbance. Workers are faced with clients whose behaviour can be aggressive, highly sexualised, self-injurious, suicidal, manipulative (a literal not derogatory term), testing; whose emotional and psychological state can be extremely variable and always vulnerable; whose therapeutic needs are many and frequently challenging to established therapeutic approaches/procedures. (See again, Sakheim and Devine (1992).) Second, and linked, clients (frequently children) present with an inverted belief system and an associated ambivalence about therapy and the person of the therapist. An example from the author's experience: a 9-year-old child insisted, with excitement, that sex with adults and the experience of pain and fear were what she wanted, and that if she did not get these from the therapist, she would know that the therapist did not care for her.

This was entirely different from the child who, because of abuse, is confused over the relationship between love and care, and sex, and needs to test out the safety of the therapist. The 9-year-old ritually abused client persisted in her belief for over three years of weekly therapy, e.g. shouting, for months, 'I want to fuck you, why won't you let me. It will be good. OK so then hit me, hit me, hit me really hard.' Third, that ritual abuse becomes clear from over many years, and that is both a responsibility and a pressure. Fourth, that the details of the abusive experiences that clients recall and voice, and the concomitant emotional expression and states, can be, to the worker, personally abhorrent and horrific, profoundly moving and, on occasion, overwhelming to every sense. The author has experience, for example, of listening, empathically, to a 7-year-old talk of eating eyeballs, then having to cope with the child's retching and with her own immediate feelings of nausea, disgust and fear, and professional helplessness and inadequacy.

It is the author's contention that it is the following three inter-related factors that make work in this field qualitatively different to work with clients who have suffered extreme, even sadistic, sexual abuse. First, clients talk of being made to abuse other children and adults from a very early age, as young as 2 or 3 years. Second, clients feel that they have always had a choice in, and responsibility for participation in abusive activities, and the forced choice between two abusive scenarios is not immediately evident to them, e.g. an 8-year-old child who is given the choice between being sexually abused herself or sexually abusing her sister. Third, before, above and through most of the abuse, and in most of the cases, lies an alternative belief system that holds that pain, sex, death, fear are revered, sought after, valued and desired, and our notions/concepts of care, gentleness, nurturance and well-being are regarded as stupid, worthless, boring, irrelevant, un-understandable.

Thus many clients (often children who have been removed from an abusive setting rather than having personally chosen to leave an abusive group), will have significant ambivalence about the 'new' setting in which they now live, and frequently demonstrate great conflict and confusion. Again, from the author's experience, one child asked with much desperation, 'Who can I believe? Who should I believe? I don't know.' Another child said very forcefully, 'It's boring, I hate this. I want to be sexy. It don't make me sad or cross. I liked it. I want to go back.'

ACKNOWLEDGING THE COST AND PLANNING FOR ITS CONTAINMENT

It seems clear from this initial and partial understanding of the stresses and distress faced by workers in the field of ritual abuse that two immediate questions should follow: (a) what system(s) could be instituted that would support workers in their professional capacities; and (b) what is the quality, degree and nature of both support and supervision necessary to promote and underpin continued good practice, and help the worker manage and cope effectively with his/her emotional reactions?

Roles and boundaries – 'a safe freedom'

For those professionals who have trained and worked in the so-called 'helping professions', the words 'maintaining roles and boundaries' are synonymous with good practice. To be clear about the extent and limitations of one's role, and the boundaries of the task and acceptable behaviour for both client and 'helper', provides the safety and security that allows and nurtures positive growth and change. It is the anchor of most agencies' Codes of Conduct, and ethical codes. With such understanding firmly in place the client is free to explore the nature and cause of his/her distress, and the 'helper' is enabled to enter the client's world without running the risk of being overwhelmed, or inappropriately involved. In the field of ritual abuse, recognising and maintaining roles and boundaries is both additionally difficult and absolutely crucial.

When a child has been abused, his/her body, will, rights and freedoms have been invaded or disregarded. When a child has been involved in ritual abuse, every taboo, every boundary has usually been crossed. Nothing is what it seems; nothing is constant; goalposts don't just shift, they disappear; the only limit that has been enforced is the limit of silence. A child or adult who has been involved in ritual abuse usually presents with deeply disturbed and disturbing behaviour; later the emotional and psychological fragility and fragmentation become more apparent. For the professional, the ritually abused client presents probably the most challenging and confrontational experience of his/her professional life, as these clients oppose, test and threaten many previously well-held roles and boundaries.

Workers in this field will seldom be on their own, as other agencies are, or become, involved. However, whilst this can be potentially supportive, it also produces the possibility of further muddle and confusion. It is my experience that the greater the number of professionals there are involved in a case of ritual abuse, the greater is the likelihood of role confusion and boundary crossing; and this in turn can quickly lead to a damaging cycle of criticism, hostility and increased stress, leading to more crossing of roles and boundaries, and so on.

This is not an argument for restricting the number of involved professionals, rather it is the argument for the implementation of a system surrounding professionals that will: (a) detail individual roles; (b) monitor and evaluate the keeping of these roles; (c) plan any changes that need to take place; (d) ensure and provide supervision and support of individuals; and (e) facilitate the maximum degree of appropriate communication between all involved professionals and agencies. Such a structure should be experienced as facilitative of good professional practice, and should not seem inflexible or inhibiting. It should also foster the notion of working together in a mutually supportive and satisfyingly professional manner. This is positive and helpful containment.

Ideally, every geographical area that has a Joint Child Protection Policy should include a stated policy and a set of procedures to be followed when a case is thought to involve ritual abuse. These procedures should include not just a framework for a thoughtful, well-planned, appropriate and sensitive investigatory process, but must include a system for supporting and supervising staff as outlined above. To set up such a system obviously involves considerable time, energy, training and the appropriation of resources; but without a professional system, workers will become increasingly stressed and overstretched, and the ultimate risk of children being inadequately protected from gross abuse becomes more of a potential reality.

Before leaving this section I would like to re-emphasise that all professionals, of all levels of seniority, have difficulty working in this field. A system is needed, not because some workers are inexperienced or ineffective, but because the knowledge of ritual abuse, the details of systematic trauma and torture inflicted on children and adults, the great psychological damage that is done, is, by its very nature, personally and professionally hugely challenging and often overwhelming. What all professionals treating such clients had in common was that they all had the sense of being profoundly shocked, emotionally battered, and significantly traumatised by what they had heard.

Support and supervision – 'acting professionally whilst reacting personally'

New knowledge takes time to become incorporated into experience. Knowledge of ritual abuse, I have already argued, cannot readily be incorporated into experience, as shifts in or re-evaluations of some fundamental beliefs have first to be made. It may be that in years to come, when ritual abuse is more accepted as a reality for some children and some adults, the task and the pressure around that task will not be so great. In the meantime, however, workers are having to act professionally at, and during, the very time that they are reacting to their new knowledge in a very personal way. They do not have time to recover from one piece of knowledge before they are asked to respond professionally to the next. This continual tension and balance between professional response and emotional reaction is not new to workers in the field of child abuse (and no doubt to other workers in other 'high stress' areas), but I would argue that in this field of ritual abuse, the tension is at its most extreme, and the balance most difficult to achieve, at least at the initial stages.

From my experience of the support and supervision I have set up for myself over the years, and the support and supervision I have given other therapists, comes the suggestion that the functions of support and supervision need to be separated, at least in part, and at least at the start.

Supervision is largely concerned with professional practice: ensuring that tasks are recognised, enumerated and carried out; that such tasks are done with professionalism, care, sensitivity and respect; that roles and boundaries are seen and maintained; that a worker's particular difficulties are identified and steps taken to improve practice in those areas. Supervision in this context is more about ensuring that policy and procedures are followed, and is usually provided by line managers who are ascribed that role and responsibility by the employing agency. This is managerial supervision, and the supervisor often has the additional role of assessing and evaluating the work of the supervisee. In the situation where a worker also has a therapeutic role with a client, it has been argued that a separate supervisor is required, who carries no managerial accountability and is therefore free to help the worker focus on the therapeutic relationship, tasks and skills.

For other workers, notably independent therapists, who do not have a pre-scribed route to supervision, it is up to the individual to arrange supervision from someone who has the required level of experience and expertise. Of course, supervision, if it is well done, will also have a supportive element, as a supervisee struggles with personal reactions to some material and needs help to separate personal reaction from the requirements of objective, professional evaluation and action.[2]

In the field of ritual abuse today there can be an immediate problem with this model, in that supervisors may not have the knowledge of ritual abuse necessary to appreciate fully either the professional actions appropriate to circumstances, or the emotional response of the supervisee. In this situation workers have often spoken of having to 'wait' whilst their supervisor 'caught up'; or, 'taking care', inappropriately, of their supervisor as he/she struggled with this new knowledge; or, worse still, meeting supervisors who could not or would not face knowledge of ritual abuse, and either minimised, ignored or denied the personal and profes-sional cost to the worker, or even denied the existence of the client's experience of ritual abuse. The argument for widespread training of ritual abuse, its nature and the psychological consequences for clients, and the personal impact on workers, was never more apparent.

Support is mainly concerned with enabling and facilitating workers to explore and understand and share their emotional and psychological reactions to their work, particularly when such work is in itself highly emotionally charged. One of the most important common misunderstandings about support is that the supporter needs to find a solution for the worker and must do or provide something that will make the worker 'feel better'. This frequently means that the supporter is busy thinking of tacks to take rather than really listening to the worker. As there are usually no easy solutions, and if there were, the worker would probably have found them, the end result is often a worker who feels unheard and not helped, and a supporter who feels inadequate and ineffectual, or feels the worker is resistant to support. My own experience of both receiving and giving support is that the simple but by no means easy task of the supporter is to listen; to encourage the worker to talk more; to share more of his/her feelings; to empathic-ally enter the world of the worker, as the worker has empathically entered the world of the client. This 'mirroring' is profoundly supportive, and the end result is a worker who has gained an integrated sense of self, and has been freed to see again, with clarity, the professional and personal tasks; and a supporter who has gained knowledge about the pressures and the process, and feels both humbled and encouraged by the strength and commitment of another. Both gain, and the subsequent work done with the client cannot be anything but improved. Hopefully, it is now clear that comments that are supervisory in nature have little place in this setting, and would probably be experienced as intrusive. It may also be the case that support could best be provided by someone 'outside' the case management structure, to minimise this possibility. Again, and obviously, supporters in the field of ritual abuse need to have, and to have assimilated, knowledge of this form of abuse, so that they can be free to respond to the worker without the danger of being themselves overwhelmed by the content of the session.

CONCLUDING REMARKS

I have argued that ritual child abuse is both quantitatively and qualitatively different to other known abuses of children. I have attempted to begin to evaluate and describe the nature of the stress and personal distress that workers in this field experience at present. Finally, I have made comments and suggestions as to how such consequences for workers can be recognised, heard and managed, so that professionals can continue to work to the full extent of their capabilities, whilst also remaining emotionally and psychologically healthy. The concepts of safe freedom and positive containment are the expression for this for both professional and client. One system that encompasses both, and cares for both, sounds about right.

In the course of the last four years I have received excellent supervision and support from a number of people. I have also had the privilege of being asked to provide supervision and support to other therapists working in the field of ritual abuse. My contribution to this book began with a statement about resistance in human beings. It seems appropriate now to emphasise, in contrast, the resilience of individuals. The resilience of our clients is known, and is not the focus of this writing. The focus here is the resilience of the workers: their courage, their integrity, their commitment, their striving for excellent, not just good, practice; their tenacity in the face of significant personal pressure, stress and distress. They, too, are remarkable and impressive people.

ACKNOWLEDGEMENTS

Margaret Pinnell, Senior Social Worker and other colleagues read early drafts of this chapter and their comments were greatly valued. The term 'a safe freedom' is Margaret's, and arose in the course of one of our many discussions on ritual abuse.

NOTES

1 The results of this survey and the later quoted discussion were first published in *Child Abuse Review* 2(4), 1993, under the title 'Ritual abuse: consequences for workers'

(Youngson, 1993). Reprinted by permission of John Wiley & Sons, Ltd, who retain copyright of this material. The interested reader is encouraged to refer to that paper for a more detailed description of the survey results, and to appreciate better the depth and breadth of other professionals' experience, particularly as it contains many quoted comments from respondents.

2   For further elaboration of models, types, and levels of supervision, and support, and the functional overlaps, the reader is referred to the excellent book by Peter Hawkins and Robin Shohet (1989).

REFERENCES

Finkelhor, D., Williams, L.M. and Burns, N. (1988) *Nursery Crimes: Sexual Abuse in Day Care*, Newbury Park, CA, Sage Publications.

Hawkins, P. and Shohet, R. (1989) *Supervision in the Helping Professions*, Milton Keynes, Open University Press.

Sakheim, D.K. and Devine, S.E. (1992) *Out of Darkness: Exploring Satanism and Ritual Abuse*, New York, Lexington Books.

Youngson, S.C. (1993) 'Ritual abuse: consequences for professionals', *Child Abuse Review* 2 (4).

Appendix

Useful addresses

Beacon Foundation is a Christian organisation dedicated to helping men and women escape from satanic cults (tel.: 0745-332444).

Cavalcade Productions (video training re trauma, multiple personality and ritual abuse), 7360 Potter Valley Rd, Ukiah, CA 95482.

Centre for Abuse Recovery and Empowerment, Post-traumatic and Dissociative Disorders Unit, The Psychiatric Institute of Washington DC, 4228 Wisconsin Avenue, N.W.Washington DC 20016.

The Cornelian Trust, 101 Harley St, London WIN 1DF, fax: 071-935-3858, tel.: 071-486-1568.

Dianne Core, Childwatch, author of *Chasing Satan*, c/o 206 Hessle Road, Hull, North Humberside, HU3 3BH, tel.: 0483-25552

International Society for the Study of Multiple Personality and Dissociation, 5700 Old Orchard Rd, First Floor, Skokie, IL, 60077-1057.

NAPSAC, Dept of Learning Disabilities, Floor E South Block, Queens Medical Centre, Nottingham NG7 2UH, tel.: 0602-709987, Director Dr Ann Craft, Co-ordinator Pam Cooke.

The National Association for the Protection from Sexual Abuse of Adults and Children with Disabilities (NAPSAC) was formed in 1992. Its aims are to promote knowledge and understanding of the issues involved in the sexual abuse (including ritual abuse) of individuals with learning disabilities. NAPSAC also seeks to foster links between relevant organisations and agencies, both to share existing expertise and to encourage professionals in mainstream services to consider the needs of abused individuals with learning disabilities.

NAPSAC maintains an information exchange network for statutory and voluntary agencies, for professionals and others through the national office and by the publication of a quarterly *Bulletin*. It also publishes a directory of members, an annotated bibliography and information sheets on specific topics. Seminars and study days are offered as part of NAPSAC's commitment to training.

NSPCC (National Society for the Prevention of Cruelty to Children), 67 Saffron Hill, London EC1N 8RS, tel: 071-242-1626.

The NSPCC exists to protect children and prevent their abuse. It has a Helpline which last year responded to 37,000 calls. Anyone concerned about a child at risk can call the free helpline – parents, relatives, friends and children themselves.

The NSPCC has over 85 child protection teams and projects, working with more than 4,300 children and their families. It also runs training courses for professionals.

The National Child Protection Helpline number is 0800-800-500.

Occult Organisation Profile, PO Box 10428, Costa Mesa, CA 92627 (tel.: 714-850-0349).

RAINS (Ritual Abuse Information and Network Support). Professionals wanting to contact RAINS phone Dr Geoff Hopkins (0782-621111, ext 4037) (Keele University) or Dr Joan Coleman (0483-474545). This is the longest-standing organisation in the UK to deal with this subject.

Reaching Out Newsletter, 1296E Gibson Rd #218, Woodland, CA 95776.

SAFE, Sue Hutchinson (tel.: 0980-625990) writes: SAFE was set up for ritual abuse survivors and therapists in order to gather information, advise, help, counsel and support. We run a Helpline which is open 12–36 hours a week and need funding to keep it open longer. We work alongside the police to protect our clients, social services and other agencies. We also work with multiple personality disorder and continue to be amazed at the way children survive and contain their pain. Our workshops deal with the pornographic, prostitution and drug aspects of ritual abuse as well as sexual torture and use of animals. In 1993 we ran six workshops and eight training days for multi-disciplinary groups as well as counselling for survivors.

I grew up with generational abusers, perpetrators of ritual satanical abuse and every day of my life in some form or other I was mentally, physically, emotionally or sexually abused.

One of the things that happened to me which disoriented and confused me related to the fact that everyday words are used for a different purpose. I was constantly told I was drinking lemonade and as it was considered a luxury in those days when I asked other children 'Do you drink lemonade?' they would say 'You're lucky. We don't have that. You must be rich.' The lemonade, of course, was urine with Epsom or Andrews' liver salts or something similar. All food and drink was manipulated in an abusive way so within the house you drank urine or blood and ate rotting meat, maggots, worms and other insects. If you spit it out you are made to eat it again. These are just minor examples. There was pornography, prostitution and major physical and sexual abuse. Let me give you an example of how mind control worked.

I was put in a sack with no clothes on and left hanging outside while passing people would hit or prod the sack or stick things in. Later on in the day things were put inside that wiggled and squirmed all over me. All the time I was asked 'Are you going to be a good girl and what are you going to do?' This meant I had to say I would be a good girl. Imagine this little girl hanging in a sack for 48 hours with no food or drink while she was prodded and punched with crawlies creeping over her. I am amazed that little girl could survive and grow up to be a human being who can still care.

Things have to change. If there is to be justice for the abused there has to be acknowledgement of what has happened to them.

VOICE, PO Box 238, Derby DE1 9JN, tel.: 0332-519872. Mrs Julie Boniface writes: After I discovered my own daughter with a learning disability had been abused by a Care Worker after living securely with us until the age of 21 I was horrified too by the way in which her legal rights were given little thought. We created VOICE because so many learning disabled people have no voice, no-one to hear or believe. VOICE supports the survivor of abuse, the families and all concerned. We try to obtain a conviction and give legal and general advice. We have now been granted Department of Health funding.

Professionals should contact local NHS resources despite the initial incredulous responses that may occur. Until there is mainstream response to this issue, very little can be done.

Name index

Subject index

abandonment, fear of 88
abreaction 288; life-history reconstruction and 40, 41
abuse: addiction to 7; anal 1, 5, 18, 87, 157, 161, 191, 215, see also buggery; of disabled children 19–20, 208–9; disbelief as 163; genital 191, 215, 73, see also genital abuse; legal process as 79; of mentally ill 19–20; organised, definition of 201, 267; physical 2, 34; re-enactment of 38, 43, 101; use of drugs in 36, 60–1, 76, 166, 192, 235, 248, 249, 275; vaginal 5, 18, 161, 191; see also ritual abuse, sadistic abuse, satanic abuse, satanist abuse, sexual abuse
accommodation, process of 7
addiction 39; to abuse 7; to corruption and perversion 22; to power 7
after-life: belief of control over 7; fear of 3
Agamemnon, myth of 47–8
alter personalities see multiple personality disorder
amnesia 34, 38, 258; hypnosis and 259–60; repression leading to 254–5; see also dissociative disorders, memory retrieval
anal abuse 1, 5, 18, 87, 122, 157, 161, 191, 215, see also buggery
anal examination 214
anatomical dolls 77
anger, of victims 19
animals: abuse of 18, 72, 87, 90; bestiality 1, 20, 121; killing of 73, 90, 197, 231; pets, killing of 5, 178, 247, 281
anxiety: impairing verbal capacities 1; persecutory 88; representation of, in abuse victims' drawings 226; ritual as

way of managing 27; role in psychotic presentation 41; separation anxiety 88
archetypal energy 140
Area Child Protection Committee (ACPC) 202–3; recognition of ritual abuse 203; reluctance to consider ritual abuse 203; reorganisation and change 204; resources 205; training 203; see also inter-agency issues, management issues
assessment 207–8
atrocities, in wartime 128
attachment: abandonment, fear of 88; corruption of 281–2; creating context for development of 88; separation anxiety 88; systems 288; theory 236; to therapist, mismanagement of 129
automatic writing, under hypnosis 261

ballet, representations of satanism in 52
bathroom, fear of using 5, 72, 84, 132, see also toilet
battered baby syndrome 204
bestiality 1, 20, 121, 122, 251, see also animals
birthdays: significance of 165, 248, 252; survivors' response to 84, 167
black magic 37
Black Mass 246
blood: drinking of 1, 3, 5, 7, 20, 90, 97, 138, 176, 242, 293, 304; fear of 189; representation of, in abuse victims' drawings 236; use of 73
body memory 38, 277
bondage, as evidence of sadistic abuse 37
brainwashing 74, 254
buggery 46, 121, 191, 214, see also anal abuse